HEARTS AND HANDS

Creating Community in Violent Times

HEARTS AND HANDS

Creating Community in Violent Times

Luis J. Rodríguez

SEVEN STORIES PRESS

New York • Toronto • London • Sydney

Seven Stories Press
140 Watts Street
New York, NY 10013
http://www.sevenstories.com

In Canada:
Hushion House, 36 Northline Road, Toronto, Ontario M4B 3E2

In the U.K.:
Turnaround Publisher Services Ltd., Unit 3, Olympia Trading Estate,
Coburg Road, Wood Green, London N22 6TZ

In Australia:
Tower Books, 9/19 Rodborough Road, Frenchs Forest NSW 2086

Library of Congress Cataloging-in-Publication Data

Rodríguez, Luis J., 1954–
Hearts and hands : creating community in violent times / Luis Rodríguez.—A Seven
Stories Press 1st ed.
p. cm.
ISBN 1-58322-263-4
1. Problem youth—United States. 2. Juvenile delinquents—United States. 3. Gang
members—United States. 4. Youth and violence—United States. 5. Social integration—United States. 6. Community life—United States. I. Title.

HV1431 .R65 2001
362.74'5'0973—dc21   2001041072

9 8 7 6 5 4 3 2 1

College professors may order examination copies of Seven Stories Press titles for
a free six-month trial period. To order, visit www.sevenstories.com/textbook,
or fax on school letterhead to (212) 226-1411.

Book design by Adam Simon

Printed in the U.S.A.

02

Acknowledgments

I want to thank the people and organizations that have helped shape my thoughts in creating intentional, whole, and just communities. They include Michael Meade, Malidoma Somè, Jack Kornfield, and Orland Bishop and all the youth and mentors of the Mosaic Multicultural Foundation, in Seattle, and Shade Tree Mentoring in Los Angeles; Chicago's Community Renewal Society's Anti-Violence Initiative of the Churches-in-Communities Unit; my fellow founders of Chicago's Humboldt Park Teen Reach, including Freddie Calixto, director of the Broader Urban Involvement and Leadership Development program (BUILD), Kenny Ruiz, who runs the Street Intervention Project of the Logan Square YMCA, and Carmen Flores-Rance of St. Lucas Church; Nane Alejandrez and the peace warriors of Barrios Unidos; Magdaleno Rose-Avila, Alex Sanchez, and Homies Unidos from El Salvador and Los Angeles; Tom Hayden and the Peace Process Network; Father Greg Boyle and Jobs for a Future; Ernie Perez, Lee Balinger, Carvell Holloway, David Sandoval, Jorge Luis Rodríguez, and the rest of Rock A Mole Productions; Debbie McGill and all my friends in North Carolina's "Word Wide" Project; Priscilla Aydelott, Lori Loschert, and the others of Youth Empowerment Services of Dinè Bekahi (the Navajo Nation), including the young women of R.O.O.D. (Ruling Our Own Destinies); Will Peters and other spiritual guides of the Lakota Nation, Pine Ridge, South Dakota; Chuck Coleman and family of the Muscogee Creek Nation, Oklahoma; Anthony Lee, his wife, Delores, and family, as well as the elders and teachers of the Dinè Nation (Navajo) in Tsaile, Chinle, and Lukachukai, Arizona; Mexika indigenous elders Tlakaelel of the Kalpulli Koakalko/Tenochtitlan, and Macuiltochtli, Tekpatltzin, Xochimeh, and everyone else at the Kalpulli Yetlanezi-Tolteka Trese of Aurora, Ill.; Chicago's Guild Complex and its publishing wing, Tìa Chucha Press; Nelson Peery and the League of Revolutionaries for a New America; Video Machete, especially Chris Bratton and Maria Benfield; Fidel Rodriguez and L.A.'s Seditious Beats; my fellow companions in the beautiful, often painful, but rewarding work of Youth Struggling for Survival, including Pat Zamora, Camila Barros, Frank Blazquez, Louise Blazquez, Julia Harmon-Chavez, Simonè Peer, Geno Tellez, Laurina Uribe, Antonio Sacre, and all our youth leaders (including my son

Ramiro and daughter Andrea, Nydia Hernandez, Jay Taifa, Victor Nambo [Tepechihuaz], Dolly Arguello, Miguel Gonzalez [Ocelotl], James Anderson, Santos Ventura, Jesus Hernandez, Hector Hernandez, Shayna Plaut, Kathy Regalado, Rocio Restrepo, Andres Garcia, Tanee Blazquez, Frankie Blazquez, Luisa Hernandez, her daughter, Jocelyn, and family; Tony, Lupe, Pepe, and the rest of the Vasquez family; and all the others over the years, including in prison; Rudy Rosales Huitziloxipe, Luis Ruan; Frank Chavez; Mike Garcia; Rudy Buchanan; Carlos Rodríguez; Katrina Coker; Ruben Chavez; Otto Sturcke, Enrique Sanchez, Donna DeCesare; Julie Parson-Nesbitt, Reginald Gibbons, Michael Warr; Julie Aimen; Jeff Biggers; Julie Campoverde; John Trudell; and all the incarcerated men and women I've visited and written to over the years. And a special thanks to my agent, Susan Bergholz; Dan Spinella and Mary Kathleen Hawley for helping edit much of this text; Dan Simon and Juana Ponce de León of Seven Stories/Siete Cuentos Press; the Cardenas and Rodríguez families—bless you all; my wife, Trini, always my love and gratitude; and much love to my children—Andrea, Ramiro, Ruben, and Luis—as well as my grandchildren (Ricardo, Anastasia, Amanda, and Catalina), who embody much of what this book is about.

I also wish to thank *Social Justice: A Journal of Crime, Conflict & Social Order* for publishing, in 1998, a version of the material in this book. Also various sections of this work first appeared as editorials and reportage in the 1990s for publications like *The Nation, Los Angeles Times, Chicago Tribune, Utne Reader, U.S. News & World Report, Prison Life, The Family Networker, The People's Tribune/Tribuno del Pueblo, Grand Street, The ROC—Rock Out Censorship*, and *Latina magazine*. Parts of this book also appeared in *Images of Color, Images of Crime*, edited by Coramae Richey Mann and Marjorie S. Zatz (Los Angeles: Roxbury Publishing, 1998) and *Cultures de la rue: les barrios d'Amerique du Nord*, edited by Genevieve Fabre (Paris: Cahiers Charles V, Universite Paris 7–Denis Diderot, 1996).

And a special thanks to the Lila Wallace–Reader's Digest Fund, the Lannan Foundation, the Illinois Arts Council, the Dorothea Lang/Paul Tayler Prize from the Center for Documentary Studies at Duke University, the Hispanic Heritage Foundation, and the North Carolina Arts Council, among others, for providing me awards, fellowships, and residencies during the writing of this text.

To the memory of

Marcos Cordoba, Erik Arellano, Eddie Ramos,
Alfredo Mercado, Arlene Osuna

killed during our intense battles for justice and peace in Chicago;

and

Walter Guzman, Nathan Allen, and
Manual "Manazar" Gamboa

mentors, friends, and peace warriors.

Contents

Introduction

What the Craziness Is

*When the culture fails to draw out the innate beauty of its children,
it's deciding to turn that beauty to violence.*

—Michael Meade

There is a wound in the land, the body politic, and the collective spirit. Healing involves going directly to the wound, not recoiling from it. The wound, the damage, can be the mother of our rebirth, the reconciliation. If revolution isn't about this, it isn't about anything.

An aim here is to help span the seemingly insurmountable gulfs in our society so that we can provide the revolutionary teaching, caring, and genuine leadership that young people today are craving—and, in many cases, dying for.

I remember the day well. On April 20, 1999, two teenage gunmen rampaged through Columbine High School in Littleton, Colorado, with shotguns, semiautomatic weapons, and homemade bombs, killing thirteen people before shooting themselves and petrifying the nation with their fury and callousness. This was the most destructive of what had been an outbreak of school shootings in less than a two-year period. Scarcely twelve months earlier two boys, ages thirteen and eleven, gunned down four fellow classmates and a teacher in a Jonesboro, Arkansas, Middle School during a prank fire drill. The previous December a fourteen-year-old shot to death three classmates and wounded five others, members of a prayer group in a Kentucky school. Earlier in October a sixteen-year-old in Mississippi killed three people and wounded seven in a rampage that included a stop at his school.

From October 1997 to May 1999, similar assaults by kids occurred in towns like Moses Lake, Washington; Springfield, Oregon; Conyers, Georgia; and Edinboro, Pennsylvania. The assailants ranged in age from eleven to eighteen. Collectively they accounted for thirty-one deaths and seventy-five wounded. Then, on March 5, 2001, after a much-welcomed lull in such shootings, a fifteen-year-old high school student in Santee, California, opened fired on fellow students, killing two and wounding thirteen. Barely seventeen days later in the same school district, an eighteen-year-old senior in El Cajon High School took a shotgun and blasted several rounds, wounding five.

These events exploded in communities that were largely white, rural, or suburban, relatively crime free, and dotted with churches. The general sentiment: These things should not have happened there.

So why did they?

For some time the tragedy of kids killings kids has blown up in poor urban core communities, kicking off a spate of draconian laws and repressive measures. The popular perception in these cases was that they were "expected." Events like the one in a poor Flint, Michigan, elementary school in early 2000, when a six-year-old boy shot and killed a six-year-old girl (the boy's teenage uncle was later convicted in this case for "leaving the gun around"), further aggravated this notion.

By designating this violence as "inner city," and only affecting black and brown communities, most policymakers, driven by interests in more powerful well-off communities, showed little empathy or connection.

But we are connected. As we can see, this destructiveness can happen anywhere. The disaffection of our young people is deep—and no gated community or relatively wealthy environment is going to buffer them from the smoldering rages.

As reported by most of the media, blame for these tragic events was easily and randomly assigned: guns, violent movies, gang affiliations, video games, lack of moral training, bad parenting, bad kids. In various ways these elements do play a role in the violence, but none can hold up for long as a principal basis for these murderous assaults.

"It's the wordlessness of the schoolyard massacre that is so destabilizing," wrote Rick Moody. "Kids with weapons let weapons do the articulating. The triggermen themselves are notorious for their inability to explain their motives.... They have found the one rhetorical strategy that supervenes all others, that makes the chatter of parents and newspapers and television commentators dumb, that replies to all questions and all controversies in a final, incontrovertible splatter."[1]

So if a few kids are having guns do their talking, what are they saying? How do we intrepret the signals, the premonitions, the initial sparks of vicious outbursts in children who seem normal? "The murderer who talks with the voice of a child puts forth the dangerous proposal that we are all capable," Moody continued. "That adolescence is often fatal. That only good luck distinguishes the guilty from the innocent."2

We seem to be in a general state of depression—a cultural malaise of isolation and meaninglessness. We are feeling more rootless and hopeless than ever before, despite the unprecedented prosperity permeating our society—where consumer products strain warehouses and retail outlets; technology and rapid service is at our fingertips; TV, video games, books, music, and movies bombard us at every turn; and access to every imaginable drug, drink, and sexual release is commonplace. It's a time when "life seems utterly devoid of purpose. No path beckons. Eventually a kind of paralytic cynicism sets in. You believe in nothing. You accept nothing as truthful, useful, or significant. You don't value anything you're currently doing and can't imagine doing something of value in the future."3

What can we do? How can we get off this continually accelerating merry-go-round? How do we regain our unmediated ties to nature, our innate purposes, and the paths of creativity and caring?

A major purpose of this book is to attempt a deeper inquiry into these issues, to engage people in an ongoing dialogue about why young people seem to be more brutal, more willing to take it to the limit, more intent on resolving issues with a total and desperate finality. This is not so much about the right "answers" as it is about the right arguments. It's time to make sense of the senselessness.

Around thirty years ago I committed myself to making sense of the senselessness of my own life. I became politically active in the barrios of Los Angeles during the tumultuous period of civil unrest in the 1960s and early 1970s. I obtained a new direction to my life, using abilities I barely discovered I possessed. Around eighteen I let go the most virulent aspects of my adolescence, including drugs, jails, and gang warfare. To survive and stay out of trouble, I worked in factories, foundries, refineries, construction sites, and four years in a steel mill. I acquired organizing skills as well as work skills. By age twenty-five, I resumed my education and embarked on the long and arduous road to become a writer and speaker—in effect, to merge intellectual activity with an active community life.

But I never forgot my youth, the most intense period of my life. The death-defying acts, suicide attempts, drug overdoses, homelessness, and staring down of bullets described a traumatized, rage-filled, and impulsive young man. It is the same craziness that makes a teenager drive ninety miles per hour down a highway. It does no good to say this is useless behavior—the point is it's so prevalent (sixteen-year-olds are more likely to be killed in auto accidents than any other age group).[4] However, as storyteller and mythologist Michael Meade has stated, "we need to ask what the craziness is."[5]

For me, the street battles, drugs, and shadow-walking stank so sweet. It was the perfume of an otherwise aimless existence. Once caught in the web of a crazy life, nobody could untangle me. I had to unravel myself.

First of all, I had to want to. I had to have a vision, a sense of destiny for my life that went beyond the adolescent rages and uncertainties. I had to gain a worldview—tied to something deep in the soil and deep in the soul. Some embrace religion. Others, political or cultural awareness. Or science. Almost always the development of a worldview is linked in some way to art—music, the visual arts, dance, writing—to the intersection of external and internal energies that impel us onto a creative terrain where spirit and body, the conscious and the unconscious, the universal and the singular, the personal and the social live through us in a delicate dance.

Once I'd found a direction, I had to remove myself from the powerful pull of self-destructive impulses. I did this by helping transform the lives of other youth in my neighborhood and other parts of Los Angeles. Giving back to others, most of whom were in similar circumstances, became my way out of the madness.

A dropout at age 15, I now returned to high school and got involved with a Chicano student empowerment group. I became active in the neighborhood community center, which included an alternative school for teens, a preschool center, family referral and counseling, and a youth activities facility. Having been an outlaw graffiti writer, I eventually learned to draw and paint. For a year and a half I painted murals—sometimes with gang youth—for the community center, on the walls of various businesses and parks, and at a children's library. I even learned Mexika (Aztec) indigenous dance steps, which I performed at the school and in a couple of community events. For a brief time I tried my hand at amateur boxing, martial arts, and playing sax and conga drums for a garage band.

Later I participated in demonstrations, door-to-door organizing drives, youth dances, and retreats. Even when I worked in industry, I continued with these efforts in communities throughout the Los Angeles area, along with my first wife, Camila, and other young revolutionaries.

As described in my 1993 memoir, *Always Running: La Vida Loca, Gang Days in L.A.,*[6] at the age of eleven, I turned my whole being over to a gang. As part of this, I took a variety of drugs, particularly aerosol sprays, but also heroin. In the gang I was not a leader; I was a good soldier. The new roles that I assumed required a more conscious participation in my life.

From 1974 to 1978 Camila and I gathered around us a number of young leaders, helping them organize activities, gain knowledge, and find places to hang out. At first they included youth from East L.A., particularly from the Aliso Village and Pico Gardens housing projects. Later, in Pasadena, we worked with the local high schools, including students from the Movimiento Estudiantil Chicano de Aztlán (MeCha—the Chicano Student Movement of Aztlán). (Prior to my marriage in 1974, I had been the MeCha organizer for East L.A. high schools.) We supported striking bus drivers and school integration efforts, and participated in youth leadership camps and demonstrations against police abuse.

In the Florencia barrio of South Central L.A., and later in Watts—where we lived in the colonia neighborhood between the Jordan Downs and Imperial Courts housing projects—we set up an arts/theater group with neighborhood youth (Camila had been active in teatro groups at Garfield High School in East L.A., like the Teatro Urbano). On some weekends children and young teens would come to our house for meetings and community arts events, where they displayed their dancing, singing, and acting skills while we showed politically charged films on the outside wall of our house.

We had a cadre of young people willing to look death in the eye, and as they became more active, they adopted a vision of a more passionate and profound existence. We also attended gatherings in other cities that gathered youth and activists from around the country. The whole world lay before us. Our efforts were fraught with blood and will. I had been a young man who only lived for and cared about my barrio. Now I was going to places like San Francisco, Denver, and Chicago, driving vans or beat-up cars across the vast expanse of this land. As new geographical horizons opened up before me, so did those in my heart and mind.

I did not know it then, but by consciously pursuing a spiritual quest—which all youth are on, including gang youth—by opening up to the world in its pain and glory, I was moving through an initiation process. I left my barrio and my family to penetrate a new source of power. By returning to the barrio and contributing to the spiritual and intellectual growth of other young people, I was forging the character that would serve to carry me along divergent and sometimes treacherous paths.

The late 1960s and early 1970s were a violent period in Los Angeles. However, they only laid the ground for a more extensive violence that would grip these streets and those of other cities in the 1980s and 1990s. But I had moved away from this. In one sense I had outgrown the gang rivalries, robberies, and street wars. Like all young people at some time in their lives, I also had to make a decision to grow up.

I won't recount here in detail all the personal setbacks I've endured over the years. Suffice it to say they involved failed marriages (Camila and I broke up in 1978), losing kids and family, drinking away my sorrows instead of facing them, failing in work, in my community commitments, as a writer, and even as a father. But by failing, I was preparing for the only success that was possible: the success that comes from having descended to the depths and learning how to gather the psychic and spiritual energies to rise out of them.

All this has gone into the writing of this book, which summarizes much of what I've learned about life and working with young people through extensive study and practice.

The majority of the lessons here came from my fifteen years in Chicago, beginning in 1985. There I participated in organizations such as Youth Struggling for Survival as well as the Increase the Peace Collaborative, the Community Renewal Society's Anti-Violence Initiative, Guild Complex's Writing Through the Prisms of Self and Community Workshops, Tía Chucha Press, the Latino Planning Committee for Peace and Justice, and Humboldt Park's Teen Reach. Only recently, in the summer of 2000, did I return to Los Angeles. A year and a half later I helped launch a center of intellectual and arts enhancement called Tía Chucha's Café Cultural (a bookstore, coffee bar, performance space, art gallery, and computer center) in the Northeast San Fernando Valley—"Where Art and Minds Meet—For A Change."

In addition, for more than two decades I have spoken at hundreds of conferences, retreats, public and private schools, universities, prisons, migrant camps, homeless shelters, worksites, churches, libraries, and juvenile facilities throughout the United States, Canada, Puerto Rico, Mexico, Central America, and Europe.

On the day that Eric Harris, eighteen, and Dylan Klebold, seventeen, slaughtered their fellow students and a teacher at Columbine High, I was doing a poetry reading and talk to several hundred students at Fremd High

School in the Chicago suburb of Palatine. Many of these students later wrote me about how my words helped encourage them to live more intentional lives. We can't forget that the vast majority of U.S. schools did not report any violence that day.

So while today there may be an alarming number of young people who are losing it, the vast majority of teenagers in the country are not committing violent acts. They are trying to negotiate their lives, with many problems, naturally, but still somewhat intact. Many of them are responding in heroic, even if mostly quiet, ways to these problems—and often without much support from adults.

In his book, *Framing Youth: Ten Myths about the Next Generation,* Mike A. Males reports that twelve- to nineteen-year-olds made up 14 percent of the U.S. population in the mid-1990s. They accounted for 18 percent of the country's violent crime (slightly more than their population), 15 percent of murders, 7 percent of suicides, 2 percent of drug deaths, 14 percent of highway deaths (reflecting the exact proportion of their numbers), 9 percent of drunken driving deaths, 12 percent of births, and 15 percent of HIV infections. Given the statistics, Males concludes that youth do not account for a high percentage of America's social ills.[7]

In fact, after studying data from the California Department of Justice—California crime figures are the most complete and consistent, as well as harbingers for the rest of the country—Males maintains that the greatest rise of violence and crime from 1980 to 1997 came from white male adults over age thirty.

To consider truly innovative responses in meeting the needs of young people, we must start with real assessments of what their situations consist of—away from the political spin doctors, sensationalist headlines, and general fear mongering going on today about children and youth.

Closing in on a half century of existence, I'm in the afternoon of this day called life. Only now do I feel I can contribute an ounce of cogency to this conversation. I am compelled to try because of the growing fissures between youth and elders, wealth and poverty, men and women, parents and their children, and the resultant rise of violence and substance abuse, home and community dislocations. There is also an astronomical and detrimental growth of prisons and law enforcement as the preferred remedies to what are essentially economic, political, sociological, psychological, and cosmological matters.

There is a meaningful connection between this ruptured social contract and the fact that so many have been pushed aside by the economy. "One paycheck away" is the defining phrase of this period—one paycheck away from losing one's home, education, and a place in the community. One paycheck away from a fall with incalculable consequences, even in times of a so-called growing economy.[8] What is the phrase that defines the opposite direction? Where is the compass to a true north of victory and reconciliation?

From the segmented and conflicted class structure in our society, a new social class is emerging. Excluded from the technologically driven economy, this class is also politically, socially, and culturally ostracized. They are the exiled, the alienated, the abandoned, the demonized. Included are those on welfare, the homeless, prisoners, migrant workers, urban and rural poor (of all races, including the working poor), the indigenous and the undocumented, but also former managers, professionals, teachers, artists, and intellectuals who have been unable to make a transition through the recent societal changes. They are the ones capitalism can no longer effectively exploit, and therefore value—the locked out as well as the locked down.

As the core culture becomes increasingly materialistic and profit oriented, it also becomes mean-spirited, intolerant, and devoid of a regenerative spirit. So, where do we turn when the center of the culture becomes hollow? As many others have poignantly remarked, to the margins, to the so-called periphery where everything is struggling and alive, to the "outcasts" and outlawed. Just as the extremities of the body energize the heart, so, too, do the peripheries of a culture revitalize its heart.

Here is where the imagination of the possible expands, where change and creation find seed and root. This is also where other social classes can make a link to the developing movement for a shared future of peace, justice, and plenitude and where the needs, desires, and longings of all the people can be realized.

However, the period of possibility we are in suggests that shifts in policy won't suffice. Instead we must reorient our thinking on how young and old are joined in the political and social matrix of the land—where the people are fully activated and their dreams, aspirations, and strivings are central to what makes up community.

As Goethe once said, "Everything has been thought of before; the difficulty is to think of it again."[9] Or we can proceed from Osip Mandelshtam's statement: "Everything existed of old, everything happens again, and only the moment of recognition is sweet."[10]

At the nexus of the sweet encounters between old issues and new demands, something indeed is being born. Our society is pregnant with such potential. It's time our institutions, relationships, and collaborations were seen as birthing centers.

So this is a good place to start: To reimagine the issues and bring complete community attention and intention to the crisis faced by our youth and, consequently, the whole culture.

The people and events discussed in this publication are real. However, many of the names and circumstances were changed to protect those involved.

Part 1:
The Violence of Youth—
The Absence of Elders

With all thy getting, get understanding
—Proverbs 4:7

Chapter 1

Throwaway Kids[1]

Out of each dead child sprouts a gun with eyes
and out of each crime bullets are born
that someday will find the place
of your hearts.

—Pablo Neruda

Pedro was a thoughtful, articulate, and charismatic young man; he would listen, absorb, and respond. He had the sharp Spanish-African features of his Puerto Rican heritage, a thin but muscular body, and light curly hair cut short except for a small "tail" at the nape of his neck. His movements were quick and well developed due to years of surviving in the streets of Chicago. In 1993 Pedro was a twenty-year-old gang leader. For most of his life, he lived off and on between his welfare mother and an uncle. He had been kicked out of schools and had served time in youth detention facilities. He was also a great human being.

For four months that year the courts had designated me and my wife, Trini, as Pedro's guardians under a house-arrest sentence. He was respectful and polite. He meticulously answered all my messages. My six-year-old son, Ruben, loved him and my nineteen-year-old son, Ramiro, happened to be his best friend at the time.

During his stay I gave Pedro books to help him become more cognizant of the world. Books like *Palante*,[2] a photo text about the Young Lords Party of the 1970s, opened him up to an important slice of history that, until then, he had never known about.

One evening, Pedro was talking with a couple of girls at the bottom of the stairs, two flights below the apartment. I had just arrived by cab from the airport following a speaking trip. Although I worried Pedro would trigger his ankle monitor—he had to stay within the hundred-foot limit—I walked upstairs, put my bags down, and began a chat with Trini. When I heard a commotion downstairs and Pedro yelled out my name, I knew he was being jumped. I ran down the stairs like a herd of wild elephants and saw two guys beating up on Pedro. I came out swinging (I hit mostly wall and a lot of air). The two guys took off as this heavy-set Mexican rushed toward them.

Pedro was down, but unhurt. I walked out and the two guys were still there. One cowered behind the wheels of a delivery truck. The other, cornered at the entrance of a Laundromat, picked up some kid's bicycle to throw at me. I confronted them both, saying that regardless of what beef they had with Pedro, as long as he stayed with my family, they would have beef with me. I'm sure they contemplated jumping me. But they hesitated and fled. In reality I was out of breath and vulnerable. Those young guys could have taken me, except that I acted as if I could hold my own.

For some time after, Pedro and I laughed about that incident. It also strengthened our friendship that he knew I would jeopardize myself to safeguard his presence in my home. His stay with us passed without further problems.

When Pedro was released from house arrest, he moved out of the neighborhood with his girlfriend and her small boy. She later had his first child. He found a job. Although he remained a leader of the gang, he also talked about struggle, about social change, about going somewhere. It appeared his life was making a turn for the better.

Then, in November 1993, Pedro was shot three times with a .44 and was hit in his back, a leg, and a hand. He lived, but he was not the same after that. During his hospital stay the same gang that had shot him ambushed and killed Angel, a friend of Ramiro's and Pedro's. An honor student at one of the best schools in the city, Angel was on his way to school. News accounts the next day failed to mention this, reporting only that he was a suspected gang member, as if this fact justified his death.

In the overcrowded room of the public hospital where Pedro was recovering with tubes taped to his body, and with fellow patients coughing and moaning nearby, I tried to persuade him to get his boys to chill. I knew Ramiro and the others were all sitting ducks. Pedro went through some internal turmoil, but he decided to forbid retaliation. This was hard for him, but with tears of rage falling down his cheeks, he did it.

Unfortunately, the story doesn't end there. In early 1994, Pedro allegedly shot and killed one of the guys believed to be behind Angel's murder and his own shooting. He was a fugitive for about a year until he was captured, tried, and convicted. In 1996 he was sent to Stateville Prison to serve a forty-year sentence.

I tell this to convey the complexity of working with youths like Pedro, youths most people would rather write off, but who are intelligent, creative, and quite decent. The tragedy is that it is mostly young people like these who are being killed and who are doing the killing. I've seen them in youth prisons, hospitals, and courts throughout the land. Given other circumstances, these young people might have been college graduates, officeholders, or social activists. Unfortunately many find themselves in situations they feel unable to pull out of until it's too late.

Youths like Pedro aren't in gangs to be criminals, killers, or prison inmates. For them a gang embraces who they are, gives them the incipient authority they need to eventually control their lives, the empowerment that other institutions—including schools and families—often fail to provide. Yet without the proper community guidance, gang involvement can be disastrous.

In August 1994 a media storm was set off when eleven-year-old Robert Sandifer of Chicago, known as "Yummy" because he liked to eat cookies, shot into a crowd and killed a fourteen-year-old girl. A suspected member of a Southside gang, Yummy disappeared; days later he was found shot in the head. Two teenage members of Yummy's gang were later convicted on charges surrounding his death. Hours before his murder a neighbor saw Yummy, who told her, "Say a prayer for me."

This is a tragedy, but without a clear understanding of the social, economic, and psychological dynamics that would drive an eleven-year-old to kill, we can only throw up our hands. While the Columbine High School killings received more attention (fifteen people dead in one day is a good reason), the fact is that in poor urban communities young people may know a dozen or so friends and acquaintances killed over a school year. They are traumatized and confused, but the consideration that these deaths receive is usually scant or, as is often the case, focused on their "innate" predilection to violent and criminal behavior.

Yet it isn't hard to figure out the array of forces behind much of this violence. Yummy was a child of very real and chosen policies during the Reagan years, of substantial cuts in community programs, of the worst job loss since the Great Depression, of more police and prisons and few options for recreation, education, or work. He was a boy who had been physically abused, shuttled from one foster home to another, one juvenile facility after another. At every stage of Robert's young life, he was blocked from becoming all he could be. Yet there was nothing to stop him from getting a gun, using it, and being killed by one in return.

No "three strikes and you're out," no trying children as adults, no increased prison spending will address what has given rise to the Pedros and Yummys of this world. Such proposals deal only with the end results of a process that will continue to produce its own fuel, like a giant breeder reactor. They are not solutions.

In 1993, along with Patricia Zamora, who at the time worked with Casa Aztlán Community Center in Chicago's Mexican community of Pilsen, we organized a nucleus of gang and nongang youth to help them find their own answers and to conceptualize their own organizational structures in their own interests. By June 1994 some thirty people gathered in my backyard, ready to start a new youth organization. They came mostly from the predominantly Puerto Rican area of Humboldt Park (my son's friends, and Pedro's homies) and Pilsen, two areas known for gang violence and marked by crowded three-story brick flats, trash-strewn vacant lots, graffiti-scarred alleys, family restaurants, corner bars and liquor stores, carnecerias, store-front churches, and used-car lots.

The group agreed to reach out to other youths and hold retreats and weekly meetings, and to organize a major conference. All summer they worked, without money, without external resources, but with a lot of enthusiasm and energy. The leadership consisted of kids with names like Pinkie, Jungle Boy, Jay Jay, Chupa, Bobo, Cholo, Satan, Puppet, Chuckie, Mexico, Frosty, and Mugsy. My kids, Ramiro and Andrea, and their mother, Camila, were also there.

Their efforts culminated in the Youth '94 Struggling for Survival Conference, held that August at the University of Illinois, Chicago. More than 150 young people and about 30 adults attended. A few gang members set aside deadly rivalries to take part in this gathering. They arrived by bus, on foot, or got rides from parents and teachers. They came from Humboldt Park, Pilsen, Logan Square, Little Village, West Town, Rogers Park, Uptown, the Southside, the Northside, and the Westside. Even students from suburban high schools and colleges participated. They held workshops on police brutality, jobs, and education, and peace in the neighborhoods.

There were a number of mishaps, including a power failure that blacked out the whole building. Yet the young people voted to continue meeting. They held their workshops in the dark or with sporadic flashes of cigarette lighters, raising issues, voicing concerns, coming up with ideas. The adults—parents, teachers, counselors, resource people, and a video crew from the Center for New Television—were there to boost what the young people had organized. Later some of them established Video Machete—a production group organized by Chris Bratton and Maria Benfield—that has grown into a major training and filming organization for youth and have presented screenings in New York City, Chicago, and Taos.[3] (Chicago has pioneered such efforts, including the internationally known Street Level Media.)

Unfortunately the building personnel told us we had to leave because it was unsafe to be in a building without power. Casa Aztlán agreed to let us move to several of their rooms to continue the workshops; I felt we would probably lose half of the participants in the fifteen-minute ride between sites. Not only did we hang on to most of the youths, we picked up a few more along the way. In Casa Aztlán's flooded basement, adorned with crumbling plastered walls, we held the final plenary session. The kids set up a round-table at which it was agreed that only proposed solutions would be entertained. A few read poetry, including Ramiro. It was a success because the young people wouldn't let it be anything else.

Over the years Youth Struggling for Survival (YSS) grew and brought together young people from twelve different Chicago communities and surrounding suburbs, including Aurora. Several hundred young people have gone through the organization's processes. Our elders base increased to more than a dozen, including several families. We worked also with organizations like Barrios Unidos of California, which organized several peace summits in the 1990s; the Mosaic Multicultural Foundation's gatherings around themes of youth, violence, and the veritable place of mentors and elders; and the Center for Youth Development and Policy Research in Washington, D.C. In addition, YSS incorporated spiritual experiences, including Mexika, Lakota, and Navajo traditions, such as the purification sweat ceremony, guided by respected teachers in those traditions. YSS set up Day of the Dead altars, honoring mainly the young people who have died in street gang wars, and, once, a Mexika-style pyramid made of bamboo and paper for a ritual pageant event in the Logan Square neighborhood.

In 1997 PBS-TV aired a segment on YSS for the series "Making Peace," produced by Moira Productions for the Independent Television Service. Viewings of the series resulted in more than two hundred community meetings across the country. And we have linked with similar groups in the United States as well as in Europe, Mexico, and Central America.

As is bound to happen in this kind of work, there were some terrible setbacks. Three of our young leaders were killed and others ended up behind bars, including Ramiro, convicted in 1998 for three counts of attempted murder.

Yet YSS's positive impact is undeniable. Over time community organizations—Alternatives, Senn/Youth Net, Youth Options Unlimited, Family Matters, Public Allies, the Chicago Foundation for Women, Chicago Association House, Youth Services Project, Strive, Yollocalli Youth Center and Radio Arte, the Quantum Project, Aspira, the Aurora public schools, and the Music Theater Workshop—hired many of our leaders. A few of our members set up their own businesses, and many have gone to college.

A number of these young people have spoken at schools, conferences, juvenile facilities, and Native American reservations. They've attended gatherings in Santa Cruz, El Paso, Washington, D.C., Los Angeles, Kansas City, North Carolina, Atlanta, and San Francisco, as well as in Canada, Italy, and Cuba.

By reaching out to assist other youth from falling into the traps of violence, drugs, and alcohol—even though some of them were still themselves active with these—they have contributed to changing themselves. One young man, who once held his brother as he lay dying from bullet wounds in the streets of Pilsen, gave an impassioned talk to children in the Pine Ridge reservation, warning them not to emulate the big city gangs, which some of them were beginning to do. "You have a beautiful culture, with great traditions," the Mexican youth said. "You don't have to end up lost like many of us. We may not make it, but you have a chance to do something about your own future." For young people who beforehand had not seen more than five blocks of their own neighborhood, to reach out so far and so wide has been crucial in helping them see the vastness of what's possible in the world, as well as in meeting other young leaders who are trying to accomplish similar goals.

YSS is but one example of young people tackling the issues head-on. There are hundreds more across America, rising in number every year. The point is that for a long time young people have organized themselves for their art, music, and well-being—on their own terms. They've already taken major steps in running their own lives their communities, even their schools. The question may then be whether the relationships between adults and young people are mutually respectful and beneficial.

I've learned that people like Pedro are not "lost causes."

But then, as a wise man once said, the "lost causes" are the only ones worth fighting for.

Chapter 2
Modern Street Gangs: A History

The state of society is one in which the members have suffered amputation from the trunk, and strut about like so many walking monsters.

—Ralph Waldo Emerson

With all the hoopla today about street gangs, you'd think gangs were a new thing in American life. The fact is they are not. What follows is a capsule history.[1] Although this history is predicated on the "criminal" aspects of these associations, we shall see how this alone cannot provide a suitable insight as to why gangs exist and have grown tremendously over the last three decades in this country. Keep in mind, too, that what sociologists and criminologists call gangs—just like much of what is thrown up from the bowels of our culture—are actually mutated forms of organization. By itself a mutated form is neither good nor bad. It's reflective of the state of chaos and uncertainty we're all in. Order and beauty can come from these forms as well as harm and destruction.

For one thing the term *gang* is unable to completely convey what we're dealing with. It does not encompass the social, initiatory, spiritual, and mythological aspects of these groupings; most people are overwhelmed by the pathological aspect, thus they only perceive a small piece of the puzzle.

The general idea is that gang members are "monsters"—predators, deviants, antisocial. This may be true to some extent, but it is not the whole truth. Some are indeed "monsters," but in the sense of being a departure from what is "usual" or normal in a social structure or species; in some cases, they are continuations of these structures on other levels. At some point they don't fit in, although they are of society's making. As Emerson says, they are amputations from the trunk.

Of course, being called a "monster" nowadays has the connotation of not being human—an animal—therefore, deserving of less than human consideration. This is the wrong formulation. It's important to differentiate between these two meanings, as subtle as they may seem.

Many groups called gangs are all about business; they are smaller versions of corporate organizations. Although largely involved in enterprises such as drug dealing, some have legitimate businesses such as restaurants, pool halls, or car washes, alongside their illegitimate ones. Many are loose and carefree, often imitating or acting like media-fed versions of gangs. Others have religious and nationality or racial connotations.

While "street gang" implies highly stylized armies of youth and adults (most "youth" gangs are actually run by adults), one can also point to "suite" gangs that carry out their criminal activities from inside plush offices.

And there are organizations of mostly youth who are considered "gangs," although they have no criminal participation. Today almost any group of youth banding together gets "criminalized"—skateboarders, ravers, Goths, political interest clubs, and others.

What we generally call street gangs first emerged in this country at the end of the American Revolution. In the 1820s these groups consisted of mostly Irish immigrant youth. New York City neighborhoods—Five Points, Hell's Kitchen, and the Bowery—bred groups like the Forty Thieves, the Kerryonians, the Roach Guards, the Plug Uglies, the Atlantic Guards, the Gophers, and the Dead Rabbits. Some also sported "colors." The Roach Guards had blue stripes on their trousers, and the Dead Rabbits had red stripes. The Whyos of Five Points were believed to be the first to include murder as a requirement of membership. Some of the groups had also entered the drug trade, trafficking in morphine, cocaine, and opium-based drugs. The Hudson Dusters were named for their frequent use of cocaine dust.

These young people lived as second-class citizens. Their parents worked in the lowest paid, most menial jobs. They organized to protect themselves within a society that had no place for them.

In 1857 the worst gang rumble in the history of the country occurred in New York City between the Dead Rabbits, an Irish group, and the Bowery Boys, who considered themselves "native" Americans. This battle-turned-riot resulted in at least a dozen dead and almost 100 injured, including police officers. The National Guard was brought in to quell the violence that lasted several days. Six years later this incident was overshadowed by the mostly Irish Draft Riots, which claimed several hundred casualties, primarily from the African-American community.

After the Civil War the new street organizations included Jewish and Italian immigrants as well as African Americans. Chinese immigrants—the target of some of the most hostile laws and practices of the Far West, including exclusion acts and lynchings[2]—organized groups like the Six Companies in California. Otherwise known as Tongs, the Six Companies were established as protection and mutual-aid societies in San Francisco; they were also immersed in prostitution and gambling. Around the same time, following the U.S. war against Mexico, Mexicans who had been forced out of their homes were organized and led by such men as Tiburcio Vasquez and Joaquin Murietta, and in Texas by Juan Cortina and Gregorio Cortez.[3] As expected, they were labeled "bandits." American Indians—led by Geronimo, Cochise, Chief Joseph, Crazy Horse, and others—as well as ex-slaves who organized were similarly branded.

And Wild West gangs and gunslingers, including a good many dispossessed Confederate or Union soldiers, were thriving at the time. They included the Wild Bunch, the Regulators, the Dalton Gang, as well as personages like John Wesley Harding, Billy the Kid, Jesse James, and Butch Cassidy. (They were, however, idealized in books, songs, and later in movies and TV.) This was also the time when perhaps the largest, most pernicious gang of all was spawned in America, the Ku Klux Klan. It was originally founded in Pulaski, Tennessee, by former officers and troops of the Confederate Army, including Nathan Bedford Forrest.

By the end of the century more immigrants and displaced American farmers crowded into the industrialized cities. In the early 1900s street organizations existed in Chicago, Philadelphia, Detroit, San Francisco, and Los Angeles. The ages of the members ranged from eleven to twenty-five years; some had members as young as six (which is roughly the situation today). Most of them were the sons and daughters of immigrants from Italy, Eastern Europe, Germany, and England.

A movement arose around this time to help these impoverished and neglected youth. In his 1997 book, *A Kind and Just Parent,* Bill Ayers describes this development:

> Jane Addams and the dauntless women of Hull House established the
> first children's court in the world on July 1, 1899, in Chicago. Their goal

was straightforward: to create a special, separate place for children in crisis, away from adult courts and the horrors of adult jails and poorhouses.... The founders strove to develop a safe haven, a space to protect, to rehabilitate, and to heal children, a site of nurturance and guidance, understanding and compassion. They envisioned the Juvenile Court functioning in the best interest of children and youth, acting in any circumstances, they said, exactly as a 'kind and just parent' would act.[4]

Most of the gangs that emerged during the nineteenth century ceased to function by the early 1900s. A "prosperity" had enveloped the country. Yet by the 1920s, Prohibition had arrived and a new level of organized criminal activity became ingrained in the political and social life of most major cities. In 1927 criminologist Frederick M. Thrasher studied some 1,300 gangs in Chicago—at the time, 7 percent were African American; the rest were of European descent. Members of these groups developed major crime syndicates. This was the era of Al Capone, of the speakeasy, of the tommy gun. The Great Depression of the late 1920s and early 1930s also brought forth a new breed of "criminal." U.S.-born and -raised, they included Bonnie and Clyde, John Dillinger, Pretty Boy Floyd, and Machine-Gun Kelly—all of them have attained mythic status in the United States. The driveby shooting and the "machine gun nest"—in which second-floor apartments were rented and rigged with machine guns to strike at enemy gangsters on the street—were first seen in this period.

Between 1910 and 1940 the African-American, Puerto Rican, and Mexican communities—whose members had arrived in large numbers from the Deep South, the Caribbean, or Mexico to work at the lowest levels of the growing industry of the North—started their own street organizations. In the early 1920s the first East L.A. barrios were conceived, such as those in Chavez Ravine (La Loma, La Bishop, Palo Verde), White Fence, the Flats, and Maravilla; in the 1930s and 1940s these groups consisted largely of the first- and second-generation children of refugees from the 1910–21 Mexican Revolution.[5] These barrio organizations are today among the oldest continuous street gangs in the country.[6]

After the criminal heydays of the Prohibition era and the Great Depression, within a generation or two the European immigrant groups had "moved up." The so-called Cosa Nostra had consolidated into a powerful organization with ties to government and business, leaving much of the low-level street activity to others. In cities like Chicago, some gangs were incorporated into the political machines of the day. The city's first Mayor Daley—father of the present mayor—brought along members of the Hamburgs, a "social club" whose main activity had been to keep African Americans out of the Irish community; they reportedly played a deadly role in the 1919 Chicago "race" riot, performing lynchings and beatings. Tammany Hall, New York's early political machine, had similar origins. With the added barrier of color discrimination, the African, Mexican, and Puerto Rican communities were not moving up the social ladder.

After World War II, with an influx of heroin and other drugs into major cities, gangs became involved in the burgeoning drug trade. Drug use among gangs grew fast; some even had subgroups of heroin users. By then Mexican *pachuco* or "zootsuit" gangs gained prominence in the Southwest and were the target of some of the worst civil disturbances in the 1940s like the 1943 "Zootsuit" Riots in Los Angeles.[7] African Americans in Harlem, Detroit, and Washington, D.C. were also targeted.

Between 1941 and 1956 half a million Puerto Ricans migrated to the United States, primarily to New York City, but also to Chicago, Philadelphia, and the northeastern states of Connecticut, Massachusetts, and New Jersey. The tenement slums of Manhattan and other boroughs became the new home of many Puerto Ricans, joining the African Americans and prompting a high level of street warfare in the 1950s.

Many U.S. communities also had their "leather-jacketed" youth gangs during the 1950s. On the West Coast, "biker" gangs proliferated, such as the Hell's Angels, which were born on the dusty streets of a steel town, Fontana, California. Other well-known biker groups included the Outlaws, Pagans, Bandidos, and Vagos. And street-corner "societies" arose around the stoops and alleys of eastern cities. Although rarely using guns, roving bands of youth rumbled on the weekends, resulting in a public outcry, as if nothing could get worse than this.

In the 1960s a lull in gang activity coincided with the apogee of the civil rights struggles and the advent of groups such as the Black Panthers, the Brown Berets, and the Young Lords. However, after a concerted government effort (including COINTELPRO)[8] to destroy those groups, and with an influx of Vietnam War veterans—mostly without jobs, heavily trained in weaponry, and some addicted to drugs—a new level of gang activity emerged.

The late 1960s and early 1970s saw the birth of Crips, Bloods (Brims, Bounty Hunters, Pirus, and so on) and 18th Street (as well as other Chicano street organizations) in Los Angeles. At the same time the Latin Kings, Spanish Cobras, Black P. Stone Nation, and Gangster Disciples increased their presence in Chicago.

This period also saw the strengthening of older Mexicano/Chicano prison groups, the oldest of which reportedly began in the 1950s at a California prison. The two largest Chicano prison associations were known in the media as La Eme and La Nuestra Familia. These groups eventually broke down between those representing barrios from northern California and those from southern California. The infamous super-max prison at Pelican Bay was purportedly created to house leaders from these organizations as well as other major prison groups.

Similar prison formations have spread throughout penitentiaries in New Mexico, Colorado, and Arizona. The massive Texas Department of Corrections has dealt with many decades of active prison gangs, involving people from all races, but most certainly from the large Chicano-Mexicano prison population. Two of the most well known are the Texas Syndicate (TS) and Barrios Aztecas. TS was originally organized to retaliate against a system-wide, prison-sanctioned group of prisoners called the Building Tenders (BTs). The BTs were created in the 1930s to control the prison population. They were brutal and often used murder.

"The use of building tenders... and their like created a savage underworld in prisons," wrote Joseph T. Hallinan, a Pulitzer Prize–winning *Wall Street Journal* reporter. "The strong ruled and the weak acquiesced; at the end of the day what mattered was power. In Texas, the building tenders functioned as enforcers for the administration, meting out beatings and other forms of punishment to inmates who got out of line. In their cells they were allowed to keep ax handles, blackjacks, brass knuckles, even knives. Many had keys to secure parts of the prison and access to confidential inmate files. They also enjoyed extraordinarily close ties to the officials they worked for. When a warden moved to a new prison, his favorite tenders often went with him."[9]

In 1976 the Texas Syndicate organized retribution. By 1983, after a federal judge issued a sweeping opinion against the state's prison system, a partial-consent decree in the Texas Department of Corrections abolished the BTs system. However, TS had by then become highly organized. The Barrio Aztecas began in the late 1980s, originally consisting of prisoners from the very old barrios of El Paso (known as El Chuco). Some of El Chuco's most infamous street organizations—El Secundo Barrio and the T-Birds (Los Pajaros), for example—were already well known in the Texas prison system. Recently groups with ties to Mexico's drug cartels have also been established.[10]

One of the country's worst prison disturbances, the 1980 Santa Fe Riot in New Mexico, was reportedly initiated by a Chicano prison organization that rapidly spread to other groups. In the end that conflagration claimed more than thirty lives, with scores more tortured, beaten, and raped.[11]

There was also the beginning of "alliances" such as the Sureño and Norteño groupings in California, tied to the *trece* (representing the southern California gangs) and *catorce* (representing the northern California barrios) formations in the prisons. In some areas this signified whether members were mostly Chicanos—youths of Mexican descent who have been in this country a generation or more—or the more recent arrivals from Mexico and Central America.

All these major alliances have extended to other states and countries: I saw Sur Trece graffiti in the U.S. Southwest, including Native American reservations, Illinois, Delaware, Mexico, and Central America; I know there are Crips and Bloods across the country and the Caribbean; and Folks and People are also active on the East Coast and some southern cities.[12] In addition there is now the phenomenon of the "hybrid" gang, for example, the growing Crips-Folks alliance in some areas, or the participation of various race and nationality groupings within formerly homogenous groups. For instance the 18th Street, started by Chicanos in the 1960s, now includes Central Americans, whites, blacks, and Asians.

By the mid-1970s the deindustrialization of the big cities contributed to a decrease in jobs, particularly for young people. Old mechanical-industrial employment was being transformed and electronics-computer jobs failed to significantly impact the areas hardest hit by the loss of work. New economic outlets, such as the now-pervasive drug trade, were fashioned.

By then drugs and guns were arriving in large quantities. In 1950 there were 56 million guns in the United States; by 1995 that number had escalated to 240 million, including many military-issued weapons that conveniently wound up on the street.[13] The technological advances in weaponry became a major factor in the rise of gun-related homicides. Up to the 1970s firearms consisted mostly of handguns such as the snubbed-nose "Saturday Night Special," shotguns, rifles, and the occasional machine gun. By the early

1980s multiround high-caliber weapons like Uzis, AKs, MAC 10s, and Tec-9s were found in most U.S. communities.

In additon, the changes in the job market brought on by new technology drew a significant number of the displaced population toward greater involvement in criminal enterprises—and a subsequent rise in the body count in the 1980s and early 1990s.

A friend once told me a story about a former Black Panther leader in a Midwest community who in the 1960s had his phone tapped, while federal agents followed him everywhere. Forced to go underground, he later entered the drug trade and eventually got good at it. However, he told my friend, soon after this nobody kept tabs on him—he wasn't followed or harassed. He later became the number one drug dealer in the area. As he said this, my friend noted a breaking in his voice; the pain, perhaps, of having been pushed away from being a committed community activist.

In the 1980s many street gangs merged with or changed into drug "crews," mostly involving crack, particularly in New York City, Washington, D.C., Baltimore, Miami, and Detroit. The drug trade became the mainstay of economic life for many communities.[14] Armed with greater firepower—and fed a rash of "gang" movies, music, and fashion—youth from every major metropolis were beginning to claim "sets," "nations," "klicas," "crews," or "varrios."

The general perception is that the majority in these street organizations are African-American, Mexican, and Puerto Rican youth. Yet young people of European, Asian, and Native American descent have become among the fastest-rising members of what are called gangs. Sets from L.A. and Chicago spread to the suburbs and rural communities. I encountered thriving groupings next to corn fields in Nebraska, and in the Pine Ridge and Navajo reservations. My own barrio gang in South San Gabriel, Lomas, has become one of the largest street organizations in the Omaha area, apparently set up by homeboys who had settled there in the late 1980s.

Refugees from war-torn and impoverished countries such as El Salvador, Guatemala, Laos, Cambodia, the Dominican Republic, and Haiti also arrived in large numbers in the 1980s, many of them participating in the growing street economy. The media has made much of Jamaican "posses" and Southeast Asian extortion crews.

In the 1990s, with the breakup of socialist regimes in Eastern Europe, refugees poured into various U.S. cities, particularly on the East Coast but also into places like Chicago and Los Angeles. Some of these immigrant youth also formed street organizations. In Hollywood an Armenian immigrant group—Armenian Power (AP)—were believed to be responsible for a dozen driveby murders by mid-1997.[15]

Another example involves Salvadorans, who numbered upward of 500,000 in Los Angeles by the mid-1990s (a total of a million refugees, a fifth of their total population, were scattered throughout the country by then). Many of their children, brutalized by a fifteen-year civil war that by 1992 had resulted in more than 75,000 killed, were further traumatized by the poverty and violence in their Koreatown, Pico Union, South Central, and Hollywood barrios. Some of these youth joined older Chicano gangs, such as 18th Street, White Fence, and Florencia Trece; others began their own, such as La Mara Salvatrucha (MS).

In the early 1990s I traveled to El Salvador with photographer Donna DeCesare to visit members of 18th Street and MS in two prisons and local hangouts. Cholo-style graffiti graced many a wall. Some of these youth greeted me with *"¡Orale, ese!"*—what any vato would say from the streets of L.A. They, too, were part of *la vida loca* in which I had once participated.[16]

L.A. gangs were also in evidence in Mexico, Honduras, Guatemala, Nicaragua, and Belize. By the late 1990s L.A. gang youth were allegedly behind gang violence and the growing drug market in the impoverished Mexico City suburb of La Neza (Nezahualcoyotl).[17] This "globalization" of the L.A. gang culture was largely created when U.S. immigration authorities started targeting Mexican and Central American gang youth for deportation after the 1992 L.A. Rebellion. In 1996 new immigration legislation also demanded the jailing and deportation of anyone who had a minimum of one year in jail (regardless of when it may have happened), forcing even more people back to countries that had no place for them.

Nationwide, thousands of undocumented prisoners have been sent back to their countries of origin—37,000 in 1996–97 alone—impacting countries that have far less resources to deal with felons and gang youth, who have been for the most part raised in the United States. (Another result of this is the number of cholos who now reside in Armenia after some AP members were deported—with *chicanesca* street names such as Negro, Topo, and Boxer.)

Over the years I also met with members of Los Solidos in Connecticut, a mostly Puerto Rican organization that in the 1990s had a deadly rivalry with a version of the Latin Kings. In fact Chicago-based "supergangs" such as the Latin Kings, but also Gangster Disciples, Vice Lords and Maniac Latin Disciples, had members scattered throughout these areas, in addition to Florida and Puerto Rico (although some were unauthorized spin-offs of the larger group). As stated in a recent *Los Angeles Times* article, "The nationwide expansion has been in progress since the late 1980s."[18]

You have to add to this the growing number of White Supremacist gangs, sometimes called Skinheads (although antiracist Skinheads also exist). By the mid-1990s in California, groups such as the Peckerwoods and Nazi Lowriders made a name for themselves following some highly publicized violent acts. The Aryan Brotherhood has been a major player in many penitentiaries across the country for years.[19]

There are also middle- and upper-class white youth who have become more active in ganglike peer groups. They include the Spur Posse of Lakewood, California, which caused a brief furor in the early 1990s for allotting "points" for the number of teenage girls with whom their members had sex; and the so-called Trenchcoat Mafia, which became vilified in 1999 when the perpetrators of the Columbine High School killings were alleged to be members. In addition I have met middle-class or rural white youth who became cholos or members of African American–based gangs such as the Crips, Gangster Disciples, or Vice Lords. And bear in mind, there have been old Irish and Italian street crews in places like New York City, Philadelphia, and Boston that continue to be active.

In the late 1980s Southeast Asian youth, the Hmong included, were carrying out hits, extortions, and robberies in their own communities throughout southern California, but also in Minnesota, Michigan, Texas, and Louisiana. I met with several of them in Fresno, California, and with a couple of tattooed Vietnamese gang youth in North Carolina. Although many Asian gang members are apparently part of groups like the Crips and the Bloods, some well-known Asian gangs include Wah Ching, Pinoy Real, Tiny Rascal Gang, Black Dragons, Asian Boys, and Asian Dragons. Since early 2000, federal prosecutors have been targeting a major Chinese American criminal gang in southern California that the government claims is one of the most sophisticated and organized in the United States.

Yet despite these developments, many so-called gangs are not necessarily criminal organizations. What some law enforcement agencies have been calling "gangs" run the gamut of social, cultural, and/or political groups of young people. In some cities, organizations such as the Ñetas (originally from Puerto Rico) or Africa Bambataa's Universal Zulu Nation refuse to be labeled "gangs."

In Connecticut I visited a maximum security prison "gang pod" where Black Muslims and Puerto Rican *independistas* were designated as gang members. Mexika spiritual circles and Nahuatl-speaking collectives in some federal and state prisons have been labeled "gangs." For years L.A. barrio groupings never called themselves gangs.[20]

In fact there is little unity among officials as to what constitutes a gang. "It's not just the names that differ," wrote Chicago reporter Andrew Martin. "Each city's gangs have different patterns of violence and activity. Each city has different ways of combating gangs. And cities differ in what they label a gang-related homicide. They even differ in what they call a gang."[21]

Another consideration is that even if someone were in a street gang, this does not necessarily mean he or she would become a violent criminal. Given that the total gang membership in L.A. County is 150,000, as estimated by police, why were there only 807 gang-related murders in 1995, one of the worst years for gang-related violence? Although any one such incident is one too many, 807 slayings seem few in light of the belief that it is easy to provoke 150,000 gang members to pull the trigger. This latter number seems exaggerated, possibly to fuel fear and justify pouring ever more public money into law enforcement (the primary source of the numbers). We have to concede that the vast majority of so-called gang members are not shooting people. In fact police often admit that a smaller core of "shooters" end up doing most of the damage attributed to a whole gang.

Furthermore it should be acknowledged that former and active gang members have played major roles in establishing truces, peace plans, and positive institutions in Los Angeles, Chicago, Minneapolis, Boston, New York City, and other cities. Besides the well-known efforts of the Crips and the Bloods, other peace organizations in the South Central L.A. area include Unity One, F.A.C.E.S., Amer-I-Can, N.O.G.U.N.S., and Mothers Reclaiming Our Children (Mothers ROC). For decades now, Chicanos have made numerous truce and peace efforts such as Barrios Unidos, the Coalition to End Barrio Warfare, the Barrio Federation, Proyecto Pastoral, with the participation of people like William "Blinkie" Rodríguez in the San Fernando Valley and Henry Toscano in East Los Angeles. Many of them in turn helped the growth of a primarily Salvadoran gang peace effort called Homies Unidos, based in Los Angeles and San Salvador.

In Chicago, similar efforts have been made by—including, but not limited to—members of the Latin Kings, Latin Maniac Disciples, Insane Spanish Cobras, Two-Six Nation, Gangster Disciples, Vice Lords, and El Rukns. Among Latino organizations, *tablas,* as they were called, were set up to negotiate peace and mediate beefs between gangs.[22] These significant efforts have also been largely overlooked.

Still the distortions prevail about youth and gang violence in this country. John Dilulio, Jr., a Princeton University professor of politics and public affairs (and most recently part of President George W. Bush's White House team), claimed in *Newsweek* and other publications that "super-predator" youth will increase in number as the number of young children increase in the United States.[23] In 1997, Youth Vision—a Chicago-based organization— tried to combat misinformation about young people by pointing out that, contrary to statements like Dilulio's, most youth are not violent or criminals. In fact among young teens, crime is on the decline.

Despite a rise in the early 1990s of juvenile arrests for violent-crime offenses—murder, forcible rape, robbery, and aggravated assault—in 1995 this rate fell 3 percent and has continued to fall. By the year 2000, arrest rates for juveniles accused of murder was down 68 percent from 1993—the lowest levels in more than three decades.[24] Today less than one-half of one percent of youth ten to seventeen years old are arrested for a violent crime.

Nonetheless there is a growing trend to use the designation "gang-related" to jeopardize due process for many young people. In various states youth offenders are given more prison time just because they are alleged gang members, even if their crimes had nothing to do with being in a gang. This practice is called *enhancement.*

Jose "Pepe" Vasquez's experience in a Kane County, Illinois, court is an example of this practice. In 1997, twenty-one years old and a YSS member, he received a mistrial for a 1994 murder case. It was revealed that police officer Marshall Gauer—known as "The Sheik"—prompted a so-called witness to finger Pepe as the culprit. In fact, Pepe had never seen or heard of that witness before the trial. A new trial was ordered and more evidence introduced to support Pepe's innocence. An out-of-state police officer even testified to the suspicious manner used by the Sheik to get help for his "witness." Four character witnesses testified that Pepe was an asset to the community. Family members and YSS attended the sentencing to show support for the youth. Even guards at the county jail, where Pepe had been locked up for several months, told how cooperative and decent the young man had been while incarcerated.

The judge ruled against Pepe, basically accepting the Sheik's word over the defendant's. On December 19, 1997, Pepe was sentenced for murder. The public defender tried to get the minimum sentence—twenty years. The judge, however, reasoned that since Pepe was in a gang—something that was never confirmed—he should get fifty years. "This will be an example to other gang members," the judge stated.

Pepe's father was a hardworking Mexican immigrant. His mother had several other children and a few grandchildren to look after. Pepe's younger siblings, Tony and Lupe, were also YSS participants. Tony, who was close to Pepe, began having problems in school and with the law after his older brother was jailed. Although the family was clear on his innocence, not knowing Pepe's fate was torturous for them.

One day, YSS elder Frank Blazquez and I entered the offices of Lawrence Marshall and Jeff Urdangan, two well-known people's attorneys who worked with the Northwestern University Legal Clinic. They were famous for helping exonerate a number of innocent people on death row in the late 1990s (some of them having spent a dozen or more years in death row before being released). We wanted to see if they would take up Pepe's case. They agreed to challenge Pepe's conviction; it was clearly a travesty of justice. Finally, on November 13, 2000, after months of hearings and after Pepe had already served 1,562 days in prison, his conviction was overturned on appeal.[25]

This, of course, is not an isolated case. As a Minnesota attorney dealing with a similar travesty that involved an African-American gang member said, "A growing list of 'gang-related' exemptions to due process is evidence of courts' willingness to buy into anti-gang hysteria."[26]

Notwithstanding the designation of "gang" to put away people not involved or barely active in a gang, the number of young people who claim to be in some kind of gang keeps on growing. Whereas in the early 1970s such street organizations were primarily situated in the largest cities—notably in L.A., Chicago and New York City—they are now spread throughout the country. In 1998 the Bureau of Justice Statistics and the National Center for Education Studies declared that nearly twice as many teenagers reported gangs in their schools in 1995 as they did in 1989, and that the increase came in every type of community.

There are complex forces contributing to this phenomenon. Within the present social-class divisions of modern technology-driven capitalism, many youths—urban and rural—are being denied the option of earning a "legitimate" living. Sons and daughters of coal miners, factory workers, and farmers are affected, as well as those coming from the shrinking "middle class" of professional and managerial positions. Everyone needs a productive and meaningful job, not just to survive, although this is paramount, but to thrive. Without this, the imbalance gets "stabilized" in gang or illicit enterprises.

Los Angeles, which has had more gang violence than any other city, experienced the greatest incidence of gang-related acts during the 1980s and early 1990s when 300,000 manufacturing jobs were lost in California. According to the Gang Violence Bridging Project of the Edmund G. "Pat" Brown Institute of Public Affairs, at California State University, Los Angeles, the areas with the greatest impoverishment and gang growth were those directly linked to industrial flight.[27]

At the same time, the state of California suffered the results of deep cuts in social programs—most of them from the passage in 1978 of Proposition 13, which decreased state funding for schools after a slash in property taxes. Since 1980, while California's population has jumped by 35 percent, spending for education has steadily declined. Yet there has been a 14 percent annual increase in state prison spending during the same period. In 1995 California's funding for prisons superseded that for education.

Almost all areas in the United States where manufacturing has died or moved away are now reporting ganglike activity. Seventy-two large cities and thirty-eight smaller ones claim to have a "gang problem," according to a 1992 survey of police departments by the National Institute of Justice.[28] It was during this time and under these conditions that the greatest rise in gang violence has been recorded.

Chicago, also hard hit by deindustrialization, is presently considered the second largest gang city in the country. Like Los Angeles, it has many multigenerational organizations; the Vice Lords, considered the oldest of the major present-day Chicago street organizations, started in 1959; the Latin Kings are supposed to have begun around 1964–65.[29]

With industry and community life disrupted or dismantled in the most industrial city in the country, gangs found fuel for growth in Chicago. For years one of the oldest and most stable Mexican communities in the Chicago area existed around the steel mills of the city's southeast side. Fathers, grandfathers, and even great-grandfathers worked the mills. Many residents eventually owned their homes and lived a relatively "good" life. However, with the massive loss of jobs over the last two decades, the community now has a thriving drug market. There are bands of unemployed youth on street corners, and many homes have been abandoned or converted to rental units.

And what has been the official response? For one thing, there has been a complete turnaround from the rehabilitation programs and redemptive philosophies that guided juvenile criminal legislation in the 1900s. Jane Addams's "kind and just parent" has become uncompassionate.

In the early 1990s police sweeps of housing projects and "mob action" arrests were stepped up in Chicago. When a suspected gang member was among two or more young people gathered in certain areas, this was considered "mob action." This resulted in 43,000 arrests through 1995.

Also known as the gang loitering law, this ordinance allowed police to break up small groups of youth from street corners and other public places. Its aim was to ward off any future mishaps from suspected gang members. Young people waiting for the bus to go to school or standing in front of their house on a hot day could be told to disperse or face arrest, jail time for up to six months, a $500 fine, and community service up to 120 hours. Many youth were picked up more than once—literally for doing nothing. One example of its arbitrariness involved my son Ramiro, who got popped for "mob action" once when a friend walked up to him to shake his hand.

The Illinois Supreme Court in 1997 ruled this policy unconstitutional on many counts, including "prior restraint." It stated that the ordinance "failed to distinguish between innocent conduct and 'conduct calculated to cause harm.'"[30]

In California several communities enacted ordinances to outlaw beepers, cellular phones, public phones, baseball bats, and congregations of young people. In 1997 L.A. area prosecutors obtained injunctions against the public gathering of three or more members of 18th Street, the largest L.A.-based gang, and other street organizations.[31] In April 1997, Governor Pete Wilson proposed a package of twenty bills to "get tougher" on violent juvenile criminals; at the same time he suggested imposing the death penalty for murderers as young as thirteen.[32]

Congressional Republicans and Democrats, along with the Clinton administration, were also looking to incorporate many state youth "predator" laws into national legislation. By early 1997 forty-one states were allowing juveniles to be tried as adults. Families in housing projects were being evicted if they had children—or even grandchildren—who were alleged to be in gangs;

this was later extended to include any renter in a poor community where there was suspicion of gang and drug activity going on.

"In the case of violent offenders or those involved in the drug trade, the young no longer would be viewed as more redeemable than adults," according to Representative Bill McCollum (R-Fla). "These are people who we want incapacitated. These are violent predator youth."[33]

Recently there have been calls to deploy the National Guard against gangs, which is like bringing in a larger gang with more firepower. In March 2000, Californians voted in Proposition 21, which gave prosecutors, instead of juvenile court judges, the power to try juveniles as young as fourteen in adult courts, making juvenile convictions open for consideration in determining a "three strikes and you're out" sentencing, as well as other ridiculous injustices. All this, and the increased prison building at the expense of colleges and jobs, is a misdirection of social energies.[34]

These are not solutions.

The situation needs to change. Most people—from the Chicago-based Mothers Against Gangs, to teachers who are forced to be police officers in their classrooms, to families trapped in the line of fire—are scared. They are bone-tired of the violence and are seeking ways out. It's time the voices for viable and lasting solutions be heard. The public debate is now limited largely to those who demonize youth, who want to put them away and use repression to curb their natural instincts to re-create the world.

First we must recognize that our battle is with a society that fails to do all it can for young people—then unjustly lays the blame on them. We must realign societal resources in accordance with the following premises: that all children have intrinsic attributes, that can allow them to succeed; that schools should teach by engaging the intelligence and creativity of all students; that institutions of public maintenance—whether police or social services—respect the basic humanity of all people; that we rapidly and thoroughly integrate young people into the future, into the new technology; that we root out the social and political underpinnings for the injustices and inequities that engender most of the violence we see today.

Sound farfetched? Too idealistic? Fine. Anything short on imagination will result in "pragmatic," fear-driven, and expedient measures that won't solve anything but will only play with people's lives. It doesn't take guts to put money into inhumane, punishment-driven institutions. In fact such policies make our communities even less safe. It's tougher to walk these streets, to listen to young people, to respect them and help them fight for their well-being. It's tougher to care.

I've talked to young people, parents, teachers, and concerned officials in Miami; New York; Phoenix; Seattle; Lansing; Denver; Boston; Hartford; El Paso; Albuquerque; Washington, D.C.; Oakland; Portland; Omaha; San Antonio; Compton; Raleigh-Durham; and Dover, Delaware. I've seen them deal with similar crises, pain, and confusion.

I've worked with various U.S. urban peace efforts and I've addressed international conferences on work with troubled and dispossessed youth, including in Taxco, Mexico; San Salvador, El Salvador; Antigua, Guatemala; Milan and Rome, Italy; London, England; San Juan, Puerto Rico; Groningen, Holland; and Paris, France.

Sometimes, talking to Teens on Target in Los Angeles, a group made up of youths, some in wheelchairs, who have been shot; or to teenage mothers in Tucson, one child caring for another; or to incarcerated young men at the maximum-security Illinois Youth Center at Joliet, I feel the immensity of what we're facing. I felt it when a couple of young women cried in Holyoke, Massachusetts, after I read a poem about a friend who had been murdered by the police; when Navajo elementary school children lined up in Dennehotso, Arizona, so I could autograph their T-shirts and coats; and when I addressed a gym full of students at Jefferson High School in Fort Worth and several young people came up to hug me, as if they had never been hugged before.

These experiences tell me we don't need a country in which the National Guard walks our children to school, or in which pizza-delivery people carry sidearms, or in which prisons outnumber colleges. We can be more enlightened. More inclusive. More imaginative.

And I'm convinced this is how we can be more safe.

Chapter 3

To "See" Again[1]

When more and more young people plan their funerals and not their futures, it spells alarm for the rest of us.

—Father Greg Boyle

Alberto walked out of his apartment building in the Pico-Union neighborhood of Central Los Angeles. He had a round mustached face and was bald, except for a long "homeboy" braid that began at the top of his head. His long-sleeve shirt covered the intricate lines and shades of tattoos on his arms. He backed out of the entrance pulling a baby carriage that held his ten-month-old daughter, Angela, whom he was taking to a neighborhood baby-sitter. Her mother, Sonya, followed. Sonya, a slight and cute girl in her late teens, had reddish peroxided hair and intense chola-style make-up.

Alberto would later hop a bus to an auto shop in South Central L.A. where he apprenticed with his brother. Sonya would wait for a friend to drive her to a small garment plant in Koreatown where she worked.

Alberto had emigrated to L.A. in his early teens. As a child during the civil war in El Salvador, he learned how to use a rifle in a guerrilla outfit. He had witnessed many deaths among his comrades and in the villages they were protecting before he grew out of puberty. Perhaps this knowledge allowed Alberto access to L.A.'s gang culture, gaining him respect and notoriety. But it also made him a frequent target of rival gangs.

Sonya earned her "gang" stripes on L.A.'s streets. She entered the country as an infant, living with her mother in a crowded Pico-Union apartment complex. She eventually dropped out of school, moving in with Alberto when she got pregnant. Sonya often worked in downtown dance halls where immigrant girls from Mexico and Central America were given tickets to dance with strangers, some of whom desired sexual favors. A forged identification

47

card made her twenty-one when she was clearly in her teens. Eventually Alberto put a stop to this when the nightly drinking and dangerous situations proved too draining for the young mother. They were hardworking and thoughtful people. When Alberto worked under the hood, tuning up a car in the shop, he seemed like a regular working stiff, happy, for the moment, to be out of the battle zone.

Alberto and Sonya were members of 18th Street, the city's "deadliest street gang," according to a 1996 series of articles on the gang in the *Los Angeles Times*: headlines such as "A Look Inside at 18th Street's Menace" were used to demonize a segment of mostly Mexican and Central American youth.[2] Alberto once dealt drugs. He had a massive "Eighteen" in old English lettering across his back. There were times when the couple would lay deathly still on a mattress, their infant daughter between them; then Alberto would edge up to the window to check for possible snipers.

But 18th Street is not a monolith. There are caring and intelligent people among their members, just as there are those who don't give a damn.

I got to know Alberto, Sonya, and some of their homies. I also met with some of their rivals in La Mara Salvatrucha. In the Normandie section of the barrio, there are multistoried art deco buildings amid streets crowded with brown-faced mothers and unemployed men, and noisy with the horns and roar of traffic and the squeals of children. The apartment hallways are dense with people lounging on fold-up chairs near their doors, with toys for their kids nearby—they'd rather not be outside and possibly get caught in a crossfire. Street parties are held next to neatly scripted barrio graffiti, below the fire escapes of smog-sooted dark buildings. Several young men in wheelchairs, casualties of the *pleitos* (gang battles), bob their heads to the incessant beat of a Spanish-laced hip-hop sound. With their scars, bullet wounds, harsh makeup, and mad-dog looks, you know many of them are hurting.

When U.S. immigration officials raided the auto shop, Alberto got deported. He called Sonya from Tijuana once or twice, but eventually he stopped calling. The last time I heard, the couple had broken up, leaving Sonya to fend for herself—a single mother in a place where single mothers abound, with little or no resources.

Politicians and demagogues often reduce the complex interactions and situations confronting most people, particularly those ensnared in poverty, to soundbites and quick fix solutions. Everything is a moral failing—"It's not about rich or poor, but about right or wrong." This thinking opens the door for "get tough" legislation.

Most of these people are not in the community as teachers or elders because they are not willing to fully address the problems. They are not vested to do anything real and lasting because they are more concerned about their career, their financial standing, or their own neck. Instead they build campaign coffers and ratings on the legitimate fear people have of violence and uncertainty. With the problems becoming increasingly aggravated and left unsolved, panic begins to grip the highest levels of city, state, and federal power. Most official responses are repressive: more laws, more police, more prisons.

In 1999, in the heavily Mexican–Puerto Rican Chicago-area township of Cicero, some of the most severe antigang ordinances were enacted: Officials could confiscate vehicles and evict people from their homes if they believed them to be members of a street gang. These measures were changed later that year after the ACLU threatened to challenge the ordinances in court. New ordinances were then established that would allow police to confiscate a young person's vehicle if he or she had no legitimate purpose to be out after 9 P.M.[3]

Equally troubling is the notion—which helps give life to these repressive measures—that we don't know what to do about the escalating violence. Judith Steele, a City Hall public safety analyst, was quoted in a *Los Angeles Times* article as saying, "We don't know what works... it's like trying to catch Niagara Falls in a teacup."

Maybe we don't know because we are asking the wrong people. Instead why don't we ask the parents? Why don't we ask longtime community activists? Or the young people themselves? Aren't they the "experts" on their lives? If policy is targeting them, shouldn't they be participating in the formulation of that policy?

In 1999 there was a dialogue organized by the Jane Addams School of Social Work at the University of Illinois, Chicago, concerning child protective services in the state. One official, representing the Illinois Department of Children and Family Services, asserted that "prior domestic abuse is no justification for abusing one's own child." Of course abusing a child has no "justification." However, if a parent was abused when he or she was younger, it is an important part of the equation. Such things can help us understand the patterns of broken relationships that contribute to the abuse of children. Why would anyone not want this to be part of the dialogue?

We must deal deeply with the circumstances and the environment in which child abuse exists and not just deal with it in a limited and punitive manner, such as the practice of taking children away from the mostly poor—and mostly African-American—families that have been targeted by such agencies. It is a way to involve such families, regardless of their economic status or skin color, to become active shapers of the policies and remedies that involve them. Looking at the history and conditions that give rise to such violence can help us to prevent it.

Michael Meade has often stated that the work of community elders is "holding the ground while youth make their glorious mistakes."[4] What brings youth and elders together is trouble. When society at large fails to develop true eldership and mentoring at the most basic community level, and when the elders are not there to provide compassion, wisdom, experience, and meaningful and lasting skills knowledge, the young usually "sacrifice" themselves to drugs, violence, gangs, and prison, many times paying with their lives.

Repeatedly administrators in youth detention centers or community programs say they want their young charges to go through a process of awareness and change, of opening up and maturing, but without any trouble. But there is no such process. Unfortunately these "troubles" lead the people with the resources to turn away from the individuals who need them most. Alberto and Sonya, and youth like them, are often lost because too many churches, recreation centers, and employers have closed their doors to them. Too many people have given up. I've heard parents plead to the courts, "Take my child—I don't know what to do anymore." But the problem is not just unsure parents. The whole community is fragmented in their response, and many children are falling through the cracks.

Young people need a place—both at home and in the community—of unconditional acceptance, where they are honored, where their natural gifts are nurtured and they can live out purposeful lives. Children and youth need the guidance and support of community as their psychological-social development occurs. Self-esteem can't be achieved by telling oneself over and over, "I'm okay." One also needs confirmation from the outside to more or less accurately estimate one's place and abilities. Such confirmation can only come from a community that surrounds young people with "hearts and hands," and provides them the initiatory experience necessary for their proper growth and tempering.[5] Properly helped, young people learn not to be helpless; properly disciplined, they can become self-disciplined; properly cared for, they care for themselves.

All youths, troubled or otherwise, have these needs. A violent and fractured community will produce violent and lost children. We need to look at the big issues: Have we abandoned our elders? Are we pushing our young people aside? Unless we address such concerns, megalopolises like Los Angeles or Chicago cannot sustain the kind of grassroots community-building that is necessary.

This is not about "rescuing" young people. We can't rescue them, because they have to save themselves, tapping into their own creative energies. They have to become masters of their own lives—with their autonomy and integrity strengthened in the process. Finding their places in this world is an intensely personal endeavor. But where is the community that prepares them, sets clear and consistent parameters, and, when the ordeal is over, welcomes them home?

We must ask ourselves the following questions:

• Where are the centers and the schools where young people can be creative, respected, and safe?

• Where are the meaningful social activities, including community-organized and community-sanctioned recreation, as well as the empowering, socially charged, community improvement projects?

• Where are the loving family environments? Where these environments don't exist, is it fair—or wise—to blame the families?[6]

• Where are the sanctuaries, the safe and sacred spaces, where their spiritual quests are attended to, their psychological and social concerns are met, and where the law, which often works against them, can be accessible and understandable so it can work for them?

• Do the young have the sense that their floundering steps, even the missteps, are part of their growth and advancement?

• How can youths contribute to social change, to bettering their homes and community, and know that their contributions are essential?

Other societies have long recognized that young people need proper initiatory experiences, rites of passage profound enough to match the fire in their souls. If not, they will turn that fire outward, burning everything around them, acting out in violent ways, or consuming themselves in such false initiations as drugs or alcohol.

As renowned social-psychologist James Hillman has pointed out, these initiations must be linked to discovering one's life purpose, one's daimon or genius. All of us have to find our own special calling. The Mexika people of ancient Mexico, also known as "the people with an umbilical to the moon," believed that every child had his or her own *tonalli*, or soul-direction, calculated by the movements of the sun, moon, planets, and constellations. They believed that there are personal and specific group destinies tied to the cosmos and integral to the web and movement of all life. The *tonalli* was kept secret by the parents and the diviners until the child was old enough to make conscious steps toward it—and to prevent anyone from blocking the child from his or her predestined path. *Tonalli* was a direction, but not unalterable; a person had to consciously participate in his or her own destiny to get there. Hillman has written that a life is similar to that of a tiny acorn in which the image of a mighty oak tree is already imprinted.[7] Like the acorn, human beings have innate attributes and faculties that, properly nurtured, can reach fruition. Our life task is to go in the direction of this calling, the pull of destiny. What eventually gets us there is character. Destiny therefore is not just about a future. Destiny is here, now. It is something you have to make happen.

Unfortunately in a postindustrial capitalist society our internal purposes are too often demeaned, denied, or crushed in the helter-skelter scramble to survive (similar to when a plague, conquest, natural disasters, or war destroys whole peoples). Today much of this creativity is expressed as madness. It appears that many of our sons and daughters have gone insane, whether they are shooting their classmates, using drugs, or becoming precocious consumers.

Any society that does not take care of the material, spiritual, and educational needs of its children has failed. A community out of balance turns out unbalanced people. So when one sees the young dying before their elders, when there are more and more violent responses to problems—whether from the powerful or the powerless—we know society has lost its vision. "Conservative," "liberal," or "moderate" are not terms that express the real content of our times, the revolutionary promise that most people are crying out for: a society humane enough to take the wondrous inventions, the advanced resources, and unleash them to heal and protect the lives of its people.

As Michael Meade has often said, the problem is not the gang; the problem is the lack of interest in the gang. We need to look at people like Alberto and Sonya again. At its root this is what the word *respect* means, from the Latin *respectus:* "to look back at, to reconsider, to see again." If Alberto and Sonya, with their wisdom born of barriers, blocks, and battering, had been given the proper support, teachings, options, and centering, they would have been more capable of becoming good parents, hard workers, and creative people. But when things looked good, when both were working, renting their own place and avoiding some of the hazards of where they lived, the law came in and undermined this partnership while it was in its formative stages, eventually forcing them to go their own ways.

The general attitude toward gangs is that they are a social disease ("they're worse than a cancer," a so-called gang expert recently declared), that gang youth have nothing positive to give. But when their needs are addressed, these youth will give plenty. Many have already done so despite the negligence. What can determine the difference is an aware, resourceful, authentic, committed, and spiritually rich community. Under favorable conditions, anyone can become a confident, competent, and autonomous person.

Is there a role for policymakers and law enforcement? Of course, but as part of a whole package, developing action around the assets of a community, not the perceived deficits. It's also time to reactivate our elders and their status. We need what some cultures have called "root doctors," those who go to the root of a problem to solve it.

Chapter 4

Being Solid in the World[1]

There is something about poverty that smells like death. Dead dreams dropping off the heart like leaves in dry season and rotting around the feet; impulses smothered too long in the fetid air of underground caves. The soul lives in sickly air. People can be slaveships in shoes.

—Zora Neale Hurston

The accused murderer placed the razor blade against the skin of my neck. He put his face up to mine, scrutinizing me for signs of fear. Another accused murderer stood next to him, grinning broadly, as a thirteen-year-old stood behind me. I had given myself the task of protecting this kid against the adult prisoners in the Los Angeles County Hall of Justice jail, known then as the "Glasshouse." I was sixteen—too young to be in an adult facility. But I had been arrested during the August 29, 1970, Chicano Moratorium Against the Vietnam War, also known by some observers as the East L.A. Riot.

From a sheriff's substation, to an overcrowded juvenile hall, we ended up at the infamous Glasshouse—two sixteen-year-olds, a fifteen-year-old, and the thirteen-year-old. In the cell next to me was Charles Manson, awaiting trial for the murders that would forever be linked to his name. Along the tier, which a sheriff's deputy called "murderer's row," were other accused killers, including the two in my cell: One claimed to have killed a teacher and another allegedly shot a youth at a housing project.

When I asked a deputy why we were being placed among murder suspects, he said we could be facing murder charges since by then three people had been killed in the disturbance—including Chicano journalist Ruben Salazar. The implication was that by our alleged participation, we could be held responsible. It was several days in hell. Fortunately all charges were later dropped.

Fortunately, too, I was able to stand up to the man with the blade, looking at him straight in the eye and telling him that he had better make sure I was good and dead, because if not, I was going to come after him. Silence followed. He removed the blade from my neck and started to laugh. Later all four of us played cards until lights out.

However, another kind of scar had been made in my psyche. Although I had been arrested numerous times since the age of thirteen, for stealing and fighting and disturbing the peace, I made a violent turn after my stay in the Glasshouse. Stabbings, shootings, and armed robberies became the gist of my involvement in the neighborhood gang. A year later I was arrested for attempted murder in an incident in which four people were shot. A year after that I faced a six-year prison sentence for a scuffle with police officers.

Ultimately I avoided a conviction in the attempted murder case (the witnesses failed to identify me). And later a judge, who decided to give me a "second chance" (in truth, a fifth or sixth chance) after receiving numerous letters of support from the community, gave me a lesser charge and county jail time for the incident with the police. It's hard to express how crucial this was; I honestly don't believe I would be here if not for this intervention.

With the careful and consistent involvement of adults, I began to study and lay an intellectual footing that I did not have before. These adults included the teacher who saw worth in the poems and vignettes I had first written in a juvenile facility when I was fifteen; the Chicano leader who ran the John Fabela Youth Center that served the South San Gabriel barrio; the high school's home-school coordinator who became like a second mother; and a former gang member who worked for the L.A. County Probation Department, and who involved me in his "get-together" retreats that have trained leaders out of troubled youth for more than thirty years. They all helped me prepare for a self-directed, crime-free life. These people brought to bear an important quality in relating to young people: the quality of their presence.

While I was writing this book, legislation was being enacted by states and Congress that would give prosecutors wide-ranging discretion to send kids charged with crimes to adult court and prison. The dangers alone warrant the end to such legislation. As the Children's Defense Fund (CDF) reported in 1999, children are eight times more likely to commit suicide and five times more likely to be sexually assaulted in adult jails than they are in juvenile facilities.

While there must be consequences for one's actions, the consequences should also include redemptive measures, healthy recreation, intellectual activity, skills training, art and rituals, human connections, and community initiatory practices. Although some juvenile detention centers may fail to manage these things, most adult prisons won't try.

Such legislation is partly a return to more than a hundred years ago when "prisons were graduate colleges for criminals," according to Otto L. Bettmann:

> "Youthful offenders were thrown together with hardened criminals, whose corrupting influence complemented the courts' general indifference to reform," wrote Bettmann. "Judge Ben Lindsey recalls his assignment as a young attorney to look after two prisoners. His clients turned out to be young boys who had been locked in a cell for sixty days with a safecracker and horse thief '…upon whom they had learned to look as great heroes.' Like grownups, children were locked up on the slightest suspicion of misdeed. In Chicago, 'upwards of 10,000 young persons were arrested, clubbed, handcuffed, and jostled around… without having committed any crime.' Such excesses nurtured in the young a disrespect for the law that strengthened the inclination toward delinquency."[2]

Our policies must heed the advice of most experts in the field who tell us that youth is the time when the psyche is most susceptible to intervention and change. "The teenage brain is a work in progress," said Sandra Witelson, a neuroscientist at McMaster University in Ontario.[3] Youth is a time when we all make mistakes and learn to overcome them. If we enshrine the concept that people cannot change when they reach adolescence, we are condemning the whole community to instability and dread.

In effect, these laws are forcing youth to take responsibility as adults without having the authority of adults. This leads to a terrible imbalance. The fact is that no legislation can make a child or teenager a mature adult—they are developmentally unable to do so even if they are still capable of committing some extremely terrible acts.

Of course, change is not easy, as my own life can attest. It's often a process of one step forward and two steps back. It may include self-sabotage, as I have done many times. In the end the help I received found a lasting berth, an opening, toward my own transformation. But it took a long time. It helps if the community works on the premise that every life has value and that with proper relationships and support a person can find the self-caring and self-discipline to turn toward an innate purpose. "[To] step in," as East L.A.'s Father Greg Boyle once said, "where others have stepped out."[4]

Unfortunately our social policies are too often about dispatching problems, not effectiveness. This usually amounts to "zero tolerance" in the courts, schools, families, workplace, and other institutions. It is a losing proposition. Crime is characterized by a web of broken relationships—economic, social, familial, and, finally, brokenness within one's self. By pushing the "problem" youth out, we are snipping the delicate threads of community that should keep us together.

The harder but exceedingly more rewarding work includes hanging in with young people, teaching them, guiding them, and tapping into the creative reservoir they all carry so that they can find the meaningful life they are meant to live.

We need comprehensive policies and strategies that flow from our extensive social experience on how people become positive and active members of the community. The foundation for this is the powerful and elemental idea that we save our communities by saving our youth.

When youths are questioned about what they believe to be the source of instability in their communities, the number-one issue is economics.[5] People can't address for long concerns about their core values or psychological and moral soundness when the economic rug is pulled out from under them. If nothing else, economics is about being solid in the world.

In other words a tree's branches cannot rise toward the sun unless the tree is firmly rooted in the earth. In many respects so, too, a human being. This is where family, community, collective-affirming values, and a stable, sustaining economy come into play. They are like the enveloping ground (earth-womb) that nourishes the growth of a self-sufficient, individual-affirming, spiritually aware person.

The word *economics* has a Greek root meaning "household management." In the seventeenth century, this meaning was broadened to include the management of a nation's resources. The concept was more fully termed political economy (they are two aspects of what should be a unified whole). Over time, the economy has been removed from the political sphere (including the civil administration of governing) and has been imbued with a certain mystery. Today the subject of economics appears to have magical qualities beyond our grasp. Looking at recent headlines about stock market downturns, recessionary pressures, and the growing number of bankruptcies around the world, it appears we can't do much about the economy. However, economic laws are not only knowable but, if we are armed with an understanding of these laws, they are manageable. Although there are some things that are beyond our control, an economy is one thing we can do something about. Young people trying to establish their own economic means are often reminded how much this is out of their hands. It's time to stop being helpless about the economy. As the old saying goes, to be truly free, you have to appreciate and respect the limitations.

The most basic economic law is the one governing polarity. We know about the polarities in our society between men and women, old and young, rich and poor, black and white. They each have their own dynamics. The key polarity in our economy involves the production of the basics of life. There is an antagonism between the social and the collaborative nature of production—the development of the tools and technology, the laborers and administration, the consumers required to keep production going—and its private ownership. Everyone participates in production at some level, but only a few reap its immense rewards. What's set aside for wages, charity, foundations, infrastructure, donations, and social programs can't balance this. This is the source of the so-called haves and have-nots. From this basic polarity flows most other social polarities.

Meantime, we have turned away from the deliberate and planned aspect of ensuring the economy takes care of our basic needs. More and more people have bought into the idea that government is not responsible for helping people (although government works for "somebody"—usually those with the financial clout and lobbying power to dictate policy). It has gotten so we can look at the growing number of people without homes or jobs and smugly claim "it's their fault," or "it's God's will," or some equally indeterminate excuse, washing our hands of the problem.

The central economic reality facing young people today is the global transformation of an industrial-based economy to one based on electronics and digital technology. This is characterized by a shift from intensive profit-producing physical labor to information-producing mental labor. We are in what people have called the Information Age.[6]

In other words, globalization is capitalism in the age of electronics.

Yet the technology is also making capitalism's essential impulse—maximizing profits by the creation of surplus value—difficult to sustain. When most workers were confined to large-scale labor-intensive capitalist enterprises, or even small sweat shops, one could practically see this surplus value at play (mostly by not paying workers the real value of their labor). This is increasingly harder to achieve when robotics and digital technology—as well as biotechnologies and nanotechnologies—make products without labor and when most social wealth derives from financial speculation, manipulation of stocks, and the oscillations of the real estate markets.

For years millions worked in factories and mills. Today these industries no longer offer viable employment options. The 1970s through 1990s saw the greatest loss of such jobs in this country since the Great Depression. A new class of unemployed or subemployed people has been formed as a result of the robotization and downsizing of the workplace.

The March 29, 1998, issue of *Parade* magazine reported that since 1989, about 4 million jobs were lost in the United States. Although at least 4.2 million new jobs were expected to be in place through the year 2000, they were mostly low-paying, part-time or temporary, service-sector positions. Currently many of the impoverished are actually working. A reexamination and redistribution of paid and unpaid labor is crucial now as less paid work becomes necessary to keep the economy growing, especially in the highly industrialized Western economies.[7]

A shift like this has not occurred in our economy since the post–Civil War period, when society moved rapidly from an agricultural society to an industrial one. In those days people who had lived for generations on farms left their homes for the promise of a better life in the industrialized cities of the North and Midwest, even though work was not available for everyone. Millions from Europe and the American South crowded into cities that did not have the infrastructure—housing, sanitation, utilities—to adequately contain them.

As a result whole families, out of necessity, established "marginal," often illegal, economies. Jails were crowded with those who tried to survive in circumstances not necessarily of their own making.[8] On the other hand, philanthropies were being endowed by the founders of some major corporations (including Carnegie, Rockefeller, and Ford). While some of them may have been compelled by humanitarian concerns (*philanthropy* means "love of man"), these institutions also served another purpose: to absolve the major architects of the economy of any blame—the steel magnates, the banking kings, and the retail and building trades giants, as well as the bureaucrats who failed to thoroughly address the needs of an expendable, and quite young, displaced population. Philanthropies or prisons—neither was a satisfactory response to the problems of industrialization.

The post–Civil War period was also characterized by strikes, walkouts, demonstrations, and pitched battles between laborers, strikebreakers, and police. The massive marches of union women in New York City's textile industry in the late 1800s, and the 1886 Haymarket bombing in Chicago— seven police officers were killed, four professed anarchists were later executed, and one committed suicide while in prison—were two of the most "notorious" incidents growing out of economic "dislocation." Others followed: The bloody battle between Pinkerton detectives and steelworkers in Homestead, Pennsylvania, in 1892 that ended with thirteen dead; and the massacre of thirty-three men, women, and children from the mines of Ludlow, Colorado, in 1914 were among them.[9]

Such social disruptions, including the massive civil rights and antiwar mobilizations of the 1960s, were telling us something: The whole of society aimed to attain equilibrium after a long period of social imbalance.

Today we are also in need of rebalancing. Economic and political refugees continue to enter the country from Mexico, Central America, the Caribbean, Eastern Europe, and Asia. Small home businesses and dot.coms have proliferated throughout the economic terrain. And for some time we've seen the "permanently" unemployed walk the land, while the safety nets put in place during the Great Depression are removed.

Again, robots, computers, and digital technologies now produce commodities where people once did. There are steel mills, assembly lines, and auto plants being run without human participation (from labor-saving to labor-replacing production). But selling their ability to work is how people make money to buy the things they need. Without work there is no money. Without money in people's hands (liquid assets), we cannot sufficiently distribute the vast amount of commodities, from food to computer hardware, piling up in storehouses. The crying need is to get money into people's hands again through credit or government assistance—both of which have reached their limits—or, as the crisis is already indicating, to distribute commodities without money.

The big economic system on which we have staked our lives, our children's lives, and our future is running out of fuel. Nonetheless, if we go by the Gross National Product, the fuel gauge seems to be going higher—perpetuated by the media, dishonest economists (dabbling in some peculiar mathematics), and many politicians. However, this is a false measure of our economic standing. The accumulation of product wealth cannot tell the whole story. In essence this is like watching the fuel gauge going up while we clearly see the plane going down.

It is all quite complicated, but you can see how far-reaching and profound the solutions must be to meet the momentous challenges of today's economic realities. Advanced technology must be aligned with the needs of the society—moreover, with the needs of our children—or it will become a source of further conflict. The direction is to actualize the potential of plenitude and equity built into the advanced productive forces. Until this is satisfactorily dealt with, the spiritual longings of young people are largely unmet or addressed in "shotgun" fashion.

The young, in particular, are reeling from the social tremors resulting from this process. Because they are unsure of where they now stand, they have an obscured vision of the future and their places in it. Their community is in turmoil and unable to generate a vision for itself. If the children seem to be going crazy, look at the veering relationships and technological upheaval contributing to the "craziness" in their world.

"In the big picture, there is an upheaval throughout the world in terms of the rapidity of change in all aspects of the culture," says Meade. "Usually, adolescents rebel against tradition; but what they face is changing so fast that they can't rebel against it. They become caught in the flood of change. The old idea is that culture represents stability and young people propel themselves away from that and in doing so find the essence of themselves. In this case, there's nothing to bounce off ... they're just bouncing along. They have a double dose of uncertainty."[10]

Many youths have already started to find solutions to the economic problems in their communities. Following are some suggestions that have come up while working with young people in various neighborhoods to rejuvenate communities lacking an independent and affirming economic foundation:

• Every institution, organization, church, school, and association in the community should ensure that young people are integrally active in their leadership. So many policies are directed toward youth, yet young people are rarely asked to help form these policies. In Youth Struggling for Survival we had young people chair meetings, take minutes, decide their activities, and plan how to carry them out. An agency director from New York City turned over a whole building and project to a nineteen-year-old—and never regretted it. Given the opportunity, most youth will develop their gifts for leadership and solving problems.

• Young people have proven they can develop sound business sense. They have demonstrated their mastery of illicit enterprises (drug crews are some of the best organized street organizations).[11] They can help manage food franchises, bookstores, and coffee shops, community stock options (where community members invest in community projects, at reasonable amounts, and where the money stays in the community), or new moneyless economies (which have been explored in smaller self-contained communities). Homeboy Industries in East L.A. and Barrios Unidos Industries in Santa Cruz, California, have created jobs for gang youth, who in turn stabilized their lives enough to give back to their families and neighborhoods. Many enterprising young artists have founded air-brushing businesses, making T-shirts and other items.

• "Give us the hammers and the nails, we will rebuild the city." With these words, sections of the Crips and the Bloods of South Central L.A. proposed to heal their communities in the aftermath of the 1992 Los Angeles rebellion.[12] First, they had to reconceive their surroundings—youth have a natural talent for this. Before they end up losing much of their imaginative powers as adults, they can still dream. It's up to the rest of us to help them achieve their healthiest and most pertinent dreams.

• Use the creativity, talents, and skills of young people to redo walls, windows, alleys, and schools. Their art—which is already being put up as so-called graffiti—should be allowed to grace any public space. There is a sense of ownership in this. For example, Roberto Clemente High School on Chicago's near northwest side is known for having gang-related problems and high drop-out rates. Graffiti decorates much of the property. However, a mural of Roberto Clemente, painted by students in the 1970s, and a more recent one by Chicago aerosol artist, D-Zine, have not been marred. For the most part, young people will take care of what they feel a part of. This should also translate into an investment in their learning. (As a former muralist, I saw how effective art can be in keeping young people's interest and participation intact. Getting paid for their work also helps them see how their talents can be linked to a viable, livable practice.)

Yet despite these examples, few adults, particularly those with the power to do so, will give young people the authority to make a lasting contribution to the overall economy, or to their education and community. Many of the people who oppose such authority are the same ones who are quite willing to send juvenile offenders to adult courts.

The groundwork for young people to become full with their destinies is the firm and invigorating embrace of community.

Chapter 5

Warning: Don't Get Involved!

People who have no heart are ignorant, because thoughts come not from the head, but from the heart.

—Heinrich Heine

In December 1997 I received a letter from Ms. Lange, a high school teacher in the town of Cicero, Illinois, who lamented a situation that is far too common in our nation's schools:

"I've been warned about keeping 'professional distance' from the gang members. Yes, I've been 'unofficially' warned to keep more of a distance!... I honestly believe this is bad advice. Every instinct and everything I've read and experienced with these boys and girls tells me they need respect, kindness, unqualified personal regard—whether they are in gangs or not. Whether they are in school or not. We aren't reaching our most needy kids... they aren't in class, I know this. But I've been warned. And this hurts so much because I know in my heart that they need to be accepted and helped from where they are now."

Cicero was one of the towns affected by two ordinances adopted in 1999 that would allow suspected gang members to be evicted from their homes within six months; anyone defying the order to move, would face fines of up to $500 a day. The town also filed a pair of lawsuits seeking to declare gang members public nuisances and asking for $11 million in damages from two major street gangs (consisting mostly of Mexican and Puerto Rican youth) for emotional stress and damage they purportedly inflicted on local residents.

When the ordinances were challenged in court for possible civil liberties violations, the town moved to change them to a curfew law.[1] However, in a town where "gangs" are not tolerated, and teachers are "warned" not to cultivate respectful relationships with their students, there is also

64

widespread corruption and illegal activity involving elected officials, the police, and local businesses.

In a 1998 article by Gary Marx and Peter Kendall, the just-suspended police superintendent—removed by Cicero's town president along with his deputy superintendent—alleged that bribes, harassments, and other abuses were routinely carried out in that town.[2] One scam reportedly involved police stopping undocumented immigrants without cause, asking for their papers, and then threatening to send them to immigration authorities unless they paid them several hundred dollars. Another involved a towing service—incorporated less than a week prior to winning the no-bid contract with the town—that towed cars for no apparent reason, then charged hundreds of dollars for the owners (mostly poor Mexicans) to get their vehicles returned.

"There would be two hundred, three hundred cars towed in a night," said the former police chief. "There are people standing in lines to pay two hundred dollars to get their vehicles back. We would watch them in line, some of them holding children, and we just said, 'This is unbelievable. What a rip-off.'" By then a third of the Cicero police force had been suspended or dismissed for corruption. Then, in June 2001, nine town officials, including the town president, were indicted on federal corruptions charges of siphoning off millions of dollars in town funds to purchase, among other things, a Wisconsin golf course and an Indiana horse farm.

Hypocrisies like these give life to that cynical observation, "Do as I say, not as I do," resulting in a deep mistrust between adults and youth. One could argue that the town authorities themselves could be designated a "gang," and may very well be eligible for evictions and compensation under their own rules.

Residents there don't have an easy time of it. Violence is a real issue in Cicero—bullets fly through the walls of flats, where even small children become victims. However, after a number of talks to young people in their schools, and to their parents and teachers in a parent-teacher training—Spanish was definitely a language to be reckoned with, although not at the expense of English—I found the students appreciative of my story and found that it could touch and invigorate their own stories. The community as a whole was bountiful with ideas, energy, commitment, and human resources.

Something has to be done. But unless corrupt officials—and their apologists—first deal with their own damaging behavior and learn to pay attention and be considerate of those they have been honored to represent, they can't lead the way.

National mobilizations have emerged to address the so-called crisis of youth—a crisis of a society at war with its youth. A growing spirituality movement for young people is sweeping the land. Part of the culture, in effect, is trying to heal itself, and we have to follow this to its natural conclusion. But for it to make a difference, it has to integrally involve the youth themselves; moreover it has to provide them knowledge of their environment and the skills to effectively negotiate within it.

America's Promise—The Alliance for Youth, formed in 1997 and headed by Ret. Gen. Colin L. Powell (before he became U.S. Secretary of State in 2001), with the support of the president, politicians, and major corporations and foundations—recognized that if we don't do something meaningful with young people, no one has a future. The alliance pledged to help at least two million "at risk" youth by the year 2000—providing them with mentors, decent health care, safe neighborhoods and schools, and a marketable skill—mostly by organizing millions of adult volunteers.[3] These elements are vital to any community. However, the year 2000 has come and gone, and this and similar campaigns have yet to serve as a real correctives to the "turning our backs" scenario.

In the July–August 1999 issue of *Youth Today,* Bill Alexander wrote that America's Promise is "long on hoopla and short on doing."[4] Summarizing a *Youth Today* survey and a three-city study of AP's progress by two youth research and development organizations, Alexander wrote that:

1. "Local AP initiative planning committees have been slow to build staffed organizations."

2. There is an apparent "lock-out of activist or policy-driven organizations from AP initiatives."

3. "Inadequate pre-planning and mapping strategies have ignored well-functioning but cash strapped Safe-Place and Mentor programs in impoverished neighborhoods."

4. "Highly publicized, overblown, and unrealistic corporate commitment promises have been quietly killed (such as United Way of New York City's withdrawal of a $50 million 'promise')."

5. "No uniform evaluation or tracking mechanisms exist to monitor a program's effectiveness."

6. AP "competes with local agencies for corporate funding and foundations grants."

7. There is "not enough tracking done to insure that pledges by national corporations filter down to local affiliates."

8. A "lack of coordination between AP's national office and its state and national initiatives."

As valiant as they may seem, there is a common element in these endeavors: to create an "army" of like-minded people who are responsible and disciplined in the abstract, instead of around their specific talents and attributes. Their aim is to control young people, especially those most in "danger" of acting out. The problem is we don't need any more "good soldiers." And we don't need an effort that may only last through the next presidential election, one that is politically motivated (AP was supposed to "end" during national-elections year 2000, although in 1999 it was extended—ambiguously—to "beyond 2000").

What is needed has nothing to do with controlling youth. Corporations and funding sources say they will be looking at reallocating funds through the campaign to programs that "work." Yet what works cannot be measured in eight, ten, or fifteen years. But, as Powell said, "If they don't make it, we're still better off than where we are now."[5]

There are already many programs dealing with young people. Far too many of them, however, are organized inadequacies. They don't seem to go deep enough; they don't get to the heart of the matter. They don't address the essence of the transformation process for individuals and society. What we need is a fundamentally different system of relationships that, as a whole, sets the conditions in which anything that can happen will happen. This system should also have the weight of historically evolved, long-standing knowledge about human development and interaction, and a sense of the cutting edge and experimental. Everyone is a "story"—a storehouse of experiences, thoughts, memories, sentiments, traits—with links to other stories. Not story as history, but as Michael Meade says, story as "symbolic liveliness." Remember, if you don't know your own gifts, you can't see the gifts in others.

A community with independent, inventive, and thinking adults who live what they say is a way for children and youth to seek out the ways they must live. It is a community that understands that kids "acting out" is reflective of something important to be addressed in the community. We can start by acknowledging the gifts that all youth bring into this world, and the need for strong communities that can organize themselves around these gifts.

Hand in hand with the many programs like Alliance for America, there is the growing phenomenon of "zero tolerance" policies: in schools, in shopping malls, at home, and also in churches. Schools are expelling students for wearing baggy pants, certain colors, or having "graffiti" on their book cases. In the aftermath of the Littleton murders, for example, students were expelled or suspended for wearing black clothing or making statements in support of the Goth lifestyle on their personal websites. A fourteen-year-old in Pennsylvania was suspended for telling a teacher in a conversation on the Columbine High School shootings that she could understand how someone who is teased endlessly could snap. One preschool child was sent home for bringing a plastic ax while dressed as a fireman for a school event.[6]

It has been getting so bad for so long that a few years ago at one suburban shopping mall, security officers turned away a troop of Girl Scouts because they violated a policy, aimed at gangs, about not having similarly dressed youth in their shops.[7]

In one predominantly Mexican school in Chicago where I used to conduct poetry workshops, zero tolerance resulted in the removal of a third of the student body. Another third of the students dropped out before their senior year. As a result the graduation class consisted of only one third of the students who had entered the school as freshmen. They got rid of the "problems" all right—by getting rid of most of the students to "save" the institution. What sense does this make? The "zero" apparently means the number of people left after all the trouble and reality has been ejected.

At a time that has seen a phenomenal rise in spiritual awakenings, in religious conversions, and in "celestine" visions, we have to ask, Why are we also seeing more children being tried as adults? Why do we have the highest rate of imprisonment in the history of the world? Why the slashing of community-based activities for young people? Why an increase in the number of schools in disrepair? Why a dearth in truly promising job prospects?

The net effect of zero-tolerance policies is that more and more adults are being forced to remove themselves from any authentic relations with children and adolescents. This was Ms. Lange's predicament, a situation many other people involved in the lives of young people have found themselves in as well.

A Puerto Rican friend once told me how his wife had baked cookies for students at the elementary school where their son was a student. A student at that school had been killed the previous weekend during a domestic dispute. As in many Latino households, baking cookies for the kids seemed appropriate. But as soon as my friend's wife tried to enter the school building with the aluminum-foil covered tray of cookies, she was met by "grief counselors" brought in for the occasion.

"You can go home, madam," one of the counselors stated. "We'll handle this."

Despite the parent's insistence, school officials would not allow her onto the premises. But what she was doing was exactly what needed to happen, where adults of the community, familiar to the children, reached out to them in real and loving ways. The counselors, even if competent, were only going to be there temporarily. These people were not known to the children and would probably not be heard from after their "job" was finished.

The disconnection today is deeper than it has ever been. This is a key issue that has yet to be thoroughly tackled in discussing the recent school shootings and other violence. Beyond providing economic stability for our children, there is an even greater need for emotional and social stability from family and community. The presence of such stability helps some people turn out strong and inspired; the lack of it in materially rich communities results in alienation and spiritual vacuity.

"Professionalism" has come to mean "don't get involved," particularly in the emotional life of a child. Teachers and coaches are told not to establish personal relationships with their students. There are millions of young people in this country who have no respectful and lasting ties to adults (including their parents). A few professionals have used such relationships to exploit, abuse, and control young people—nobody wants that—but when all teachers are told to cut such ties, how are children and teens to know what a healthy personal relationship with adults looks and feels like? Under the present conditions an abusive adult can take advantage of any needy young person seeking such a relationship.

Young people can be manipulative. This is normal and we can handle it (besides, what adult doesn't manipulate?). But in trying so hard not to get "used" by children, we set the conditions for their being used by adults—which is more widespread, dangerous, and with enormously tragic ramifications. A majority of those whom I've talked to in prisons and mental institutions and who are or have been on drugs relate having been abused by at least one adult when they were young.[8]

We are seeing the wholesale abandonment of young people, particularly those who require more guidance, resources, patience, and caring of community.[9] Regrettably many of these youths have already been abandoned by the economy. But the other important truth is that "well-off" communities are affected by this process as well.

Only once has a young person said to me, "Why don't you inner-city people pick yourselves up by your own bootstraps?" This happened in 1994, when I was serving as a poet-in-residence for five private schools in Bryn Mawr and the wealthy Main Line communities of Pennsylvania.[10] The parents of these children—almost all white—contributed at that time around $17,000 a year for their schooling.

Of course, the kids were great—all children are wonderful. They were extremely attentive and the art on the walls was evidence of their immense creativity. They had read my poems and were prepared with smart questions. Many of the kids in the Spanish-language classes were better versed in my first tongue than I was.

Interestingly the students had a 100 percent graduation rate and a 100 percent college entrance rate. One teacher told me the reason for this was that "we won't let them fail." Those children didn't just feel empowered, they felt entitled. It's not that they were more gifted or more intelligent than the children in my neighborhood. Some of them, in fact, were quite troubled. They had a high drug and alcohol abuse rate. When I was there, rock musician Kurt Cobain had just committed suicide and there was a suicide watch in the high schools. I even witnessed one of the largest federal busts of a methamphetamine lab in the country there (the lab was located in the basement of one of the mansions).

The difference was that the children in Bryn Mawr were expected to succeed (which is its own distorted pressure). In my neighborhood, however, they were expected to fail, and if someone manages to succeed, they are often considered special, "not like the others," establishing a breach between that youth and their community. The young man who wondered why us "inner city" folk lacked the fortitude to "pick ourselves up" didn't even see how many resources and support systems existed for him to make it. Nobody does it alone. The self-made person, the so-called rugged individualist, is mostly farce. We all need help.

Unfortunately the stimulus of this economy—investing to make profit—becomes the leading metaphor in our relationships with children: If they don't appear to produce "value," then society has determined they are not worth any "investment." Yet even when they are considered worthy of such an investment, their true value as human beings is subverted for the superficial ones of power, status, and profit.

Chapter 6

The Power of Hanging in There

The trouble with America's children is America's adults.
—Marc Klaas

Francisco was fifteen when he was kicked out of high school, following a shouting match with a teacher in the school's cafeteria; he had already been removed from another school prior to this. His mother managed to get Francisco into a third high school, but only after jumping through a number of hoops because the administration didn't want him there. Then, after less than two weeks, his mother received a phone call from the principal: "Ms. Acosta, please pick up your son. He's no longer welcome in our school."

The school accused Francisco of talking back to a teacher. There was no doubt the young man was difficult—I mean, three schools in one year. But he was also smart—he had tested "gifted." He could also be generous. He was the kind of child who would give away his toys to more needy friends. Still, he had some deep-seated emotional problems, triggering uncontrollable rages that required hours of counseling.

But Francisco was being undermined by members of his own community, and not just the gang leaders and drug dealers, who often use people like Francisco as lookouts during drug sales, for "missions" against rival groups, or robberies. You can expect as much from these guys. (Many community efforts involve diverting the energies of such leaders to more positive, community-based concerns.) No, Francisco was also having problems with the "good" guys. The principal who expelled him is a case in point.

When Ms. Acosta arrived at the school, she tried to persuade the principal to take her son back, albeit under supervised conditions. He adamantly refused. They had a zero-tolerance policy. One mistake, and he was out.[1]

The upshot was that Francisco did not finish high school, although he had many things going for him. What he needed to get through this situation was a unified collective of caring adults who would hang in there with him. It's true that Francisco also needed to see how he contributed to his own failures. But this couldn't be done when those most needed to help him do so had removed themselves from an integral and trustworthy place in the boy's life.

I've faced this kind of intolerance many times with the youth I work with. YSS used to meet weekly in a northwest-side community center. There was even a boxing program that some of our young men signed up for and were enthusiastic about. The kids, who included gang youth, didn't cause any problems, always cleaned up after themselves, and were respectful. They looked forward to going there. One day the center's director called me into a meeting.

"The group can't meet here anymore," he declared. "I've heard you have gang members in the group. We don't allow any gang members in our facilities."

Because I was a volunteer, there wasn't much I could do. Clearly, zero tolerance determines action against people on the surface of things, not on content. There is no "day in court," no listening to the "other side" (which, at least on the books, is supposed to be fair practice in the case of adults). If the director had bothered (as I had suggested) to get to know the kids, he wouldn't have had reason for concern. Needless to say, this was a setback for the youth, who had already gone to two other places where they were treated about the same. We didn't give up, though, and we eventually found a place to meet, but it was disheartening to keep facing this refrain from our so-called community elders.

If anyone had taken the time, he or she would have seen that Francisco had some "sense" to his behavior. If anyone had bothered to look, he would have seen how this accomplished young man, who, his mother says, was always smiling, inquisitive, and helpful when he was a toddler, could become "incorrigible."

Francisco was born to a young couple—his mother was eighteen, his father twenty—living in a poor neighborhood of southeast Chicago during a period when the vast industrial backbone of the city had begun to shrink. His father worked in factories and foundries, although he was also frequently unemployed. He drank too much and was often not at home. His mother had her own issues of abuse from when she was a child. She stayed home to take care of her three children, including Francisco, while her husband worked.

But times were hard—the couple argued all the time. The father often stormed out the door, while Francisco cowered in his room, wishing it would all go away. Within three years his mother had an affair with one of the neighbors and the couple separated. Things only worsened. Mother and children moved to the mostly Mexican Little Village community, which had a vibrant cultural life and many struggling families but also a thriving world of gangs.

Francisco's mother had relationships with numerous men, as if they were the only source of her self-worth. She married another man who turned out to be an alcoholic and physical abuser. One winter she found herself in a battered women's shelter with her children. Francisco's father was not around and only visited on some weekends. He also had numerous girlfriends. He wrote letters, but soon found work in other cities, and for the most part failed to be there during the child's most trying times.

Francisco's mother found it hard to leave this other man, who also humiliated and abused the kids. Francisco was beaten for the most minor infractions, such as failing to put the plastic covering over the kitchen trashcan. At one point this man forced Francisco's mother to hold her son while he beat him; she felt helpless, scared, but the effect was to push Francisco away from his mother, the one consistent source of love for him. That was the day that love had broken.

Between the ages of nine and twelve, Francisco ran away often. He began to hang out with the local peewee gang members. By thirteen, he was stealing and doing "jobs" for one of the large Little Village street associations called the Two-Six Nation. By fifteen, he had been beaten into one of the main sections of the Two-sixers, as police liked to call them. His trajectory could have been scripted by any sociologist.

But something deeper had been overlooked. While the abuse, the neglect, and the poverty cannot be dismissed in assessing someone's disruptive behavior, what about the passions and callings impelling much of what Francisco was doing? Who was paying attention to see how to interject themselves into the fraying quilt of his life and say, Here's where you were meant to be; here's where the thread was going. Francisco needed nurturing and preparation so that he could feel thoroughly engaged in life and impassioned by his abilities to reform the world through his own gifts.

Instead, disjointed and disassociated, as many young people feel, Francisco was further abused by the impatient and angry response of the adult figures in the community. The degradations and shame—abuse followed by guilt is typical behavior of adults who abuse children physically or spiritually, either individually or institutionally—grew with each encounter. Something began to die in him.

Another problem when we don't "hang in there" with our most disruptive youth is that other youth who may not be in need of as much help can end up feeling less secure about themselves and our relationship to them. "If these adults can't handle [the most troubled youth]," a young person once told me. "What will they do when I lose it?"

Eventually an English teacher took a liking to Francisco, who enrolled in an adult education class in his early twenties. Recognizing both the young man's potential and his quick response when yelled at or disrespected, this teacher patiently helped Francisco study for his General Equivalency Diploma (GED), which he earned without having to spend hours in class because he already knew much of the material. Next, the teacher obtained a community therapist to give the young man help in understanding the basis of his emotions so that he could stay on track with his goals. It took time, but Francisco was helped. He also became a father, and vowed not to repeat the mistakes his own family had made. That teacher, who saw a genius, not a gangster, in Francisco, filled a void this young man was desperately seeking to be filled.

Unfortunately too many adults go overboard when trying to "straighten out" kids. One of the most damning examples occurred in 1997 and involved the handling of a five-year-old girl in Pensacola, Florida, for allegedly assaulting a fifty-one-year-old school counselor. A warrant was issued for her arrest. She was taken to jail, booked, fingerprinted, and had a mug shot taken. The day before, a six-year-old boy was arrested and handcuffed in his kindergarten class in Lakeland. The spring before that, police in the Tampa Bay area made separate arrests of three elementary school children, including a six-year-old girl. As a *New York Times* reporter wrote, "for misbehavior, elementary school children are facing adult standards."[2] It's bad enough that children are growing up too fast in this culture, but we are beginning to enshrine this situation in our laws, policies, and practices.

Middle- and upper-class schools or institutions don't experience this level of intolerance (or if they do, it's usually in a more measured form). Though their students also get into trouble, there usually is a helping and patient response for them. But even in those schools this is changing rapidly; lawmakers and school officials are reevaluating such responses after violent incidents like that of Littleton, Colorado.

I also know this level of intolerance doesn't exist for many adults.[3]

Most parents don't want their kids suspended or expelled; they want them in school because being idle, bored, in the streets, with nothing meaningful to do is worse. School should be one place where much of a child's imaginative and emotional needs are met, where classrooms are captivating places of calculated intensity, adventure, and discovery.

It's not to say that a home cannot be the center of a child's emotional and psychological balance. It can be. Parents should attempt to make their home a place where children can find peace, parameters, and personal accountability. But parents cannot provide this alone, particularly since in many households both father and mother work full time. The fact is poor and working parents need help too.

Poor families are not the worst when it comes to providing a nurturing home, and certainly not poor single moms. I have known many such moms in the housing projects of Chicago and the wood-frame structures in Los Angeles—from trailer parks to the rez. Most of these women, with little or no support, have raised wonderful children. We can't underestimate or misrepresent the role mothers have had to play—particularly in a period that is characterized by the absence of fathers.

At a gathering of teachers, students, and parents in Loudon County, Virginia, the issue of poor families—particularly female heads of households—came up. Some participants claimed that single moms were directly responsible for the rash of violence among youth. They insisted that if families were set up right—a mother and father and all the right values—everything would be just fine.

But a number of single, mostly African-American mothers then stood up to say their children had turned out just fine—some going to college and raising their own families—even though they didn't have the "right" family structure. There were also some Salvadoran families who explained how they had traditions, strong family ties, and that despite this their children were joining gangs and getting into trouble.

Most Mexican, Puerto Rican, and Central Americans come to this country with strong extended families. But I have seen how poverty, discrimination, and lack of options have undermined these relationships. And there are many poor African-American and white families where a legacy of slavery and generational poverty have largely dismantled family units.

Strong families matter. I happen to be married to a woman who grew up with ten siblings and two parents. Originally from Jalisco, Mexico, the Cardenas family became part of the migrant stream in California; they eventually settled in a large Mexican community in the Pacoima section of Los Angeles. My wife, Maria Trinidad, lived in the same house for her elementary-, middle-, high-school, and early college education. The family was tight-knit, traditional, and quite valiant. Her father was a gardener who maintained a strict but loving hand in family affairs; their mother was consistent and steady, a model of Mexican strength and values.

Although their neighborhood was poor and quite rough, none of the family members joined gangs or got into drugs. Except for one brother who accidentally drowned at sixteen in Mexico, the rest graduated from high school, and many of them obtained advanced degrees. My wife has a B.A., graduating cum laude, and a teacher's credential (she taught elementary school for ten years); she has worked as a bilingual writer-editor and as an interpreter for the courts. She has a brother who works at Pasadena's Jet Propulsion Laboratories. Another brother owned his own real estate business and became the first Latino State Assemblyman for the San Fernando Valley. Other siblings include a child psychologist and a construction supervisor for a major phone company.

However, as fine an example as this Mexican family may be, they cannot possibly translate their experience as the "end all" for everyone, even though we may draw some vital lessons from them. For although they were relatively safe, there were also issues about "seeing" the individual gifts and interests of each child (and parent). Usually in large households, parents have to find one thick, mostly psychic, rope to pull all the children along—as is done in a massively grander scale in armies. But this is usually accomplished at the expense of the particular strands of destiny and purpose that each member of the family possess. I believe the Cardenas siblings have admirably dealt with these aspects, particularly with their own children (my wife and I have tons of bright and active nieces and nephews). There's much we can learn about such families—both the good and the bad.

It is vital to understand the vibrant dynamic interactions between the various family members and not enhance or discredit the relationships out of preconceived notions about families. Today too much policy disregards the actual dynamics that exist in a child's life. Too much policy is being shaped out of prejudices and preconceptions.

The main point here is that hanging with kids also means hanging with their often beleaguered and overwhelmed parents. This notion that only family can "save" a kid fails to see how families are also affected and influenced by what happens in the community. Yes, parents should provide their children strong anchors in a truculent sea of pain and doubt. But too often, even when this happens, others in the community are not in step.

The problem of school officials misapplying their authority could well be extended to almost anybody in authority. We need real, reliable, and clear authority, the existence of which can help young people establish their own authority, and, at a certain point, become the authors of their own way.

Unfortunately what we have today is usually an imposed authority whose goal is to mold people to an abstract and archaic set of values and relations. The thick rope. This type of authority plainly has no relevance, and people are bound to challenge it, for good reason.

There is a way, however, in which authority can meaningfully relate to young people so that children and youth don't just link to traditions, family, community, and a set of predetermined values and relations, but also discover these things for themselves. This guidance is provisional; to accept this kind of authority is eventually to outgrow it. The goal is not to pull people along from the outside but to prepare them so that they are driven by their own center.

Thinkers and scholars of various backgrounds, including C. G. Jung and Joseph Campbell, have identified a very long period of dependency for human beings, one that stretches from birth to adulthood. We know the human body begins to mature to adulthood around age twelve (earlier for girls, later for boys) and reaches its highest point of development in late teens or early twenties (earlier for men, later for women). No other animal has such a lengthy period of dependency. If we are to survive it, we require strong and healthy relationships with an extended community of adults—family, extended family, village or community, tribe or city—and an understanding of the mores and values of the larger culture.

This period is one of adjusting to society, to the individuals and groups that have fed, clothed, and housed the child. Campbell calls this the adaptive stage of life—a period of acculturation, whereby the individual is taught not only the primary rules of the social order but also, in most cases, the belief systems and rituals.[4] However, just because a person reaches a certain age, say eighteen or twenty-one, does not mean he or she has matured enough for this responsibility. Maturity is not marked by any single event, such as graduating from high school, getting a driver's license, or marriage.

Young people have to be readied, if this maturity is to take hold in the psyche, by experiencing a dynamic tension between actual responsibility and authority as their emotional faculties and intelligence develop. Adults should turn certain aspects of young people's lives over to them as part of the process. At the same time adults must maintain control of those aspects that young people are not yet ready to control. The key is to know what to turn over and what not to at different junctures of a child's growth.

Helping children discover values for themselves is more empowering than if you impose them. But if you feel you must take action, then you have to take full responsibility for that action. For example, most parents now accept that a young person's room belongs to him or her—and adults generally respect the child's privacy. You can model the virtue of keeping things neat and orderly for your children; this is important. But you can't really decide what posters should go on their walls or how they arrange their clothing. However, you might, for example, step in and say you don't want them listening to certain music, reading certain books, or watching certain TV programs. These are still areas where adults can reasonably make a good case for intervention (better you than the government). Young people may not like it, but you have to be ready to thoroughly defend your decision. Arbitrary and unilateral decision making is not a good way to teach young people how to think and decide things for themselves.

One parent I worked with was constantly stepping into her daughter's life, making decisions about almost every aspect of the girl's world: what she should wear to school; how her hair should be cut; who her friends should be. Ms. Thomas's motivations were not necessarily wrong. She worried that her daughter, Shaunda, would make the wrong impression or decision and get hurt.

Ms. Thomas, a church-going African-American activist in the community, had good reason for concern. She had seen too many neighborhood women fall by the wayside. Her own sister, Shaunda's aunt, was a crack addict and prostitute. Many girls were becoming pregnant at increasingly younger ages. Gangs and drugs pervaded much of the area's culture.

However, Ms. Thomas wanted to mortar any cracks on the walls of her daughter's life. She did not seem to understand the proper relationship of those things that are not up for Shaunda to decide and those things that are. The daughter may have been safer because of her mother's constant intervention, but she was not becoming self-reliant. This prompted Shaunda to rebel. At a youth gathering, Shaunda cried during a talking circle while expressing the lack of trust her mother had in her. She said she was tired of being constantly hounded.

"I want to get away—make my own mistakes," Shaunda said. "I'd rather mess up and die, if I have to, than have my mother keep telling me what to do."

While this may seem extreme, it's important to point out that what we do as parents can incite these kinds of emotions. The finality and pain of having a child commit suicide, for example, is not always commensurate with what may have sparked it. But by then, what does it matter. This is why every issue, however insignificant it may seem, has to be properly attended to.

For Ms. Thomas to rebalance this situation with her daughter, she would need to slow down, listen, and begin to turn over some authority to Shaunda. She would also have to set up a bridge of trust between them. An adjustment needs to be made. This is not about what's right or wrong; as I said earlier, Ms. Thomas loves her daughter, and I truly believe she wants the right things for her. This is about adjusting up or down, right or left, in or out. Just as you tune up cars, every once in a while you also have to tune up relationships.

A full life is made up of mistakes and missteps as well as the proper decisions in the proper direction. In this sense it's like finding the right frequency on the radio—sometimes we're off, sometimes we're not, but our "station" is constant. Did I go too far or not far enough? Did I turn too much this way or too much that way? The more aware one is of one's path—and of the external forces that push or impede one's footing on such a path—the more one can make the correct changes in attitude, skill, and style to stay forcefully on that path.

This is a dilemma we parents have to deal with every day: The safer we try to make our kids' surroundings, the more we may be taking away from what they need to be strong. But we don't want to go over to the other side either: allowing teenagers to make most of the decisions and take unnecessary risks makes them more responsible than they're able to be and correspondingly lowers their level of safety.

Clearly defined parameters and expectations would help Ms. Thomas and Shaunda. There will be decisions that children will have control over, particularly around issues that will not be detrimental to them regardless of what they choose. However, brushing one's teeth, getting up early enough to prepare for school or work, eating right, and bathing—these are decisions that are made for the child and cannot be compromised. Whether to smoke, drink, take drugs, or have sex—these are also areas where parents should maintain control, even while providing the necessary education so that children can eventually make their own healthy decisions in regards to these issues.

Furthermore, the structures have to change as a child gets older. We should invite young people to express their thoughts and feelings so that they don't become disruptive and counterproductive—there has to be a built-in emotional release valve. Being firm and consistent about the big and important issues should help parents become flexible about the smaller and not so important ones. Children learn what they live. And by actually living what they believe, parents can do better than merely preaching or cajoling children to do the right thing. Morality is not an abstract notion, it's a decision to act in the face of a moral dilemma.

However, the ability to get their children to do what they should is an option parents won't have unless they understand the actual limitations of freedom, the nature of human development, and the way of properly motivating their children. You can't go through a raging blaze to save a child just because you want to. However, if you understand the nature of fire—how it works, how it can be contained, and how extinguished—then you can apply the necessary techniques and possibly save the youth.

When a child makes adultlike mistakes, we still have to remember that the gravity of the mistake (even murder) does not indicate a corresponding level of maturity. The ability to be responsible for any act has to be measured by the mental and emotional state of the person at the time the act was committed. Mistakes do not have to be considered "adult" to be grave; they are grave because of the nature of the act itself, regardless of who commits them. We seem to presume that a child who does a horrendous thing is making an "adult" decision and therefore deserves an adult punishment. This simply does not apply: If you're not an adult, you cannot make an adult mistake.

Putting handcuffs on five-year-olds is totally out of sync with their stages of development. Trying children as adults doesn't help either. As much as I abhor seeing eight-year-olds with a 9-millimeter automatic weapon in their hands, as I have seen on the streets of Chicago, it does not change the fact that they are still eight years old.

Growth doesn't stop unless we force the issue, unless we decide that a child should pay for these mistakes with their lives, which says a lot about how we appraise their lives. To teach a child the severity of taking life means showing them by our words, our actions, our proclamations, and our concerns how much we care about them. They are still in an adaptive stage, which means that we can use all these opportunities (even crisis is opportunity) to assist them in meeting the demands of this stage. The overwhelming majority of children won't kill or maim. But if they do, God forbid, then we must always maintain the universal principle that there is still room for growth.

This is where prevention has its role: From infancy to adulthood, we need to teach, not threaten; to respond with measures that are instructive and revelatory, not punitive and repressive. When people are older and presumably know better, and punitive measures are utilized instead of instructive ones, we still need to remember that learning is a lifelong endeavor. You can't ever say that someone is done learning.

Chapter 7
Hungers and Angers

My humanity is in feeling we are all voices of the same poverty.
—Jorge Luis Borges

Rick, a young white high school student, had a problem with a school board psychiatrist assigned to evaluate him. On the day this young man was to meet with him, he showed up in white shirt and white pants. He had a short haircut, but he left a long section of blond hair down his back. He sported a nose ring and a multicolored wrist tattoo. He looked stylish, to be sure. The psychiatrist, with much disdain, wrote that Rick was narcissistic and needlessly drawing attention to himself. The boy's exuberance—which is typical for young people who are coming into themselves—was viewed as a deviance that had to be crushed.

Rick, whose parents were artists, grew up seeing how affectation, the aesthetic, the graceful and sublime, have the power to hold and enthrall. But he was also undergoing an identity crisis in school. The facility was divided between the children of well-off professional parents and those of a blue-collar section of town—a source of conflict in the hallways, classrooms, and playing fields. Rick lived in-between those areas, not rich but not poor.

Rick wasn't sure which way to go, considering that his school had large numbers of both blue-collar and professional students. Something about the well-off students repelled him—they didn't seem "cool" enough. But he also recoiled from the harder blue-collar kids; he didn't like the disruptive things they did to stand out and be noticed.

He tried to walk a middle road—appearing cool, yet not falling into the anxieties this often entailed. It was a tightrope act. In time he had friends from both groups. Yet something about Rick didn't want to disappear into the crowd, to be lost in the sea of styles, tattoos, piercings, and accents. Something in him also wanted to be noticed for who he was. His humor proved to be the key. However, Rick usually tried to be funny at inopportune times, such as during class. A teacher accused him of not taking life seriously (a terrible thing, apparently), so he was dispatched to the office, and from there to the resident shrink.

Like others his age, Rick was trying to find his place in the world. Identity is important, but it gets muddled or cramped with issues of race, social class, and status—"preppies" versus "trash." Even these lines get blurred. Students are more likely divided between "the functional and the dysfunctional," as one teacher claimed. There is an ongoing tension between an individual's expression and his or her ability to fall in line with the rest.

The adaptive stage for any young person has to take into account not just the physical and biological needs, but the spiritual and psychological needs as well. There are hungers of the body; there are hungers of the soul.

Like everyone else, Rick needed peer relationships. Although some parents speak disapprovingly when they refer to "peer pressures," it is in the collective that young people start to become self-actualized beings. "Wanting to belong," therefore, becomes a natural and healthy aspect of a teen's life, especially when one's personal identity is most clamoring to breathe. As Orland Bishop, a cofounder of Shade Tree Mentoring in Los Angeles, once remarked, "Intimacy for youth is found in the other; intimacy for adults is found in the self."

We don't always realize that a part of the end of the adaptive stage, when a young person enters the threshold of maturity, is the development of an ego identity. The form this development takes can be quite disconcerting. It is the time when a young person may exhibit outlandish traits and responses, and may be determinedly independent and foolish. Alas, this too is part of growing up. It is hardwired in the brain. It cannot be denied any more than it is possible to deny the growth of whiskers on a boy's face. As many have said before, all adolescents are chemically dependent: they're on hormones.

This is a time when it becomes vital to stand by them so that they can seek their own unique place in the world without causing damage. To deny or suppress this development altogether results in severe ego identity problems when the children become adults. I once heard the head of a new college for home-schooled children in Virginia, speaking on television, say that the school's aim was to help children "skip the adolescent stage" and all its alleged foolishness. It simply doesn't work that way.

How often have we seen adults who have not outgrown their infantile posturing or adolescent hungers and angers? Partly this is because most adults today never received adequate recognition when they were young. I have witnessed this in the men's gatherings I've done with adults and youth, where some of the older men get extremely upset at the attention given to the young men.

One can't dismiss the important work that therapists can and must do. However, therapists who see only the worst in people, who view the trauma in their patients' lives not as a possible door to self-realization and fulfillment but as a trap to deviance and pathos, are doing a major disservice to our youth. Small wonder many troubled young people don't trust, and often don't benefit from, counseling sessions they are required to attend. Far too many counselors and therapists use their expertise and "concern" to push their patients to so-called acceptable behavior, back into a predetermined social line. Some young people have told me how they feel their souls shrink in such settings rather than a genuine expansion of soul-seed and soul potential.

James Hillman wrote,

> Psychology, as the specialty named after Psyche, has a special obligation to the soul. The psychologist should be a keeper of the great natural preserve of memory and its innumerable treasures.... We invented psychopathology and thereby labeled the memoria a madhouse. We invented the diagnoses with which we declared ourselves insane. After subtly poisoning our own imaginal potency with this language, we complain of a cultural wasteland and loss of soul. The poison spread; words continually fall "mentally ill" and are usurped by psychopathology, so that we can hardly use them without their new and polluted connotations: "immature," "dissociation," "rigid," "withdrawn," "passive," "transference," "fixation," "sublimation," "projection,"... "resistance," "deviate," "stress," "dependence," "inhibition," "compulsion," "illusion," "split," "tranquilized," "driven," "compensation," "inferiority," "derange," "suppression," "depression," "repression," "confusion"—these words have been psychologized and pathologized in the past one hundred fifty years.... So Psyche requests the psychologist to remember his calling.[1]

Hillman has also said that therapy should be "a cell of revolution."[2] This means not aiming for the transformation of a troubled person into an "idealized" person, which doesn't really exist except in fantasy (movies, books, TV, cartoon, comics, and so on). But deeper into one's own nature, "becoming more and more oneself," while at the same time embracing the active and significant role such a person should have in his or her society.[3]

Another major symbol of authority we must talk about is the police. There has been a virtual state of war between the local police and many youth in the barrios of Chicago's Humboldt Park and Logan Square, where I lived for many years, and Los Angeles, where I grew up. It is also the state of things in many cities throughout the country. The police killings in New York City of mostly blacks and Latinos, including the 1999 death of Amadou Diallo, an unarmed West African peddler who was shot forty-one times, dramatizes this point.

Not all police officers are into the war. I've worked with a number of truly caring law enforcement officials over the years. But the fact remains that far too often the police act like the biggest, baddest gang on the block, with more firepower and the weight of law (even if misapplied at times) behind them. With community backing, many police organizations aim to eradicate street gangs by whatever means they can, including breaking the law. Troubled youth only have their defiance, which can take the form of some terrible violence, sometimes against the police but mostly against themselves.

The problem is you can't stop gang warfare with gang warfare.

Apparently some people in the federal government agreed. In 2000, the feds forced the Los Angeles Police Department to accept a consent decree in the wake of some extensive corruption. The situation came to a head in the so-called Rampart Scandal. A member of the LAPD's Rampart Division's gang suppression unit, Rafael Perez, was sentenced February 25, 2000, to five years for stealing eight pounds of cocaine. To reduce his sentence, Perez told investigators he and fellow officers routinely framed innocent people, shot unarmed suspects, and stole drugs for resell. Another officer, David Mack, who once served as Perez's partner, had earlier been convicted of a bank robbery that netted almost $800,000. By November three other Rampart officers were found guilty in cases surrounding the investigation. However, by December a judge had overturned their convictions, a rarity in criminal cases, prompting outcries of undercutting the jury system of justice.

In one highly publicized case Perez and another officer, Nino Durden, in 1996 allegedly shot an 18th Street gang member named Javier Ovando in the head and chest. The pair then planted a gun and accused the youth, then nineteen, of trying to attack them. Although paralyzed, Ovando was subsequently sentenced to twenty-three years in prison. During the investigation it was found that Perez and Durden had framed the young Honduran immigrant, and the conviction was overturned. By then, however, Ovando had served two and a half years. Finally, in November 2000, the city awarded Ovando $15 million in the single largest police misconduct settlement in L.A. history. By then the city had already made payouts in other Rampart-related cases to the tune of $30 million.

These cases were only the tip of the iceberg. The corruption went beyond the Rampart Division and antigang units, embroiling the whole department. By the end of the year more than seventy police officers had cases pending against them that included the wanton killings of people—innocent or otherwise. Officers often partied after people were killed. They gave each other plaques to reward such actions. They even sported their own tattoo: a grinning skull with demonic eyes and a cowboy hat with the words "Ramparts CRASH," the name of the antigang unit. "Intimidate those who intimidate others," was the CRASH unit's motto. But in taking away the dignity of those they policed, officers put their own dignity on the line.

Let's not forget there are many good people who are police officers: Bless every one of them. There are creative policing strategies being implemented across the land. But they simply cannot be given the task of cleaning up the mess that government, schools, parents, churches, and some community leaders have left behind. Most police departments are overburdened when it comes to dealing with the worst aspects of our communities: the dead bodies; the battered faces; the torn homes; the deadly accidents.

When society makes law enforcement the solution to violence, drugs, and theft, we are putting too much burden on men and women who are not trained or prepared for this. They can't take the place of good parents, counselors, ministers, teachers, friends, managers, or mentors. They can't replace the power of community-directed initiation practices and life-affirming rituals in people's lives.

There is also a built-in danger when the police department is the most cohesive force in a community. We have seen it in the destitute areas of our country. One crucial counterbalance to the misuse of police power is a strong and unified community. We can't see violence—or any crime—as just a law enforcement issue. Besides, the police only get involved at the back end of a problem: when the shootings, beatings, and stabbings have already happened; when the home or store has already been robbed; when the elderly citizen has been mugged or the young woman raped; when the wife has already been beaten up by an irate husband or a child's been abused beyond recognition.

Much more has to be done at the front end.

Let's look at the growing sale and use of illicit drugs in this country. Such activities are seen as criminal, and therefore under the purview of law enforcement. A torrent of "get tough" legislation on drugs has been passed, including intractable sentencing. In Illinois—following a pattern in other states—women convicted of nonviolent offenses (mostly for drugs or related crimes, such as shoplifting and forging checks) make up two-thirds of incarcerated females. More than 80 percent of these women leave small children behind. Because they are not looked after decently by the powers that sent their mothers away, they end up lost themselves—and the pattern continues.[4]

Despite billions of dollars allocated over the last twenty years, the drug war has not stopped the drug trade. It has, however, served as a boot on the neck of the American people, particularly the poor.

We know that the detrimental effects of drugs and alcohol on people can be attributed to a genetic propensity—some people are more affected by drugs and alcohol than others. Environmental factors are also key—most addictions are responses to early-life traumas, poverty, and isolation. For these people, doing drugs or abusing alcohol is not a simple matter of choice, or else there wouldn't be such a massive "recovery" industry in this country. Substance abuse is primarily a health issue, as well as an economic and cultural one. Given these circumstances, people need treatment and education, not prison. They need stable living options as well so that selling drugs does not become a viable survival strategy.

By having the police practically become sole heirs to these problems—some believe they are the "thin blue line" keeping the "barbarians" from dragging down all that's good and decent in society—we are forcing them to respond in a brutal and deadly fashion. Too many of our children are harassed, beaten, and sometimes killed by police. There is no justification for this behavior. Police officers have to be taken to task whenever deadly force is used against members of any community. The power of life and death must not be given to any governmental or public maintenance institution. There are a myriad of ways to respond to most crisis situations without having to shoot somebody.[5]

Many incidents involving police action against youth have been characterized with great violence, including murder. These actions have to be brought out into the open. Exposing and effectively acting on these unlawful police actions will help restore a balance between community safety and our civil liberties. It's appalling that we are consistently forced to choose "one or the other" when policies are formulated.

One such police action involved the possible murder of a young community leader and YSS member, although it's been called a gang-related homicide. Antonio was a striking Indian-looking youth with great leadership qualities and highly charged emotional responses to the injustices he saw growing up in Pilsen. With guidance and support he was capable of becoming a responsible member of the community, possibly even involved in political office. Despite not knowing English, he had quickly learned how to express himself and was extremely articulate. I saw him practically grow up in YSS; angry and wise, he proved to be a consistent and caring member of the group. Many of the boys and girls from the streets of Pilsen who took part in YSS did so in large part because of Antonio.

When Antonio first came to this country, he was threatened by local gang members. For years this community was known for having rival street organizations on almost every other block—some of the bigger ones were La Raza, Ambrose, Latin Counts, Bishops, Satan Disciples, and the Gangster Party People. Eventually Antonio joined a group of youth for self-defense. However, Antonio's greatest threats came from the police who were supposedly there to protect the community. He would be routinely beaten, humiliated, and shaken down. Apparently Antonio came to know about a local police officer who actively dealt drugs and guns in the community. He had also witnessed a shooting of an alleged gang member. As Antonio and others related the story, the youth lay on the ground while the police refused to call an ambulance or let anybody help him. When an ambulance finally did arrive (after neighbors called), the police held it up for several minutes. The boy bled to death where he lay.

The Community Alternative Policing Strategy (CAPS) was implemented in the city in the early 1990s. A goal of this effort was to bring the community and police together to help fight crime—an admirable effort. CAPS may have worked in some instances. However, it failed to live up to its stated purpose in too many others; when the antigang loitering law was being challenged, CAPS groups were organized to support it.

Devon, a social worker in the Mexican community, thought it would be a good idea for Antonio to attend a CAPS meeting and perhaps say some-thing about the way police treated the youth in Pilsen. Unfortunately Anto-nio didn't let the YSS elders know he was going to such a meeting. He went and, according to Devon, stood up and complained about the dirty police tactics in the community. He also talked about the alleged drug-dealing cop. Devon told me he saw officers with scowls on their faces scribbling in notepads as Antonio spoke.

The following Tuesday we had a YSS meeting at my house. Antonio showed up drunk and disruptive. After the meeting I took him aside and asked him what the problem was. Antonio wanted to know if he could move in with me (at the time, I had a number of young people staying at my house). He said that he felt his life was in danger, and he wanted to get out of the neighborhood before anything happened. He did not give any details. I assumed he meant enemy gangs were after him. I agreed to work something out and help Antonio move in that weekend, asking him to give me a call.

I never heard from Antonio again. On Sunday morning I received a call from another YSS member, who told me Antonio had been killed the night before. The initial word in the neighborhood was that a rival gang had cor-nered him and shot him five times with hollow-point bullets (this is extremely lethal police-issue ammo). His arm was practically torn apart from the blasts.

Then, over the weeks, more information came to light. Apparently two men wearing ski masks had stepped out of an alley. Witnesses said they were built like men, larger in size than most teenagers. Although several other peo-ple were around Antonio, the assailants walked up to him and made sure all the rounds struck only him. They fled and did not say anything; they didn't mention the name of any rival gang, which usually happens in inter-gang conflicts.

Devon, who lived across the street from where this happened, said he saw several police cars patrolling the area just minutes before the shooting. He also went to the hospital with Antonio's mom and aunt, where more strange things occurred. One of these involved Antonio's friends, who had put the badly injured youth into a car and begun the drive to Cook County Hospital. This hospital has an emergency trauma unit; it was also where most uninsured people in the city go.

But en route, Antonio's friends were apparently stopped by police and told to go to another, supposedly closer, hospital. Not knowing what to do (and not suspecting that the police had anything to do with the shooting), they diverted the car toward the other hospital. This particular hospital, however, did not have an emergency trauma unit—which the police had to have known. Antonio was left in a gurney in the corridor for hours.

Devon and Antonio's family finally arrived there, after first waiting at the county hospital to no avail. The doctors refused to let the family members see Antonio, whose body could be seen lying on a gurney without any IVs or emergency staff around him. He may have died in that very corridor.

Devon came to me in a distraught state with this information. He felt responsible for what may have been a police-ordered hit. We had no direct proof of this, however, which thwarted our efforts to get an official inquiry. The official word—just like the word in the street—was that a rival gang had killed Antonio. In fact several youth were picked up for Antonio's murder. Only one was eventually charged. This young man was later found dead in his cell, an apparent suicide.

These kinds of incidents happen too frequently in cities like Chicago to be dismissed without inquiry.[6] They happened too often in smaller places like San Bernardino, California, where I was the cop-and-disaster reporter for the daily newspaper for two and a half years in the early 1980s. At the time, San Bernardino had the second highest per capita murder rate in the country as well as the worst vehicular accident rate—I saw enough dead bodies in car accidents, gang wars, murders, suicides, fires, and drug overdoses to cover a small war.

Growing up, I had lost four friends to police violence. At Antonio's wake and funeral, his dark Mexican mother, wrapped in an Indian shawl, screamed. His short and stocky father, with the callused hands of a laborer, stood sturdy and silent like a statue, although seemingly capable of breaking at any moment. I felt submerged in the grief of all these deaths, fearful that I would not be able to surface. At the time, Antonio's younger brother was in prison for a murder he didn't commit. This was too much for this family, any family, to carry. Yet in places like Pilsen it was all too common.

Hundreds of young people have related similar stories. In many cases an angry exchange precipitates a police beating. Kids in schools as well as in the streets have to show great restraint in dealing with adults—no anger or strong emotions are allowed—so many of them have gotten in trouble just because they can't hold their tempers. This is difficult for adults to do (most adults don't show the same restraint toward youth or children); it is much more difficult for teenagers. I have often heard police officers remark to angry young people that they "need an attitude adjustment," preferably at the police station (you hear the same words in movies and TV programs). But why? For what purpose? To save the social order? As the result of some officer's own pathology? In one northside high school the police substation in the building—now commonplace in many communities—is called "the beating room" by the students.

For years I've facilitated workshops at the Audy Home, Cook County's Juvenile Temporary Detention Center, known as the largest youth institution in the world. While I knew many good teachers and staff members there, there were still too many youth being reprimanded and punished just for getting mad. Many of them had been removed from family and friends and often traumatized by past abuse and neglect. They were afraid and alone and just didn't know how else to act. As Robert Bly has observed, there's too much "temperament, but not enough teaching" from adults to young people in today's culture.[7] So young people respond in kind, and we can't stand it. Humor or anger, we seem unable to withstand the expressive powers of our young people.

James Hillman has said that "any big emotion signals value."[8] It is not just indicative of something wrong, it is also about something important. Outrage cannot be seen as needing to be squashed. It has to be seen as symptomatic of a profound crisis—a schism, for example, in the spiritual center of a child. But they are also outcries about great injustices, social imbalances, and a generally deteriorating environment. Earthquakes in nature are about cataclysmic changes beneath the ground. So, too, are the outbursts of people, particularly the young. What they signal cannot be pushed aside or ignored.

Once, I met with the staff of a youth psychiatric treatment center where I raised concerns about how they dealt with my emotionally explosive son, Ramiro, who was placed there for three months when he was fifteen years old. Ramiro was constantly put in leather restraints, drugged, and removed from group activities. I felt that when the anger erupted was precisely the time that staff, with proper training and patience, could do something positive in addressing the motives for his anger. After they "calmed" him down, Ramiro would refuse to talk about the problem—until the next outburst, when the process would start up again. After I had outlined my observations, a staff member responded with "we cannot sacrifice the institution for one person." So they would sacrifice my son? I firmly believe the test of any viable organization dealing with our children should be that they will do all they can for one child—or else they can't be trusted to do this for any.

Although police abuse is considered an aberration, there is a great deal of unexamined pathology in many individuals on the police force just as there is among members of gangs and distraught people in impoverished communities. Individuals involved in domestic disputes—some of whom have actually been killed by police—are usually agitated and crying out for help, not bullets or chokeholds.[9] We forget that what sparked most civil disturbances across the country over the past forty years has been wanton police violence against members of relatively powerless communities. "Police departments are not... mere passive mirrors of the social order, nor could they be, because such orders are complex and embody conflicting interests and values," writes Paul Chevigny in *Edge of the Knife: Police Violence in the Americas.*[10]

It appears that the various segments of the adult community are not only failing to work together, they are often completely at odds. In fact, when these conflicting interests are at play, they are literally at war with one another. Young people see this and may ask, quite legitimately, how can anyone expect them to come together when adults can't seem to stop fighting for one minute?

Whether I like it or not, I have to see police officers as members of my community. Too often, however, they don't live there. An officer once told me while investigating a violent incident near my home, "Look, I can go home after this and not think twice about it—you have to live with this nonsense day and night." Precisely. This is my neighborhood. I'm vested here. But a police officer may not be, although such people continue to maintain a level of authority over the rest of us.

The fact is police cannot fill the voids in our relationships. Today a significant section of the community have turned their backs on kids. What's needed is for us to be meaningfully and consistently active in kids' lives. We have forced young people to find their own way, then demonized them for doing so. We can't go back to the repressive police tactics that have characterized anticrime efforts.

Peace is a process. It's a plan. It's a way of life.

Police, therapists, teachers, lawyers—they've all become "professional," and in the process many of them have lost the "dreaming" that first brought them to their particular callings. Unfortunately too often they discourage dreaming in our children and youth. To have peace, we have to get back to this dreaming, to the original pull of our passions, to the spirit that brought us into these lines of work in the first place.

An important aspect of elders is that they, too, have passions, fire, and dreams—only they have them largely for others, while young people have them largely for themselves.

Chapter 8
Fear and Fury

The word was born
in the blood,
it grew in the dark body, pulsing,
and took flight with the lips and mouth.

—Pablo Neruda

Gilbert, seventeen, was arrested for shooting at a gang rival. I got involved in his case, visited Gilbert in the county jail, tried to solicit bail money, and located a lawyer who could do him justice without costing his poor family a load of money. From the outside someone may ask why I would embroil myself in a situation that clearly indicated Gilbert had, with deathly intent, shot at an unarmed person, even if this person was a perceived enemy.

But Gilbert's home life had to be understood in order to comprehend why he would do such a thing. Gilbert was a handsome, bright young man of Puerto Rican and Mexican descent. He lived in Humboldt Park, which was rival gang territory. His own father, who did not reside with Gilbert, was a founding member of the rival gang. His mother, alone and on welfare, was too stressed out to handle the two boys and two girls in the family (and, later, four grandchildren from the teenaged girls), all of whom joined local gangs at one time or another.

Living in the wrong neighborhood meant Gilbert had to run down the steps of his apartment building to avoid confronting enemies before entering a vehicle. He scanned the scenery wherever he went, every time he happened to be in my car. Gilbert faced danger at every corner, although he tried not to show it.

Things worsened when his cousin, who lived only two houses down, was shot in the chest after answering a knock at his front door. Although his cousin survived the incident—the bullet barely missed his heart (another cousin was also shot and survived), Gilbert felt more endangered than ever. What's more, his twelve-year-old brother was hit in the leg during a shooting incident in which Gilbert was the intended target.

One day Gilbert happened upon a rival gang member talking to his sister. In their younger days this particular sister sometimes would set up Gilbert for beatings by rival gang members after they had argued, which aggravated the fact of this encounter. Something went off in Gilbert. A blinding rage that he could not explain simply overwhelmed him. This reaction is often called "flooding"—a rush of chemicals causing palms to sweat, breath to shorten, and the head to feel as if it will explode. Sometimes the eyes bulge and veins pop out of the side of the neck.

As the young man walked down the street, Gilbert stopped the car he was in and began firing a gun toward the rival. The good news was no one was hit. The bad news for Gilbert was that a police officer happened to drive by and witness the shooting. The youth had acted so impulsively that he hadn't even thought about who may have seen him or, even worse, who else may have been hurt by stray bullets. Having a gun had proved too much for Gilbert.

He was later convicted, but because of the lack of any prior major incidents, he was allowed to participate in one of the new boot camps the state of Illinois had set up (his lawyer fought for this, although these boot camps were supposed to be for nonviolent felons).

To many people's surprise, Gilbert graduated the boot-camp program with its vigorous regimen and Marine-trained staff. I was impressed. I probably couldn't have done that myself. He looked good when he was released; he was thinner and physically fit. It looked as if Gilbert might have learned some regulating strategies to deal with his frustrations.

But then I met his parole agent.

The first time we met, the parole agent was polite. He related a terrible story about a young man who lived only two streets from my house. I had read in the newspaper about this guy, who was in his early twenties and also a boot-camp graduate. While on house arrest with an ankle monitor, the dude went off for some reason and beat his three-year-old daughter to death. Gilbert's parole agent had been this guy's parole agent as well. The agent mentioned to me that the majority of those who come out of boot camp end up going back to prison. He did not like the boot camp program—and, I later learned, he did not like anyone who had been in one.

Whenever the agent came to visit Gilbert, who was on house arrest for four months after boot camp, I noticed that afterward Gilbert would be quite agitated, though he wouldn't say why. One day I was at his home when the parole agent came by to talk with the boy and check around for anything illegal. From another room came a terrible harangue. The agent kept calling Gilbert demeaning names. He said that he was a born failure and that he'd never last on house arrest. Gilbert tried to keep cool—he didn't want to be given a violation. But when the agent left, I saw how disturbed Gilbert was.

Some people might conclude the agent was challenging Gilbert so that he would learn not to respond angrily when others harangued him in this way. I don't buy that. The net result of all this would be to set the young man up to fail.

If this agent also did this to other parolees, I wondered how many exploded? I wondered how many ended up violating their parole by attempting to strike the agent or just tell him off? Or how many kept the resentment pent up inside, and then one day, triggered by something mundane and minor, ended up hurting someone close to them, even a child?

I couldn't shake the feeling this agent may have helped push that young man who had killed his baby to the breaking point. We know many people have been driven to psychotic states or to suffer emotional stress. We know that most prisons, but also some of the boot camps where a person's very being is torn down so that it can be built up by drill officers, take almost anybody to the limit.

The parole agent acted as if his behavior had nothing to do with a parolee's state of mind. It's a ploy of the mind to distance oneself from others one may be hurting, so when the object of one's assaults reacts in a bad way, one can walk away thinking he had nothing to do with the behavior. "Where's his personal responsibility?" I can hear the agent say. But we also have to ask, Where's yours, sir?

We know that many young people express their rage with violent fury. Almost anything can set them off. Mostly this happens when they feel wrongfully challenged, disrespected, or misunderstood. Many of the young people I've worked with were highly sensitive to a variety of dangers around them. They confront a steady stream of abuse at home, in school, and on the street, which heightens their levels of fear, resulting in an acute state of awareness. Chemical changes occur in the brain as a defense mechanism against habitual threats. These kids sometimes react like frightened animals. The oldest known responses to these situations are called the three Fs: "fight, flee, or freeze." It is now recognized that children who have been severely beaten in their families, who live in poor and violent settings, or who have been abandoned or neglected exhibit certain traits akin to soldiers coming back from war. They also suffer from posttraumatic stress disorder (PTSD). According to *Increase the Peace: A Primer on Fear, Violence, and Transformation*,[1] brain chemistry adjusts to dangers and threats. There is a rush of chemicals called neurotransmitters, such as adrenaline (the fight mode) or noradrenaline (the flee or freeze mode).

"For children who live with violence and other abuse, fear is a shadow that follows their every step," the primer states. "This fear doesn't just make them feel uncomfortable and need new ways of coping. It can also cause permanent changes in the way their brains and bodies work."[2] The primer outlines how this change in brain chemistry occurs in children whose survival mode is based on real and perceived threats. "When people spend a lot of time in danger, their bodies start making more and more adrenaline and noradrenaline. They even form new pathways in the brain for [the chemicals] to travel."[3] Jumpy, anxious, on edge—you've seen people like this.

According to an article that appeared in *Pediatrics* magazine: "It is increasingly clear that violent injury during adolescence causes psychological disability that may contribute to the established high risk of these victims for reinjury, death or reactive perpetration of violence."[4] When the dangers are ones that never seem to cease—bullets at all hours of the night, sometimes coming through walls; shouts and beatings in the street by other youth or adults, such as the police; and ongoing sexual, physical, and emotional trauma at home—the coping mechanisms take on more complex turns.

Chemicals in the brain can help these children cope. Serotonin helps keep instincts and emotions—including sexual desire, appetite, mood, sleep, and aggression—under control. Endorphins raise feelings of pleasure, calm, and well-being and help lower levels of pain. However, these chemicals may also be taxed to the point that some children start feeling "detached" from the world, unable to "feel," and therefore unable to respond properly to the dangers—and the consequences—of their actions. Under these circumstances these actions are heavily directed by chemical reactions in their brains.[5]

There is a way to treat children and people with PTSD, or the most severe psychotic breaks. Some people can relearn how to think and respond properly by "imprinting" over the previous configurations of the brain that were the result of trauma. But this takes time, resources, and unfortunately money. It is especially true in the most deprived communities that the people, knowledge, and patience required for this therapy are not available. Prison—the main way to address these issues when they involve the poor—is not treatment. In fact the prison experience can exacerbate the symptoms with new levels of fear and pain. Essentially some prisoners are resocialized around the pathologies, instead of the other way around.

Unfortunately, carrying a gun is routine in our neighborhoods. Yet what is not understood is that most youth don't carry guns to attack people; they carry them for "protection." I'm sure this is the same rationale a young woman jogger may have for possessing Mace or a more lethal means of warding off would-be rapists. We don't always see that many of these youth have weapons for the same basic reason. The root of this is fear, not aggression.[6]

Gilbert eventually managed his parole time without a hitch, learning to work and keep a job while focusing his attention on the more positive aspects of his life. We referred him to the Jorge Prieto Family Mental Health Clinic in the Little Village barrio. On the staff is Puerto Rico–born Dr. Antonio Martinez, a well-known expert on torture and the effects of trauma on families and communities, who has worked with torture victims from places like Central America and Africa. Dr. Martinez found that many families in the poor urban areas of the United States exhibited symptoms similar to those in more impoverished war-torn countries.

Over the years Dr. Martinez has helped teach young people like Gilbert and their parents the science behind their rage and the skills required to control and redirect their anger. Like most people who do this work, Martinez knows the key is to remove people from the source of the traumas as soon as possible. However, this is something most poor people find nearly impossible to do unless other areas of their lives—work, housing, and health care—are also attended to. It requires a whole-community approach.

The March 30, 1998, broadcast of *Nightline* on ABC-TV focused on conditions inside the maximum security administrative segregation unit of Estelle Prison just outside Huntsville, Texas. Host Ted Koppel interviewed prisoners and officials, including Warden Fred Figueroa. At one point Figueroa responded to Koppel's concerns about releasing a prisoner who had been isolated and perhaps driven to psychosis in one of the Ad Seg units, where prisoners are locked down for twenty-three hours a day, with nothing but a cell, a bed, and a toilet.

"The implicit message here is you've got men who are so incorrigible, so tough, so violent that they can't make it here in the general prison population where they're surrounded by people just like them," observed Koppel. "But once they've done their time in Ad Seg, they're out on the street. I'd be a little concerned if one of those fellows was moving into my neighborhood, wouldn't you?"

"Oh, yes, sir," replied Figueroa. "I'd be concerned."

"And what's the answer?" Koppel asked.

"There's no hope for that individual, in my opinion," Figueroa continued. "He was aggressive for wanting to get into Ad Seg, and he was probably aggressive before he came to the penitentiary, and he's going to continue to be aggressive when he gets out."

"But if anything, he's a little meaner, a little tougher, a little more psychotic than he was when he got here in the first place," Koppel said.

"Yes, sir. I'm not going to argue that point either."[7]

There's something daunting in this—as if the only solution is to continue to isolate prisoners, continue to drive them crazy, and then continue to endanger more people when they are released. There is a vast body of literature and a great number of experts who know how to work with such cases. But once these experts become part of the penal system, this knowledge, this collective understanding, is no longer brought to bear. Years of practical and scientific knowledge are rendered null and void.

It's hard to change people. When people do not want to change, of course, no one can truly make them. But the ideology driving any institution has to be that no life is useless. Everyone has something to give. Everyone. Change is internal and therefore natural—people are going through changes all the time.

We cannot keep working on the assumption that change is impossible, that people are hopeless, and that we have to accept, even to the endangerment of the entire community, our inability to apply the great knowledge we have to ameliorate this situation. If those in power feel that people and situations are hopeless, that feeling permeates the very psyche of that community, particularly the most susceptible, its youth.

Unfortunately it goes further than that. Many officials, regardless of their stated rationales, are participating in the abusive relationships and detrimental policies that end up looking like the very things they are trying to "remove" from society.

Here are three rationales abusers often use to justify their actions (these observations about the so-called criminal mind do not just apply to "criminals"):

• Blame the victims: They are responsible for what's happening to them, not the abuser.

• Demonize those who are being victimized—they are no good, they are scum. By using such terms as *animals*, *monsters*, or *less than human*, abusers show less regard for the people they are abusing. If they saw these people as they really are, they would see a part of themselves, which is the starting point for any empathy with others. Making someone an "enemy" is a powerful way of removing oneself from the human link we have with them. Just as in any war—which includes wars between police and the poor, between gangs, and between races—we justify our actions in relation to our enemies. Serial killers who stalk and kill women often exhibit an intense hatred for them. The mind relieves itself from association and pain by saying, "Who cares about them? They are enemies. They deserve what they get."

• Deny one's participation in the abuse by saying: "I don't care." There are many emotional states one may be in while committing a violent or abusive act, including fear and hate. But the overriding one is a deep and overwhelming disconnection. This is the rationale behind driveby shootings. Shooters don't have to look into the eyes of the victims in a driveby. If they did, they'd have to see the victims' pain, their mothers crying, how just like them they are.[8] Gang youth and prisoners respond in these ways. But preachers, politicians, teachers, and parents also justify in a similar fashion their efforts to degrade or turn away from needy young people, gang members, or prisoners.

War is a defining metaphor for most arguments, conflicts, or dissensions in our culture. It pervades our daily language and infects our conceptions about relationships as well. According to George Lakoff and Mark Johnson in their book *Metaphors We Live By,* "The conceptual metaphor, ARGUMENT IS WAR… is reflected in our everyday language by a wide variety of expressions: 'Your claims are indefensible.' 'He attacked every weak point in my argument.' 'His criticisms were right on target.' 'I demolished his argument.' 'I've never won an argument with him.' 'You disagree?' 'Okay, shoot!' 'If you use that strategy, he'll wipe you out.' 'He shot down all my arguments.'"[9]

"It's important to see that we don't just talk about arguments in terms of war," continue Lakoff and Johnson. "We can actually win or lose arguments. We see the person we are arguing with as an opponent. We attack his positions and we defend our own. We gain and lose ground. We plan and use strategies. If we find a position indefensible, we can abandon it and take a new line of attack.... It is in this sense that the ARGUMENT IS WAR metaphor is one that we live by in this culture; it structures the actions we perform in arguing."[10]

So when we use the images and metaphors of war for our campaigns—the war on drugs, the war against poverty, the war against so-called predator youth—we are designating an "enemy" who must be eradicated at whatever cost, and objectifying the enemy in order to further depersonalize the struggle.

"Our best hope for survival is to change the way we think about enemies and warfare," writes Sam Keen in his book *Faces of the Enemy: Reflections of the Hostile Imagination*. "Instead of being hypnotized by the enemy, we need to begin looking at the eyes with which we see the enemy."[11]

I have been to a number of juvenile facilities where "killer" kids are housed. Most of them don't look any different than any other kid their age. Gang youth may exhibit a certain stance, may have tattoos and scars, but for the most part they are still children trying to figure life out. The fact is that many of those who have committed murder at such young ages come from so-called good families. They were not necessarily bad students. They probably had a healthy dose of values. Many went to church or temple. The majority of these youngsters happened to be at the wrong place, at the wrong time, under the wrong circumstances. Perhaps they got drunk, perhaps somebody gave them a gun and somebody else said, "We have to get our enemies." Swept up in the swirl of the moment, with lowered inhibitions, boom!—someone is dead.

Although there are youth who are strongly pathological, they can be helped. The problem is you can't always recognize when a kid tells you to drop dead or to get out of his life that he may be saying the exact opposite. Unfortunately we have lost the art of reading these signals.

The warden at Estelle Prison in Texas is wrong when he says "there's no hope" for certain prisoners. There is far more evidence to show that hope is a primary component of this intricate machinery called a human being. The story of Pandora's Box tells us this truth: The same box carrying the seeds of all the troubles and anxieties of the world also brought the one sustaining virtue, hope. We are the Pandora's Box. Moreover, hope is connected to despair—the more desperate one is, the more the beacon of hope can shine.

We as a society have allowed the warden to justify his hideous position. "The community is with me," "Most people want these kind of prisons," "Everyone knows the Bible says 'an eye for an eye.'" Yes, we are all in consensus, according to certain polls and political statements. We also participate in these injustices.

The same thing happened during the period of slavery. For decades most voting white males with property (the only ones who could vote then) supported "the peculiar institution" of slavery. "This is democracy," someone may say. However, a real democracy would have enfranchised the slaves so that they could become the sole determiners of their sovereign conditions. But just because most people agree to something doesn't make it right. Likewise, this society should empower the powerless to enable them to solve their problems. It's better to stand with a few and be right than to stand with millions and be wrong. Under most circumstances, this is a true hero's stance.

Chapter 9

"Don't Give Up on Us!"

With no name, no face:
the death I want
bears my name,
*   it has my face.*
It is my mirror and it is my shadow,
the soundless voice that speaks my name,
the ear that listens when I am silent,
the intangible wall that blocks my way,
the floor that suddenly opens.

—Octavio Paz

When I first met Jeremiah, he didn't care whether he lived or died.

A tall and muscular African-American man in his early twenties, Jeremiah had just finished serving a stint at an Illinois state prison when he came to a YSS retreat near Chicago's Cabrini Green housing projects. The night before, he had been jumped by rival gang members—Jeremiah arrived at the event with one eye closed, his mouth cut and swollen. He soon found a spot in the corner of the room, pulled several chairs together, and laid his head down to sleep.

One of the elders asked why I didn't throw Jeremiah out. "It isn't right that he's sleeping while the other youth are busy working," the elder insisted. I didn't disagree, but I had other concerns in mind. I felt that at least here, within eyesight of the group, Jeremiah could be looked after. The others didn't seem worried about Jeremiah sleeping while they talked and made plans for their ongoing activities. Many of them have been on the streets, drugged out, dodging bullets, running ragged down wet cobblestone alleys. They seemed to understand that Jeremiah was safe, at least for now.

Jeremiah's great gift was words. He was a muse's instrument; verbs and nouns flowed through him like rushing water. He was filled with stories and ideas, humor, pain, and a pervading beat. Somehow, because of my own passion for words, Jeremiah and I clicked. There was much that Jeremiah already knew. What I had to teach had more to do with direction.

But like many of his peers, Jeremiah was also good at undermining his own efforts. He got involved in a few more fights and shootings after our first meeting. He drank too much. As a young father, he also had ongoing battles with the mother of his kids (and probably like most young men, with women in general). There were days that seemed like one more brick on a solid blank wall—nothing changed, nothing seemed to matter.

Jeremiah didn't trust adults in general. He had a bad relationship with his father, who divorced his mother when he was young, and an ongoing war with his mother, who raised him and his sister by herself. He challenged us to try to hang with him, to see if we could catch up, to see if, like most adults he knew, we'd jump ship.

I was determined not to be the one who jumped, although I often cautioned Jeremiah that for the most part he was bound to give up first. "I won't be navigating the boat of your life," I'd say. "You have to put in a hundred and ten percent—not 'meet me halfway,' as some people say. This is your life. If you're fully committed to your own aims, I will then help the best way I can." He liked this response. It reminded him that his life belonged to him, that he held the reins in his own hands. Because he had been criticized heavily by his mother and by his father, he never liked anybody telling him what to do or pointing out his mistakes. So through teachings based on his own experiences, and the results of his own actions, he finally opened up and saw the ways in which he was contributing to his own failures—and successes.

There were, of course, ups and downs. His troubles with the law and with gangs were always a strain. He had a hard time returning calls or showing up on time to events (he usually did show up—a big plus). Eventually we got him to stay with us for a while, and another time we sent him off to California to slow down, work, and get his bearings. In time we grew close. Within a few years Jeremiah became a leader of YSS, eventually serving as chairperson of the board. By then he was working with another community organization, mentoring thirty to sixty youths of his own. He tried to help others, including homeboys of his caught in the same web of rage and defeat that he had been entangled in. When we went around soliciting funds for YSS, Jeremiah, in his articulate and poignant way, won over many a funder. Once in a protest rally outside Chicago's federal building, he delivered a powerful talk to several thousand youth and community leaders.

In time I sensed that Jeremiah was letting go of the face of death that seemed to dog him. He was beginning to demonstrate a lust for life. By the time he was in his midtwenties, I could see that living had a much greater purpose and momentum for him, although the dangers around him persisted for some time.

Teachers, therapists, police officers, parole agents, child protective services workers, prison personnel, and parents can make a difference in young people who have lived similar lives. Such people can be such powerful influences on youth that when they do right by them, they do immeasurable good; but when they do wrong, they can do incalculable harm. We have a tremendous amount of responsibility as members of the community for the condition of our young people.

Some of the youth I've worked with have cited parents as the people they most have problems with, often due to abuse and neglect. They usually say things like "they don't listen to me," "they're too tired," or "they're too drunk" or "drugged out" to care.

I remember a compelling session in late 1998 with several young Mexican, Puerto Rican, and Guatemalan women at the Antonia Pantoja Alternative School of ASPIRA in Chicago. We were recording for Radio Guatemala the impact of drug use by parents on their children. There was story after story of mothers who prostituted themselves down the street where their children had to walk to school; of fathers who drank and abused their daughters; of how cocaine, heroin, alcohol, and marijuana mediated any parent-child relationship; and their stories brought tears to those who sat in on the discussion. One girl continued with her studies, even making the honor roll, despite having a mother hooked on crack.

For years I mulled over everything I had done, attempting to contribute some positive lessons in regard to being a father in my children's lives, particularly for my oldest son, Ramiro. "I am their father." I'd remind myself. It was important to know this, and not to become immobilized with self-pity or remorse for things not done. Remorse— a"torment of conscience"— is an important part of change, but it can be a paralyzing sentiment when people are not allowed to go beyond its initial impact.[1] It allowed me to establish a rapport with my children that should last a lifetime, and this is invaluable. I'm most thankful that I overcame much of my own infantile ego and obsessions so that I could begin to cross a very important bridge toward our healing.

Good, strong parents have been trapped in powerlessness. Any father and mother who has had to go through some trying times with their sons or daughters—who may be in gangs, on drugs, or on a psychosomatic roller-coaster ride—knows how difficult it is to relate properly and respectfully to their children. Parents need to be a strong presence in a young person's life, and to do this they need the strength and embrace of the community as well.

None of us lives in a vacuum. All our actions or inactions have ramifications and impose consequences on others. People make choices, but if someone believes he or she has no choices, the choices will choose them. We will have to pay a price for our decisions down the road. This is also true for the people who set the parameters for the choices to be made. If they are wise, the consequences should result in good things, but if they are not—as is most often the case—then they cannot escape the wrong they have wrought. If we want others to be responsible for their actions, we have to be responsible for ours. There can be no real personal responsibility in an environment of social irresponsibility.

A community must think before attempting to shape the behavior of young people. If we treat people like animals, for the most part they will act this way. If we treat people with respect, patience, caring—being firm and consistent or flexible and open as needed—they will more likely respond in the same way. One of the most profound lessons of life—the Golden Rule— is to treat people as you want to be treated. It's the essential idea in most religions and belief systems of the world. Where are these lessons in the criminal justice system? At home? In schools? In the street?

In the summer of 1996, YSS youth, along with others from various organizations, put out their first newspaper, *Increase the Peace,* largely through the efforts of Patricia Zamora. The lead headline was, "Don't Give Up On Us!"

"We know that at times it is hard being a parent and that it is a struggle. Everyday there are lot of issues that are being confronted by the youth and many of your very own sons/daughters feel that parents are giving up too easily. We feel that parents have no hope for us. But there is!" wrote fifteen-year-old Irene Correa in the front-page article.

You must not give up on the youth, because that's the only hope we've got. Your sons and daughters are the coming generation and we're the only thing you have to try to make positive changes in this world. We must come together and form bonds to let the youth know that our parents really care for us.

Parents have to be open-minded and realize that their children are struggling, too! We, as one, have to come together and face these issues slowly but surely. Hopefully, parents reading this newsletter can have a better understanding of how our children feel towards our society-based problems, and to know that we really care about these situations.

Through this, we can finally fill in the gap that is missing with loss of communication between parents and children.

Remember—Don't give up! We are the future.

We can't always ease the suffering our youth may have to go through. But they need to know there are family and community praying and struggling with them. Some parents think their job is to excuse the actions of their children when they do wrong, while too many think they should write their children off. Neither of these responses is appropriate. The middle way, the gap between the two conflicting poles, where the tensions are most acute and probably the most ambiguous, is where we must increasingly find ourselves if we are to be true to our children. Keeping to this middle course—acting with integrity—may be the hardest thing we have to do.

There is a strong push in this country to cut off those who are serving time in our various penal institutions from their communities. Far from being a community-directed and ritualized banishment, this severing of ties serves to fracture our society even further. Prisons are purposely built far away from the urban centers where most convicts' families live. Long-distance collect calls are far more costly than for the rest of the population, making contact sporadic and causing more isolation. This situation tends to create more estrangement between members of the community. Fathers are cut off from their children, husbands from wives, mothers from their kids, brothers and sisters from one another.[2]

Too many people in prison don't have anyone else to turn to but family. Without these ties, many of them fall in with convicts' societies, including prison gangs, that necessarily arise to offer convicts protection and meaning—often at the cost of their very lives, if not their souls.

Many adults—parents, teachers, police, and other authority figures—have contributed to the dilemmas and terrors of young people, culminating in their responding in some very terrible ways, as did those two young men in Littleton. How many humiliations, beatings, and betrayals do some of these children have to endure, how much of being "wrenched and buffeted... by systemic thugs,"[3] as one writer put it, before they finally explode?

We know these kids are not "angels," but they're not "devils" either. Simplistic labels like these only contribute to the confusion. They are extremely capable human beings whose every life crisis can serve as a stepping-stone to a fuller and deeper life. In a community of properly initiated, aware, and vibrantly committed adults, mentors, and elders, they would have gone through much of their troubles without hurting themselves or others.

"Societies that attend to the initiation of youth provide rituals that require everything else come to a halt," writes Michael Meade. "Questions hang in the air: Will this generation of youth find a connection to spiritual meaning and beauty that will keep the light at the center of the tribe burning? Or will they be a generation of possessive, power-driven people? If the elders of the society do not seriously consider these questions, if they forget about or ignore the matter of initiating their youth, sooner or later there is bound to be a spontaneous eruption of inner forces among the youth themselves: a move toward physical violence, possessiveness, and brutality."[4]

This may shed light on why fifteen-year-old Kip Kinkel, a seemingly normal kid from Springfield, Oregon, walked into his high school cafeteria on May 21, 1998, and opened fire with a semiautomatic rifle, shooting twenty-four students. Perhaps the lack of a truly encompassing, consistently attentive, and responsive community may explain why Kinkel, a C-average student and average in most other ways as well, would murder his own fairly well-adjusted and loving parents and place numerous, homemade bomb devices in his home.

Kipland Kinkel was most definitely part of the community, linked by so many strands to its character and history—good and evil, light and shadow, love and hate. But what would the residents of Springfield say? Would they react like the school principal who said to *Rolling Stone* magazine, "I don't think it's a stigma on our community. It's a statement about a poor kid with a tortured soul."[5]

The people of Springfield or Littleton are as decent as any other people; these communities came together to mend. But like so many communities in this country, the disarming quiet of tree-lined streets, picket fences, and weathered storefronts may hide more than we think. Even in the most peaceful homes, violence invades everyday through TV, movies, video games, and newspapers. Although the vast majority of kids in such places would never hurt anybody, let alone murder, violence is very much a product of who we are and what we have created.

There are no simple answers. There never will be. But we can figure this out. Whether we are ready or not, we're going to have to look into the nooks and crannies of our own souls as well as those of our communities and society. When more and more communities undergo this kind of horror, and when we remember that for generations the so-called inner city has been waging a protracted war against children, then it's time to look at the very heart of what our culture has become. Something deep, central to our lives, is askew. This is not about throwing blame around; it's about being true to the demands of the crisis, of challenging ourselves to meet the actual levels of pain, loneliness, and fear.

Young people, even in the midst of a society rife with fear, anger, and hatred, exhibit a great range of spiritual, artistic, and intellectual powers, as well as extraordinary resiliency.[6] But they need a constant reminder of these talents and strengths. Too often they are "corrected" rather than encouraged. Our job, then, is to learn how to use our strengths to overcome our weaknesses when solving society's problems; too much current policy and practice (including imprisonment) uses people's weaknesses to overcome their strengths.

Drawing on their vast inner resources, our children can learn to negotiate whatever barriers are thrown in the way of their personal and social growth.

Much Madness is divinest Sense—
To a Discerning Eye—
Much Sense—the Starkest Madness—[7]

PART TWO

THRESHOLDS AND TRAJECTORIES

In every child who is born... the potentiality
of the human race is born again.
—James Agee

Chapter 10

Doors, Story, Purpose[1]

I would retrieve the secret of great combustions and great communications. I would say storm. I would say river. Tornado I would say. I would say leaf. I would say tree. I would be watered by all rains, dampened by all dews. I would rumble onward like frenetic blood on the slow stream of my eye my words like wild horses like radiant children like clots like curfew-bells in temple ruins like precious stones so distant as to discourage miners. He who would not understand me would not understand the roaring of a tiger.

—Aimé Césaire

A few times over the years I've entered the guarded gates of the Fred C. Nelles School for Boys in Whittier, California, to talk to "wards" of the state incarcerated there. Nelles is a California Youth Authority (CYA) facility for young men ages ten to sixteen, whose crimes range from incorrigible criminal behavior to murder. I've addressed assemblies of youth, dressed in their "blues," many of whom were members of Los Angeles–area gangs. The majority at Nelles were Chicano/Latino; the rest were mostly African American.

On the faces of these wards, some of them marked with tattoos, I saw the pain, the emptiness, the shame, and the pride that I felt some thirty years before when I myself was part of a Los Angeles barrio gang. Some were defiant; others, victims. Some were brave; others, scared. They were emerging men and immature boys.

I spoke to them as honestly as I could, as soft and hard as the occasion required. I didn't preach. I didn't tell the wards what to do. I tried to summarize what I lived so that they would learn to assess their own lives—where they've been; where they're going—so that they could see assessment as an important part of any purposeful existence.

During one of my visits in 1993 I heard about the Nixon Unit, where some of the "worst" cases were supposedly segregated and locked down—kids, some as young as ten, who have murdered, raped, and maimed; often these were the ones who couldn't get along in the main population. I asked to go there. At first Nelles officials weren't sure about this, but, after arguing the case, I was allowed to speak at Nixon.

When I got there, the place was fairly dark. I asked that the lights be turned up. The two-story tiers held rows of thick-steel doors. When they were opened, the youth came forth, a few with baby faces, some squinting as if they had not seen light in days (or due to sleep, which, for many, is how they spend most of their time). We gathered just below the cells, under the watchful gaze of uniformed officers. I talked, they listened mostly in silence, occasionally interjecting thoughts and ideas. They appeared to be thinking. Perhaps feeling. They laughed. A few had tears in their eyes. One officer later told me he had not previously seen these kids show any emotions except rage. At the end of the session a sixteen-year-old Chicano came up to me and shook my hand. "I've never been as proud of being a Mexican as when I heard you speak here today," he said.

I then asked the youth why he was *torcido* (imprisoned).

"For two murders and eleven murder attempts," he responded.

As far as the criminal justice system was concerned, this young man was not going anywhere. But I sensed he was already on a journey of discovery and social clarification. Looking at this mythologically, he was embarking on the first leg of a hero's path—sinking to the depths of his psyche, facing his own shadow, clarifying the monstrous within (the Minotaur in the Labyrinth), entering a place of renewal (with guidance from an external power), of having part of him die (the infantile ego) only to emerge a changed soul, prepared to return with gifts for his community.

But in the predominant culture there are no lasting or trusting metaphors and symbols to help our young along this journey—especially youths like those at Nelles, who have broken the law or committed horrendous acts.

The hero's quest exists in most cultures, tribes, and nations in one form or another as a universal pattern, an archetypal story. Yet today we have failed to bring this out—"Pokemon" and "Power Rangers" do not adequately convey this crucial mythic image. In modern society even our religious symbols—as rich as they are—have been largely removed from the mysterious and the truly glorious. Many of the symbols have been gutted of their significance, used by rote, with little or no imagination, risk, or engagement. Yet most religious rites exist in forms that can be useful in the initiation of young people. Practiced wisely, they can help an initiate move on to the next stage, reborn into a "spiritual" life that is more conscious and mature, a natural step after their mostly incubated existence as children and adolescents. The whole psychology of youth is transformed; there is ritual death of the infantile personality and resurrection as an adult—born anew to their own natures. They die to the ordinary and are resurrected to the deeper transcendental qualities of their world. This, then, becomes the elemental pattern to one's growth, flowering, and decline.

Such rituals are vital for enabling human beings to enter a realm of meaning. It's a journey we all have to undertake, but what we see, what we encounter, how we find the character and courage to come back, are deeply personal. We need the guideposts, we need the helping hands, we need the hearts opened to our cries, but we have to go through the ordeals ourselves.

Mircea Eliade, whose pioneering work on initiation rites is considered a foundation for the modern study of these kinds of rituals, writes,

> The term initiation in the most general sense denotes a body of rites and oral teachings whose purpose is to produce *a decisive alteration* [italics mine] in the religious and social status of the person to be initiated.... Among the various categories of initiation, the puberty initiation is particularly important for an understanding of premodern man. These "transition" rites are obligatory for all the youth of the tribe. To gain the right to be admitted among adults, the adolescent has to pass through a series of initiatory ordeals: it is by virtue of these rites, and of the revelations they entail, that he will be recognized as a responsible member of the society. Initiation introduces the candidate into the human community and into the world of spiritual and cultural values.[2]

There's another important aspect we have to consider for any modern initiation practice: helping a person find himself or herself, his or her particular attributes, voice, and calling as artist and creator. Initiation today is as much about laying a road for the possible future of the initiate and our community as it is about conveying the traditions and stories of the past, the affinities between people and their deities, and the community's sense of wholeness and fulfillment.

Prisons, the profusion of new juvenile "predator" laws, or zero tolerance have nothing to do with these types of transition rites and initiation processes for young people—and therein lies a key to their failure.[3]

Presently we are witnessing the greatest rise in the number of young people adjudicated to adult facilities. While juveniles, age seventeen and under, made up less than 1 percent of the total adult prison population in 1997, this percentage was three times more than in 1979. By 1998 an estimated eight thousand juveniles were in adult state prisons, according to the Bureau of Justice Statistics.[4] "This increase largely has been fueled by public fear and lawmakers' responses: Get bad kids off the streets in a way that, unlike much of the juvenile justice system, will keep them off for a long time," writes J. Taylor Buckley.[5]

Such fears led California voters in the spring of 2000 to propel Proposition 21 into law, giving prosecutors, instead of juvenile court judges, the power to try violent felons as young as fourteen in adult courts. Early in 2001 a California Court of Appeals struck down a key portion of the juvenile-crime initiative, ruling that prosecutors should not decide unilaterally whether teenagers are tried as adults.[6]

According to the National Center on Institutions and Alternatives (NCIA), the transfer of juvenile offenders into the adult prison system, at increasingly younger ages, is producing a momentous strain on existing criminal justice resources.

"The adult prison system, focused on punishment and failing on its own accord, is ill-equipped to handle this new challenge. Yet critics complain that the juvenile court and its focus on rehabilitation, job training and 'second chances' has failed its mission. A single problem is driving this policy nationwide. The problem is violent juvenile crime, especially juvenile homicide. The problem is so serious it terrifies entire neighborhoods and leaves little children planning their own funerals," wrote Eric Lotke and Vincent Schiraldi in an NCIA report. [7]

The report then states that juvenile homicides, although generally increasing, are still highly site-specific. "Six states account for more than half of the country's juvenile homicide arrests, and just four cities account for nearly a third of the juvenile homicide arrests. These cities, Los Angeles, New York, Chicago and Detroit, contain 3.7 million juveniles, just 5.3 percent of the juveniles nationwide.... The problem is so site-specific that fully 82 percent of the counties in the country had zero known juvenile homicide offenders in 1994."[8]

The report concludes that transferring juveniles to adult court doesn't help, but may actually hurt.

> Legislation under consideration at the federal level adds new offenses to the list of those that lead to transfer to adult court, and requires states to transfer some 14 year old children to adult court in order to qualify for federal funds.... In order to examine whether increased transfer was associated with decreased homicide by juvenile offenders, we compared the per capita transfer rates with the per capita youth homicide rate in each of the fifty states and found no correlation. The data do not show that states with higher transfer rates have lower youth homicide rates. Connecticut has the highest transfer rate in the nation, and it has the same youth homicide rate as Colorado, whose transfer rate is nearly zero.... Rather than reducing juvenile crime, recent research has found that transfer to adult court is associated with higher rates of recidivism.[9]

Trying juveniles as adults is not new. We have stark and dramatic experiences to draw from—the dire situation when America routinely tossed youthful offenders into jails alongside hardened adult criminals prior to 1899. As I recounted in Part One, in that year the first children's court was established in Chicago "to create a special, separate place for children in crisis, away from adult courts and the horrors of adult jails and poorhouses."[10]

Instead of going back to a time before this enlightened approach was first undertaken, we should work to make real the concepts and concerns that the first juvenile courts were formed to achieve.

In March 2000, during a ten-week residency/tour of North Carolina,[11] I visited the Western Youth Institution (WYI) at the request of a courageous volunteer, a senior citizen named Millicent Gordon, who after she retired brought the arts to the incarcerated youth there. A devoted Christian, Ms. Gordon spent many hours with them as a way of giving back and living Christ's example of compassion and healing.

WYI is a sixteen-story block structure in Morgonton, North Carolina, with a backdrop of tree-covered mountains, next to the Foothills Correctional Facility. The guards are burly, the bars and walls are gray, and the place is loud. Some eight hundred youth, ages thirteen to nineteen, were housed in that facility. I was told every ward started out on the top floor. As they accomplished what was expected of them, they would move to lower floors until they hit the first floor, then out the door.

Unfortunately many of them were having a hard time leaving the top floors.

After my presentation I invited the people assembled in WYI's chapel—about 150—to ask questions or offer comments. Most of the responses came from staff, which was fine. They sought orientation and insight. I have come to believe that staff is as much in the dark as are most of the youth about what to do with their lives. The messages from policymakers and the public seem to be that these offenders should be treated harshly, no breaks, "don't coddle." Yet many staff were compelled by their humanity to strive for a deeper and more relevant approach in working with their charges, though few seemed to know what to do.

I regretted leaving the mostly black faces of North Carolina's largest youth facility. For a short while I had opened up their conceptions about what's possible. I hoped that Ms. Gordon and some of the staff might have grasped what I said about initiation, the power of art and intrinsic destinies, and how words and ideas can save lives. People like Ms. Gordon, by emphasizing the arts, are tapping into initiatory practices as old as humanity itself. Every culture around the globe, at one time or another, had profoundly meaningful rites and practices for these purposes.

At the North Carolina Correctional Institute for Women, I was brought to tears at the poems and stories the women wrote, particularly when they expressed the pain of leaving their children behind. At the Perquimans Detention Center in the Albemarle, a big fifteen-year-old girl who had been locked down in a tiny cell for weeks, stood up following my talk and performed a self-penned rap that rocked the joint.

And at the Foothills Correctional Facility next to WYI, I met a respectful and easygoing twenty-one-year-old, David Bowman, who was also an accomplished poet and writer. David helped pull together an anthology of poems from the prison and was taking numerous writing and music courses through a local community college. He even wrote an article about my talk to three hundred prisoners there that was published in the local daily newspaper. One of the staff later told me that David was serving two life sentences plus sixty years.

This is one of the poems that Bowman had published in the anthology:

We make these doors by spreading pain.
They spring from our ill-gotten gain.
Every door has a name,
some are hatred, greed and shame.
All these doors we control.
Opened and closed by our soul.
So beware of what you do,
Lest a door open for you.

When someone says poetry or any art has saved his or her life, this is recognition of an initiation process.

It was a former prisoner and heroin addict, Manual "Manazar" Gamboa, who first inspired me to enter prisons and juvenile facilities to conduct writing workshops. I met Manazar in 1979 at a Barrio Writers Workshop in East L.A. He had spent seventeen years in various California institutions, including Folsom, Soledad, and San Quentin, and some twenty years as a heroin addict. During one session, he said that poetry saved his life—I wanted to learn this truth from him. In a year's time I attended workshops he facilitated at the Chino Men's Colony. Since then I've given talks, interviews, and workshops in many prisons and juvenile facilities—both male and female—throughout the United States, in El Salvador and with juvenile offenders in Rome, Italy.

After doing all I could to avoid a long prison term and removing myself from gang life in the early 1970s, this has been my way of giving back. But I also do it because the prison world continues to engulf my world—my son Ramiro, friends and family, some of whom are serving long prison sentences sometimes for minor offenses (one friend is doing twenty-five to life for allegedly stealing six-hundred dollars' worth of merchandise) or for offenses they didn't commit (such as Pepe Vasquez).

In November 1999 I again visited CYA institutions in the southern part of the state, through the auspices of the arts program run by CYA's arts coordinator, Shelly Wood. These included Nelles, but also the Heman Stark Youth Training School (YTS) in Chino and the Southern Youth Correctional Reception Center and Clinic in Norwalk.

At each site we gathered a circle of young men together to listen to one another. You can teach in such a circle—by example, by one's own story, and by touching on the stories of others. I spoke briefly of my own experiences in gangs, jails, and my twenty-seven-year battle with drugs and alcohol (by then I had been sober for more than seven years).

I stopped using drugs and committing violent acts by age nineteen. I hid out for two and half months in a run-down housing project in San Pedro, away from my old haunts and friends. I studied intensely about my society, about methodologies, and about art. I cleaned out the drugs in my system, exercised, and ate right. Then for the first few years after that, because I was still vulnerable to unsavory situations, I stayed away from them.

This was not easy. I had to work long, draining hours in hot, humid, dangerous, and filthy places. I had relapses. I drank too much and had numerous auto accidents in my early twenties—most were minor, but a couple of them were total wrecks in which, by the grace of the Creator, I walked out with hardly a scratch.

I also had temptations to rob and seek revenge. I failed to deal adequately with relationships, including those with the women I loved and with my own children. The drag of drugs, the madness of a traumatized life, the simplicity of caving in, the pressure to give up, the draw of the suicide road—all of these kept coming back to me. So many times I felt like becoming enmeshed again inside the silky, weblike threads of la vida loca and letting things fall where they would. "So what?" I would say. "Who cares? It won't hurt just this once."

But despite continuing to use alcohol and not truly trusting people and family until I was close to forty years old, I finally made the turn. I know it's possible to change from a life of depravity, weakness, and addictions, even if many other people who may have tried have failed to do so.

I also spoke about the changes I made to remove myself from these debilitating addictions and about the work I was doing with youth all over the country, including through Youth Struggling for Survival.

And I talked about my son Ramiro. Some of the young men were about Ramiro's age—in their early twenties—and like Ramiro, many of them had children in the world, children they were not sure how to help, guide, or even how to stay in touch with. Despite all the problems my son and these men faced, the state of their children seemed to be the most pressing.

Almost all of the wards had great aspirations—to be artists, writers, rappers, to raise a family, to work and live a good life. Many of them said they wanted to complete prison programs so that they could get out. One young man—a tall African-American youth with handsome features and a sly smile—said his purpose was to become "the best drug dealer in the world." Nobody responded to him in a negative way.

In these kinds of circles listening requires taking in whatever is given, even if it seems like nonsense. One of the other youth later asked me what I thought about the aspiring young drug dealer's statement. I said he was probably just trying to get a rise out of us. But even if he was serious, such a goal had nothing to do with his inner purposes and passions. But let's assume that some aspects of what he was saying were intentional (to be an entrepreneur, for example, or even just the need to take a contrary position); these parts, too, have value when taken seriously. Unfortunately it was just as likely that the young man had fallen prey to society's expectations of youths like him. It was almost as if he had said that the main purpose of his life was to be the best damn slave on the plantation. Such expectations don't arise out of one's inner life. Rather they're the most palatable of the limited options offered certain people by this society.

One seventeen-year-old, who had been incarcerated in a CYA facility since the age of eleven for a driveby shooting, was slated to leave soon. However, he admitted he was having a hard time handling the notion that he would be out in the world. Just before he was to be released, he broke into one of the facility's classrooms and stole some fairly insignificant items, such as rulers and pens. This meant he would have to stay longer. He actually felt more at home there, having spent some important developing years in CYA, than his real home. This young man was simply not prepared to leave; he had no vision of a proper path to follow, nor the strength and support to do so.

Today we often praise the self-made individual, the person who walks his own path, the lone stranger. "I did it my way," crooned Frank Sinatra. We've seen this same sentiment expressed in the Westerns among the Rambos and Dirty Harrys, and to a certain extent, in the Jerry Seinfelds of film and TV. Such personalities appear not to abide by the dictates of their society. "Show me," he or she might say. "I want to draw my own conclusions." These types of people are moved by what are called "lived judgments." Through experiential means they arrive at their own values—the prelude to any real commitment. "It doesn't mean accepting what's given you," Joseph Campbell says. "It means evaluating."[12]

This is an important quality to possess. But however highly esteemed the myth of the "individual" may be in our culture, it is in fact not taken seriously. Those who don't quite "fit in"—not just the lawbreakers and malcontents but also those close to their creative center—often end up in correctional facilities, mental institutions, and other marginal spaces. We idealize "the individual" on the one hand; then, when we truly meet one, we want to put him or her away.

In reality, very few people can truly claim to be self-made. We need others to impart trust, to provide support, and even to discipline us. We need others to acknowledge us and in other ways to hold up the "mirror" at the right time. We are in fact surrounded by models and mentors. Some of them are blessings, others curses, but whether "good" or "bad," many external sources, including TV, music, books, and movies, help shape our individuality.

While many people turn their individuality over to others in an effort to "belong"—a crucial need of human beings—what makes a strong community in the final analysis is the association of self-appointed and self-driven persons. This is what it means to achieve *communitas,* a community of people with equal rights and status, although distinct and diverse qualities.

And what of the rest of us? Mostly we are living what Joseph Campbell called "inauthentic lives." In our culture we no longer search for the "holy grails"—those vessels of inexhaustible vitality that characterized the myths and lives of most other peoples and times. We don't know how to fulfill that which has never been on this earth before, namely our unique potentialities. We've forgotten that pain is where our life is. We don't express the spontaneity of our innate natures; nor do we remember that what impels us is compassion and love, not just ego, so that we may act not because of rules or what we are told but from the impulses of our own noble hearts.[13]

In *The Wasteland,* T. S. Eliot captured the sense of soulless duty, the purposeless purpose, the heavy heart with the weight of other hearts:

> *After the torchlight red on sweaty faces*
> *After the frosty silence in the gardens*
> *After the agony in stony places*
> *The shouting and the crying*
> *Prison and palace and reverberation*
> *Of thunder of spring over distant mountains*
> *He who is living is now dead*
> *We who were living are now dying* ...[14]

Prison is a "wasteland" culture, where all incarcerated are forced into the same mythological plain, given the same directions to enter the same story. For a few this works; the prison experience is enough to take them through the initiatory ground they are seeking. But it doesn't work for many. There is a detour in the initiatory passage, surrounded by metaphors and symbols that don't go deep enough; it is a break in their own story. [15]

A friend of mine once argued that the prison experience should be a long, stark, and terrible one so that people are forced to do the right thing. Then only the "bad" people, he reasoned, would want to end up there. Sounds good. But that's only if we are all the same, with the same psychological, social, and cultural pressures and with the same adaptive mechanisms. Many people accept the notion that "no excuses, no exceptions" works; however, in small families it rarely works and in large societies it never does. The myriad realities in the United States alone—with different social classes, races, religions, language groups, sexual orientations, and neighborhoods—makes this literally impossible, especially if you take into account the nature of the political state as we know it.

The fact is, with the large number of prisoners—besides the two million behind bars, there are another four million people on parole, probation, house arrest, or alternative sentencing—increasingly more families are within the parameters of the prison world.[16] Although prisons should be the hardest places to get into, for many they have been easier to enter than schools, colleges, or decent jobs. This is largely due to the many vested interests striving to maintain a thriving prison industry. According to the Criminal Justice Center, in 1994. it cost $22 billion to build and maintain prisons in the United States. By 1997 the price tag was close to $30 billion. Whole communities and businesses are dependent on them for jobs and for profit. For example, in Huntsville, Texas, site of a complex of eight prisons, including the most active death row in the country, nearly 6,700 of its residents split up $18 million in monthly paychecks. Twenty percent of the town's population now lives behind bars.[17]

Private industries also gain immensely from prisons when a captive workforce becomes the most profitable game in town. According to Eric Bates, in *The Nation*, January 5, 1998, "The stock of the Corrections Corporation of America (CCA) is publicly traded on the New York Stock Exchange. Its performance is in the top twenty percent of stock market returns over the past ten years." There are powerful hands directing the construction of more prisons in the United States, and at the expense of the poor people—black, brown, and white—who are the ones who end up in them.[18]

Joseph T. Hallinan writes, "This [privatization] surge alarmed many of those who ran the nation's publicly owned prisons. If left unchecked, they warned, privatization could put them out of business. Among those who feared this trend was John J. Armstrong, commissioner of Connecticut's Department of Correction. Although his state had not a single private prison within its borders, Armstrong nevertheless warned of the perils they presented. 'Competition,' he told a trade publication in 1996, 'is the word of the day. And if we're not competitive, we'll be gone.' By 'competitive,' Armstrong didn't necessarily mean better. He meant cheaper. Competition with private prisons is based almost entirely on cost, not quality. The emphasis is not on producing an improved inmate, one who will commit fewer crimes when released, but on producing a cheaper inmate."[19]

Another aspect to consider is the phenomenon of gated communities, where more than four million people now live. With imposing guard houses, regular security checks, electrified fences, and other elaborate systems to keep out "graffiti writers and gang members, of course, but also nonresident children selling candy, federal census takers, and other outsiders."[20] These, too, are a kind of prison.

"You may pass a law punishing every person with death for burglary, and it will make no difference," said Clarence Darrow in 1902. "Men will commit it just the same. In England there was a time when one hundred different offenses were punishable with death, and it made no difference. The English people strangely found out that so fast as they repealed the severe penalties, and so fast as they did away with punishing men by death, crime decreased instead of increased: that the smaller the penalty the fewer the crimes. Hanging men in our [jails] does not prevent murder. It makes murderers."[21]

Certain basic premises behind the "get tough" policies need to be examined. One of the ideas often bandied around is that some people are born to make bad choices. But if they are 'born' to make such choices, where is the choice? Conversely, if nobody is really born bad, he or she must choose to be bad. Could we argue, then, that these people must have chosen the consequences of their actions as well, including removal from community, ostracism, prison, and even death? This fails to recognize the sociological forces behind any so-called personal choice. Most arguments today seem to assume that the environment is at best only slightly significant in determining how lives are led.

"Behavior evolves as a function of the interplay between person and environment," writes Urie Bronfenbrenner in his ground-breaking work, *The Ecology of Human Development.* "One would therefore expect psychology, defined as the science of behavior, to give substantial if not equal emphasis to both elements on the independent side of the equation, to investigate the person and the environment, with special attention to the interaction between the two. What we find in practice, however, is a marked asymmetry, a hypertrophy of theory and research focusing on the properties of the person and only the most rudimentary conception and characterization of the environment in which the person is found."[22]

In real life there are choices and predetermined factors that have to be taken into account. Nature and nurture. Instincts and what we are taught. Genetic propensities in the body and in the psyche, as well as the environment that contain or propel them. All this and their intricate connections, too. So when we focus on individual choices and behavior modifications, we're dealing with at most 50 percent of the puzzle.

What about the effects of one's home setting, whether it was in a single or two-parent household, home care versus day care, with or without social or religious training, and peer relationships? If you're poor, if you're black or brown, or an immigrant—where you fit within the class and race matrix of society—you may be branded as mediocre, as having fewer gifts (or no gifts) to contribute to one's family, one's community, one's world. Poverty, race hatred, emotional instability, and severed relationships pressure and pound many of our youth; a few develop some extreme charactor flaws, while others develop character greatness. The results depend on the quality of their interactions.

The other half of the equation are the behavioral tendencies, personality traits, and inborn temperament of a given individual. We also have to look at personal history—was there parental abuse at home, instability, a blurring of authority and responsibility, incest, intense sibling rivalry, rape, physiological handicaps? You have to take into account how these aspects conflict, converge, support, and nullify one another in the process of a person's growth.

Were there enough positive "correctives" to counter this? Was there a community to process this? Was there the resiliency in the human soul to withstand this? And if not, what can be expected from such a person?

These circumstances are compounded by a strangling double (triple or quadruple) standard of justice, whereby certain laws and social norms simply do not apply in the same way to those who can "buy" their way out of a predicament. Again, I have seen this many times, whether in universities or in prisons—the "higher learning" option for many poor people. People with money fare better.

But for the rest of us who may not have such means, the legion of prosecuting attorneys, judges, clerks, police, and their pool of "experts" (also, on other levels, the media, organized religion, schools, and so on.) tend to outrun, outgun, and outspend most poor defendants.

You can begin to see how "choices" in people's lives are not so clear cut.

Chapter 11

Human to Human

Let there be a panorama of open eyes and bitter inflamed wounds
—Federico García Lorca

If initiation practices do occur in our culture, they are mostly unintentional, governed by other interests and concerns, and too often superficial. "Everybody undergoes initiation," I've heard people say in retreats and conferences. This may be true, but for initiation to be deep and transformative, it should be deliberate and integral to community.

All people make mistakes, but the ones who learn from them are most often enabled to do so because they're guided by the nurturing embrace and teachings of community, and this is almost solely dependent on social standing and the value placed on one's life. To demonstrate this, let me tell you the stories of two "killers."

The first story has to do with a fifteen-year-old Southern, middle-class young man of Scottish-Irish descent. In the 1950s he got into a fight with an African-American man, whom he ended up killing by mistake. The kid also happened to be a good student and had never been in trouble with the law. Authorities eventually let him go without a trial, since the act was deemed to be a case of self-defense. Years later, right out of university, members of the federal government located this young man and asked him if he would be willing to be trained as part of an elite team of scientists working on technologically advanced tactical weaponry. This was during the Vietnam War. He accepted. His work eventually led to the manufacture of new instruments of war, including the night-vision goggles that enabled the finding and killing of hundreds of Viet Cong guerrillas in their dense jungle encampments. They were later used, among other things, to track undocumented people along the U.S.-Mexico border.

127

This man became rich, powerful, and a supposed asset to his community. He raised a family and eventually retired. I met him during a men's retreat in 1996. A nice fellow, he ended up leaving after a hot exchange of words among the men concerning race. He was also the only one who raised his hand when the facilitators at the event wanted to know who had never stolen anything in their lives.

The other "killer" was an eighteen-year-old Mexican migrant worker who had traveled from El Paso, Texas, to Omaha, Nebraska, in 1956 to find work. After weeks of back-breaking labor, he cleared about two hundred dollars on payday and decided to go to a local bar. This was a time when racism was so engrained, particularly in the outback corridors of the country, that it seemed natural. The youth was the only nonwhite person at the bar. After a couple of drinks he walked out and was confronted by two white men. They told him to turn over his money or he would be killed; one of the men held a long knife at the youth's throat.

The migrant worker did indeed turn over his money, which he hated to do, but he figured he could always work again for more—but not for his life. Then one of the men turned to the other and said, "Go ahead, kill him." A scuffle ensued. The knife was dropped. The youth somehow picked up the weapon and managed to stab both robbers, one of whom died. The trial was swift. Despite witness accounts and his own words, the Mexican was found guilty of murder. He was given a sentence of twenty years to life.

Apparently this man had been a conscientious church-raised youth who also had never been in trouble before. But he was a poor working stiff and a Mexican to boot. After serving twenty years he went through parole hearings every two years for another twenty years. In 1997, after forty years incarcerated at a Nebraska state penitentiary (where I met him during one of my visits there), he was finally released. During this time, however, he had lost family, he had lost home. All he had known for two-thirds of his life was a barred cell. When we talked, he struck me as a soft-spoken, decent human being.

Here were two similar self-defense cases that ended with quite different results. These happen to be cases I'm personally acquainted with. Despite whatever exceptions may exist, this situation is repeatedly played out in the criminal justice system. Skin color, economic status, and social position do matter. In case you've had your head buried in the sand, you should know that justice is not blind in America (or rather, because it is blind, it cannot see the hypocrisies).[1]

"A criminal justice system is a mirror in which a whole society can see the darker outlines of its face," writes Jeffrey Reiman.[2] Moreover, Reiman adds, "among acts that are defined as crimes, it is still true that the well-off folks who are guilty of white-collar crimes are treated more gently than the poor ones who are guilty of nonviolent property crimes. And it is still true that better-off offenders are less likely to end up behind bars than poor offenders, even when they have committed the same offense. The failure of the criminal justice system has a pattern: The poor feel the full clenched fist of the criminal justice system, while the well-off are rarely touched by the system at all, and when they are touched it is oh so gently. In short, it is still true that the rich get richer and the poor get prison."[3]

Of course, this reality destroys the so-called deterrence factor attributed to incarceration. When pathologies arise from an impoverished environment, places like prisons become rites of passage for young people, not deterrence. One teacher told me how astounded she was by an insight one of her students offered in a Miami ghetto school about looking forward to prison.

"Aren't you scared?" the teacher said, "I would be."

The youth replied, "But it's not for you."

For the most part, people who are deterred by prison probably aren't in prison.[4] But for those who see incarceration as directly tied to their cultural identity, whatever fear exists is reduced.

If the chief function of prison is to serve as a "correction," then how does one account for the similarity in background shared by such a large number of prisoners? Perhaps their so-called criminal activity results not from an individual pathology but from an environmental pathology. If individuals exhibit personality disorders, so do communities, since communities consist of individuals. By the same token, no individual is truly isolated from community, even if it is a toxic, impoverished, and spiritually diminished one.

When more and more poor people, including whites, end up in prison, we are not solely talking about putting away people who have made "bad" choices. We are talking about putting away those who—due to their adverse relationship to the production capacities of a town, state, or nation—don't have a "productive" place in society. You can't simply say these people have removed themselves from such a place when it was never theirs to occupy from the start.[5]

When the primordial contract of a community to take care of its people is already shattered, it's easy for so-called criminals to see the law as fair game to be broken. When the expectation that a child should be protected, taught, and helped by family, relatives, the neighborhood, schools, city, state, and country breaks down (this is where class and race discrimination does most of its damage), then faith in the system and its rules, mores, and laws is harder to maintain, and increasingly more difficult as a child gets older. "If society doesn't think I matter, I don't matter," declared one juvenile offender I met. He does matter, of course, but this is a powerful notion. To overcome it, in most cases, people have to work together to provide the young person with the relationships and resources necessary to convince him that he does matter.

What you did as a child—no matter how bad—can be overcome, transcended, as an adult, but only if the path has been properly followed and gone through to its end. For many, the seemingly insurmountable obstacles are the very catalysts for such change. However, when people are given twenty, thirty, forty years of incarceration—life sentences or the death penalty—we help to enshrine the concept that real change is not possible. And we do this at great peril to our society.

A practice like "three strikes and you're out" institutionalizes what has been happening to a particular segment of the population for years. Under these kinds of laws there is no change or redemption. There is also no transcendence, no moving away from the hold of the patterns, ideas, and ties of the adaptive stage. Most detrimental, there is no transcendence of the circumstances of one's birth: poverty, race-based valuation, or other obstacles.

The circumstances of the two "killers" dramatizes a certain reality: We have a multitiered system of justice in this country. Both through my work with youth and as a newspaper, magazine and radio journalist for two decades, I've seen the slipshod manner that some police and detectives use in dealing with homicides in "inner city" areas. Unlike the movies, where characters like Hercule Poirot look under every rock and rug for clues to a murder, we have communities where police see a dead body and then arrest the person most likely to have done the deed, whether the evidence is there or not. Beating confessions out of suspects is not uncommon. If this particular suspect doesn't have a good alibi—and no decent lawyer—he will probably do the time.

Scientific advances can now help solve crimes even if they occurred in the distant past. In the hands of good lawyers, such evidence has been used to prove how many cases were badly mishandled by investigators in the first place. This is why many innocent people have been released from death row and maximum-security institutions over the last few years. My wife, Trini, worked for four years as an interpreter in Chicago's criminal courts; she finally quit after witnessing too many Spanish-speaking people being shafted because of language differences, no money, and a confusing court system.

"Many public defenders didn't care about being thorough in these cases," she commented. "It wasn't that these people didn't do what they were accused of, but they weren't given the full attention that others were given. I had to be the advocate for them, asking them the questions that the public defenders wouldn't ask. I wasn't supposed to do this, but somebody had to do something." She claimed many convictions were quickly obtained with sparse evidence.

In 1990 I interviewed four Mexican nationals in Illinois who were convicted in a case *Chicago* magazine called "one of the more stunning multiple murders to have occurred in Chicago in the eighties."[6] On Thanksgiving Day 1981, six undocumented immigrants were gunned down in a neighborhood people called Little Guerrero (for the Mexican state most of the residents originated from), on the city's near northwest side. Four eventually died. A family feud with origins in Mexico had seeped across the border, across vast expanses of land, to this northerly city by the lake. One lawyer called it, "the Mexican version of the Hatfields and McCoys."[7]

Almost immediately four *guerrereños*—Rogelio Arroyo, Ignacio Varela, Isauro Sanchez, and Joaquin Varela—were taken into custody. They spoke no English. They feared the police. They feared deportation. They hardly understood what was happening to them. In a matter of months they were tried and convicted; all were given life sentences, with no hope of parole.

For years these men sat in prison, mostly forgotten by the media and the authorities. But the community did not forget. One woman, Margo De Ley, a research administrator at the University of Illinois in Chicago, pursued the case, meeting with the convicted men, family members, and eyewitnesses. It appeared the police didn't properly investigate the murders. Their reports differed completely from what others surrounding the case had to say. When I talked to Isauro, he said the police stopped him just before he entered the crowded tenement apartment he was staying in, yelling in a language he didn't understand. He was arrested. His side of the story was never heard. Investigators nonetheless gave the courts their version, even if largely unsubstantiated. Unfortunately a judge and jury took this at face value and convicted the four men. Three of the men had a bench trial; the fourth faced a jury.

De Ley and others, however, did their research. In short order—it didn't take long to figure out what actually happened when the right questions were asked—they discovered the real killers. One of them, Gilberto Varela, had fled to Mexico and was living there when he finally confessed. In a telephone conversation in March 1990, Varela detailed the circumstances leading to the four people being killed. Eventually Varela wrote a letter stating his part in the murders and also naming three other men. With evidence, witnesses, confessions, and other information, the four falsely convicted Mexicans were finally released in 1990, having served nine years in a maximum-security facility.

Soon after, I talked to the four men in a small Mexican restaurant in the West Town barrio of Chicago. They were gentle and courteous. I asked if they had any anger toward the authorities for what was done to them. "No, I give thanks to God to have my life back," said Ignacio, also known as Tio Nacho. "The problem is there were many others in prison like us, who didn't belong. I pray for them."

Parker J. Palmer wrote in his 1990 book *The Active Life*[8] that there are people who feel they are exempt from all this, who deny that their life bears any resemblance to other people's, especially those lives that are damaged and hurting. They act as if they have some power that no one else possesses, some superior qualities, as if they were smarter, more skilled, and more virtuous than most other people. "[T]hey have none of the brokenness, none of the humility, that makes it possible [for them] to act for and with other people," writes Palmer.[9]

Unfortunately these seem to be the same people who support and enforce some of the most insidious prison and law enforcement policies: the "regular" schmoes at the corner sports bar; the "good" family men and women we hear so much about; that amorphous group of "everyman" and "everywoman" that many powerful politicians and religious figures like to cite to give weight to their positions.

That's the picture you get, anyway, reading newspapers, watching TV or listening to the radio. This "consensus" holds much of the country's politics in check and keeps our society from imagining other possibilities; it allows this country to be the largest jailer in the world and one of five that executes juveniles; it makes us "too busy" to care, despite having real people's lives on the line and the future of our human community at stake.

But not everyone agrees with the consensus.

In the July 16, 1998, airing of *Justice Files* on cable TV's Discovery Channel, a show entitled "Behind Bars" highlighted various aspects of the present prison situation. One of the segments discussed the work of the late Doris Tate, mother of murdered actress Sharon Tate (a victim of the Manson-family serial killings in the late 1960s). Moved by the grief of losing her daughter in such a terrible way, Ms. Tate spent many years going to the Vacaville Prison in California and reaching out to convicts so that they would see the suffering they caused when they murder or hurt people. When the TV reporter asked whether she felt her work really made a difference, she responded that it did, and added, "Out of sympathy, one of them will be affected." While she spoke, cameras panned across the room. Several convicts began to cry at the video image of this mother talking about the loss of her daughter to violence. Several participants later expressed that they had never felt such sorrow about what they had done to others until they attended Ms. Tate's workshops.

"Human to human," is the way one convict described such a program.

Most corrections officers, politicians, and the general public may not accept the fact that these approaches—including the imaginative arts—are very effective in helping rehabilitate violent criminals. If done well, with consistency and follow-up, they are healing. "Everyone deserves a chance to [show] themselves to be worthy of repairing wounds," another convict stated. And this healing must be integral to any consequences.

I have seen how sweat lodge ceremonies, Eastern spirituality, poetry and theater workshops, and truly redemptive Christian services have helped such men and women see something about themselves, their own pain, and from this the pain of those they had not thought about—their victims. Remorse would eventually come, but only after the process had taken its course, by tapping in to each person's own humanity.

Unfortunately these and other programs—college education courses (deemed the most successful in keeping convicts from returning to prison), art supplies and workshops, weight training and planned physical activity, job training, and ongoing psychological counseling—are too few, and becoming fewer. Therefore when released, convicts are often worse off than they were when they first entered.

The prison workshops of Manazar Gamboa, but also people such as Lynette Seator, Judith Tannanbaum, Shelly Wood, Michael McLaughlin,

Michael Meade, and Toni McConnel (a former federal prisoner who wrote *Sing Soft, Sing Loud* [Flagstaff, Ariz.: Longoria, 1995] about her own prison experiences), include the following "human to human" principles:

• Giving people a sense that they are important. We need them not as takers and manipulators but as strong, autonomous, wise, active, and caring people.

• Opening up options of skills, practices, arts, and knowledge so that they have many ways to go, many places to turn to, without going back to crime and violence.

• Teaching skills having to do with managing their emotions, as well as proper parenting, neighboring, partnering (learning to deal with lovers and spouses in respectful and loving ways), and community volunteering.

• Validating their different heritages, their experiences, their suffering and their ability to overcome such suffering, and the power they have to make decent and wholesome choices.

• Providing them with pathways of transcendence that should be with them wherever they go. They need the tempering of heroic character, persistence of aims and goals, and a vision of the "long haul" versus only doing things "day by day."

• Making sure there is adequate treatment for drug-and-alcohol abuse problems, as well as other health maintenance resources. Learning how to take care of oneself spiritually and physically is most helpful in valuing life, ones own and that of others.[10]

• Offering them stories, mythologies, poetry, and ways to read and engage them as well as provide a dynamic and vital sense of ritual in their lives. Drumming, martial arts, songs, and meditative practices are all part of this dynamic.

Compassion is what rules such approaches. It is so strong that it can reach every heart in a room, no matter how hard or how shrouded. Compassionate feeling with and for other people is a quality that leads to responsive rather than reactive action.

Over the years I've talked to prison personnel in juvenile and adult facilities who understand the logic of caring and hanging in there. Once coldhearted and willing to dismiss their charges, many of these staff are now conscious of the connections they've had with the wards and prisoners. One

CYA employee told me directly, "We've tried what the state has demanded of us. We've tried the remorse road. We've tried the punitive recovery programs. The steps programs. And nothing is working. We need to do something else completely different, something that truly engages their whole being."

What would work is a new vision. In many cultures, order is linked to death while chaos—things moving into shape—is linked to vitality. Not understanding this takes out the poetry and imagination required to truly live the spirit of our ideals. We are told to "live" the Word, and not be bound by the Word, to reside in its expansiveness and not in its narrowest confines. We must do deeper and more extensive work, have deeper and more extensive relationships, and look at adversity as a place of renewal and strength.

"For God hath not given us the spirit of fear; but of power, and of love, and of a sound mind" (II Timothy 1:7).

Chapter 12

The Truth of Consequences

What is madness but nobility of soul at odds with circumstance.
—Theodore Roethke

Efrain had been a gang member in East L.A. since the early 1970s. For almost twenty years he was also a heroin addict and in and out of prisons. Then, like many *veteranos,* he became tired of the nonlife he was living—chasing the bone through a maze of fly-infested trash-strewn alleys, knocking on peeling backdoors as his body burned and hands trembled, shredding limbs in search of a vein, beyond the demands of weary partners who'd leave, and the fever for the drug that wouldn't leave.

Eventually Efrain found solace in the Church. A dramatic and drastic intervention had to be applied. Only the all-consuming passion of a born-again relationship with Christ seemed to penetrate the wall of ruin that surrounded this man's every move, choice, and outcome. Soon Efrain preached on street corners, in the graffiti-covered abandoned houses and vacant lots of barrio youth, to the sunken eyes and rotten-toothed grimaces of hardened junkies.

At one point, Efrain went to Chicago to reach out to more people. The same fellowship group he was affiliated with in L.A. had a church and apartment building in Humboldt Park, in the middle of one of the country's most intense gang communities. A number of reformed L.A. gangbangers and addicts came with Efrain. Mostly Mexican and cholos, they looked markedly different from the predominantly Puerto Rican Cobras, Jivers and Disciples they now encountered. For one thing, the East L.A. guys had more elaborate tattoos and a more severe street attire. Yet this didn't deter them as they dispersed throughout Humboldt Park's street, witnessing for Christ.

One night, as Efrain and his "brothers" were sleeping, he awoke to the sounds of a dispatcher's voice on a police radio. He looked out the window to see several police officers searching two teenage girls and a guy, their arms stretched onto a brick wall. Efrain went back to bed; just a routine roust-ing, he thought. But in a matter of minutes automatic gunfire ripped across the din of traffic, the yelling, and children's wailing. This time Efrain peered out and saw the young man with a hand at the small of his back and the other over his stomach; both girls had their hands over their temples. There were no police in sight.

Efrain and the others ran out. He rushed up to one girl, who was flat on her back, blood streaming from a wound in her head. Efrain held the girl in her arms, putting one finger over the hole to stop the bleeding, and recited a prayer while she convulsed and fell into unconsciousness. The police finally returned, but Efrain said they took their time getting the three shooting vic-tims into an ambulance. Before the morning broke, the two girls were dead.

Deeply affected, Efrain worked even harder to reach the local youth on any corner, stoop, and gangway he could find them. One night we got word that Chicago police officers had arrested Efrain. They had accused him of trespassing. Efrain had barely stepped onto a sidewalk in front of a business, when officers surrounded him; a business owner he had never seen accused him of intimidating clients—he had only been passing out tickets for a play about gang members finding Jesus Christ. The arrest, apparently, was an excuse to block him and the other brothers from witnessing. We had heard that a number of police officers had taken it upon themselves to descend on these L.A. guys and intimidate them.

Efrain recounted that after the two officers handcuffed him, they pushed him into the backseat of the squad car and drove to the nearest police sta-tion. On the way Efrain started to quote from the Bible. The officer on the passenger side turned around, red-faced, and exclaimed, "Stop that crap! You can't fool us. We know you gangbangers haven't changed. You can't change. It's a game you're playing, pretending to be Christian and all."

Efrain responded that he had changed. That he had gone from an addict's life, caught in the street's evil clutches and hurting his family and everyone else around him, into the arms of Jesus. He figured the police officer was most likely a Christian and would understand.

"Bullshit!" the officer replied. "I'll tell you why we don't believe you can change—because if we did, we'd be out of a job. As far as we're concerned, 'once a gangbanger, always a gangbanger.'"

Efrain continued to recite scripture to the police officers. Five times he was interrupted and accused, among many things, of being "spooky." After he was processed, Efrain said one of the police officers came up to him and apologized.

This exchange illustrates a major obstacle to reform. Many jobs, particularly in law enforcement, but also in some areas of social programming, depend on people not being able to transform their lives. For police, fear of change sometimes justifies beating up suspected criminals and manipulating paperwork and crime scenes to put them away. It is an ideology that shapes itself around their immediate concerns as guardians of the social order.

In 1998 one of YSS's elders tried to introduce indigenous sweat lodge ceremonies into the Cook County Jail—one of the largest jails in the world, with several blocks of buildings, and a new electronically controlled maximum-security facility—on the edge of the Little Village barrio. Used in many prisons and youth facilities where Native Americans are housed—and growing in popularity among Mexican prisoners and others who have reconnected to their own indigenous roots—this ceremony has a powerful way of working on people in prison, helping in the recovery from drugs or alcohol, or just for general healing. It has been used for years with violent gangs, non-gang youth, and their families.

The elder, who also worked with several Native American organizations in the area, met with the jail's deputy director. He explained how the sweat ceremony helped to spiritually engage and transform prisoners, through a purification process utilizing the natural elements of fire, air, water, and earth.

He carefully detailed how the *inipi*, the Lakota-style lodge, is made using bent willows with specially prepared "prayer ties" hanging from the top. Inside, a hole is dug in the center of the ground. After the participants have encircled the hole, stones that have been in a fire for several hours are placed inside it. A lodge chief—or roadman, as he may be called—pours water over the stones, which are interspersed with sage and cedar, thus filling the lodge with steam. Heavy blankets or tarps draped over the structure keep it in total darkness and stop the steam from leaving the lodge. Prayers and sentiments are said and chants and songs are sung for as long as there is inspiration to do so. Generally, this goes on for "four rounds" (each round is marked by opening a flap in front of the lodge to let the steam out).

The jail's deputy director, however, was not impressed. After the elder spoke, the deputy director burst into a tirade about the fact that he had been working in the jail system for twenty-five years and his experience showed him that criminals who reached the age of eighteen would never change.

He was not a bad guy. His opinion fitted perfectly with his position, and there is some truth to it. The way most jails are set up, conditions don't allow for young men and women to make radical positive changes. Mostly they only allow for the worst in people to prevail.

Still, the concern remains: What about people who have been lost, who have committed crimes and have hurt others, who've become addicted to a variety of vices, who are past their adolescence and entrenched in manners of being—can they change?

I met Rudy Rosales in 1994 when he invited me to the Nebraska Maximum Security Correctional Center in Lincoln. For some time Rudy had been organizing community and prison exchanges for celebrations like Cinco de Mayo under the auspices of Mexican Awareness Through Association (MATA).

Rudy was a "homeboy." He had lived in many neighborhoods where I had lived, including Florencia in South L.A. and in the San Gabriel Valley. He knew several of my homies and some of the social and lowrider clubs from that area. He also came out of the Chicano movement in the late 1960s. He had been a member of the Brown Berets and was part of the contingent that took over Catalina Island in protest of U.S. policies toward Chicanos in the early 1970s. He fought in Vietnam. But after this experience, and as the activism of the movement days waned and jobs become less and less a reality, he moved into criminal activities the way many old soldiers—both from the *movimiento* and the war—had done. Eventually, for an illegal confidence scheme Rudy was embroiled in, he landed in Nebraska's correctional system.

But a seed had been planted from his community involvement; something within him never gave up the struggle for the people, for justice, and for their eventual empowerment. So decades later, from jail, Rudy was still figuring out ways to lift up his people, to unite the scattered groupings and individuals, and to activate a new cause based on the present conditions facing Chicanos and indigenous people in this country. MATA, a cultural-social organization for the growing number of Chicano-Mexicano prisoners there, was his vehicle for doing so.

Under Rudy's leadership MATA featured various speakers, *folklorico* dancers, poets, filmmakers, community activists, and students from the universities nearby. While I have been in a few exchanges in other institutions, I found this one to be well organized and at a high political and cultural level. The prisoners in turn, greeted the various guests with hospitality and respect. They listened to the talks and spoken-word presentations, and even had their resident *banda* musical group for entertainment.

Rudy's energy was amazing. Even though he was incarcerated, he managed to have his own office, typewriter, and library. He was able to bring together many students, community groups, families, and prisoners through his grant writing and networking. He established good relations with the African-American and Native American cultural organizations in the institution. Rudy did more things to pull together ideas, activity, individuals, and organizations from behind bars than many people were doing on the outside.

By the late 1990s, however, Rudy had become a persona non grata at the joint. A new prison administration began a clampdown on groups like MATA. The political climate called for more control in the prison and the curtailing of programs or activities not directly linked to this control.

Rudy became a prime target. He was placed in controlled units, removed from MATA as well as the general population. People on the outside whom Rudy had helped and brought into the institution were told not to contact him. For the most part they turned away from him after prison officials claimed he couldn't be trusted.

Unfortunately the strain proved exhausting for this warrior, who was already in his late forties and suffering life-threatening ailments. At one point, prison doctors denied Rudy his medicines for high blood pressure and diabetes. Largely due to the neglect of prison health officials, who did not respond to his situation in a timely and professional manner, Rudy suffered a stroke that left him partly paralyzed.

I kept close ties with Rudy. When his younger brother was killed in some beef in California, I tried to help him with letters and phone calls as he sorted out his feelings of hatred and revenge. When his mother died, Rudy wrote a eulogy that I read at her funeral, which he could not attend. In time Rudy decided to take his battles to the courts.[1] He initiated a $1.5 million lawsuit that became one of the largest ever sought against the Nebraska prison system. Even though the suit was not settled as of this writing, on several return visits to the prison I was able to see that his efforts had resulted in positive changes for other prisoners. State legislation had been introduced to reform the prison health care system because of Rudy's case. But the struggle is far from over.

In 1999, at Rudy's request and with the help of the prison's chaplain, we were able to hold a special indigenous pipe ceremony with Pipe Carrier and Mexika teacher Tekpatltzin (Frank Blazquez) on the prison grounds. The Mexika elders in Mexico had given me permission to do these ceremonies, so I accompanied Tekpatltzin to Lincoln.

After going through security checks, Tekpatltzin and I met with Rudy. His paralysis had mostly diminished by then, and he was using a cane to get around. We spent some time talking before we were allowed to gather on the main yard of the correctional center. The sky was strikingly blue that day, interspersed with spirals of dense white clouds. With guards surrounding us—and as other prisoners looked on from behind their barred windows, some carrying on with their own prayers and chants—the three of us performed a beautiful ritual there, one I will never forget.

These rituals helped Rudy turn to a more calm and meditative place within himself. He removed himself from any criminal activity and the harsh prison politics. Rudy's spirit for what is just and equitable, linked to a writing and organizing genius as well as strong leadership, is another example of how people can maintain their integrity and dignity, even in the worst of conditions.

We can agree that if someone commits a crime, they should do the time. And we can agree that the courts have major concerns to address in their deliberations: the safety of the community, a measure of justice for the victims, and consequences for the convicted. However, we need to agree that the consequences should be appropriate and meaningful. Most courts fail to make sure the "corrective" measures have a redemptive impact on the convict and the overall interest and safety of the community in mind. This is why prison sentences need to be followed up and taken seriously.

We need new models of restitution so that what one "owes" the victims and society is not about money, taking away their freedom, or even so-called "community service"— some school offenders in Chicago washed police cars or picked up trash. We need restitution based on innate gifts, through which people can truly evolve into their art and into their lives.

I'm not talking about giving people more time for their crimes, but enough time. Enough of a certain kind of time, a certain ritualized and sacred time. The consequences have to be adequate—not beyond the point of "who cares what happens to me." One, two, or three very well monitored, instructive, and resourceful years away from the community may do more good for certain people than ten or twenty years of idling away in a four-cornered cell.

Likewise, five to seven years for more serious offenses may be just right if the time is seen in qualitative terms, with the long-range interests of the community and the individual in mind, and if the educational, emotional, psychological, spiritual, and skills development of the convict are truly taken into account.

The real problem cases, those "too far gone to turn around"—an assessment trained personnel should make, not just a court employee or guard—can be isolated and treated appropriately.

If everyone goes through the same amount of time, under the same high-security, low-level conditions, regardless of what they are capable of overcoming, then there can be no change. Change, or what is often called rehabilitation, is unlikely if people are getting twenty-five years to life under the "three strikes" law for stealing small amounts of merchandise. Take the infamous case of twenty-seven-year-old Jerry Williams, who received a twenty-five-to-life sentence in 1994 for stealing a slice of pepperoni pizza. (This sentence was later reversed.) In California by early 1998 some fifteen thousand people, mostly poor black and brown, were sentenced under the "three strikes and you're out" law passed by the state's voters, although 85 percent of them were for nonviolent crimes.[2]

Rehabilitation is harder to achieve when laws concerning "minimum" terms or "truth in sentencing" compel judges to give certain crimes no less than twenty years' incarceration, regardless of mitigating factors. It cannot happen when convicts have to serve 85 to 100 percent of a sentence with no leeway for good time or truly redemptive improvements on their part.

A prisoner once provided me with this insight: He wondered why his father, who had abused him terribly as a child; or his mother, who often abandoned him to do drugs; the schools that had put him down; the police who beat him up; and a foster care system that resulted in his younger brother being stomped to death by a foster parent; never paid any consequences of note for what they had done. But as soon as he committed his own violent act—he was serving a minimum twenty years for an armed robbery—he was put away in a harsh maximum-security facility.

"I feel bad for what I done, but I can't stop feeling cheated for how this world has treated me. Would I steal and hurt people again? Probably. This punishment only made me hate more—hating a system and a world that was never there for me when I needed them, or for my brother, but gets all up in my face when I mess up."

The inconsistencies are too vast to ignore in such cases and make a farce of the whole system. We need to try to comprehend what is actually behind this.

Most parents are usually warned not to give a child consequences that are inappropriate for the trust or rule that was violated. If the consequences are minor, the reason for them does not sink in. On the other hand, if the consequences are too harsh or too long, it usually breeds resentment and a distorted sense of what's fair.

Why doesn't this basic concept apply to the judicial system when it is handing down sentences? When the consequences become dismissive, excessive, or out of whack, they become meaningless. And when the consequences become meaningless, so does the criminal justice system that is responsible for implementing them.

"This would assure us that a good portion of the prison population would experience their confinement as arbitrary and unjust and thus respond with rage, which would make them more 'antisocial,' rather than respond with remorse, which would make them feel more bound by social norms," wrote Jeffrey Reiman.[3]

And when time is served, what happens? Part of initiation is to be welcomed back to the community after the ordeal has been overcome. But most courts won't have anything to do with a convict after the sentences have come down. Too often these men and women are forgotten and left to their own devices. Those who happen to complete their time without a hitch may step out of a prison gate with a few dollars in their pocket and a bus ticket, but no home, no job, no "community" to truly go back to.

Where is the judge who sentenced the person with such resolve? Or the prosecuting attorneys? The jurors and victims? Where is the community whose laws have been breached? So the convict goes down the road alone, very likely not reaching a substantially different destination. There's a rupture in the initiation process. And real change is often not possible.

There is a saying that goes, "If you do the crime, you have to do the time." And a youth once said, if you're already doing the time—in poverty or in a dark skin—you might as well do the crime. But something else has to happen as well. It's true that certain people have to be put away so that they don't hurt anybody, but why does the prison experience have be harsh and demeaning? The fact is that everything we do has consequences, good and bad. Consequences are not punishment—they are the result of certain acts or nonacts, the effect of some cause, the price to pay for what has been done or not done. A key component of the "price," in my view, has to be restorative and healing for both the prisoner and the community.

The brutal isolation of prisoners, the taking away of what little dignity they may have, the weakening of whatever self-control they may muster—all these components of our current correctional system only increase their potential not for change or restitution but for aggression and violence.

Johnny was a Los Angeles gang leader, in his early thirties, who wrote me while he was doing time in a California correctional facility. Apparently when Johnny was around three years old, he witnessed sheriff deputies kill his stepfather on the front lawn of his house. When Johnny was eleven, his drug-addicted mother first shot him up with heroin—it would eventually consume much of his life. He got involved in various crimes, including extortions of local businesses and strong-armed robberies. In prison, he became an enforcer for one of the Chicano prison organizations in the state, for which he allegedly committed a number of murders. When I met Johnny, his tall muscular body was heavily tattooed from his neck to his legs.

But on one arm and through his shirt near the collar one could see deep swirling scars across his skin. In one of the many wars that frequently exploded in the joint, Johnny suffered burns to 60 percent of his body when an enemy soldier threw a handmade gasoline bomb into his cell. Despite this intense involvement, in time Johnny grew weary of what his life had become. He wouldn't turn against the gang; he was not a *rata* (rat or snitch). He didn't want to betray anyone. He only wanted out.

Johnny found comfort in Buddhist teachings. He had a mentor in prison and read many books about this practice. He also came across my book and he contacted me. He had a facility with words and a wisdom that you knew was hardwon. Few could claim what he could claim. Yet I also found in him a striking intelligence and a caring soul.

When Johnny got paroled in 1998, I went to see him during one of my Los Angeles visits. He had a girlfriend, Lisa, who seemed to understand Johnny's efforts to change. She stood by him through thick and thin, including during a frustrating time he had relating to his thirteen-year-old son—there had been too much estrangement between them to overcome right away. We talked about this, and I recounted my own troubling experiences with Ramiro. During this time Johnny was writing many pages of his life story. He hooked up with a recovery program, got involved in a rock band, and even had help in getting some of his work published in local publications under an assumed name.

However, Johnny had trouble letting go of heroin. He relapsed a few times, once just before I came to visit him. I didn't put him down. I knew about these things. I encouraged him to keep trying to stay clean. He continued with the recovery program, where other men in similar predicaments helped. Music and writing became an important part of his healing. So was the Buddhist practice.

One time, we drove around for a while and stopped to sit down on the water-battered rocks along Malibu Beach. As waves crashed frothy and free below us, we talked. About life. About the proper way of relating with women. About addiction. About art. He saw me as a "big homie," a teacher, as someone who could help counsel him. I saw him as someone who had found a redemptive path and had gathered some internal resources to traverse the lonely and harsh road ahead.

But Johnny also had problems with the prison organization he had been active in. He told me he had a couple more stints to do in the county jail so that he could finish off what he "owed" the state (one was for testing "dirty"). Each time, however, he was placed in the "high power" unit of the jail, where the so-called most dangerous criminals were isolated from the general population. This proved to be problematic when he came across his former associates. He expressed his anxiety during these periods in his letters to me. At one point he managed to stave off an attack. He knew his days were numbered, his time on this earth short, unless he could finally get away for good.

After his last jail time Johnny decided he would leave the city. By the time I returned to Los Angeles, Johnny and Lisa had found another life in another part of the world, apparently many miles and so many brutal experiences away from here—they wouldn't tell me where. I regretted not having gotten to see them before they left, but I understood what they had to do. Johnny's life was so deeply enmeshed in the criminal/prison world that he was a danger to himself and his family. He had to leave. In essence he knew too much.

All I could do was pray for Johnny and Lisa, that they would be fine and make something decent out of their lives. I prayed that eventually he would get his story told, that he would become the complete artist and, therefore the complete human being, he was destined to be.

What follows is a 1998 letter Johnny sent me during his last county-jail stint. I share it to show how insightful and intelligent such "bad" people can be when they're genuinely making a lasting human-to-human connection with themselves and others:

Hey Big Homie!

What's going on, carnal? Well, as you can see, this song remains the same. I'm in a much better state of mind this time around for some reason. I think it has something to do with where my mind was at before I came in. I was mentally ready for change, so when this happened, the change wasn't what I expected. But I accepted it immediately.

Anyways, the climate here ain't nothing nice. They're dropping like flies around here. And so young, too. It messes me up to see "me" die like that. So willingly. So full of false pride, pumped up with fear and self-hatred. Talking and walking like lions and then sacrificing like lambs.

This cycle is so treacherous, homes. It makes you want to put your hand out to help someone. But then when you do that around here, "it" grabs you and pulls you into its madness. And when that happens it's like riding the rapids without a boat. You have to just ride it out and hope you don't drown in the process.

So instead I just sit here and watch "it." And I listen to it quietly…and I try not to attract too much attention to myself so that "it" doesn't notice me. And maybe, if my luck holds out, I won't be called on to sacrifice myself, or someone else, to this hate factory that we have become products for. We're processed on its conveyor belt like fuckin' twinkies.

Having to stay quiet and inactive—while my brothers die and maim each other like clockwork—is agony. We have, over the years, turned this system into our higher power, into our house of worship. And we have sacrificed everything for its room and board, and our own brand of brotherhood … everything—ourselves, each other, our freedom.

And every Monday, when we all get our canteen, we throw a spread for what might be our last supper. Our rituals are no different from any other place of worship. The only difference being that we don't seek eternal life. We seek eternal war and our own damnation. In the name of God and His Kingdom. His name is death and his kingdom is insanity and hell. And we are his loyal servants, soldiers, and victims....

We are losing many of our leaders to the prison industry. We are losing many warriors. We are losing much of our future.

Long and punitive incarceration as a corrective measure is the conventional way of attempting to solve the larger problem. Another idea is that simple "just say no" programs or heavy proselytizing will change people at the drop of the hat.

A couple of teachers at a Chicago-area high school once reproached me for telling four hundred students at an assembly that I'm not "antigang." What I said was that for many poor young people cut off from any other meaningful direction, joining a gang was often a natural and rational decision to make.

"You're supposed to convince them gangs are no good," one teacher scolded. "Now they're going to think that gangs are okay."

The issue was not whether gangs are "good" or "bad." The truth—a truth most youths understand—is that gangs often fulfill a need, particularly when it comes to respect, community, and even love. This is especially true when a group of young people don't believe they can find these things anywhere else.

My strategy was to take the natural and positive aspects of what gangs do for youths to the next level of where they needed to go, while letting go of whatever is destructive and unhealthy. This is an ancient quest, as well as a painful process for many young people, especially when their whole value system, their social identity, is indistinguishable from a gang's.

Today's society is not sufficiently preparing young men and women, particularly the most troubled, to move into the transcendental stage of their life—a time in which they go out into the world, find themselves and in the process carve out their own unique place in it. Instead there seems to be a kind of mass arrested development. People end up living unfulfilled, mediocre, and confused lives. There is a kind of psychic paralysis, in which we are being fixed in old habits, concepts, and activities. Some of us grow old with the sense that life has been about climbing a ladder, rung by bloody rung, but up a wrong wall.[4] Yet everyone, at one time or another, has felt the inexorable pull of destiny within them, occasionally moving them toward an unseen purpose.

Change is possible at any age. But there are periods when a great door appears to open up for a tremendous turn in one's life. Many adults may feel like the man who once declared at a community meeting in northern California that "those between fourteen and twenty-one are too out of it to be taken seriously," but the truth is that the period from adolescence to adulthood is actually a threshold time.

The beginning years of the transcendent stage are the time when developing an art, a skill, or a practice is instrumental in harnessing the newly felt impulses pouring out of one's soul. This is the time of the student, when one surrenders to teachings and has the self-discipline to submit to tasks. This stage may begin around the late teens and early twenties, but it can last from 15 to 20 years. A community—with its elders and mentors—should be fully aware of what's going on; if older, and apparently wiser, tribal societies could do this, why can't we?

Such awareness requires strict attention and an ability to draw upon the energies and resources of a community. Unfortunately in the day-by-day scramble to "make it" that characterizes our present existence, there is very little commitment to ensure that every young person is helped through these stages of development, except in the most superficial manner.

"The crucial word here is 'focus.' The adults had something to teach: stories, skills, magic, dances, visions, rituals. In fact, if these things were not learned well, the tribe could not survive," wrote Michael Ventura. "But the adults did not splatter this material all over the young from the time of their birth, as we do. They focused, and were as selective as possible about what they told and taught, and when. They waited until their children reached the intensity of adolescence, and then they used that very intensity's capacity for absorption, its hunger, its need to act out, its craving for dark things, dark knowledge, dark acts, all the qualities we fear most in our kids—the ancients used these very qualities as teaching tools."[5]

As "advanced" as we have become in this society, we have lost much of this knowledge. We have let fear dictate our policies, apathy and indecision rule our actions, and the money value system (with its expedient and superficial impulses) permeate our daily concerns. The natural intensity of adolescence is now seen as dangerous and deviant—we fear it, and the growth of the U.S. prison industry is proof of this.

"This fear is used to scare everybody into being inhuman," Michael Meade once told me.

A few years ago a similar fear was behind the "scared straight" programs in which youth offenders were confronted by convicted felons with the brutal and unglamorous details about what was awaiting them in prison. I'm sure many young people decided not to go this route, after having the stark realities of incarceration pushed into their faces. But there were far too many who were not scared. Unfortunately many young people see prison, like gangs and violence, as exciting, powerful, and a life of living on the edge. Intense boredom and meaninglessness will drive what are otherwise reasonable people to do some detrimental things in order to have such a life.

More effective is what an inmate named Gypsy, whom Rudy introduced me to at Nebraska's Correctional Center in Lincoln, called "cared straight." What young people are looking for—a heroic, deeply felt, carefully monitored, and properly recognized existence—needs to be taken seriously, given real shape, and allowed to go where it's going to go. If you have to "scare" people to do this, you've missed the point.

In mid-1998 a *Christian Science Monitor* article appeared about the work of Youth Struggling for Survival (YSS) in Chicago.[6] It outlined how some of our youth, after years of hard work and learning, using art, rituals, retreats, spirituality, skills development, and political education, became leaders in their own right. It also describes how they were sometimes hired by other agencies to mentor similarly troubled youth.

"In contrast with other organizations, YSS wanted us to do things for ourselves," commented Jay Jay Taifa, a then-twenty-three-year-old former gang leader and ex-convict, who was a youth mentor at a not-for-profit agency in Chicago's diverse uptown community.

But later in the article, George Knox, director of the National Gang Crime Research Center in Chicago, questioned the "long-term value of groups such as YSS that offer recreation, jobs, and other incentives to gang members." Instead, he argued, the emphasis should be on grade-school prevention programs. "I wouldn't send the message to the good kids out there that all you've got to do is screw up and you'll get all sorts of attention," he said.

What Mr. Knox doesn't understand is that even if you do all you can at the grade-school level, intervention/prevention has to continue as the child moves into preadolescence, adolescence, and early adulthood. Each stage requires a discerning and determined community-based interaction, or a young person may go off onto a harmful course, despite having been a good and disciplined child in grade school. Each stage has its dangers and pitfalls, but also its opportunities and challenges.

We can't afford an either/or position that only guarantees more human fodder for a multi-billion-dollar prison industry. Besides, with all due respect to Mr. Knox, many of these gang kids *are* good kids. In YSS, which also includes teens not in gangs, the gang youth were among the most disciplined and consistent. What's more, those young people whom we have designated as more stable and "trouble-free" may appreciate that we are seriously dealing with those who are reeling in turmoil.

Don't be fooled: Trouble has many faces, many features that come out in many interesting ways. Yes, the squeaky wheel gets the grease, but this is because it found a way to express its need. Conversely, those who don't "squeak" as much may turn out to be more troubled than Mr. Knox and his cronies comprehend, to their detriment and ours.

Therefore the message should be: If you're in trouble, let us know you're in trouble so that we can indeed provide "all sorts of attention" and help you do something about it. If you're not in trouble, I'm sure you'll feel good knowing that those who do need help will get it.

One time in 1993 a homeboy of mine, whom I had not seen in twenty years, organized a reunion for whoever was still around from our time in the South San Gabriel barrio. By then the neighborhood had changed considerably. Gentrification had claimed many sidewalkless streets, weather-worn homes, and crumbling fences. New asphalt and curbs now graced what were formerly dirt roads. There were freshly stuccoed homes, landscaped yards, and townhouses. There was even a mansion in the middle of the old barrio.

Thousands of Chinese, Korean, and Japanese families had moved into the Monterey Park, South San Gabriel, San Gabriel, and Rosemead communities (and throughout much of the main San Gabriel Valley corridor, particularly along Interstates 10 and 60). Former white middle-class sections now sported Asian calligraphy on business signs. Many of the poorer Mexican areas were knocked down and rebuilt. There were new shopping areas, motels, and banks. In Hacienda Heights an exact replica of a massive and beautiful Buddhist temple from China was constructed, the largest such temple in the West. The high school I had gone to, which in the early 1970s was roughly 40 percent Mexican, 50 percent white, and 10 percent Asian, by the mid-1990s was 60 percent Asian.

The shifts in the community, interestingly enough, did not destroy the barrio gang, Las Lomas. In fact in twenty years the gang had become larger, spreading to areas where it did not previously exist, even incorporating some of the disaffected Asian youth.

The remaining Mexican streets were still destitute, but now, instead of being solely surrounded by middle-class whites, there were middle-class Asians and the older Mexican families that had moved up. Because I had been gone so long, I did not know the new homies. A few were the sons, daughters, and grandchildren of people I used to hang with. But most of the names and families were different.

There were rumors about some of the older *veteranos* in the gang, how a few had integrated into the largest prison organization in the state; how others may have forged ties with Mexico's drug lords; how, since there were no real jobs for former Chicano convicts, some had become hitmen for Asian extortion gangs; and the fact that the war between Lomas and Sangra, our main rival, was still being waged.

My friend could only find three former homegirls for the gathering. He also contacted the home-school coordinator for the high school we went to, who was like a mother to all of us. She was still an employee of the school district, only now at another high school. It was a great reunion. It was so good to see these old friends, the other survivors.

The friend who had organized the reunion had become a refrigerator repair man, with children and grandchildren of his own (although we were both only in our late thirties). Two of the homegirls were now in law enforcement—one worked at the Nelles School for Boys the other homegirl was a security guard. They had children who, like my son Ramiro, also faced some dangerous times. A couple of the kids were joining gangs or getting into other trouble.

These friends had gotten their lives together. They had jobs and families. No longer as poor as when they grew up, they were nonetheless just barely "making it." But they seemed strong and mostly happy. They were the ones who had escaped death, drugs, and *la pinta* (prison). But we never forgot who we were or where we came from. We never forgot the old neighborhood, both the good and the bad times. We reminisced about all of this with laughter and some heartache.

We talked about some of the other homies we knew. Most had left the area. Many were in prison. A few more had died, and I had not been aware of this. There had been a terrible rise of heroin addiction, which had claimed many of the old soldiers. One of the homegirls became mentally ill and homeless; she was often seen in the streets fighting with others. Later, I found out about one guy who had become a truck driver, a family man with kids and grandkids. But I had heard this guy had killed at least two or three people during the late 1960s and early 1970s. I suppose he, too, had escaped the worse aspects of the barrio warfare; he ended up becoming a regular dude—although, like many of us, probably drinking and raging too much.

This visit opened up the door for me to talk at my former middle school, and a few elementary schools, including one in Sangra. The next day I spoke at the local schools. Some people told me not to go to the elementary school in Sangra because of the ongoing warfare. In fact two months before I arrived there, some guys from Sangra had beaten, stabbed, and shot to death a young man from Lomas.

But I was no longer at war with Sangra. I owed a visit to members of this community—a Chicano community worthy of the same consideration as any other. If someone were going to hurt me for this, so be it. I had to do it.

The visit to the children of Sangra turned out to be warm and friendly. The children listened. Many of them, I could see, had already been traumatized by living among several generations of a gang community. But they were also smart and gracious. We had a good time after all, and I did not shy away from saying where I had lived and why I had changed.

After twenty years of not setting foot in these neighborhoods, it was time for me to walk among my people, to talk to their youth and parents, and to heal. I visited one of my old grammar schools in Rosemead, which had been converted to a combined elementary school, middle school, and high school. The gangs were active there, but we had a good time nonetheless; I remember their respectful interest. I also talked at Century Continuation High School in Alhambra where Lomas and Sangra, in a strained effort, attended classes together. And Vail High School in Montebello, at the time the largest continuation high school in the state, which had a number of gang youth, including some from my old neighborhood. I visited one of the other local elementary schools in the area, which still looked as worn down and neglected as I remember it. It had rained the day before my visit, and the play area and several classrooms had been flooded—just the way it used to be so many years before.

Since the reunion I have gone to barrios throughout East L.A. In some of these there are the rival gangs of Las Lomas. I was reaching out, trying to make right for what in my heart had been some terrible wrongs. Of course the difficulties were vast, considering that many of these wars continued on and in many ways had worsened. But each visit brought me to a more quiet, gentle, and loving place. Every child's face, every teacher's concern, every mother's cry brought home the importance of continuing to fight for peace and justice in our communities.

I mention all this because there have been a few instances—few compared with the support I've received—in which people have questioned why I have not been "punished" fully for my crimes as a youth. Despite several arrests, I escaped hard-time prison sentences for shootings, firebombings, stabbings, and robberies. Why, then, someone might ask, shouldn't I pay my "debt" to society?

Why would anybody want me to? Punishment is not the same as justice. The penal system was first visualized by the Quakers and other apparently enlightened people during the early period of this country's growth as being about rehabilitation and true transformation. I know many people whose punishment it was to serve long sentences, but who have not therefore been able, despite being willing, to follow a redemptive path.

In fact many of us who "escaped" such punishment, and were able to find a healthy and meaningful purpose in our lives, are today honoring our personal changes by giving back to others. Many of those involved in the urban peace movement of this country include former prisoners, gangbangers, addicts, and abusers. I have seen how these hardened characters have become wise and compassionate, patient and steady. This has happened to me and to many of my colleagues, including my homeboy Rudy and people like Johnny. People who have robbed, shot up heroin or hit the crack pipe, and even killed now have a vital place in their communities. This is a powerful, beautiful, and encouraging thing to witness.

Besides, many former gang leaders and drug users often have more impact than any police officer, school official, or outside youth organizer will ever have. These are the "peacemakers" who still have an ear to the ground. They struggle daily with the most troubled youth, defusing confrontations, taking them to sports events, cultural outings, or the woods. They link them to work or alternative schools. They involve youth in projects that then enrich their communities by active service.

They continue to do this work despite having attended too many funerals, seeing too many of their charges sent to prison for extraordinary amounts of time, and having been shortchanged by government and business representatives time and time again. Some have lost their own children to violence or prison. Some have faced character assassinations. Yet regardless of the setbacks, they're still putting their lives on the line without fanfare or meaningful support.

It's time to bring these leaders to the table, to set up the proper mentoring and teaching so that they can become agents of peace instead of war. It's time for politicians, businesses, schools, churches, and law enforcement to align to what these street workers and peacemakers have been doing to make peace in the community a reality. The fuller your imagination, the fuller will be the response.

For years I've sat across from convicts and kids, some of whom have done some terribly destructive things, helping draw out their poetic and artistic spirit. I've looked them straight in the eye and said, "I can see your beauty." And just those words, minimal though they are, have allowed some of the most hardened psychic shells—mostly constructed out of the sinews of their survival strategies—to crack. Perhaps these shells will close up when I leave. But if the intellectual, social, political, economic, and spiritual forces were attuned to these needs, I believe that shell would be hardpressed to continue imprisoning the daimons within. Few ever do this kind of work. Few have had a large enough imagination.

However, I'm not saying, "If you get it together, all will be forgiven." Nothing is ever that easy. Change is supposed to be difficult. It requires great courage and much character, a lot of study, a removal and a reconnection, consistency, maturity, and constant analyzing; it requires making the right choices whenever they come up. It means getting back up when you've relapsed. It means facing your demons, but also facing those people whom you have hurt. It means lurking in the scariest part of your own soul and staying there so long that the tears refuse to stop and you feel you can't breathe for drowning in the darkness. It takes much time, effort, and a whole lot of people whom you seek out from a place in your psyche that you can't even name.

Everything we have—every resource, expert, program, plan, therapy, and concept—has to be utilized to help each and every person who is undergoing this process. They may not all make it because the complicated pieces needed for success may not all fall into place. But at the very least the love and support of family and community have to be firmly and consistently there so that we can save more than we lose.

I'm not saying let's build policy around illusions; I'm saying let's change the environment and unhealthy dependencies so that illusions are not necessary.

My honesty about those events in my life that were harmful and abusive has been part of the healing. But I also recognize how important mentors and teachers were to this process; how important it was that I found an art and a practice; and how important my participation in many expressive, political, and community activities was to transcending the destructive aspects of my life.

I'm not being invited to speak at venues throughout the country because I've done everything right. Rather, I'm allowed to do these presentations because I've done many things wrong.

So what possible good would punishing me—or others like me—do? I made my amends. I didn't need society's heavy hand. I made them out of my own accord, which is the best way for such things to occur. Most of my work today with youth, the homeless, prisoners, and the unemployed, is voluntary. I "sentenced" myself, in effect, to a lifetime of real community service.

Chapter 13

A Handmade Life

Who will compute the lonely nights made less lonely by your songs, or by the empty pots made less tragic by your tales?

—Maya Angelou

Soon after the 1992 uprising that followed the acquittal of four police officers in the Rodney King beating, I flew back to Los Angeles to assess the level of crisis for a number of articles I was writing. Friends and family, as well as participants in the fighting, burning, and looting that had destroyed hundreds of businesses and homes, told me about the armed National Guardsmen who patrolled the streets, and of massive green tanks that lingered at intersections like mammoth toads. Makeshift fences surrounded blackened and crumpled steel beams on lots filled with burned debris. These lots were oddly interspersed between untouched structures in the South Central, Koreatown, and Pico Union neighborhoods that I visited. In front of their homes or on street corners, people were selling items apparently taken during the melee as a sort of "fire sale."

Several people including my brother, who worked as a repairman for the phone company at the time, were unable to immediately communicate with their loved ones, causing much consternation since all the households were watching the destruction on TV. A friend who worked as a night security guard in a downtown bank was kept inside the building for hours; she recalled fearfully observing from the rooftop the growing rings of fire dangerously approaching the area around the bank.

These people were unharmed. Unfortunately that was not the case for others. In the end sixty people were killed, hundreds injured, thousands arrested, and billions of dollars lost. As sizable as it had been before, the chasm between the powerful and the powerless widened greatly.

Soon after the fires were quelled, a healing process began. Some celebrities and politicians organized spontaneous cleanup crews. Others started outreach efforts toward the various racial communities that had been thrown against one another. New businesses and projects were begun to help bring the poorest Los Angeles communities into the future, including technological training and resource centers. A major result of the uprising was the growth of a highly organized unity beyond gang lines, community lines, and racial lines.

Unfortunately the official Rebuild L.A. only benefited the most powerful and connected people in the city. And whatever healing had been mobilized became undermined by an insidious move to obstruct any future unity among the poorest communities. Blacks and Latinos, who have historically been pitted against one another for jobs and resources, were now more at odds than ever before. This antagonism, particularly acute in the streets, in jails, and among the gangs, was now as active as ever in the angling for control of whatever programs, benefits, and funds were being allocated.

Today, ten years later, except for some highly publicized cosmetic construction and neighborhood projects, nothing has fundamentally changed in Los Angeles.

An important outcome of the uprising, however, was the formation of groups like Rock A Mole (rhymes with "guacamole") Productions. It was the brainchild of Mexican "soul" singer Ernie Perez, who had a mixed-race band at the time called Blackasaurus Mex and later became part of the Boxing Ghandis. He grew up in South Central L.A. Besides Perez, the initial crew consisted of *Rock and Rap Confidential* editor Lee Balinger, Afro-Cuban activist and musician Jorge Luis Rodríguez (who ran a not-for-profit art gallery and performance space in Pico-Union), onetime Los Lobos producer and longtime Chicano educator David Sandoval, and African-American jazz and hip-hop trumpeter Carvell Holloway.

Rock A Mole Productions aimed to infuse street-level creativity into organizational expressions addressing the needs of the poor, bringing music and the arts directly into the healing process. It produced CDs of talent from South Central L.A. and the East L.A./San Gabriel Valley areas. The first was called *L.A. Underground;* it garnered some airplay in the city, and its original music was used in a couple of films and documentaries. It featured musical acts like Strokely, with African-American rapper Brother Bank and trumpeter Holloway, and the Mestizo Soul band with the fantastic stylings of Chicano saxophonist Fre Ballesteros. *L.A. Underground* also included a young Chicano rap group from the San Gabriel Valley called the D.O.P.E. Mob, consisting of four young street dudes: Wicked (Joey Perea), Chaos (Jesse Carlos), DJLA (Justin Corona), and Drastic (Henry Diaz).

In addition Rock A Mole established several free music, art, and spoken-word festivals that involved aerosol art, video art, prison art, live music, poetry, and painting, bringing together thousands of people of all ages, all races, all walks of life. These festivals also showcased the massive talent from some of the area's most neglected communities. *The Ultimate Song,* Rock A Mole's first documentary, is about the role of music in the struggle to end poverty in this country. They also created the "Just Health" theme song for the newly formed Labor Party's Just Health campaign. Hours of efforts for most of these projects were done without pay. Just love.

"All the laws in the land will never conquer what we hold in our hearts," stated Ernie Perez in Rock A Mole's literature. "Art, like poverty, is everywhere.… Art, like the billions of poor people on this planet, has the power to transform reality. The unification of art and common struggle will truly be our lifeline in this century. Without it, we are simply factions. With it, we are a force to be reckoned with. With it, we can get up and out of poverty once and for all."

Perez composed the music for D.O.P.E. Mob's rap called "The Valley of Death." This recording detailed the violence and mentality that pervaded many of the San Gabriel Valley's hardened barrio gangs; at the time the San Gabriel Valley was believed to have more gang violence than any other section of L.A. County. The words, like much of Chicano rap in those days—Cypress Hill, Frost, Lighter Shade of Brown, and Aztlan Underground—interspersed Spanish and *calo* (the barrio street lingo) with English.

Gangsta Rap was all over the musical map. While in the beginning it was about rapping a reality that had resonance and appeal, eventually it got coopted; the stories lost their flavor, their truth, their impact with the constant posing, misogyny, and stark brutality. It was being mishandled and misdirected by those who only wanted to profit from it.

Hip-hop tells the harshest truth in the most lyrical flows. However, commercial interests have used it to caricature the ghetto/barrio life. The music industry is the main force behind the acts willing to be the most wild for money, guns, and jewelry, sending to the edges—and deeper underground—the more conscious, jazz-inflected, and complicated rap acts such as Public

Enemy, KRS-1, Common, Black Eyed Peas, Dilated Peoples, the Roots, Mos Def, Slum Village, and Jurassic 5.

Yet the real stories have to be told. Censoring them only points to their essentiality for millions who have nowhere else to see their lives reflected or cared about. Reality put into poetry has already trasformed that reality—regardless of how violent, evil, and explicit it may be.

So in 1997, D.O.P.E. Mob came to the Chicago Humanities Festival to perform at the famous Orchestra Hall. Along with a Chicago Westside African-American group called 180, they rocked the audience of some four hundred people, including a busload from the Southside's Robert Taylor Housing Projects, the largest subsidized housing complex in the world.

D.O.P.E. Mob was a smash at the event. Later that night YSS leaders hooked up with the guys to share with them some of the realities about Chicago's mean streets.

Unfortunately by early 1998, when I brought several YSS members with me to take part in Rock A Mole's cultural festival in L.A. that year, only one member of D.O.P.E. Mob was still around to perform "The Valley of Death." Most of the others were in jail. But for a time those young men, probably not given much of a chance to contribute in other circumstances, positively impacted the people around them with their stories and their truths, while pushing their art to new heights of expression.

Art is the most powerful means of dealing with violence. This is certainly true in prison, where the most brutal aspects of the streets tend to be reinforced, where oppression is internalized and society's values are inverted. A convict can be rewarded for being a snitch, for betrayal, while an upstanding person can be heavily punished, hounded, and broken in prison. Dignity is not encouraged or valued. There is no hero's redemption in prison.

"I knew that prisons were social institutions, presumably founded and maintained by society to cure the criminal of his criminal ways," wrote Kate Richards O'Hare, in a piece published in 1920 about her own prison experiences (she later became the assistant director of the California Department of Penology, where she helped reform a barbarous state prison system). "Yet when I arrived in prison I found that by the workings of the prison system, society commits every crime against the criminal that the criminal is charged with having committed against society. We send our criminals to prison to teach them not to lie and defraud, and the prisoner is forced to live one long lie, and can exist only by becoming party to fraud.... We send thieves to prison to teach them not to steal and rob and all prison life is thievery and robbing.... We send people to prison to punish them for murder, yet the prison system murders... not only the bodies of men, but the minds and souls of them as well."[1]

During poetry workshops and talks in correctional facilities, I try to emphasize not only the liberating aspects of poetic or artistic expression but also the concept of a place where dignity can flourish. The arts and poetry are more than just something to do while doing time—they are some of the most powerful means of linking again to feelings, other human beings, and perennial patterns (to learn how to swim, as it were, in the "collective unconscious," as the renowned analytical psychologist Dr. Carl G. Jung terms the ocean of inherited archetypal images and dream experience we all carry). These workshops are where the hurts, loneliness, fears, suicidal thoughts, hate, and the accompanying self-hate, find a language. The arts are the best way of dealing with violence.[2] However, the arts shouldn't just be relegated to a "program." They should be integral and vital to any community.

In the mid-1990s, in a rural Illinois prison, a buffed Puerto Rican man in his forties came up to me; in his hand was a dog-eared copy of *Always Running*. Some twenty years before, he started a gang in Chicago's Humboldt Park community that became one of the leading street organizations in the area. A prison guard told me, with a look of disgust on her face, that this person was one of the "worst convicts; a known killer, manipulator, and gang enforcer."

"I want to tell you how much this book meant to me," he said when he approached me. "I really appreciated that you tried to help your son get out of trouble."

Then, haltingly, he proceeded to tell me why he felt this way. It turned out he had two sons who, when they got older, joined the same gang he had started when they were babies. While the man was in prison, the gang warfare in the streets escalated. In the course of time both of his sons were killed. However, he was still incarcerated and unable to attend their funerals. As he told me this, I could see a tear forming in his eyes. For whatever he had done wrong in this world, he had experienced the pain of his actions with the death of his own sons and his inability to do anything about it, or even to be there at the end.

He had a moment to speak his heart, to link with someone who faced a universal father-son dilemma, and just as fast he closed it and walked away.

Writing workshops have helped prisoners like him express what they feel and think without making them show the kind of vulnerability that would place them in extreme danger. Many of the men and women write about the children they left behind. One Latino prisoner in North Carolina wrote a poem to "Nancy," a daughter he never knew. Others talked about their African, Mexika/Native, Puerto Rican, or Irish roots, about the small mundane images and thoughts that represent freedom to them, and about their often hidden but very real pangs of regret.

"Creativity is like your blood," wrote Julia Cameron in her popular book, *The Artist's Way: A Spiritual Path to Higher Creativity.* "Just as blood is a fact of our physical body and nothing you invented, creativity is a fact of your spiritual body and nothing that you must invent."[3] In *The Right to Write: An Invitation and Initiation into the Writing Life,* she speaks of a "hand made life," one that anyone is capable of accomplishing regardless of what schools, our parents, and social norms have taught us.[4] What a concept—that the power to transform, make whole and beautiful, is in our hands.

Rock, rap, aerosol art, breaking, techno, grunge, house, swing, jazz, jitterbug, bebop, salsa, quebradita, low riding, prison art, and tattooing—all have their foundations in the creative capacity within everyone. We can't help it. Yet too often such expression has been dismissed and even outlawed.

"If you think of the primary function of art as a spiritual-emotional expression, and you take away the capacity for people to express what they really have to express, you start to force the violence into action," said Michael Meade. "What do people think is coming through rap music? The otherwise unexpressed rages of a culture, the disappointments, the deep angers. I mean, people have it all mixed up. They think that when you hear it, you're hearing a problem. It's a way of the culture saying the artistic imagination, the musical songs of these children, don't count—that's a crucial mistake."[5]

The culture—caught in a stranglehold of dead values, dead images, dead and brutal interests—can't reconcile most of this new and vital expression: the rage of it, the fire and truth of it. Heavy metal. Punks. Cholos. B-Boys. You name it. These forms terrorize most people, perhaps because they force many of us to own up to our dark secrets, failures, and fears. Instead people are prepared to write off a whole generation rather than bear the intensity of their souls. This criminalizes those with the weakest ties to the capitalist machine. The media—popular books, movies, and newspapers—distance the outcasts and so-called cultural deviants from the rest of "civil" society (even though this society is uncivil as its core). How many films and TV shows have we seen where poor black or brown criminals run the dark world while demonstrating great weaknesses as human beings and then are later crushed by the powers of goodness and "whiteness"?

Of course this is fantasy. But fantasy feeds reality. Some people don't seem to know when the fantasy ends and the reality begins. Their values are being formed by their "experiences" in the cultural imagination (not really their own).

The solution is not to start closing down movie houses or bookstores or censoring TV programs—censorship isn't the answer here. It's about having an in-depth and abiding dialogue on the vital issues that can later be translated into TV, movies, and books with real resonance and meaning. (You can't always do this, however, if you're trying to make a fast buck).

Despite the cutback of many creative endeavors, mainly due to a lack of money or the fact that they are not commercial enough, poor people have created new outlets for self-expression. As the open mike of the deprived, hip-hop is extremely influential. It reaches beyond all boundaries and cultures—there are Hip-hop festivals in Havana, Milan, Paris, Tokyo, London, Mexico City, Warsaw, and Johannesburg. I believe that much of the attack hip-hop is often subject to is because of its worldwide impact.

If creativity is the most viable alternative to violence, then we have to allow it a full flowering—or else violence will become the poetry of a generation.

> *Your exact errors make a music*
> *that nobody hears.*
> *Your straying feet find the great dance,*
> *walking alone.*
> *And you live on a world where stumbling*
> *always leads home.*
>
> *Year after year fits over your face—*
> *when there was youth, your talent*
> *was youth;*
> *later, you find your way by touch*
> *where moss redeems the stone;*
>
> *And you discover where music begins*
> *before it makes any sound,*
> *far in the mountains where canyons go*
> *still as the always-falling, ever-new flakes of snow.*
>
> —William Stafford [6]

Chapter 14

Governance and Gangs[1]

I have seen many changes since I was first initiated into the barrio....
But nothing has had so much impact as how many homies have
passed away.... It's about time we value our lives, and think about
our future, about the future of our children.

—Alex Sanchez, director of Homies Unidos in Los Angeles

One of the most healing experiences I've had involved a meeting between
Walter Guzman and myself during a talk at a Barrios Unidos gathering in
the Beach Flats barrio of Santa Cruz, California. Guzman was a member of
the Sangra barrio when I was part of Las Lomas in the early 1970s. Two Chicano neighborhoods on the western edge of the San Gabriel Valley, Sangra
and Lomas had a deadly rivalry that lasted over fifty years. Grandparents, great-
grandparents, and even great-great-grandparents participated in its terrible
legacy, and it has resulted in hundreds of mostly young men and women killed
or wounded over several generations.[2]

There were instances in which Walter and I may have shot at each other.
Several of his homies were hurt in battles I participated in and vice versa.
Although active in the community, Walter gradually became addicted to
heroin. But he eventually recovered from the drugs, moved to northern California, and worked for a drug rehabilitation program. He also became part
of Barrios Unidos, serving as chair of the board for many years.

Barrios Unidos had by the 1990s established one of the largest and most
effective peace movements in the country, including BU Industries, which
hired many needy young people in creating art products and T-shirts. Directed
by Nane Alejandrez, a former gang leader, Vietnam War vet, and ex-addict,
BU also helped bridge the rifts that divided the just-arrived Mexican families from the older, more established, Chicano ones. This peacemaking also

included working within the deadly rivalries of Norteño and Sureño street organizations in the juvenile detention centers, streets, and prisons.

Walter came to a talk I presented to the youth and parents of Beach Flats and sat in the back of the room. Right away I recognized him. I didn't know what to expect. Was he bitter? Was he going to attack what I said? Would he walk out? I kept talking.

When I finished, Walter raised his hand to speak. I motioned to him and in an older lived-in voice, he talked about the war environment we were both from, how he had read my book and recognized the people and places there, and how much this had affected him. He remembered the intensity of the time and the names of those I honored in my dedication, including some of his homeboys. While I was president of the Chicano activist group in my high school, Walter held the same position at the high school near his neighborhood.

Later at a bookstore where I was doing a reading, Walter presented me with a braid of sweet grass as a peace offering, a Native American gesture— both Sangra and Lomas have indigenous ties to California and Mexican tribes. Walter later told me how one of his homeboys had been designated chief of a small local tribe after the former chief, the homeboy's father, had died, and how this literally transformed a tattooed, cholo-styling, ex-convict into a wise, sober, and respected person.

At this I hugged my former enemy and began to truly believe that peace could be born, even if only as a small flame between two weary warriors. The war between Lomas and Sangra was as devastating as any between two rival groups in this country—if we could embrace, maybe there was hope for others.

We shared tears together, for so many dead and for so many forgotten, and we vowed to fight together for peace in the barrios, if not always at the exact place or time. Walter Guzman, this dedicated and selfless man, became a good friend.

Unfortunately the toll of years of drug addiction, prison, and street life recently claimed my dear friend. In early 2000, at age forty-six, Walter passed on due to conditions associated with hepatitis C.

Later that summer in Los Angeles I met his mother, sisters, and other members of his family during a Youth Unity Gathering. It was held at Proyecto Pastoral of the Mission Dolores in Boyle Heights, across the street from the concrete ruins of the Aliso Village Housing Projects (they were being torn down to make way for new structures, apparently including condos and townhouses for the well-to-do). Former enemies, we talked. We cried. Walter became the bridge across our river of hate.

This is a small part of the various community peace efforts that have been going on for some time in the barrios, ghettos, and reservations of America. Over the years rivalries have continued to rage, but there have also been instances of former enemies reaching out to stop the carnage.

One of the best-known peace efforts involved the Crips and the Bloods of South Central L.A., in the Watts community. A truce between them had already kicked off before the Los Angeles Rebellion. As the fires from that disturbance shimmered, TV's *Nightline* and *The Larry King Show* broadcast interviews with Kershaun Scott of the Crips, known as Little Monster, and Cle Sloan of the Bloods, known as Bone. Together these young men addressed in the most articulate of terms the deeper issues of economic displacement, political impotency, and the historical inequities fueling the anger. Despite a gang war that had claimed hundreds of lives, these and other leaders were prepared to put down their weapons to help rebuild the city.

I attended a few of the Crips-Blood meetings. I read about the various rallies held in parks, churches, and mosques, with Crips and Bloods tying their blue and red bandannas together. I heard told how gang members, without support or resources, dressed in black—a neutral color—had marched into rival housing projects in Watts; they were unarmed, singing chants and shouting peace slogans, beginning the truce process in the late 1980s. Along with my son Ramiro, I was on the Oprah Winfrey show in early 1993 with truce leaders from Los Angeles and Chicago, including the late Tony Bogard, who played a role in founding the Hands Across Watts Foundation. I later met people tied to Amer-I-Can, Communities in the Schools, the Association of Community-based Gang Intervention Workers, the Community Self-Determination Institute, Chicago's Unity in Peace, and other truce-active organizations. I got to know Jitu Sadiki, Twilight Bey, Aqueela Sherrills, Elegba Earl, and DeWayne Holmes, activists in the Crips-Bloods truce movement, and Holmes's courageous mother, Theresa Allison, who helped found Mothers ROC.[3]

At one meeting with community leaders, a young Crip asked of the older veteran organizers there, "Show us the ropes, and we'll do the rest." This was a sound proposition, one that is being ignored every day in this country. Show us the ropes, and we'll do the rest—a clarion call for elders if ever there was one.

The political terrain of the country has dramatically changed since Los Angeles exploded. The deadliest and costliest urban uprising in the United States in more than one hundred years mainly brought about state-led repression and a deeply cynical "outbreak" of unswervingly defeatist politics.

Unlike what happened after the 1965 Watts Rebellion, when billions of dollars were pumped into economic and social programs for the urban core communities, by the mid-1990s a Democratic administration and a Republican-held Congress, despite their so-called differences, united on abandoning these very communities—backing off from federal safety nets, including welfare and subsidized housing—and on redirecting social energies to prison construction and gang injunctions.

Their response took the form of cutting back on what they called an unwieldy, costly, and ineffective government, canceling funding of programs that were supposed to assist those unable to obtain employment, education, or social mobility by any other means, while authorizing billions of dollars for police, prisons, and so-called prevention programs.

The immediate payback, which would mellow most people from protesting or caring about these cutbacks and dismantlements, was in tax relief or in programs such as vouchers for private schools (while the public schools only fell further behind). Of course such cynical approaches are short-lived and become costlier down the road.

Much of the new policies embodied juvenile crime legislation that wended its way through Congress in 1997, 1998, and 1999. The provisions in these packages included putting more children into adult jails, even as truants and runaways; juvenile records would be open to the public; stiffer sentences could be sought for "gang" crimes; and children could be expelled for bringing tobacco, alcohol, or drugs to school. In addition the focus of spending was on punishment, not prevention. In 1998 the proposed prevention funds were $50 million to $100 million, whereas for punishment they were $450 million to $500 million, even though studies from the Children's Defense Fund confirmed that crime prevention efforts were three times more cost-effective than increased punishment.[4]

In the face of this, new forces were arising in the land.

A segment of the so-called marginalized and disenfranchised have been stirring for some time. In the past they have been written off as the disadvantaged, even as "illegal." They have been labeled criminals and dismissed. You could either feel sorry for them or hate them but the point was not to get near them. They must now be reckoned with as a political force.

From welfare mothers to people with AIDS, and the physically handicapped, from the homeless to the homies, thousands began flexing their organizational muscles and using them on the streets in pursuit of their own economic and political interests. The uneasy but crucial unity in Los Angeles between the Crips and the Bloods is indicative of this development.

Another is the Kensington Welfare Rights Union (KWRU) from the devastated communities of North Philly. In the 1980s KWRU tore the boards out of abandoned buildings so that their members could find shelter, and organized tent cities in protest of policies that pushed out the homeless while good structures were being shuttered. By the year 2000 they were leading marches and summits against poverty that have included participants from around the world and well-known entertainers such as Steve Earle and Jackson Browne. I have worked with their leaders, including the tireless organizer Cheryl Honkala, in Philadelphia and other cities where the poor have organized for the benefit of the poor.[5]

The stirrings of "the bottom" of society aim toward certain goals:

• The end of poverty in the midst of plenty
• Real education predicated on the powers and gifts everyone possesses
• Productive and viable employment
• Access to the most advanced health care in the world
• Decent housing for all
• A real voice in the policy decisions that affect their lives

This is why organizations like KWRU and Rock A Mole Productions were formed: to demand the leading place of the destitute and disenfranchised in the changing social fabric. Such demands were also being articulated in cities and rural areas across the United States where similar stirrings have occurred. And gang youth were very much a part of these stirrings.

How was this possible when the police and most of the media portray gangs as drug-dealing, inner-city terrorists?

This was possible because these street associations are not homogeneous. There was no single leadership. To be sure, there have been gang members who cared nothing about unity. For years their violent acts dictated the lives and determined the deaths of thousands of young people as communities were pulled into the warfare.

Other gang members, less publicized, became politicized with every police beating, every inequity, every injustice. Years ago these gang members, along with others in the community, began work on uniting the gangs. Until the 1992 uprising most of these efforts were individual. Since then, unity efforts have been carried out on a larger scale, with whole neighborhoods participating. A nationwide urban peace and justice movement was set in motion.

The fact was that gang members grew tired of the killings. Many of these killings touched everyone, particularly when children were getting hit. This is why, in the aftermath of the uprising, graffiti appeared expressing such sentiments as "Mexicans & Crips & Bloods Together." Police later erased most of the unity-related scrawl.

The gangs became political through observation and participation. Although many of the youth don't read, they witnessed politics as it was played out every day. What the King beating did, what the uprising did, was to help them cross the line of understanding about what's really going on.

The Bloods-Crips unity was also about who will rule South Central L.A. For years now the community has been dotted with hundreds of liquor stores and storefront churches, schools and streets in disrepair, and manufacturing industries that have been shut down. Under these circumstances you have to ask, Who really controls this community?

Not the community. Not when they've had little or no say in the zoning laws that allow a proliferation of liquor stores and hardly any space for community centers, movie theaters, bookstores, and computer learning centers.

Although the people of South Central shared responsibility for their conditions—proportionately more of them were in jail than any other community in the city—they didn't have decisive control over their lives. This was another example of the breakdown in the integration of responsibility and authority. Those with the authority, including the police and city, county, and state officials, failed to take any responsibility for the situation in South Central, thus abdicating any claim to leadership.

It was precisely when the gangs came together that the police tried to break up as many unity rallies as they could, arresting gang leaders and inflaming the ire of housing-project residents, where many of the rallies were held. The LAPD told the media that the gangs were going to turn on police officers, even ambush them. Yet no police officer had been hurt at any of the rallies.

Soon after the rebellion, local law enforcement circulated a flyer among themselves—and the media—that proclaimed the Crips and Bloods would "kill two cops for every gang member killed." It was incendiary and a forgery. Most gang members who saw the flyer told me the writing style was not even close to the style in the street. The flyer appeared to be yet another example of cartoon propaganda that had characterized previous allegations by police.

Meanwhile, early in the 1990s the federal government mounted the largest investigations ever to destroy gangs. Government officials began to target key people associated with the Crips and the Bloods. It appeared that the FBI was striking at L.A. gangs for political, not criminal, activity; its intervention was directly tied to the truce and other similar community efforts prior to the uprising, on April 29, 1992.[6]

I have to emphasize again the role that the government played in undermining many peace or political efforts among street organizations. One tool being used was the Racketeer Influenced Corrupt Organizations Act (RICO). This is the same act that helped put reputed crime boss John Gotti behind bars. With RICO the federal government indicted alleged leaders of La Eme in California and Texas. In southern California the indictments followed a no-driveby decree that La Eme instituted in the summer of 1993, which actually resulted in a 25 percent drop in driveby shootings in various parts of L.A. County.

I was around the MS and 18th Street areas of Pico Union when La Eme first organized this peace effort. Sure, I read about the terror and the taxing and the drug deals that La Eme supposedly exerted among many of these gangs. But I also saw a level of leadership that many of the youth were hungry for—"organize us," they were saying, "for our *gente,* on one level, and for the peace, on the other."

Even though law enforcement officials and prosecutors were stating in the media that the decree was about La Eme extending its control of the drug trade to all L.A. barrios, I witnessed the effects from another angle. In the streets, former members of various barrio gangs were now feeling a heavy weight lifted off them. Many were venturing outside their underground enclaves for the first time in years. They were now able to sit on their front porches or in neighborhood hangouts.

Wars between various factions were being stopped, including some that had been in existence for several generations. Former enemies—up to about three thousand representatives from various barrio street organizations at any one time—were meeting in parks and other locations throughout L.A. to implement the parameters of this peace.

And while a few of the older Chicano street organizations were the first to pull out or not take part in these efforts—most notably the barrios of the large Maravilla district of East L.A.—there were still enough groups involved to make a significant impact.[7]

It is true that the illicit drug trade continued, but the fact that fewer strangers now came at you in a vehicle with guns in their hands amounted to something: Many innocents were spared; needless and careless gunfire was severely curtailed. For the first time a semblance of calm and even hope visited these streets. There was also a decline in fear and in the grave uncertainties that had marked barrio gang life for decades. It was an important start that could have been built upon.

This particular peace was short-lived. A lot of it had to do with internal struggles within the prison structures as well as between the various barrio groupings not aligned with La Eme. However, a big contributor to the curtailing of this peace effort were the government indictments, under federal racketering laws, of twenty two alleged Eme leaders and associates in early 1995 (thirteen were later convicted), and another forty in 1999. Among the intricacies of the streets, law enforcement and other government forces have played a role in keeping gang wars alive. As one Pelican Bay prisoner wrote, "A level of leadership in the streets has been removed, and now younger vatos are instigating wars to make a name for themselves."

This is a widespread tactic. In Chicago a lull in gang violence was often broken by suspicious shootings (for example, masked men with high-powered weapons), police dropping off gang members in rival territory, or some other manipulated beef. In L.A. County some sheriff's deputies reportedly did their own driveby shootings in order to ignite certain gang battles; a few were indicted in the early 1990s.

The point is there wouldn't be the level of gang and drug violence in our communities if not for the role of police and other officials. The Rampart police scandal is proof of this, although it's only a small part of the total picture.

There were several results of the undermining of the Crips-Bloods truces and of the barrio gang unity efforts by the police and others. One of them was that in 1995 L.A. experienced the largest number of youth killed by gangs in its history, close to 810. Gang-led peace efforts were discredited at the same time that resources, jobs, and societal support were pulled out. These efforts could have worked. But they were labeled as failures when they began—then everything was done to make sure they would fail.

The problem is that our society cannot truly have street peace unless significant sectors of gangs are integrally involved in shaping it.

In the rest of the country indictments were issued against the El Rukns (formerly Black P. Stone Nation) when they were major players in keeping "crack" out of Chicago; after their indictments in the late 1980s crack could be found almost anywhere. And indictments against the Gangster Disciples of Chicago (the largest street gang in the city) came down after they helped bring a large number of African-American youth to march for jobs and after announcing they were now to be known as Growth and Development, a social-empowerment group. Although the GDs have been around since the 1960s, and alleged to be tied to the drug trade not long after that, no federal indictments came down until Growth and Development was established.

Let me reiterate: Although criminal activities tied to factions of El Rukns and GDs, Crips and Bloods, and La Eme and Nuestra Familia were well documented, it appeared that the indictments occurred only when these organizations began to politically mobilize their members or help bring about a measure of peace.

Similar indictments have been leveled against the Almighty Latin Kings, a mostly Mexican–Puerto Rican street organization based in Chicago (a spin-off group on the East Coast began to be more politically active, particularly in the New York City area). Remember that the Young Lords in Chicago, a street organization that arose at the same time as the Kings in the 1960s, were virtually destroyed after they became a politically strong Puerto Rican rights organization. The Latin Kings thrived, on the other hand, because at the time they primarily turned away from politics and maintained themselves as a street gang association. Now that sections of the Kings have become more politicized and community-minded, the feds have moved in on them.

This pattern of government activity is not new or surprising. After the 1965 Watts Rebellion, several African-American gangs united, some of whom became the L.A. chapter of the Black Panthers. The federal government also intervened, including orchestrating friction between the Black Panther Party and the United Slaves organization, which led to a shootout at UCLA in which two Panthers were killed. It was the breakup of these unity efforts (and the removal of teen posts and jobs programs during the long night known as the Nixon era) that eventually set up a vacuum that led to the birth of the Crips.

This in turn led to war with groups such as the Brims, Bounty Hunters, Rabble Rousers, and Pirus, who later came together to form the Bloods.

The government did the same with organizations in East L.A., especially following the Chicano Moratorium Against the Vietnam War of 1970. This time government activity involved the covert and overt dismantling of the Barrio Federation (which tried to unite most of the Maravilla district gangs) and other barrio unity efforts, including the militant Brown Berets organization (the Berets were reportedly disbanded in the mid-1970s because the group was so infiltrated with agents, nobody knew whom to trust).

Elsewhere the feds infiltrated the Independence for Puerto Rico movement, many of whose leaders are still serving time for their political beliefs and activities. A similar response occurred during the Wounded Knee protests in 1973 and the 1975 shoot-out in Oglala, which led to the killing of two federal agents and a Native American. This case resulted in the false conviction and incarceration of Leonard Peltier. There have been a number of books, including South End Press's *Agents of Repression,* that outline the politically motivated efforts of the FBI and other government agencies to destroy—including with the use of government-sanctioned "goon" squads—groups like the Black Panthers, Brown Berets, Young Lords, and American Indian Movement.[8]

So in addition to breaking up any gang unity in South Central L.A. after the 1992 L.A. Rebellion, a special U.S. Immigration Service Violent Gang Task Force was established to detain and deport many Mexican and Central American youth with criminal records. The general sentiment among law enforcement was that the gangs—African American, Mexican, and Salvadoran—were the main culprits behind the uprising. Thousands of young people were then sent back to countries that had few resources and little if any understanding of who they were.

Yet despite the array of local, state, and federal forces poised against gangs, peace in the streets was being organized in almost every major city with the help of gang youth. Barrios Unidos now has almost thirty chapters throughout the country. Urban peace summits were called throughout the country—the first major one was in Kansas City in 1993—that included representatives from the West Coast, the Midwest, the South, and the East Coast. In 1997, Homies Unidos was founded in El Salvador, under the mentorship of Chicano activist Magdaleno Rose-Avila, former director of the Cesar Chavez Foundation in L.A.[9]

Members of the Bloods and the Crips have continued their truce, especially in Watts, although much of the truce elsewhere has since broken down. One Crip told me this was largely due to the government and business community not recognizing their efforts, despite some heroic incidents: One Crip, whose cousin had been killed by gunfire, walked into a Bloods-held housing complex to say he was tired of the war and was willing to die, if need be, for peace; he became a truce leader.

In East Los Angeles' Aliso Village and Pico Gardens housing projects (the largest federally subsidized housing units west of the Mississippi), desperate mothers, many of them untrained and unable to speak English, organized themselves to march down the streets, carry out strategic night walks, communicate with the most active gang youth, and witness police arrests so that they wouldn't abuse the youth in their often deadly neighborhoods. In the Northeast San Fernando Valley, a mostly Mexican impoverished area with a number of rival gangs, the work of William "Blinkie" Rodriguez (who lost a sixteen-year-old son to gang warfare and who has another son in state prison), helped lead a 70 percent drop in gang shootings in the mid-1990s.[10] And again there's the example of East L.A.'s Father Greg Boyle with Jobs for a Future and Homeboy Industries.

There are many such stories that don't get told, many such efforts that unfortunately cannot all be spelled out here. I truly believe that when the rate of violence goes down, as it has in the last few years,[11] it has much to do with these efforts. Churches, schools, parents, teachers, street workers, youth, and, yes, law enforcement, have played vital roles in this decline. But most certainly this is due to the work of peace activists around the country who have not turned their backs on the most troubled youth.

Of course the violence will rise. These statistics tend to go up and down, although in general, when compared with the population growth, the rate of violence is lower than in previous periods. We cannot idealize peace any more than we can idealize street warfare. To think that in a few years there would be total unity and peace after generations of fighting is unrealistic. There are still many unresolved disputes. But the violence levels have been definitely affected since peace efforts began. The government and the police should stop undermining these efforts and stop fanning the emotional flames that will only bring on more death and injuries.

Not long ago a Chicago community organization was attacked by Mayor Richard M. Daley, police officials, and the media for inviting the Rev. Jesse

Jackson to hand out community service certificates to alleged gang youth. They claimed the organization and Jackson were "honoring" criminals. But those awards were for the positive contributions these youth had made, to instill in them a new criteria for self-respect and personal power. Such attacks only make more problematic the already difficult work of keeping these young people alive and in peace.

In addition an international controversy was sparked in late 2000 when the Crips cofounder, Stanley "Tookie" Williams, who was serving a life sentence in San Quentin for four murder convictions, was nominated for a Nobel Peace Prize by a member of the Swiss parliament. Martin Fehr nominated Williams because he felt the former gang leader had truly changed his life and had saved many other lives with a series of children's books and an Internet project aimed at getting kids out of gangs. There were those, however, particularly in law enforcement, who felt such a man should never get this honor.

"We should never elevate gang members to statesmen," said Los Angeles County Sheriff's Sgt. Wes McBride, president of the California Association of Gang Investigators. But others, such as Melvin Farmer, a former Eight-Tray Crips gang member and current peace activist, disagreed. "When do you pay your debt—when you are dead?" he asked.[12]

Despite these and other obstacles, Bloods, Crips, GDs, Latin Kings, Norteños, Sureños, and others around the country have found common ground, a unified aim to end the violence. Whether society is ready for this or not, it is the only path not littered with hypocrisy and blame. This struggle includes hard work, training, mentoring, and rethinking the world, something many police and some government officials would like the public to believe gang members are incapable of doing.

Some are taking responsibility. And they are making a demand for the authority to carry it out.

At the same time, because society has not helped these organizations to obtain peace by providing them with basic necessities, such as jobs, a new crop of gang leaders has emerged who are determined not to be part of any peace process. Even the OGs and *veteranos* can't reach them. They sell drugs, they instigate battles, and they have been known to shoot their own members who try to pull out of the madness.

"I'm afraid we're seeing a new kind of gangbanger that can't be reached," one street organizer told me after a seven-year-old girl and a teenager were killed in a November 2000 driveby shooting in East L.A. "After they shot those kids, a few of them sat on a front porch, cleaned their guns, and laughed at the mourners."

Can they be reached? Sure, but not without a determined and multifaceted struggle. I recall similar cases of "unreachable" youth in my neighborhood during the 1960s and 1970s, when the community centers and viable alternatives had disappeared. I'm sure this was true more than 150 years ago when the Dead Rabbits and the Bowery Boys were terrorizing sections of Lower Manhattan. Some of the combatants can only be reached with tangible and long-lasting solutions. When these continually fail to materialize, when we fail to move in a solid and significant manner to create peace,this is the kind of wall we will face.

When the community exploded in Los Angeles, the slogan that best expressed the outrage was "No Justice, No Peace." It's a reality that has to be addressed: Wherever social injustice exists, there can never be true social peace. But based on this, we still have to envision and create paths for peace. For another reality hits us as well: As long as our communities are at war, we cannot adequately organize for and implement true justice.

On August 24, 1996, YSS set forth a Chicago Youth Peace Plan that was distributed for a few days afterward during the Democratic National Convention. The youth worked on this plan for several months. They organized a gathering at the University of Illinois, Chicago, campus to finalize the main points. The plan included problems and solutions.

"We the youth are demanding our right to be heard and to fully participate in rebuilding our communities, cities, and country," the plan's introductory statement read. "[YSS] organized the event to bring young leaders together to help change the inequities of our society. This is a first step. We are prepared to take this plan and its essence as far and wide as possible. We are willing to change as long as we know that our actions and feelings are respected and needed for society to change."13

The issues they addressed were divided into four categories: education, discrimination, economics, and laws and rights. Some of the solutions included more funding for school structures and materials, ongoing treatment programs, the end of trying youth as adults, the removal of police officers and metal detectors from schools, and more Peer Jury programs.

At the end of the plan YSS stated, "To All Adults: Please value and respect all children and youth! To All Young People: Follow Your Dreams!"

At this meeting, then–California state senator Tom Hayden was among our guests. Senator Hayden also invited YSS to take part in a commemoration of the 1968 Chicago Seven Trial, in which he was a defendant. At the Arie Crown Theater on August 25, sponsored by *The Nation* magazine, about thirty YSS youth and elders addressed close to two thousand people who had come to see Bonnie Raitt, Jackson Browne, Crosby, Stills & Nash, Jesse Jackson, Dolores Huerta, John Trudell, and many others remember and honor the spirit of that time. YSS came to honor the spirit of this time.

Nydia Hernandez, then a seventeen-year-old resident of Humboldt Park and of Puerto Rican–Guatemalan descent, was chosen to make a short speech at the event. "We believe that every solution must have the youths' genuine input, including in every policymaking body in government and in the community," Nydia said. "This is valuable because we have dreams, we have visions, and we have the energy to make positive and lasting social change. We are determined to have youth be in control of their own lives by taking responsibility through clear and decisive actions."

We then passed out hundreds of copies of the plan. Nydia and others later organized crews to get copies of the plan to Democratic-delegates (who were well protected from the public), mostly by passing them out in the lobbies of hotels where delegates were holed up. At one point Nydia showed the plan to a well-known celebrity reporter covering the convention. This person's response was typical, unfortunately, of many adults who may believe youth are the "whatever" generation. "All these gripes," she said after looking at the plan. "But what are you going to do about them?"

The celebrity then turned around and walked away. As callous as this may have seemed, Nydia and the other YSS youth took her words to heart. Looking at the problems and solutions, they tackled the various ways they would contribute to make the plan a reality.

And that's what YSS began doing, again without resources, funds, or paid staff. Unfortunately there weren't many major media paying attention. There weren't many accolades or much of a rush of support. The celebrity reporter never returned to seek out Nydia or another YSS youth to see how they were doing. In fact the mere fact that these young people spoke out in such positive terms tended to get in the way of preconceived notions anyone may have had about "predator" or slacker youth.

For example a press conference had been called prior to the Arie Crown Theater event. More than two hundred media people were there, including journalists from several other countries. Cameras rolled, flashes flashed, and pages of notepads flipped over several times as journalists feverishly tried to capture the words of such notables as Bobby Seale, Dave Dillinger, and Tom Hayden.

Then I was introduced to say a few words. With me was a Puerto Rican gang leader from my neighborhood and his brother, members of YSS. I walked up to the podium and all of a sudden the video recorders were turned off, notepads closed, and camera motors stopped whirling. Reporters actually walked away.

I thought this might be a scene for a comedy. But it wasn't funny. For the most part the media representatives there were not concerned about YSS, the work the youth had done to prepare their document, or their presence. I'm sure that if I or the gang leader had sworn, stuck out a gun, or robbed someone, they would have been all over us. But here they practically ignored what was essentially a positive and powerful message.

This didn't deter us. We were doing this work whether the media paid attention or not. And people like Hayden and the publishers of *The Nation* went out of their way to make sure we had a place in the proceedings, for which we were most thankful.

But the incident with the media does say something about what some people may consider "news" in this country—"if it bleeds, it leads." These shallow viewpoints have become detrimental to the important work being done to prepare youth to be autonomous, competent, and confident for most of their own lives. (I say this with the caveat that there are indeed many journalists and broadcasters who do positive and meaningful reportage outside of the sensational and negative.)

YSS's efforts have now been part of larger mobilizations of youth in Chicago, including the 1999 Youth Summit (which also involved a major pre-summit, and various local forums, discussion circles, and meetings) at the University of Illinois, Chicago. An estimated eight hundred youth and adults attended that significant gathering.

Organized by the Community Justice Initiative with the support of a cross-section of organizations and individuals, the Youth Summit has taken to another level what YSS and other groups—Youth for Change, the Southwest Youth Collaborative, Alternatives Inc., Senn Youthnet, Voices for Illinois Children, and Center for Youth and Society, among others—have been initiating in the Chicago area for many years; it is a movement of youth and adults together for the social, political, economic, and cultural betterment of all people.

These are striking examples of leaders who don't just complain about the problems and throw blame around, but who work hard, with immense patience, spreading knowledge and leadership so that a just and caring community is built from the ground up.

Another example of this was the second National Urban Peace and Justice Summit, held in October 1998 in Kansas City, Missouri. Some two hundred people were in attendance. Whatever conflicts, feuds, or rifts may have existed among those who gathered there, it didn't take long for them to overcome the divisions and focus on the tasks at hand.

It was a ten-year-old girl who helped unite them.

Shanelle Cooper, a fifth grader from Kansas City, Kansas, was killed the day before the summit in a driveby shooting while she stood in the front yard of her home. This tragedy reinforced why the various ministers, imams, Pipe Carriers, community activists, and leaders of warring street organizations from across the country came together here to say: "Let's put aside our differences and get to work for peace."

About fifty summit participants took part in a vigil at Shanelle's home the first night of the summit. With tears and a broken voice, Elizabeth Ayala, from Barrios Unidos, told the gathering how sitting there in the Cooper home brought to mind her own two-year-old son back in Santa Cruz, California, and the realization that such a tragedy could happen to him or to any other child. She talked about how Shanelle must be seen as everyone's daughter, and how we must stop the many forms of social violence that are tearing apart our families, destroying children, and undermining whatever struggle for justice we must undertake.

The following day at the Metropolitan Spiritual Church of Christ, Shanelle's father, Darnell Cooper, spoke to summit participants, thanking them for consoling his family. This was a tragic way to begin any proceedings, but in the work for peace in our communities this is the one constant: Our children are dying. While some die suddenly, others are killed slowly, daily, by conditions that trample their souls.

Activists and leaders came from Los Angeles and Chicago, the cities with the largest numbers of deaths due to gang violence. Many others traveled from northern California, Ohio, New York, Indiana, Illinois, Arizona, Massachusetts, Missouri, and Minnesota. They included activists from El Salvador and Native American reservations who have made peace their passion and principle. Although the participants were mostly black and brown, there was an implicit understanding that street violence was no longer a "big city" phenomenon or a black-and-brown issue.

Surrounded by healing circles, prayers, rituals, workshops, inspirational talks, and memorials, various participants also fashioned an Urban Peace Initiative. This would be a guiding policy for work at the local as well as national levels around economic development, political empowerment, ending police abuse, court advocacy, and stopping the growth of prisons in the country.

At the Peace and Justice Summit, we pulled together our energies, our voices, and our families to make peace a reality, to have justice in our time, and to see that everyone has adequate food, shelter, and clothing as well as spiritual centering. The peace we were talking about is war by other means—organizing to make our economic and social needs the human rights issue of the new century. The summit was a powerful beginning that should reverberate throughout the United States, and the Hemisphere.

I was heartened to see these major movers and shakers at the summit, proving that it was indeed a gathering of the leading peace warriors in America. I was also pleased that spiritual movements and churches were actively involved.

But most heartening was the participation of leaders from some of Chicago's largest Latino gangs. We had arranged their presence at the Summit through a collaborative of Humboldt Park, Logan Square, and Little Village community and church organizations. These leaders represented sections of the Almighty Latin Kings, the Maniac Latin Disciples, the Insane Spanish Cobras, and the Two-Six Nation. Wars between them have led to countless deaths over the years. The mistrust they had for each other was formidable.

The collaborative organizers and I had our doubts about whether they would sit in the same room together, let alone be part of a national assembly. But in the course of the proceedings we saw them converse, share stories, and possibly begin to see a path for peace in their devastated communities. One evening we walked into a diner where we spotted the four "enemies" sitting together, talking and laughing while munching away at huge servings of hamburgers and fries. It was a sight some of us thought we would never see.

Beginnings are the most fragile period in any process. To strengthen the resolve that came out of the summit requires an immense amount of resources, funds, ideas, and sweat so that peace and justice breaks out in every barrio, every hood, every reservation, and every community of this land. Far too often the peace won't hold. But each time this happens, we must take up the peace banner even tighter and higher. We have to keep working, becoming more experienced, more knowledgeable, and more successful each time.

Youth and other members of our communities have to be sovereign over their lives, their neighborhoods, their country. The community has to work with those gang leaders and members who hunger for peace and change; it has to provide the strategies and methodologies that help keep them on the peace and justice track. The efforts of MATA, Barrios Unidos, Homies Unidos, and Rock A Mole are all part of this. So is YSS's Chicago Peace Plan. And so is the urban peace movement in this country and in other parts of the globe.[14]

Youth have to see the hero's pattern in what they are already doing and in who they already are: They themselves are the heroes. It's unjust and inaccurate to make heroism a quality of only those who possess a certain skin color, or who embody certain values, or who come from a certain social class or background.

There are many people caught in the steely grasp of the prison culture. There are many thousands like Shanelle Cooper or the members of D.O.P.E. Mob trying to link to eldership and the skills to struggle, to think, and to triumph, who are waiting to be seen.

We—especially those of us who have already gone through this process—must provide the necessary sustenance for the visions of the young. No more prisons. No more mediocrity. No more mind slavery to archaic images and symbols. While almost everything seems to conspire to say that we're stuck in the economic-social paradigm we're in and, that there's nothing we can do about it, we have to say most emphatically it doesn't have to be this way.

"Somewhere in the course of youth, fate must be felt," Michael Meade writes. "The eruptions of youth, often judged dysfunctional and anti-social, may well be revelations of life's calling. These uncertain voices ask strangely for 'education,' for a leading out and for the cool hand of the mentor. Instead, the uncertain call is met with fear, condemnation, and punishment. What society does to its youth, it also does to itself and to the continuity of culture."[15]

PART THREE
STRETCHING OUT YOUR LIFE

For all those who have faced death,
and have chosen life.
—Jack Kornfield,
from a Buddhist prayer

Chapter 15
Abundance or Scarcity

To produce without possessing; to work without expecting; to enlarge without usurping: This is the supreme virtue.

—Lao Tzu

Since 1994 I have been working with the Mosaic Multicultural Foundation's national conferences, in which men of all colors, professions, and economic classes gather in idyllic and forested sites for weekend to week-long sojourns. There we delve into the deep and often perplexing issues of race, class, gender privilege, sexual orientation, and the "violence of youth and absence of elders."

Mosaic utilizes rituals, stories, poetry, drumming, song, dance, and traditional cosmologies from Africa, India, Asia, Ireland, Christianity, and Native America, including Mexico and Central America. Through art and intense dialogue we deal with the starkest rages—many of the men have committed great violence against their families, during the Vietnam or Persian Gulf wars, and in gangs or prison. We also attempt to recognize and challenge the seemingly impassable "giants" within men's psyches. Many of these men have been spiritually incapacitated, governed by internal gatekeepers and bad "kings." Blocked from their resolve and confused, they have become overgrown bullies who are often irresponsible and mostly unresponsive to the deep pain of severed relationships between men and women, young and old, white skin and dark skin, and the poor and well-to-do.

By giants I mean those psychological barriers pertaining to fathers, mothers, family, acceptance, cowardice, fear, and forgiveness that seem to bind our souls in quick-setting mud, immobilizing us, restricting our movements, keeping us from truly transcending the wounds of our lives. By internal gatekeepers and bad kings I mean those rulers or judges within that often hinder us from drawing out our intrinsic gifts, of meeting the challenge of our calling and our personal heroic path. (A king can also refer to the nobility we all carry.)

These mythological images, which many saw as the stuff of children's stories and bedtime fare, have in recent times been used to plumb the deepest hollows in our souls. They've become psychoactive. The ancient stories, from all cultures, not only excite the imagination and our own stories, but they play a dynamic role in our awareness and development. Dragons, horses, birds, giants, kings, twins, serpents, dwarfs, gold, seas—all represent tangible qualities, places in our psyche, relationships, and pursuits that become vital again, especially in today's mythologically sparse culture.

Michael Meade founded Mosaic in 1989 after years of working in the men's movement with internationally known pioneers such as Robert Bly and James Hillman. Mosaic events, however, are not limited to what many may believe to be the parameters of this so-called movement. Even though these conferences are about men meeting, challenging themselves and each other, learning, teaching, opening up, and imagining, in their essence they are about our full humanity.

Meade decided to reach out to men who do not usually have the privilege and funds to participate in such events—inner-city youth, as well as young people from suburban white communities. Costs are usually covered by donations, grants, and other assistance whenever it can be obtained.

Mosaic men's events deal with about 70 to 120 men at a time, building strong relationships, while opening doors to perceptions and sensitivities not otherwise experienced. Here the men confront their own demons and *daimons,* giants of the culture—racism and male supremacy—and the whirlpoollike pull of class, status, and narrow material interests.

Because of the brutal history of this land—as a society, and even as individuals, we have murdered, raped, plundered, lied, and exploited one another to achieve whatever place of exaltation and power we believe to be our destiny—those of us in Mosaic have dedicated our time and souls to reestablishing a cohesive and humane cultural stream and a new system of human interactions. We cannot go forward as a people until there is some degree of conscious reckoning with how we have pursued power, riches, and control in this country, and until a personal commitment to sacrifice and struggle has been exacted. We cannot dismiss the fact of our atrocious past. We cannot become complacent or satisfied with the mostly superficial remedies offered by the present culture.

Human slavery, the official theft of land and cultures, the domination and degradation of women, wars of conquest, and the corporate control of government and social relationships are all part of the "greatness" that this country may proclaim. Unless we understand the deeper implications of this, our past acts become the ghosts that continually steal from us the fulfillment of our best and dearest ideals.

Although this may have resonance for some, it more than likely conflicts with many of the views of the general American population. And so it has to be. While pulling together the threads of freedom, equality, justice, and democracy inherent in our history and culture, we also need to distance ourselves from the destructive and inhibiting factors that have made this country far from what it claims to be. There are many among us who sing in discordant voices, who don't mouth the same old songs of hypocritical self-interest or patriotic platitudes.

We are living in politically and spiritually confusing times. There are sweeping changes in the economy and in politics that are widening the gap between classes, genders, and generations. The Mosaic retreats and my work with Youth Struggling for Survival have allowed me "to glimpse new grounds of meaning where life can be renewed and purpose restored," as Meade has written.

Whatever we do, we have to see the process of restoration as a shared task. Regardless of our perceived differences in beliefs and values, we have a common future and this should inform how we can proceed, and how we can broaden the roots, mysteries, truths, memories, and stories of the past to guide us.

Parker J. Palmer, drawing on an American-rooted spirituality largely based on Christian precepts, makes an important distinction between the abundance we can share as a people and the presumption of scarcity that permeates almost every political and religious conception here.

"The quality of our active lives depends heavily on whether we assume a world of scarcity or a world of abundance," writes Palmer. "Do we inhabit a universe where the basic things that people need—from food and shelter to a sense of competence and of being loved—are ample in nature? Or is this a universe where such goods are in short supply, available only to those who have the power to beat everyone else to the store?"[1]

The politics of scarcity are evident in how people are treated in government offices or whether their garbage gets picked up or not. It's also behind major concerns like the stock market (many lose so that others can win), welfare reform, affirmative action, discrimination (including so-called reverse discrimination), immigrant rights and bilingual education, the struggle for workers' pay and conditions, and the existence of homeless men, women, and children in places where buildings are allowed to sit idle.

The politics of scarcity are right smack in the middle of the phenomenal growth of prisons in this country—where some people profit from the "prison industry" while others pay for their mistakes with their lives. Presently, most parolees are effectively convicted for "life," regardless of their sentences, when they are barred from jobs, educational opportunities, or social benefits, thus forcing them into prison.

"Given the sort of action that dominates our world, it is apparent that many of us, and our institutions, have chosen the scarcity assumption," argues Palmer. "How else can you explain such practices as grading on the curve, an educational device that treats A's and B's as if they were diamonds, while treating C's and D's as if we had warehouses full of them? How else can you explain the fact that competition (a way of allocating scarcity), rather than cooperation (a way of sharing abundance), is widely regarded as the only way to conduct our affairs, to make things happen? How else can you explain the fact that our country so fearfully clings to its habit of overconsuming the world's resources, as if letting other people have a fair share would mean national suicide? At every level of our lives the assumption of scarcity, not abundance, threatens to deform our attitudes and our actions."[2]

This assumption also fuels the strained relations between races, men and women, and those who have and those who don't. If we see the world as a finite pie, a metaphor used in the 1960s with the suggestion that African Americans and other oppressed peoples should "get theirs," then there are only so many sections to slice up, and damn those who didn't get their piece.

So when police say, "Once a gangbanger, always a gangbanger," they are assuming that young people have only a finite capacity for change. So, too, the teacher who pushes failure by claiming, "You're never going to amount to anything," as if only a few can succeed. Or the politician who says, "It's time to defend victims' rights," but they trample on the rights of others as if there were only so many rights to defend at any one time.

Racism is definitely a scarcity issue: Only the superior "race" can control, have most of the wealth, and own most of the arable land, even if race as a concept is scientifically and spiritually unfounded. The same can be said of class politics, male supremacy, and regionalism.

Of course by abundance we don't mean accumulation. It's not about quantity but quality. It's not just about the "material," although society should meet the basic physical needs of people so that they can adequately and thoroughly advance their ongoing spiritual, cultural, intellectual, and aesthetic development. It's in how we live and in how we relate, in what brings forth the most and best from people, from the earth, and from ourselves.

Abundance in this sense is how it exists in nature, like the abundance of creative capacity in each human being. You already know that as soon as you tap into this creativity, it can never be used up. Yes, creativity can be hindered, forgotten, dismissed and belittled—even for a lifetime. But it's always there.

Or the abundance in the land. Properly taken care of, the earth replenishes itself through its own processes of birth, growth, death, decay and new birth. It keeps yielding and providing. I recall once hearing about the Owens Valley in California. As a result of years of intrigue and outright theft, much of the water now being used by the Los Angeles area was siphoned away from this fertile valley until it became a wasteland. Go there now: Very little green exists. The ground is largely dry and cracked.

But there was a time when the native peoples lived, hunted, and grew food there, a time when the Owens Valley was alive with waterfalls, rivers, trees, bushes, plants, nuts, crops, and animals. The natives did not take more than they needed. They lived within nature's own cleansing and birthing cycles. When a land developer from L.A. saw this, he exclaimed, "What a waste! The Indians are not taking advantage of the vast wealth this land possesses." Soon after, the people were driven from the land, farmers came to exploit it, and then massive pipes were put into the hillsides to redirect its water to the dry L.A. basin.

In fact it wasn't the native people who wasted the land. It was the very ones who exclaimed in horror how "dumb" the natives were. Ultimately these people took the land beyond its own capacities to grow.

Nature does have its limits; yet if our approach to it is nurturing, balanced, and harmonious, then nature's built-in process will respond in kind. Seeing nature as our university, we can learn how to make economic and material needs plentiful through processes that keep people healthy and spiritually alive for generations to come.

The real poverty today is not being aware that abundance is everywhere; the real wealth is in knowing not only that this is possible but that it is the very nature of things. When you venture into the deepest oceans, enter a canopied forest, or walk among the greenery and color of acres of wild-flowers; when you see photos from space and see the mists of galaxies, or even look through a microscope at the tiniest organisms pulsing and multiplying; it's hard to reconcile the shallow and limiting concepts of scarcity with the bounty that is nature. Nature is ever-evolving, growing, present. Yes, things die, but only so that other things can live. This is nature's master plan—and it works, providing us with smells, sights, sounds, and textures that illustrate how ample, beautiful, and fervent the world actually is. For indigenous people, for those attuned to the generating forces of the universe, nature is the Great Mystery, the source of all life, of learning, and of the future.

One of Mosaic's teacher-elders, West African shaman Malidoma Somé, often makes a similar point when discussing the importance of recognizing the element of "earth" in our lives. Here's a statement used in the retreats to summarize the essence of this element (from the five-element cosmology of the Dagara people of Burkina Faso and Ghana):

> Earth is both the ground of origin and the destination; the point of stepping off and the place of arrival. In the earth realm each wanderer is firmly welcomed as a familiar body who has returned home to be recognized, touched, and remembered. Authentic identity requires struggles to find one's place on earth and in the community, one's sense of self and openings to the "other." When grounded with experience, earth energy keeps expanding the community to include others and "otherness." When in touch with earth, fragility finds strength, restlessness becomes rest, and the hollow wasteland of the self becomes full and abundant. Like the earth itself, those who receive abundance must give continually or their riches diminish, their resources disappear, and the wasteland returns.

Earth acknowledges everybody and everything, as Somé often points out. It accepts without prejudice or judgment any foot that tramples its soil, whether rich or poor, black or white, disabled or abled. It is where the dead are buried, and all that they did or did not do, the things they had accumulated, the rewards or debits, no longer carry great weight. It is where everyone is welcomed.

The earth reminds us seasonally of its immense generosity—the awakening of plants, flowers, and trees in spring; the fall harvests taken from ground prepared with foresight and hard work. Most ancient rituals were an affirmation of the renewal processes in nature; they were also our way of participating through conscious acts in keeping these processes on track and constant. But today we are acutely aware of the bounds imposed by our excesses, the consequences of turning away from such rituals and preparations—and of exploiting the land and people for the enrichment of a few.

With today's global warming patterns, periodic El Niño and La Niña effects, and shrinking rainforests, we seem to be paying for our lack of respect and connection to the earth. This is our true "original" sin, for which we are being punished daily as we become more conscious of the diminishing returns from earth's beneficence—and from our taking.

Besides the earth element, the Dagara recognize four other elements that make up the universe (and each person). These are fire, water, mineral, and nature. Fire stands for vision, passion, the ancestors and authority; water for reconciliation, healing, and the coolness that comes from heartfelt grief; mineral represents story, poetry, and memory—the stored knowledge of the world and its people; and nature, which includes the air, trees, and greenery, symbolizes change. Michael Meade points out, "In our culture, there is a lot of mobility, but little change; trees have little mobility, but a lot of change."

Each person also carries the elements as properties in their physical-spiritual being: fire in the belly, the burning visions that drive us to action; water in our sorrows, the healing tears, and in our blood; mineral in our bones, the home of ancestral memory; nature, consisting of the modulations of our breaths and our capacity for change, including the growth of our bodies and minds; and earth, our flesh, including the "womb," where new life gestates, where we are renewed.

Everything around us is essentially made up of the same basic elements.

Most peoples honored these elements and their connections, living through them and deriving mythologies, deities, and rituals that reflected an ongoing and conscious effort to remain integrated and aligned with the cosmos as they understood it.

Native Americans, according to their traditions, also emphasized our bonds to one another, to nature, and to the universe. *O mitakuye oyasin!* say the Lakota. *To all my relations!*

"All species keep a genetic memory that is stored in the cells of our body," writes Tlakaelel, a Mexika/Tolteka elder from central Mexico and a spiritual leader of the Mexicayotl (Mexican Red Road) indigenous movement. "The species is interconnected and shares a common consciousness."[3]

The sweat lodge ceremony, the oldest ritual known to exist on the continent, is a purification ceremony that embodies the elements that many tribes considered essential to life. Fire is used to heat up the stones, which are considered grandfathers and grandmothers, the ancestors. The red-hot stones tell their stories, their memories, when water is poured over them. Water is the healing source, the cooling agent, of peace and tempering. Air is in the steam, carrying the prayers of the participants to the Great Spirit. The lodge, made of willow saplings or packed dirt, represents earth, the mother womb, and our rebirth.

Running through all this is the generating principle of all movement and life—the unity and strife of opposites, represented as the "complementary pairs," as Diné (Navajo) Roadman Anthony Lee calls it, of Female and Male energies. Among the Mexika this is evoked in the Nahuatl exclamation, *Ométeotl,* which translates as "Two Energy," the male and female—light and dark, up and down, the conflict and complement of every essential relationship—in all things.

Why do people participate in these ceremonies? Among other reasons, it is because they want to remember that human beings are *not* dominant over everything else. Such forgetting is the most disgraceful thing we can do. Unlike animals, our brains have the capacity to change or destroy the very environment that bore us. The rituals and myths exist to remind us that we are responsible to and for one another, as well as to the whole; that we all suffer whenever any of us suffers; that we rejoice when any of us triumphs; that community and individuals are one, part of the greater "community" of living energies that inform and form us during our short time in this world.

The difference is that for humans this is a mostly conscious thing, whereas for animals, microbes, and other living organisms it's instinctual. Thus we have to be taught, which accounts for the relatively long time our young are incubated in family, schools, and community.

Christianity has lessons about this, too. Parker Palmer talks about abundance and scarcity using the New Testament story of the Miracle of the

Loaves and Fishes, which recounts how Jesus fed five thousand people with five loaves of bread and two fishes. "Hunger and food, both literal and metaphoric sorts, are the dominant images in this story," writes Palmer. "I want to translate these images into the generic terms of scarcity and abundance. The crowd that seeks a teacher does so because it finds truth scarce; Jesus teaches to reveal truth's abundance. The disciples, asked to feed the crowd, are sure that food is scarce; Jesus performs a 'miracle' to reveal how abundant food is even when there is none in sight. In this story, as throughout his active life, Jesus wanted to help people penetrate the illusion of scarcity and act out of the reality of abundance."[4]

Some people may consider these concepts weird or alien. The concepts are infinitely older, however, than the five hundred years of capitalist economic development in the world—the single greatest deformer of values, relationships, and the earth itself—which we have almost totally succumbed to today. Capitalism is a *system of scarcity* that controls the distribution of goods and services, and manipulates the conditions for demand to increase profit. While we consider our modern society "civilized," it has spawned its own defining statements to govern these dealings and interests—"Dog eat dog," "Only the strong survive," and "Every man for himself." These concepts exist not only in the corporate world and in international politics, they're pervasive in sports, entertainment, and the arts. They are also very much at play among gangs and illicit enterprises. The irony is that the "primitive" way is the way of abundance.

It's time to reassert what human beings have known since time immemorial: If we don't take care of one another, we can't reap the abundance inherent in everyone. If we don't take care of the earth, it will not take care of us. Look around you. We continue to pay a tremendous price for not meeting our responsibilities.

In the year 2000 a number of Mosaic Foundation's teachers and staff met to expand the work we've been doing with youth and elders in the men's retreats, in our national and international talks and workshops, and with the community ritual events that have involved women and men. The Foundation's vision to bring together the broken pieces of the culture needed some attainable strategies, bold steps, and real champions at every level of activity. We reasserted that youth are key to this vision.

To help centralize their role in community, Mosaic established what Michael Meade called Voices of Youth, a temporary means for creative expression. This mobile vessel would go outward, working with various organizations and individuals. We also brought in another piece called Voices of Community, which brings mentors and elders into a creative process to shape and sustain mentoring as vital and necessary for our youth.

The goal is "to sow seeds of authentic community" in place of the fragmented and alienated "communities" we see today. Our resources are the rich and powerful stories, myths, songs, poems, plays, and rituals that we've inherited from all our ancestors, which, ultimately, are the same for everyone.

Our purpose is to allow youth to express their emotions, experiences, ideas and voices—with all their pains and doubts, as well as their nobility—so that they can be clearly heard and felt, taken in, and transformed through a haven of words and "harmonic resonance."[5] By this means, community finds its direction, its balance, its umbilical chord to the sustaining power of nature and the source spring of new life.

"Although current cultural problems are pressing and often tragic, the first step on this journey is a step back, away from the present; back to the ground of traditional societies and tribal imaginations," wrote Michael Meade in a brochure for a Mosaic event, Seeds of Change, held in October 1998 in Leaf River, Illinois. "The interest in 'old ways' and tribal ideas is not an escape from the present or an idealization of the past. Rather, it is an attempt to retouch radical roots that can nourish new ideas and inspire change where obstacles appear insurmountable and despair appears inevitable."

Chapter 16

Dying for Something to Live

First the earth was formed, the mountains and the valleys; the currents of water were divided, the rivulets were running freely between the hills, and the water was separated when the high mountains appeared. Thus was the earth created, when it was formed by the Heart of Heaven and the Heart of Earth, as they are called who first made it fruitful, when the sky was in suspense, and the earth was submerged in the water. So it was that they made perfect the work, when they did it after thinking and meditating upon it.

—The Popul Vuh

A group of teenagers gathered noisily outside the old brick-walled building of the community center on the edge of the Pilsen barrio. A younger group, perhaps seven to twelve, stood outside; a few were on what I call "ghetto bikes," the small one-speed bicycles that many kids here ride to get around and sometimes use in driveby shootings.

In a large room inside the center, chairs were arranged into several rows of widening arcs facing the front of the room. Slowly the teenagers entered and sat down. Some squirmed in their seats. Two younger guys made faces at each other and traded insults. A few stood outside the door, eyeing the clock, as if scheming about ways to sneak out of the place.

The kids chuckled and chortled, snickered and sneered.

I was one of three speakers. The center staff wanted the presenters to talk about violence and how these kids, many of whom were in gangs, could be persuaded to do something constructive with their lives. One speaker was a youth worker in an uptown agency; the other a mother who had lost a seventeen-year-old son in a gang shooting.

After the room filled, Rocío, a YSS member who also worked at the center, introduced us. Rocío was one of the leaders whose passion it was to do youth work; when she finished college, she became a well-known coordinator of youth programs in Chicago. She was self-driven and quite capable of whatever she put her mind to.

The first to speak was the mother, who looked to be in her late thirties. She was a handsome woman of Mexican descent who spoke clear English. She appeared to have been perhaps a generation or two removed from the old country. Her talk was straightforward—no flowery words, no flourishes—but there was little joy in her eyes or in her voice. I understood why. There is perhaps no greater sorrow than the one that comes from losing a child, especially for a mother.

Before she talked, she took a beautiful vase imprinted with flowers from a large bag and placed it on a table in front of her. She said a few words and then directed our attention to the vase.

"This is my son," the woman stated as she placed her hand on the vase. "These are his ashes. I carry him now wherever I go. Although he's been gone for more than a year, I won't ever forget him, nor how he died. I wanted you to see this. I wanted you to know what suffering these deaths bring to mothers like me. My son will never come back. He's gone from this world. What keeps me going is the knowledge he is with God. His ashes now are all I have of him on earth."

There wasn't a sound from the group. She didn't need a lot of words to say what she felt. The vase, her slightly trembling hands on top of it, the matter-of-fact tone, said plenty. With this, she cut through whatever abstractions and theories, platitudes and phoniness may have crept into the room. All kidding and playing stopped. She arrested the restless. This mother apparently went from community center to community center, school to school, and church to church to speak against violence, her son's remains in tow.

Something sacrificial—from the original Latin adjective of sacer: "dedicated or consecrated to a divinity, holy"—in the sense of a sacred giving, was evident here. I don't know anybody else who would do what this woman did. I can't say if this was the most appropriate thing. People may want more "closure" from her, for her to "get over it," as if they can't be bothered with someone's pain beyond the initial mourning period. Perhaps manipulation can be detected, although I didn't sense any. She had turned this tragedy into something that could give back life.

This made me think about something. What if behind all our talks, proceedings, and gatherings, stood an invisible Congress of the Dead, as Malidoma Somé once vividly described it, of the children who were taken away, killed by bullets, hunger, suicide, neglect; of the aborted and the forgotten. What if they met in an otherworldly legislative session, determining outcomes, suggesting laws, demanding real sacrifices lest more of them are elected to serve. This mother had, in effect, brought one of the legislators to that meeting, demanding a certain kind of attention, not to be feared, but to be acknowledged.

The community needs to take risks—the proper risks—to effectively engage and bring back our youth and to reinvigorate the culture, but few are willing to take them. Liability laws, as well as zero-tolerance policies, impede a fuller approach in working with children and youth, particularly from community centers, schools, and other public and private institutions. We need to accept and work with the inherent dangers in establishing a viable and coherent community of children, youth, mentors, and elders. There is no way around this. I once heard my friend Orland Bishop say, "We have to access something within ourselves that has a regenerative capacity. Not what we can get from each other, but what we can give. Nurturing is latent. It grows by giving. From adults to the young, this nurturing has to be strong enough to pass through a psychic bridge. There is a powerful relationship of sacrifice to the nurturing of youth."

Everyone accepts that there are dangers involved in the birthing of a child. Besides the great love and joyful energy in birth, it can also be violent, with pain, screams, and blood. It has to be this way. This is true of all great combustions and ignitions, from the Big Bang to a car engine. So, too, when young people are being "born" into their lives, entering the first stages of adulthood and their self-being. But in this case, we'd rather avoid the mess. Yet when we don't do the proper sacrifices as an embracing community, young people tend to sacrifice themselves. For any sacrifice to be regenerative, the appropriate parties have to let the right thing die for the right thing to live.

The issue is not who's stronger, the adult or the child, but who's more willing to surrender to the vitality of these relationships.

So when a police officer stops a young man on the street corner, or the teacher points to the raised hand of the student, or the parent enters a child's room to complain about the noise levels, they've entered into a relationship with that person. If they're not conscious of this, of the responsibilities such relationships require, they may be contributing to some damage.

When those at the fringes of society—the so-called underclass—are empowered, educated, radicalized and liberated, all of society will advance. With all their pressing problems—and they are true problems; you can't romanticize the "poor and downtrodden"—these particular communities carry the seeds of lasting justice and peace, "the seeds of change," precisely because they are the ones directly confronting the official injustices and violence. Ultimately all of society will have to be brought into the fray. When the peripheries of society are carrying most of the emotions and the imagination, this is really a call not for abandoning a center but for a *recentering*. And it is from these very places that healing can occur.

As novelist Richard Stern writes, "Every feeling that you have, every negative feeling, is in a way precious. It is your building material, it's your stone, it's something you use to build your work. I would say the conversion of the negative is very important.... Don't duck pain. It's precious, it's your gold mine, it's the gold in your mine."[1]

Betrayal and suffering are the stuff of life, of drama, and of all good stories. They are also the openings where greater knowledge, deeper grace, and a fuller person can evolve—where wounds are the wombs of our new birth. In fact some of the most effective and lasting changes have been initiated by persons like Mahatma Gandhi, Martin Luther King, Jr., Malcolm X, Cesar Chavez, Nelson Mandela, and Pedro Albizu Campos, who recognize not only the faults of a historically evolved system but also of their own.

Robert Bly writes, "If colonial administrators begin by attacking the vertical thought of the tribe they have conquered, and dismantling the elder system, they end up dismantling everything in sight. That's where we are. We are the first culture in history that has 'colonized' itself. The inner dome of heaven has fallen. As for the gods, they are... in the garbage. To say we have no center that we love is the same thing as saying that we have colonized ourselves. What we need to study, then, is how a colonized culture heals itself."[2]

There is nothing heroic in denying the past, but there's nothing heroic in getting stuck there either. The paradigms of pathology and dysfunction can be paralyzing, becoming hitching posts where we conveniently tie up all our arguments and solutions. To heal we have to go through the wounds and not get trapped in old hatreds, prejudices, excuses, and abuses. We have to get beyond them, past the stalemates and blocked passages.

Some adults cringe when young people talk about the injustices and blame "the system," as if they were only trying to render themselves powerless to handle the personal end of a problem. This may be true for some but not for all. Some are developing a social consciousness necessary for them to see their place in the world and, properly guided, to gain a vision integral to entering another *kind* of world.

Perhaps, instead of accusing these youth of making "excuses" for their behavior, we should clarify how racism, poverty, rotten schools, brutal police, and abusive parents have shaped us—and how, in knowing this, we may shape them. We need, as Malidoma Somé makes clear, "to become the page on which the language of healing is written."

Each one of us must take personal responsibility and own up to our acts, especially those that have been harmful to the community and that threaten the compact whereby we treat one another as we would want to be treated ourselves. But responsibility also means to respond to and nurture each of our arts, each of our gifts—to not let anything take us off our trajectories. The true goal is to follow the threads of our lives out of the labyrinth. The ground of one's own suffering is also the ground of one's most meaningful expression. So while the worst thing that can happen is *not* to find your gift, the second worst thing is to find it. "Choose your troubles," says Meade. "A gift is trouble, but the right kind of trouble—a most elegant suffering."

First we must struggle for personal change as part and parcel of social change. We must take personal responsibility for our environment. When someone says "I'm only taking care of Number One," that person is missing a vital part of the collective and unitary aspect of being human. Yes, take care of number one—heal thyself—but for the purpose of healing one's world. The individual and the collective should be like gears working properly to keep the whole machinery of community going. By engaging this process, we begin to overcome the environmental traumas and barriers that have a hold on our psyches and our decisions. If someone is truly concerned about healing or eradicating the vicious patterns and inequities, he or she should get organized, get active, and take the proper steps to get stronger, more knowledgeable, more skillful, and more spiritually and psychologically balanced.

For many of the youth I've worked with, being clear about the role of the system in their lives and their capacity to contribute to change in that system is a major part in helping them to become the strong, caring, and transcendent people we claim we want.

It would be better if we listened to them rather than prevented them from attaining this level of awareness.

Throw yourself like seed as you walk, and into your own field,
don't turn your face for that would be to turn it to death,
and do not let the past weigh down your motion.

Leave what's alive in the furrow, what's dead in yourself,
for life does not move in the same way as a group of clouds;
from your work you will be able one day to gather yourself.

—Miguel de Unamuno[3]

Chapter 17

Premises and Principles

Moderation in temper is always a virtue, but moderation in principle is always a vice.

—Thomas Paine

In the fall of 1997 a dozen leading national youth-oriented organizations met in Washington, D.C. to discuss what is known in the field as "best practices." The host, the Center for Youth Development and Policy Research, had been inviting YSS to a few of the these events over the years, asking us to summarize what we have learned and where we need to go. It was an honor to be with courageous and hardworking people in the various foundations, programs, schools, and not-for-profits attempting to deal on a daily basis with youth and the violence surrounding them. They don't get much credit in the media or in politics, but they are truly frontline fighters.

When it came to talking about the basic premises or principles under which we worked, the discussion got more animated. We all had different ideas and approaches (mostly variations on the same things) on how to work with youth. What I wanted to know was what primary principles we could agree to that would guide and direct our efforts. This was not an easy thing to decide on, but attempting to do so proved how invaluable it was to try.

One problem is that we live in a vast country with many regional and local concerns. Despite the fact that we are all dealing with many of the same problems, it is hard to break from parochial ways of working with youth. The goal was not to undermine any organization's particular approach, but to find common ties to which we could all agree and basic principles by which we could all abide, despite our local differences. It was a struggle, but in the end, after a few days of breakout groups, arguments, and frustrations, we formulated some of these principles. They included the following:

- Don't give up on youth.
- The survival of each depends on the survival of all.
- To whom much is given much is expected.
- No decisions will be made without those affected being part of the decision-making process.

These were elemental premises we could stand on. Such wisdom, of course, can be found in all religions and spiritual paths. These are the universal and elemental ideas that touch all humanity. They can guide our day-by-day exchanges and decisions when we are confronted by the more immediate and local ideas that only apply to a particular place or period of time (and often in detrimental ways, such as "Kill or be killed").

"Every adult has a responsibility to nurture, guide, and support young people as though they are our own," stated a 1998 paper from the gathering called "Core Beliefs and Values," by the Center for Youth Development and Policy Research. "This commitment insures we will never give up on them, lest we give up on our hopes and dreams. We accept them for who they are, not what we want them to become."

Having primary beliefs and values doesn't mean we give up thinking, evaluating, and adjusting. Problems arise when a few people try to impose their values on others as absolutes, largely removed from context and imagination in any values-teaching and values-sustaining work with youth.

Suffice it to say we don't do enough in establishing basic principles among the agencies, not-for-profits, and organizations working in the most marginal communities. If corporations, unions, and major religions can come together and work out pacts with each other, we should do the same in our work with the most troubled young people. Keeping the principles and premises guiding our work in front of us at all times helps contain the overblown egos, narrow viewpoints, petty politics, and greed that constantly creep into this work. Without clarity and vigilance, some of the stronger personalities, who may not necessarily be aligned with these principles, can run roughshod over the important relationships so painstakingly developed by any institution or church. Remember, the principles of agreement, our covenant as Christians often say, have to be the leading aspects in our work and associations.

On occasion I've tried to establish working principles with school administrators, teachers, law enforcement officials, parents, clergy, and other adults. Once, at a meeting of principals and teachers of a large California school district, I asked them to ponder this concept: *Every child has value and every child can learn.* Simple enough, but you would be surprised how many of those officials and experts did not really agree with this. If you were to pursue the issue long enough, you could practically divide a room as if you had asked where people stood on O.J.'s guilt or innocence.

While at first most teachers and administrators may seem to have no problem with such a statement, digging deeper into the issue will tend to draw out other factors that may mediate or subvert a clear-cut position. The "what ifs" will inevitably lead to more modified versions. This is fine. This is dialogue. But ultimately we go through this process so that we can come back to the original concept in a more aware, determined, and engaged manner—to make it *real*, as some young people like to say.

These premises and principles, for the most part, have been what has guided us in YSS since its inception. The basic concept of the group is *youth and adults working together for the benefit of youth.* The key is proper, respectful, and integral relationships, which young people and adults can struggle over as the cornerstone for community building and accountability. Because this is mostly a voluntary organization, any agreements between its members are vital and need to be continually affirmed. It's these agreements, built on trust, that keep us together. This is how people establish common aims around common interests.

One of our concerns was that many young people in our fairly poor and often condemned communities were learning about life—sex, getting initiated, dealing with work, responding to anger or affronts—from other young people. They simply did not have enough adults to show them the way. The few adults around them were often immature and quite abusive. And as we have often seen, children cannot adequately teach children. They will only convey the same low-level knowledge and experience they have accumulated—or the various misconceptions that tend to swirl around them.

But what can we expect from them when the adults who should interact with children and youth on a basis of true caring and lasting participation just don't have the time or inclination—or are too afraid—to do so? How many people simply walk away from a group of young people standing on a corner with nothing to do?

YSS actively relies on the principles agreed to during the Center for Youth Development and Policy Research gathering. In addition there are several more, fashioned from the twenty-five years of experiences of some of the individual adults in YSS as well as the expertise of the youth themselves.[1]

• The relationship between youth and adults must be based on mutual respect. On the part of adults, this requires patience, listening, and allowing youth to become their own persons. For youth, this means opening up to the acquired wisdom, skills, and knowledge possessed by adults. Presently too many adults are inconsequential to the lives of young people.

• Mentoring is important, but what we often miss in the equation is how youth seek and determine their own mentors. If adults with wisdom and craft knowledge are not available, these youth will usually seek mentors from among those people already in their lives, often the gang leaders and drug dealers they see everyday.

• An adult mentor has to teach something, and it has to be specific. This may include aspects of life—how to act, how to respond to various crises, how to be firm and flexible as needed, how to address anger and other emotions. It's about accepting and learning from mistakes as well as triumphs. But we also end up teaching particular things, depending on what an adult's expertise may be. In YSS we try to have a diverse group of adults with various skills and experiences so that the various interests of the youth can be somewhat matched. Youths usually find teachers who have the qualities and skills they most admire in themselves. They want to go where their mentors have already gone. It's the *love* of the same thing that unites them. For example I have mentored many young men and women around language expression, particularly poetry. They were usually people who admired the quality of turning complicated and difficult feelings, ideas, and experience into powerful, engaging, and condensed language. It was evident they were also close to the power of poetry within themselves. The concept was to go from passions to practice. The mentor then "feeds" the initiate into the world and into a new way of life.

• We've also incorporated a concept called "the two-legged walk of the mentor"—walking with one leg in the present and one in the future. One leg in mud, one on solid, clean ground. One leg in dreams, one on earth. One in the fire, one in water. One leg in knowledge, one leg in ignorance. One leg in light, one in darkness. The point is to carry both sides of a contradiction with you. If opposites struggling, intermingling, and mutually interacting is the motor of all life, then one also has to "walk" in this way. This methodology may also serve to help youth in their own traction.

• Although young people run the meetings and determine their activities, the adults in YSS are quite active too. Having passive adults around active youth does not work. However, to be an active adult does not mean over-powering the youth, making decisions without their consent, or taking over meetings. Too many adults in youth programs end up doing adult pro-gramming "for youth." I've been to sessions where adults are literally run-ning everything, determining direction, and—even when this is not so obvious—using intrigue and deception to maintain their control. Keeping the proper balance is hard, but it is something we have learned in YSS, with many errors under our collective belt.

Having adults working together with young people requires a certain partnership that has to be constantly and positively reinforced. The part-nership is not "We adults have the power and authority over you, even if we pretend we don't." It's more like, we adults have been through something, have walked a certain path, have learned something about this process, and have acquired some skills that young people may need while discovering their own trajectories. Remember, "Show us the ropes, we'll do the rest." This is a good summary of what I'm talking about.

The adults are active in certain key ways with young people: (a) listen-ing (active listening is an art—but it has to be sincere and engaged); (b) pro-viding guidance and direction when needed; (c) teaching, including organizational skills; (d) helping young people with their needs, which has to include emotional support when called for; and (e) providing resources, treatment, job prospects, court advocacy (where adults hold sway over any young person), while including their parents (who are often in great need of the same things).

The young person can then feel empowered to achieve his or her own goals.

With patience and persistence, some of the skills the young people have learned in YSS include the following:

• How to organize meetings and activities—retreats, conferences, com-mittees, and other gatherings.
• How to start up an organizing newsletter, as well as developing other communication tools—speaking, talking to the media, writing grants.
• How to link with others in the community, to network and establish lasting ties—through dialogues with parents, speaking in schools, and par-ticipating in community-based networks.
• How to understand the political economy of the country, city, and com-

munity (the environment in which they are working) in an ongoing, relevant, and vibrant manner, using tools such as discussion circles, but also having experts and community leaders periodically address their concerns.

• How to use cultural expression, including art, for paintings, mask making, skits, and performance poetry, as well as T-shirt designs, brochures, and banners.

• How to defend oneself by knowing the law and develop coping skills in dealings with police, teachers, other youth, and parents. It's important to have legal advice when needed and to have ties with public defenders, probation officers, police, and juvenile court officials. Most young people are capable of knowing the law, their rights and their responsibilities, but most are kept ignorant of them and end up suffering needlessly for it.

• How to address traditional, indigenous, and spiritual concerns, arming young people to do so for the rest of their lives. Young people are on a spiritual quest; it is part of their entering a transcendent stage in their lives. We introduce many indigenous traditions because they relate best to the abundance of the earth and our place in it. These traditions also link directly to *this* land, which has a history of tens of thousands of years during which it was peopled—and millions of years before that when it was formed.

Our approach in YSS is *holistic,* an often-used word that may have lost some of its vitality over the years yet for us continues to be of grave importance. The whole of a child, the whole of an adult, the whole of the relationships, and interactions with the environment—all open and closed systems have to be taken into account.

This includes, but is not limited to, the following fundamental areas pertaining to young people: (a) their psychological development (with proper counseling for the most traumatized); (b) their political clarity and empowerment; (c) their economic knowledge (including how to start a business and/or not-for profit enterprise); (d) their social skills (the confidence to voice concerns in authoritative terms, to communicate effectively at any level); (e) their healthy physical development, including organized sports; and (f) their spiritual growth (including culture and the arts, but also the need to be spiritually grounded).

In many ways groups like YSS can be a smeltery where character is forged in the crucible of study, interactions, and personal and social struggle. With proper tempering, corrupted and hurt scraps of souls come out as burnished gold. Moreover, the more scrappy they were before, the more golden they can eventually become.

Utilizing various forms of talk, the arts, storytelling, and presence, YSS works with youth and adults to address the crucial issues and conflicts of their lives. We have "conflict sessions" or talking circles in a safe space where the thoughts and feelings of the participants can be expressed, acknowledged, and respected. Everything said is strictly confidential to protect the participants but also to ensure greater honesty.

By opening with poems, stories, and drumming, our retreats establish a ritual space where these issues can be dealt with without harm, violence, or impasse. We introduce these in a way that heals, deepens thought, pushes around ideas, and solidifies personal and community meaning, with a consciousness of the universal and elemental between us.

The purpose is to have each young person feel and truly become indispensable to his or her world.

Chapter 18
"What You Be About?"

Every word is a doubt,
Every silence is another doubt.
Nevertheless
The intertwining of both
Allows us to breath.

—Roberto Juarroz

Steven Guerra, a former gang member and convict, who has run many violence prevention programs for youth, and is a former director of the Jane Addams Center/Hull House in Chicago, tells how young people, when confronted by each other, ask a question that embodies the key issues they face in their lives, "What you be about?"

In that greeting they want to know, *Where have you been? Where are you now?* and *Where are you going?* These concerns are the same ones that any effective youth program or organization should address. As an example, YSS has tried to help young people begin to know their own personal histories, "where they've been," by exposing them to their own cultural roots, as well as teaching them some of the more recent history that often has not been adequately taught.

They are also exposed to the political and social realities that face them, and that might confuse and perhaps disarm them, thus keeping them from taking affirmative steps in their lives. With this understanding, they can begin to deal with their own callings to greatness, something that all young people carry but don't always recognize.

In my writing workshops I sometimes work with youth who have no desire to write or even have the basic skills to do so. I ask them to write the first things that come to mind based on three scenarios. The scenarios change, but the three basic ones are: (1) You are in a forest. In front of you is a path. Tell me about the forest. What does it look like? How do you feel? Where is the path going, if anywhere? (2) You come across a house. Tell me about the house. What does it feel and smell like? Is there anybody else in it? Who and why? (3) You come across the most important person in your life. This could be someone you love or hate. Tell me about this person and why you've included him or her.

I give them from five to fifteen minutes to put down their thoughts. Afterward they are invited to share what they wrote.[1]

Each scenario stands for something. The path in the forest represents where you feel you are going, or not going, as the case may be. If the forest is thick and formidable, the path may be lost or unreachable. If the path is clear and accessible, it often indicates a strong sense of direction.

The house represents where a person may be at the moment. If the house is old and creaky, this is generally how you feel about your present situation. If the house is bright and colorful, full of rooms (possibilities in life) and airy, then you are probably in a good place. If it's solid, made of stone and hard materials, you may feel solid inside.

The part about the most important person in one's life has to do with relationships. Most people write about their mothers or other family members. Mostly there's a positive tone. Some people may get deep and bring in abusers or enemies. Or friends and lovers. A few bring in comic book, movie, or TV characters such as Bart Simpson (this says a lot about their relationships).

These are not thorough psychological tests but an informal way to discuss the concerns and feelings of the participants. Keep in mind that these scenarios are heavily influenced by moods, recent events, even what they ate that morning. By sharing their thoughts through images, people open up to themselves and others in ways they would not have done if we just asked them directly, "Where are you going?" We try to do a cursory analysis of what they wrote so that the participants can see how the description, stories, and people in their lives have deeper meanings than what is usually understood about them.

The responses are always fantastic, whether they are students in elite schools or incarcerated juveniles. Sometimes they weave each scenario into a continuous story. Mostly they go from one scene to another without any segues.

Once I did a series of poetry workshops in a predominantly Mexican high school in Chicago. Security personnel with walkie-talkies roamed the school, often yelling at the kids for lingering or not showing them the proper ID (they had to have them hanging from their necks). At one point I heard one security person exclaim to a student, "An earring! Go to the office. You know we don't allow earrings in here."

There I conducted a writing workshop for a particularly unruly class of alleged troublemakers. The assigned teacher would take roll call, then leave the students to their own devices. When I arrived, papers were flying about, students were away from their desks, and there were loud voices and laughter in all directions.

When I finally got everyone to sit down—by engaging each individual, not just the whole class—I had them do the writing exercises I just described. They goofed around a lot, but I finally got each student to read his or her paper. The first three students played it off. Then I called on the most disruptive kid in the class. He toughened up and read his scenarios. As he read, however, he got more serious. Some of the other students strained to listen over the noise from the rest of the room. When the student reached the last scenario, he mentioned that the most important person in his life was his grandmother. It turned out, however, that his grandmother had recently died.

As this young man talked about his grandmother, he began to break down emotionally, much to our surprise. Yet, without embarrassment he continued to read. By this time the whole room had become quiet. Tears flowed down the faces of a couple of girls. This young man's courage and honesty transformed that classroom. Even the teacher couldn't believe her eyes. After he sat down and we discussed his paper, others became more serious and participated in the exercise with greater intention.

When I left the classroom, the teacher told others in her department about the "miracle" that had occurred there. It may have been a miracle, but it doesn't require intangible means to achieve it. It was about establishing a place of trust, dignity, and careful attention. Call it a miracle if you want, but it's one that can happen any day in any school with any student in America. And when the voices of troubled youth are released, when they are truly heard and honored, I believe a path out of whatever trouble they may be in clears up inside them.

The rate of suicide is extremely high among the young, and, for the most part, young people who are on the verge of committing that desperate act are usually unable to adequately and thoroughly answer those three fundamental questions for themselves: Where have you been? Where are you now?

Where are you going? I recall traveling down a desolate road with a young Navajo girl and her teacher from Kayenta in the northeast section of Arizona. The teacher had told me how suicidal this girl had been recently—the Diné, like other American Indians, have especially high suicide rates. As we talked, the girl pulled out some poetry and began to read. The words were harsh—images of death and despair. But in that reading, she connected with two people in a car who silently prayed that this girl would never end her beautiful, poetic life. She seemed to find her voice, and, I believe, a path. She is now a college student in another state.

Unfortunately, at the point when most people decide to commit suicide, doors appear to close, and good people and good answers begin to disappear. A. Alvarez has noted, "[the suicidal person] enters a shut-off, impregnable but wholly convincing world where every detail fits and each incident reinforces his decision. An argument with a stranger in a bar, an expected letter which doesn't arrive, the wrong voice on the telephone, the wrong knock at the door, even a change in the weather—all seemed charged with special meaning; they all contribute. The world of suicide is superstitious, full of omens."[2]

The "madness" envelopes them. These psychic malfunctions are manifested as breaks all around them. The mind is fractured, as is most everything. Gang youth, too, find so much to propel them toward the life they are enmeshed in. They find signs to support their own needs in this regard. They exaggerate or idealize their relationships ("My homies will never let me down"), and they commit themselves in ways that appear unreasonable and beyond the call of the situation ("I will kill or die for my nation"), although this can be quite rational when the process is understood.

Simon Wiesenthal, a former concentration camp internee during the Nazi occupation of Europe, says something similar about the way the camp inmates viewed everything around them: "At that time we were ready to see symbols in everything. It was a time rife for mysticism and superstition. Often my fellow prisoners in camp told ghost stories. Everything for us was unreal and insubstantial: the earth was peopled with mystical shapes; God was on leave, and in His absence others had taken over, to give us signs and hints.... We often clung to completely nonsensical interpretations if only they gave us a ray of hope for better times."[3]

Over the years I've been to a number of funerals of gang members. One of the things that strikes me about these funerals is how each gang member, although in great sorrow, also "finds" himself through each death. Gangs carry out certain rituals: placing gang memorabilia such as bandannas, gold chains with gang symbols, and photos into a casket; pouring beer on the ground; or shooting off rounds from a firearm. This behavior is far more normal than one may realize.

Smokey, eighteen, was ambushed and killed by his enemies while sitting in a car in the parking lot of a hamburger stand. At the funeral, after the priest had had his say, Smokey's homies kneeled down around the wooden casket draped with the gang colors, and put their hands on it in the shape of the sign of their gang. Then they recited a prayer some gang member had composed. This helped to unite them in their grief and to affirm them in their gang. Unfortunately, this camaraderie appears to have occured at the expense of their dead homie. Each death brought them closer together. It's evident the deaths are an important, albeit mostly unstated, reason for the group. A new life for the gang seemed to be born with every new death. This is when gang members move from just being friends you hang out with and love to a death cult. They have mythologized the deaths around them, including their own "deaths" as marginalized members of the community. It's important to understand that the police, many political and religious groups, and soldiers in wartime do similar things; every "martyr" galvanizes the group.

One result of this is the idea among some youth that they, too, want to die so that they can have such a funeral, such attention, such love. What they should receive constantly while alive they now seek in their deaths.

In Chicago the gang symbols often serve to express for the members an exalted sense of themselves for the members—crowns, stars, Playboy Bunnies, hearts, tridents. Gang names represent courage, strength, and power—disciples, kings, lords, saints, cobras, eagles, and dragons. They usually combine these with words indicating madness—*insane* or *maniac*—or strength—*almighty*. They are emboldened by this terminology, but also use it because they are out of kilter with a society that has relegated them to a far less exalted place.

In Los Angeles the Chicano gangs have been primarily structured around neighborhoods or *barrios*. The major Chicano gangs in L.A. have taken form for the purpose of protecting and raising up their neighborhoods (although this function has changed somewhat as barrio gangs have expanded to larger areas). They have also added symbols and words—such as *c/s* (*con safos*, meaning "you can't mess with this"); *rifa* ("to rule"); and *por/vida* ("for life")—to demonstrate they are invincible, immortal, and powerful. In reality they are quite mortal; their gang involvement usually lasts for a short period, and of course they are quite powerless in the face of true political and economic control in the larger society.

The African-American sets in Los Angeles were also mostly neighborhood- and street-based: "Rolling 60s," for the numbered 60 streets in South Central L.A.; "Eight-Tray" for Eighty-third Street; or "Pirus" for Piru Street in Compton. Exceptions always exist, but you get a sense the gangs were trying to find a special place for themselves, either as an ideal state or within the perimeters of their immediate community.

As gangs in Chicago and L.A. became more intertwined with death and criminal activity, they began to see themselves as dark forces, with death being integral to their aims and the sacrifice of any member the life blood of their existence. Some gangs in Chicago began to add *Darkside* or *Twilight Zone* to their names to make the gang identity more mysterious and to create a certain aura of fear. Their enemies, of course, would respond by belittling them.

A few gang members have told me how they risked getting shot or dying so that they would go out in a "blaze of glory." (It's important to note here that most gang youth join to be part of something and are not as willing to sacrifice themselves as are some of the more troubled participants.) They looked forward to taking this risk, and were even willing to end it all as long as they got a reputation for craziness and putting themselves into the mouth of destruction. Although the other aspects of gang life are still important—family, belonging, and protection—there is a growing sense that the worth of one's life is dependent on a significant closeness to the gang. Being able to kill or die for the gang appears to be the only viable way of sealing that closeness.

These choices may actually be that of the spirit *wanting* to live, not the other way around. Here the spirit may feel trapped by the dispirited circumstances. When hopelessness seems overwhelming, how can one interact positively or impact on those circumstances? Suicide or a self-created "heroic" death may be the result. There's a kind of internal pressure for the body to die so that the spirit can go on. This is a powerful pull indeed.

The symbols end up becoming the vehicles through which a person might perceive himself or herself in a deeply meaningful drama. It's apparent that for present-day gangs (this is not just exclusive to urban youth; a similar process can be witnessed among so-called Satanist groups, Goths, or neo-Nazi gangs), much of this exists and expands because such symbols, meanings, and intensities are not found or addressed anywhere else. But they may also overwhelm the gang member, so that actual paranoia and other psychological states take over. In the end that person lives or dies for what is, in effect, quite meaningless in the overall scheme of things.

Needless to say, even those young men and women who do not go to these extremes fall prey to inadequacies. Having money, the coolest clothes, the best cars, the best schools—these things do not always translate into having a solid, full, and vital life. Dispirited circumstances often come in lavish surroundings—where all needs are met except those most internal. The following is a poem, source unknown, given to me by Anne Schultz, a teacher of teachers, that illustrates what can happen to so-called normal people. It's called "About School."

> *He always wanted to explain things,*
> *but no one cared.*
> *So he drew.*
> *Sometimes he would just draw*
> *and it wasn't anything.*
> *He wanted to carve it in stone*
> *or write it in the sky.*
> *He would lie out in the grass and*
> *look up in the sky*
> *and it would be only the sky*
> *and the things inside him that*
> *needed saying.*
> *And it was after that he drew*
> *the picture.*
> *It was a beautiful picture.*
> *He kept it under his pillow*
> *and would let no one see it.*
> *And he would look at it every night*
> *and think about it.*
> *And it was all of him and he loved it.*
> *When he started school he brought*
> *it with him.*
> *Not to show anyone, but just to*
> *have it with him*
> *like a friend.*
> *It was funny about school.*

He sat in a square brown desk
like all the other square brown desks
and he thought it would be red.
And his room was a square brown room
like all the other rooms.
And it was tight and close.
And stiff.
He hated to hold the pencil
and chalk,
with his arm stiff and his feet flat
on the floor, stiff,
with the teacher watching and watching.
The teacher came and spoke to him.
She told him to wear a tie
like all the other boys.
He said he didn't like them
and she said it didn't matter.
After that he drew. And he drew
all yellow
And it was the way he felt about morning.
And it was beautiful.
The teacher came and smiled at him
"What's this?" she asked.
"Why don't you draw something
like Ken's drawing?
Isn't it beautiful?"
After that his mother bought him
a tie, and he always drew airplanes
and rockets
like everyone else.
And he threw the old picture away.
And when he lay out alone looking
at the sky,
it was big and blue, and all of
everything,
but he wasn't anymore.
He was square and brown inside
and his hands were stiff.
And he was like everyone else
All the things inside him that

needed saying
didn't need it anymore.
It had stopped pushing. It was
crushed.
Stiff.
Like everything else.

This poem was reportedly handed to a high school English teacher the day before the writer committed suicide.

Chapter 19

The Power of Now

There are days we live
as if death were nowhere
in the background; from joy
to joy to joy, from wing to wing,
from blossom to blossom to
impossible blossom, to sweet impossible blossom.

—Li-Young Lee

When young people begin to feel that their lives are insubstantial, it's hard to convince them that this is only a phase in a stage of their lives, that they are meant to overcome all this, to overcome the idealizations and delusions and to come to grips with their own makeup and that of their world. Caught in the hold of their adolescent intensity, they feel as if the force of their engagement in their present reality cannot ever be matched by anything else, particularly anything that may occur in the future—something that really doesn't exist for many young people.

Trying to get these young people to stretch out their lives, to see themselves in ten, twenty, fifty, or even sixty years from now seems almost impossible. But to place oneself at the end of one's life, say at eighty-five, and imagine the kind of life one might lead then can be an interesting exercise. Some young people may see themselves as eighty-five-year-old homeboys. But more likely they will see themselves dead or in prison by age twenty. For too many of them this is as much as they can envision of a future.

Everything is focused on now, today, including their present enemies and loves. "It's Now or Never," as Elvis Presley's song proclaims. A few, when they break up with their girlfriends or boyfriends, truly feel their world has fallen apart; they feel there can be no one else for them, as if the entire spectrum of their possible life mates was now exhausted; they go crazy trying to get back to them (usually to no avail), or want to die because they can't.

These reactions are normal—most young people go through them—but they don't have to lead to a drastic conclusion. The inner focusing, this slowing of time to a big present, is part of a very critical stage of life: a coming into themselves. Their confusions about who they are and where they're going should signal the importance of these very issues during this period of growth. Young people generally "lose it" because the rest of their community has forgotten what it went through and refuses to carefully clarify what all this means for the young.

Many young people tend to turn over everything they have of themselves to a group or another person, even someone they may love dearly. Girls do this with their boyfriends, risking abuse, humiliation, and sometimes death by putting all their worth into someone's else hands (witness the many tragic double suicides among young men and women). Many do so with a group, identifying body and soul with it; they become willing agents of people who have other interests, doing things they most likely wouldn't do by themselves.

"Now or never"—this can be quite a powerful concept. History, future plans, phases, and stages have no relevance. Life happens at this time or it doesn't happen at all. Nothing else matters. The moment is magnified to an eternity.

"This is the way it has always been, this is the way it's always going to be." Using these words, some gang youth have explained to me why they stay tied to a gang, accepting its most detrimental aspects. "I will be for my barrio forever," they exclaim. "Homies for life—can't stop, won't stop."

But we know, especially those of us who have been through this, that these are not accurate statements. For the most part today's "gangs" are of quite recent origin—less than ten years for many; no more than twenty or thirty years for the older ones (although in Los Angeles and parts of the Southwest, some barrio gangs have been in existence since the 1920s). And gangs won't necessarily be around in the future, particularly when members get older and find themselves pulled by other concerns.

If a gang member survives the intense experiences encountered—without dying, being disabled, or serving a long prison term—he or she can consider leaving the gang. This may involve marriage or living with someone, having kids, getting work, or seriously attending to a formal education.

Dolores was a hard-core gang girl from the Little Village barrio of Chicago whose boyfriend was killed by a rival gang. She was allowed to leave the gang only if she would go to college. In fact Dolores's homies pooled together their funds to help her with tuition. She was a freshman in Eastern University in Illinois when I met her. She expressed much love and pride for her homies, who seemed to be watching out for her best interests, when probably nobody else would. It was also, I presume, a way to give back to her for the loss of her boyfriend. This is more prevalent than most people would believe.

A "governor" of a section of a major Chicago gang I knew encouraged the younger gang members to quit the corner and go to school. Another major gang leader gave his young charges incentives of money and praise if they stayed in school.

And there was the gang leader who strategized to rise to the group's highest levels to save his younger brother and sister who were also in the organization. His plan was to get out as soon as his siblings got out. But there were things about the gang that began to entice him.

"I remember sitting in my apartment," he stated. "In front of me was a table with stacks of one-hundred-dollar bills; I had gold down my chest and on my wrists. I was thinking about the big buys to make, about the nice four-by-four I wanted to get. Then I realized: The disease had gotten into me. I was supposed to be helping my brother and sister, but I got pulled into the money, the drugs, and the fast life. This is what happens when you have nothing and then all of a sudden you're surrounded by dough and respect. I stopped and thought, 'I'm getting out of this. I ain't helping nobody like this.'"

He eventually convinced his siblings to leave the gang. He, in turn, moved on to a healthier and more constructive life.

While organized groups of youth called gangs can be very destructive and violent, they are also known to stop and arbitrate violence and provide a positive protocol toward each other. In YSS we often noted that gang youth were much more serious and bent on protocol than those not in gangs. Violations of gang rules can often result in some serious beatings, most charges were dealt with by fines. The fact is many gang youth weren't just out there getting high or creating havoc; rather, they aim to shape the chaos around their lives into some kind of meaningful framework. Although a street gang can't properly take these structures to where they need to go—because they lack the skills and the proper environment—their efforts show that even the so-called worst kids have a sense of what community and caring should consist of.

Rituals, rules, and procedures were expressly spelled out in the "bibles" and official writings of almost all the Chicago-area gangs. Most of them emphasized self-respect, loyalty, and the avoidance of drug use or violence against family and neighborhood. This discipline, however, does not diminish the very real hazards of gang life.

Much has already been written and dramatized about these hazards. But the fact remains that there are relatively few instances of deaths or severely crippling "violations" or "going to court"—beatings or fines that Chicago and Los Angeles gang members administer—against those who want to leave a gang.[1] Although most gangs state that membership in the group is "for life," the way most gang youth leave this life is by *maturing out*. By a certain age their brains catch up to their physical development. For the most part, street gang membership is for adolescent youth. In some cases there are older men pulling strings and calling the shots; they exploit and use the younger members for violence or drug sales. I'm also aware that there are major criminal activities linked to street gangs (especially around drug sales), often directed from prisons. But in the main, unless they are crews associated with more sophisticated criminal organizations, street gangs consist of mostly preteen, teens, and early adults. Solidarity and camaraderie still reign as the primary motivation of gang participation.

All of this is linked to an environment in which young people's limited conceptions of themselves or the future are due to a social neglect that tends to give them a sense that they don't matter. Consequently a past and future don't matter. Only what they do now, what they experience now, has any meaning. Without a sense of belonging to a larger human tree, they are like windswept leaves with no trunk and no roots. I've had teen mothers tell me the reason they wanted babies was not because of love for their partners or because of long-range commitments, but because they wanted to have them before they leave this world—at age sixteen or so.

For these young people, there are no apparent bridges from the adaptive to the transcendent stages of their lives, from the physical to the conscious-spiritual, from their micro existence to a sense of their place in the cosmos—its energies, laws, and magnificence.

We can blame young people for their lack of vision and clarity all we want. But unless we actively and effectively challenge the debilitating premises that are based on archaic modes of existence, we contribute to a world that seems to "push" and propel more and more young people to suicide, death, prison, and addiction.

Chapter 20
The Way of Discipline

No bird soars too high if he soars with his own wings.
—William Blake

For three summers, from 1997 to 1999, I facilitated the Writing Through the Prisms of Self and Community workshops for the Guild Complex (in 2000, they were taught by Quraysh Ali Lansana and Anna C. West). Funded by the Lila Wallace–Reader's Digest Fund, along with other donors, the purpose of these workshops was to take twenty to thirty young writers from various public and private schools, alternative schools, homeless youth shelters, and violence prevention programs and help prepare them for a writer's life.

The Guild Complex already incorporates youth in its many presentations, readings, and programming, including the "Musicality of Poetry" events, the Gwendolyn Brooks Open Mic Awards, and its internationally acclaimed "Poetry and Video" festivals. With some 150 events a year, the Guild Complex features special evenings including hip-hop nights, women's voices, poetry slams, and panels on issues affecting young people and their community. On top of this, the Complex brings in some of the leading poets and writers from around the country to do readings, workshops, and other presentations. Many of their voices were published in *Power Lines: A Decade of Poetry at Chicago's Guild Complex.*[1]

The Guild Complex developed as a not-for-profit literary and arts presentation organization from Chicago's most famous independent bookstore at the time, Guild Books. Unfortunately with the encroachment of chain bookstores and rising rents in the area, Guild Books closed its doors in the early 1990s. It was a great loss to the city and its many writers and readers. However, the Guild Complex continued on its own and has now become one of the largest and most respected literary arts organizations in the country.

Michael Warr, who spearheaded the effort behind the Complex and was its first director, described the organization this way: "At the Complex, we rejoice in mixing and shaking things up. Whether it is a night of Adrienne Rich and Patricia Smith, the sonnets of Shakespeare with the soulful voice of poet Angela Jackson, dance improvisation to poetry, the solo voice of Li-Young Lee, or the poems of Rumi behind percussion, each event establishes a link based in human experience and voice.... [Here poets] mix revolutionary chants with appeals of love, Dow Jones averages with blues, outrage at injustice with razor-sharp satire, a Jimi Hendrix guitar solo, protesting racism and war, a child's cry against abuse, and shouts of joy in a b-flat note."[2]

Most significantly for the Prism Workshops was my experience at Centro de La Raza in Seattle, under the auspices of the Bumbershoot Literary Arts Festival. In the fall of 1993 this collaboration commissioned me to work with about twenty-five poor and urban children from local neighborhoods, for two weeks—eight hours, every day. We worked with them and their poems, inputing verses into computers and then helping them revise the texts. We also set up an impromptu stage from where these kids—ages six to sixteen—could practice their deliveries. Working with Amy Denio, a talented saxophonist, original music was written and woven into the program. Our first presentation was at the Quinalt Indian Reservation on the western edge of Washington State. Then as a special treat at the festival some five hundred people witnessed a strikingly powerful presentation of all the kids' voices with a live band, while each stood on the stage wearing a specially-made T-shirt with the name of the project: "Tempesta—An Urban Rhapsody."

The Chicago Prism Workshops were eight weeks long, two days a week. We were able to pay the participants a modest stipend and to introduce them to other writers who have made an income from their craft. At almost every session older writers in various genres—poetry, fiction, journalism, screenplays, theater, TV, and radio—addressed the group about the writing process, as well as the strategies and steps they use to make writing their living.

Although many of the youth were chosen—after being recommended by teachers, youth workers, probation officers, and community organizers who knew them—because of their high motivation for writing, most still lacked the discipline and skills required to make this writing work for them. Taking the young people's expressiveness to levels of craft required another kind of teaching and mentoring approach. It was important to be careful not to push away the participants' ideas, sentiments, experiences, and feelings, and to help them crystallize these into well-written, engaging, and originally compelling works. Their writing had to be able to stand up on the page, the stage, the broadcast booth, and the screen.

In the workshops we had the usual suspects—the pushed-around and pissed-off. There was a lot of grieving and grievances that had to be let out. The workshops allowed them to do so not only on paper but also up on the Chopin Theater basement stage in West Town, where the Guild Complex held most of its events. We went from developing the themes of their writing and presentations to research (mostly from their lives, but also from reading as much as possible) to organization (what makes writing flow: the ebbs and tides, ins and outs, its pacing) to its execution (the delivery on paper as well as in performance).

At the end of the eight weeks we provided the participants with certificates and held community-wide presentations to showcase their work to their parents, their teachers, writers, school principals, funders, and heads of youth agencies. Much of this was videotaped with the assistance of Video Machete. Here's an excerpt from a newspaper article that was written about these presentations:

"Hello everyone," said Dolly Arguello. "I dedicate this poem to my cousin and I feel I may cry. He died a month ago. Please bear with me," she went on, speaking softly into a microphone, telling of a street shooting, of an ambulance late in arriving, of a hospital that failed to inform the victim's mother, Arguello's aunt, before he died the next morning.

In "Soul's Song," Edith Bucio told of a girlfriend who found love, briefly, in a bar.

"'He's the best thing that's ever happened to me,' she told me once and then left for months and came back belly-rounded and alone," Bucio's poem reported.

Others talked of problems with shaping an identity, of battling past "the weed of despair," of "feeling snowed in, in a dark cold cave. Trying to get out. But where am I trying to go?"

Michael Pogue talked "of a lost love and her soft black hair and endless eyes."[3]

One of the early Prism Workshop poems was written by then seventeen-year-old Olga Chavez. It was called "Untitled, or I can't roll my *r*'s like a real *mejicana*."

> *The tips of my fingers*
> *are hard and yellow.*
> *I can flip tortillas from the obsidian fire*
> *of wood burning stoves*
> *made of ancient stones*
> *gathered in streets*
> *generations ago.*
> *I can grind maiz and chile*
> *and serve the food with love*
> *on separate matching plates.*
> *My hair flows in dark arroyo,*
> *trenzas braided backwards*
> *like my Grandmother's crooked hand used to do.*
> *It is the only way I know how:*
> *Long brown figures*
> *scooping tiny piñones*
> *from snake riddled tree trunks.*
>
> *I am choking on the languages*
> *drowning in the waters of el Rio Bravo*
> *darker than my hair.*
> *With my grandmother's bitterness*
> *and my mother's demise, I am*
> *a consumer of my father's dreams.*
> *I float on scraps of boxes*
> *my cousins filled with grapes and*
> *marked reproachfully with an 'x'.*[4]

There is a need to awaken something latent and powerful within all children and youth, which poetry and the arts do better than anything else. But there's another consideration: joining what has been roused and liberated with the rigor of craftmanship. We need mentoring that does both, and it may not necessarily come from the same mentor. Whatever a person's art is, it should also become his or her practice in order to maintain a balance in the psyche and the soul, so that an individual's longings and the needs of society intersect.

Here's what the Mosaic Foundation has written about the importance of practice:

> Since ancient times, practice has served as a gateway to the "other world"—the spirit world, the realm of ancestors, the unseen world. Devotional prayers, songs, and dances; the crafts of poet, diviner, healer, mentor, mediator and pilgrim all weave the threads of inner life with the invisible "world beyond the world." Practice can be seen as the core project in the life of a person. Practice is the attempt to find the same "way" again and again. Through practice a dream is touched repeatedly and held. This requires discipline, for practice makes us a disciple of some way in the world. Over time, practice involves a re-making of oneself; a re-inventing and crafting of oneself over and over. This making and inventing serves the re-imagination of the world. The soulful contortions, dramas and struggles that arise through practices are the very stuff that intrigues the inspired breath of spirit into life. On the other hand, a practice adds to the continuity of personal life as well as the life of community. The ways of practice invites the intensity of youth, the arts of mentoring, and the rituals of the elders. Through practice, we serve what we see and cannot see, we touch the Tree of Life and Death, we die and live again. There may be no better time to consider the ideas and images of meaningful practice than this time of rapid change and spiritual confusion.[5]

Besides teaching about art and the creative process, it is important to teach youth concepts and skills that would allow them to "stretch out their lives" and envision and strategize for a future. We need a practice but we also need the particulars for forging the circumstances from which such practices can thrive for everyone. There are other concepts that have to be understood. Key among these are the following:

• Nothing can be done without organization. You have to organize to get what you want.

• Nothing can be done without strategy and tactics. Know how to maneuver in the world, and keep your principles and dignity intact.

• Nothing can be done without politicization. Understand and work with the power relations in society, community, and family.

• Nothing can be done without education. Institutional schooling, but also learning from life experiences and decisions, and attaining some life-affirming skills.

• Nothing can be done without culture, expressions that say a lot about who they are and where they may be going.

• Nothing can be done without unity—across gang lines, color lines, language lines, and gender lines. Your interests can be truly met only when you unite with others who have the same interests and concerns.

• Nothing can be done without communication—speaking and writing well, to clarify to yourself and the world what you are about and why.

However, all of this requires a measure of self-discipline; it is the only real and lasting basis for any discipline. In 1994 *U.S. News & World Report* published an open letter I wrote to my son Ramiro and my daughter Andrea—then nineteen and seventeen years old, respectively. The topic was "Self-Discipline."

As teenagers, you have a lot of dreams, a lot of needs and desires. But you'll also need to build a foundation from which these can be realized, and because of this I wish to talk to you about the value of self-discipline.

When I was a teenager, I joined a youth gang.... For me, the change came when I got involved with social causes.... [I]t mattered to me that I was doing something important, and that I had responsibility for what I did....

[T]his was not a journey without conflict or setbacks. I spent two decades trying to become an independent, committed and intelligent human being, and there were many times when I toppled into rage and despair.... There are no perfect people, but there are people who, when confronted with the necessity of change, apply themselves. To be the father you both deserve, I had to say: "No more excuses!"...

This is not solely a personal battle.... [Our lives must be] a convergence of freedom and necessity, of self-interest and collective concerns, of individual choices and forces beyond our will. Such intersections have rocked this world....

For me, self-discipline allowed me not to be dismayed, not to lose heart, not to compromise with the unjust and the inequitable. It allowed me to truly own my own life.[6]

Self-discipline is most operative when it's tied to an art, skill, or craft. Understanding this is extremely vital in any work with children and young people. Once young people turn to an art emanating from their own essence, they will most likely become disciplined in attempting to achieve a level of mastery in that art.

One's practice therefore is the unity of vocation, avocation and evocation—*work, interest and calling.* There's no such thing as an artist in general. One's art has to be specific, achieved through ongoing, incessant, and ever-evolving work.

Sifi Earl White, an African-American martial arts instructor who teaches in South Central L.A., points out that when the British wanted to know the name of the physical movements some people were practicing in China, the response was "Kung Fu." But this means "hard work," which was true of any skill or practice.

Hard work is best achieved from within. I have seen young participants in various genres get better and better at what they do, almost without prodding, once the art flowed from a powerful place intrinsic to their natures. On the other hand, any young person who was forced to attend a workshop because of a parent, probation officer, or a teacher rarely stayed with the discipline, unless he or she somehow found a way to internalize what was being taught.

This is also linked to our work with rituals. Smaller, less elaborate, rituals are often done to begin and end meetings in YSS, and in our retreats and conferences. It may include something basic like the burning of sage ("smudging") and praying to reinforce the seriousness of what we are trying to do. As mentioned earlier, we have also introduced traditional rites such as the sweat lodge. But most importantly, we have involved youth in helping shape new and *emerging* rituals, through which they address the violence and pain in their lives within a collective imagination.

One night, in a Mosaic retreat near Atlanta where a substantial number of youth from Chicago, New Orleans, Los Angeles, and Atlanta were present, we set aside time for these young men to create their own funeral rite. They combined Christian, indigenous, and street traditions. Candles were framed in a cross on an altar; sage was used to smudge anyone entering the ritual room; and a symbolic bottle of beer was used to pour a memorial to the dead (in Africa, this is called "libation") while each youth, in their own words, "rapped" a fitting tribute for all the other men to hear. Fire, mud, masks, shrines, songs, dance, and drumming have been used by the young men in other rituals during subsequent events.

Another time, younger and older men were asked to form groups according to where they felt they stood in regard to their personal crisis: the beginning, the middle, or the end. A couple of the men moved between groups. Many felt they were in all three. Others weren't sure. But by being required to decide, and to discuss why, they were eventually able to understand a little deeper the trouble they were in. These groups then established collective rituals to deal with their respective places.

One of the most healing rituals we did through the Mosaic Foundation, in conjunction with leaders and organizations linked to the peace truce between rival gangs in Watts, was a drum, prayer, and song procession in February 1999 through the Jordan Downs Housing Projects. The purpose was to help reignite the then seven-year truce, to expand the peace to other communities, and to have a common ground of healing for all of us.

We went to three sites where young men had been recently killed. Those sites were then circled with ash and a lit candle was laid on them. Praying, singing, and drumming punctuated the ritual. Many small children, gang youth, mothers, fathers, and community activists, African-American and Mexican members of the projects, and youths and elders from throughout L.A. and other cities participated.

It's important to note the advent of other art forms linked to video production; home recording studios; microradio stations; multistreamed turntables; and the vastly improved computer programs that put out the most advanced graphics, sounds, and designs. Through many diverse outlets the voices and stories of youth are finding new forms of expression while also universalizing what they often thought were narrow, unique sentiments and experiences. With groups like Video Machete or Street Level Media, young people have learned how to interview others and capture images that essentially bring to life their concerns. Once, I attended an event organized by Street Level Media that had various TVs, some stacked on top of each other, simultaneously showing videos to music, spoken word, and live aerosol art acts.

There are also pioneers of low-power microradio stations—mislabled as "pirate radio"—that normally broadcast at 10 to 100 watts and have a range of no more than a five-mile radius.[7] Liberation Radio's Napoleon Williams and his wife, Mildred, who were ultimately hunted down and shut down for their on-the-edge, political, and "illegal" broadcasting, set up their station from their one-room home in the poor African-American community of Decatur, Illinois. They were liberating the airwaves and challenging private commercial enterprises that acted as if they could buy and control anything—including what gets sent through the skies.

M'banna Kantako, who began his low-power radio broadcasts out of the John Hays Housing Projects in Springfield, Illinois, often documented police abuse and aired police radio dispatches to alert the community about misconduct in the projects, sometimes as they occurred.

I saw the effectiveness of this firsthand. One time *People's Tribune* writer Tony Prince and I had gone to Kantako's place to talk on the air to the African-American residents of Hay Homes. After we finished, we left Kantako's apartment and walked around the block to our car. As soon as we turned the corner, several squad cars and police officers confronted us. Without hesitation the officers pushed us against a wall and searched us brusquely. One accused me of being a gang leader because of my tattoos, and they generally harassed us. They asked Tony why a "white dude" would end up in a place like Hay Homes.

As the officers scrutinized and taunted us, residents began to step out of their homes and converge at the scene. They eyed the officers and their conduct. Although they didn't make any threats against the police, their watchful presence proved intimidating nonetheless. In a few seconds the officers returned our wallets and told us to leave. M'banna Kantako, whose wife had seen us get stopped by the police, broadcast and mobilized the people to act. This probably saved us a ride to the police station.

There was also the heroic work of California's Black Rose, founder of the Zoom Black Magic low-power radio station network of the 1980s. Black Rose set up a then six-hundred-dollar operation out of his home in Fresno to play the music he liked that did not get played on the large commercial radio outfits.

Long the targets of the Federal Communications Commission (FCC), Kantako, the Williamses, and Black Rose hold a special place in the development of low-power microradio stations everywhere. Members of Kill Radio and Radio Clandestina in L.A. have taken these concepts to a higher level, broadcasting from moving vehicles with roving signals to keep officials who are trying to clamp them down off track.

These and other free microradio station operators throughout the country, such as Free Radio Berkeley, put out of business by a federal judge, finally forced the FCC to allow such radio operations to exist, although at very controlled levels. However, on December 18, 2000, Congress voted to turn down licenses to hundreds of small, low-watt local radio stations after months of lobbying by the powerful National Association of Broadcasters, which represents corporate interests.[8] While the struggles of low-power radio to be truly free is far from over, their examples should be known by all who care about how creativity can be impaled by so-called regulations and official entities in cohoots with the major broadcasting companies.

In addition there is now a growing number of "living room" studios (the technology and low costs are making high-level recording equipment accessible for more and more people). I know many collectives of musicians, poets, and rap artists doing their own sounds and CDs, irrespective of any ties to major distribution or production.

With the recent controversy over free music downloads sparked by MP3 and Napster (although as I write this, these efforts were being bottled up by the courts or coopted by major players in the music industry), it's clear that technology is creating previously unknown modes of expression and distribution without an "industry" or "middle man" to reap most of the benefits. So our battles must also demonstrate how the technology can expand everyone's art, story, image, and truth into a multitude of endless possibilities.

To accomplish all of this involves self-discipline. In essence, ritual and expression through the arts help pull everyone into the rhythms of the universe, into the inner workings of all nature, from the minute to the most massive aspects, from the DNA imprint in our genes to the massive whorl of galaxies. Once we tap into the interacting push and pull of complementary energies, we begin to put ourselves in accord with the world, into the timeless patterns and root formulas that ignite all life, and thus restore the power within each of us to better such a world.

If more of this were done with the community's full attention, we wouldn't need so much Ritalin, Prozac, and lithium. Nor would we need so many juvenile detention centers and mental institutions.[9]

Essentially, we are trying to prepare our youth to be *rulers,* over their own lives—often the first places where they stumble—and in their communities. They must be given full governance of their activities, with the guidance by older and wiser people. They must be allowed to try things out, make mistakes, and learn from them, with the help of those who have been there and are truly committed to staying there. They must have access to all the social and technological resources so that they can shape a future by knowing specifically what is required for that future.

Sovereignty is important to fully empower a person. In teaching youth, we have to demonstrate in real and loving ways what an autonomous, mature existence looks like. Here are four major areas to cover as part of such an existence:

1. One has to be truly authoritative (not dominating), confident, and a strong enough presence—a leader among leaders, not a "leader" among followers. In this kind of leadership, intellectual and creative prowess takes precedence over brute strength.

2. One has to be compassionate, caring, and a great lover of people and things, including those people who are most intimate in one's life. One has to learn that love is not to be parceled out or used sparingly or to get something else. Love, like the abundance in the earth, the imagination, or truth is everywhere. And if you love somebody or something, you have to take care of this (you don't hurt the ones you love). Love ennobles people. Love is both the call of the wild and the most civilizing force in humanity.

3. One has to become a special kind of artist. To be the creator and exhibitor of beauty in places that normally may not appear to be beautiful. Creating beauty is true magic. It is striving for harmony and balance. Traditional Navajos, who believe in the balance between complements—between *hocho* ("ugliness and disorder") and *hozho* ("beauty and order")—have a prayer that says, *"May you walk in beauty: beauty before you, beauty behind you, beauty above and beauty below—beauty all around you."* Everyone has to learn how to make beauty out of what may at first seem ugly (especially one's losses and wounds).[10]

4. One has to become a warrior, fighting for what is right, for one's family, community, and world. A warrior is not a bully. Warriors use strategy, tactics, communication, and art instead of violence and pain; warriors understand the power of stealth, the art of maneuvering over one's apparent "enemies," making them impotent so that they no longer have control over you. You don't destroy enemies; you embrace them in such a way that they are no longer detrimental in your life. Here is where courage and character are most required.

Any of these considerations will require collective as well as self-study, methodologies, planning, meaningful activities, and a group to assess, evaluate, and formulate new ideas, strategies, and plans.

Because of our own journeys as adults we know what directions young people's ideas and experiences are generally taking them. One of the things we periodically have to do is to help young people summarize their experiences and discover the significance of their thinking and actions, especially when they can't sufficiently do it for themselves. This is a delicate process; you have to be careful not to impose your own interpretations.

As elders, we lay down strong foundations for young people in order to help them develop and mature. We know that change is constant, forms are in flux, ideas are variable and fluid. And true flexibility is only possible when a strong and adequate basis is set down beforehand.

Although youth have established a number of rules of conduct for themselves in YSS, we have two basic ones. Within these seemingly simple expectations, much magic and momentum can emerge:

- Everyone respects one another.
- Everyone participates at some level.

Over the past few years I've gone a number of times to the Audy Home, Chicago's Juvenile Detention Center, to give talks, poetry readings, and workshops, usually with the support of one of the teachers, Julia Campoverde, or through B.U.I.L.D, Inc., a nonprofit youth leadership and violence prevention organization. In April 1998, National Poetry Month, I arranged for Andrew Carroll, of the American Poetry and Literacy Project, to bring several volumes of poetry to the incarcerated youth, including one with one hundred great American poems, African-American poetry, and translations of Spanish-language classical works. The young people in the Audy Home ate the books up. Here's part of a letter I received, one of several, after that visit:

I am writing to let you know how I appreciate you coming to talk with us and giving us those [poetry] books. As you know, people really don't give us things or come to talk with us because they feel we are bad people just because we're locked up. But you don't feel that way—and I want to thank you.

I've always had a rewarding time with the young people at this facility, which is part of the oldest juvenile justice system in the world. However, there were instances when I had to demonstrate to staff the power of this work. One teacher whose class I visited yelled at and degraded the young men under her care. Just before I was about to start my workshop, she began to berate one or more of her students. She acted more like a guard than a teacher. She also appeared skeptical that my workshops would do any good. But as soon as the workshop began, when I had the young men write down their feelings, stories, and thoughts, she witnessed a change in the voices and demeanor of her charges. They opened up, sometimes quite eloquently and movingly. At one point, during a reading of a student's work, she had an incredulous look on her face. Afterward she told me, "I didn't believe these guys had it in them. I thank you for opening up my eyes."

Another time, at a juvenile hall in northern California, with the help of young people from Barrios Unidos, who had been doing talks and workshops in a number of similar facilities, I talked to about fifty incarcerated girls. As I talked, some of the girls cried, others recalled reading my books and connecting to my words. At one point, though, the main staff person there began to put down the girls, although they were polite, intelligent, and actively attentive.

"What do you do," he asked rhetorically, "with kids who keep dummying down, not asking questions, or taking part?"

He was insulting the girls, making them feel inadequate, fragile—many were already in terribly fragile states, they were runaways and often victims of abuse and rape at home—and under his control. I got angry at this guy, but also at the people in the community who, whether they know about this or not, allow such adults to verbally and emotionally abuse our children in these facilities. The law states they can't sexually or physically manhandle them, but there's more than one way to tear into a child or teenager.

I use my talks at juvenile facilities partly to help counter the prevailing notions that often drive young people to end up in these institutions in the first place. For example, I read poetry once to a large group of Audy Home wards. Most of them really got into it, but one guy raised his hand and wanted to know, "Is there any money in that?"

"Well, there can be, since I'm a professional poet," I responded. "But I have to say that poetry for the most part isn't about money."

"Well, if it ain't about money, then why do it?"

"Because it's about your soul—an internal purpose. Because it's about art and expression."

"I don't care about that. 'If it don't make dollars, it don't make sense,'" the youth declared, echoing the words of a rap song of the time.

Where would someone get such an idea? From us, of course, from the society he was born into; from TV, movies, books, and probably his own family. It comes from looking around him and seeing how money works, how it "talks," how powerful it can be, especially to poor people who know firsthand how degraded and powerless one can be *without* money. This is why poetry, art, expression, and creativity are so marginalized in the culture. Unless it's about money, the arts are almost totally neglected.

Still, art, music, and poetry keep rising up, often more vibrant than before. People do art because money is *not* everything. It's about what really matters, their soul and their heart's intention.

Yet, it's difficult to tell this to young people who have bought into the very system that is eating them alive. The young man who challenged me about my poetry and its money-making prospects sat in a juvenile prison. Look how far such a line, "If it doesn't make dollars, it doesn't make sense," has gotten him.

The point is that somebody has to teach young people something deeper about themselves, the economy, the world, and a future. When we're not around, unfortunately, they are still learning anyway, only it's probably the wrong end of a wrong message.

Sometimes people equate discipline with conformity, the blunting of edges, homogeneity, and social order. Trini and I once had an argument with a friend of mine about a fifteen-year-old high school wrestling champion in Illinois; according to news reports, this young man was banned from the wrestling team in late 1998 because he insisted on wearing his hair in a stylish Mohawk. "That's a bunch of baloney," exclaimed my friend. "He's just a fifteen-year-old punk!"

"Wait a minute, what if he took this stand on principle so he could still hold on to his spirit and dignity?" Trini asked.

"For a stupid Mohawk!" yelled my friend. "Come on! If we allow him to do this, then every fifteen-year-old will want to do this. What you'll get is chaos."

"What you may get is a self-empowered young person, who, whether he is wrong or right, will at least own part of his life," I responded.

"For example, this incident may help the kid to find the strength to defend his own interests in the future," Trini added. "Of course, such stands are risky—but what is the alternative: to be safe, but lack the courage of your convictions?"

"I don't care what you say, he's a punk and he should get his ass beat," continued my friend. Like him, when someone can't rise to the level of an argument, they tend to go to the most common emotional denominator, as if the weight of an emotion is more powerful than a sound point.

"You don't know for sure when such a decision will positively impact his life," I tried to explain. "Sure, we can let young people know the ramifications of their choices. But we can't always say they are ruining their lives, or the social order, for that matter, by making such choices. Besides, chaos exists today regardless—there's nothing sacred that this teenager is undermining. I actually believe the present so-called order could use more such young people."

We didn't get too far into this dialogue. My friend insisted on fear mongering ("We'll have chaos"), name-calling ("He's a punk"), and emotional outbursts ("That's baloney!"). But I do believe the talk was revealing and fruitful. I understand that his position—although, in my view, wrong—was typical of that held by many people. His views couldn't be dismissed just because I disagreed with him. While it's important not to lose our cool and our sound judgments when young people do things that appear silly or perhaps crazy, we should still struggle to gain insight and clarity. One possible insight is that the most immediate, expedient response to such incidents may not be the best one.

Let's not forget that some of the best artists, musicians, thinkers, and writers in our culture—including Einstein, Van Gogh, and Beethoven—were known to be "bad" students or bothersome rebels. John Lennon, for example, was kicked out of kindergarten. They were often called dumb or told they would "never amount to anything." But as John Keats wrote, "Do you not see how necessary a world of pains and troubles is to school an intelligence and make a soul?"

Bryan and Tierra were two Arizona teenagers who loved to write. When I heard about them, they had recently been arrested—for writing poetry.

I met them when I visited the Salt River Pima–Maricopa Reservation in March 2001. The community is surrounded by the dense sprawl of the Phoenix-Scottsdale metropolitan area. However, as if entering another country, you cross the reservation borders and it becomes desolate and underdeveloped.

During my visit I spoke at the Desert Eagle Secondary School following an awards ceremony. Parents, teachers, and students, as well as leading members of the community were in attendance. I met the students of the Writers Fund, including Michelle Washington, who was a strong poet and editor of the school's literary publication. I was impressed with the work these students and Carmen Tenney—who helped bring me here—and other teachers were doing with words and art.

But arrested for poetry? In the maddening atmosphere we're in, I've heard of students who were reprimanded, suspended, or expelled for writing threatening or "disturbing" poems. Some later faced more serious repercussions. In this case Bryan and Tierra were reportedly removed from their classrooms, handcuffed, and escorted by police to jail.

Bryan, eighteen, had written numerous poems about violence, killings, and suicide. One poem was named for a teacher. In it Bryan talked about chopping off the teacher's limbs, torturing him, cutting off fingers, and pulling out internal organs. It was a hard read. But it required careful and unwavering attention. Bryan was crying out for help as much as for solace. Instead the police were brought in. Bryan spent a couple days in the reservation's adult tank before a judge threw the case out.

Perhaps other kids thought of doing what Bryan wrote about. Perhaps he was rightfully angry, but putting it on paper stopped him from acting on it. Maybe after writing these sentiments he felt differently about this teacher and didn't have a need to do anything else. Meaningful dialogue and relationships could have resulted from this unsettling situation. But most paths were cut off except one: shutting down his voice.

Bryan had wanted to meet me, but he was incarcerated when I spoke at the school. Despite this, one of his writing teachers arranged to bring him later to where I was speaking. I found Bryan to be interesting and gentle. Yes, he was probably capable of doing many of the things he wrote about, but so are most people. Unlike me when I was his age, Bryan wrote out these feelings and did not do what he felt like doing.

Tierra was a sixteen-year-old girl with dark skin and eyes and a head full of dark hair. I met her at the Salt River Juvenile Center. Although I didn't get a chance to read her work, I understood it had references to gangs. I asked her what kinds of charges she was facing. She said, "Criminal misconduct and malicious mischief."

She was one of three girls incarcerated at the juvenile center. About fifteen young men were also staying there at the time. I was scheduled to speak to the whole group, including rival gang members who had not been in the same room for some time.

Accompanying me was Priscilla Aydelott, a teacher and fellow writer who had brought me there through PEN's Writers and Readers program, as she had done since 1996 to various parts of the Navajo reservation, as well as Phoenix, Tucson, Nogales, and Flagstaff. Carmen Tenney was also with us. Pizza and soda were brought in. After all the youth were gathered, dressed in bright yellow institution-issued clothing, one of them read a poem and another introduced me. Homemade tattoos peeked from under shirt sleeves or alongside almond-shaped eyes. Closed cropped hair with long tails graced many of their heads. All were brown-skinned indigenous, O'odham and other tribes, Mexican or mixed.

We had a respectful dialogue. They asked good questions. They were quiet and attentive. Many were familiar with my books. I read a couple of poems. Afterward we sat around and conversed informally. I mentioned to Tierra that she shouldn't let anyone or anything stop her from writing. She smiled shyly and said she wouldn't.

Most of the kids in the detention center only get to school once a week for two hours. For many this is the only time they get out of their cells. A counselor can only see a few of the youths once a week. There are no TVs or radios—there is total stimulus deprivation. One young man had been held there for over a year. Under such circumstances, coming together like this, although nice, could lead to problems. A couple of the adults and I felt that the informal part of the afternoon was going on too long. We were right. Pent-up rage that had been simmering for a long time boiled over. During a lull one of the boys struck another boy. Within seconds other youths began to throw blows. A chair was tossed and broken. A handful, including one of the girls, went over to where I was standing to stay out of the melee. Everyone else appeared to be fighting. I saw Tierra and the only other girl scratching and punching each other.

Several guards rushed into the small room. One of them held a youth on the ground and used a free hand to shoot pepper spray into the eyes of another. Other fights continued while officers from the police station next door came in to assist. Pepper spray fumes filled the area. Priscilla, Carmen, and I, along with staff and the uninvolved youth, were inadvertently Maced. It took a while, but none of us could leave until all the youths had been subdued and removed from the room. Several of them, hit hard in the eyes with spray, were yelling and cursing. Finally we were allowed to exit after everything was contained.

Holding a napkin to my face, I felt good breathing in the fresh desert air. One young man was also taken outside, hands cuffed behind his back, to have his face hosed. The teachers and some of the staff felt bad about all of this, not only because of the disruption to the program they had organized, but because they knew there would be a lockdown with other punishments and very little, if any, processing. With hardly any place to take their fears, their angers, their loneliness, these kids were bound to explode again.

Right after the mini riot one of the boys offered an apology to me as guards led him out. Later, several others wrote letters of apologies that a staff member, Leif Hallberg, kindly sent to me. One of these was from Tierra.

> I am like an angel with red eyes, horns, and pitchfork. I liked that you didn't know me or my past. You were like new eyes, so I was good because that's how I wanted you to see me. But still the bad came out. You probably knew I was bad or done wrong because I was in here. But you didn't see me do wrong, like a brand new gun holding in a bullet.... I am writing to tell you how sorry I am for acting so ignorant. I really didn't want you to see that part of me.... I want to thank you for visiting us and letting us meet you. It was something I was looking forward to. I really enjoyed your stories and poems. You inspired me to keep writing more.

During the fighting I didn't feel in any danger. It was just something that had to happen—some beef, like so many beefs in poor communities, schools, and institutions where all the proper outlets of expression are blocked and the psychic breathing spaces become cramped. I knew there were good people and good staff at this particular facility—people who really cared, who tried to involve the youth, and who reached out. But as in most such places, the punitive qualities proved overwhelming.

As we were about to leave, Priscilla expressed sadness for the young man whose face had to be washed down. At one point she asked the O'odham sergeant there if she could give the youth a hug. He stared at her briefly, and his heart must have opened, because he said, "Go ahead, but do it quickly."

Priscilla went up to the youth, whose head was down, sitting on a brick planter outside the detention center, surrounded by guards.

"I don't know if you're up to it, but I'd like to give you a hug right now," Priscilla said. "Is that okay with you?"

The young man looked up at her, and without uttering a word nodded his head and let Priscilla embrace him, as if he had needed this for a very, very long time.

Chapter 21

Looking for the Milky Way

I believe the poet's responsibility to poetry—to shelter and advance not just the art, but the conditions in which the art occurs—has never been more obvious.... What do I mean by this? I mean the most practical, neighborly responsibilities—those of warning and witness and presence.

—Eavan Boland[1]

I am going to commit a subversive act. I am making a political declaration. I am throwing down the gauntlet.

I declare—as many have before me—that poetry is for everyone. Poetry goes beyond borders, beyond hostilities, beyond the pale of twilight mist (might as well be a little poetic). And poetry can be as devastating as lightning when it speaks of what is otherwise inexpressible to power, to ignorance, to guns.

I've lived the violence of this age, this easy rage, over turf, money, drugs, pride, and so-called national interests, for which many have died. But when there is poetry in one's life, the rage becomes petals imploding in the hand. Poetry liberates and many have also died for this. I'm talking about poetry to wake the dead, to rouse the slumbering heart. Poetry as a prowl into primeval pain.

I've carried my poems into the corridors of maximum-security prisons and into the palaces of higher learning. From Soledad to the Sorbonne. My verses have gone with me into the alleys and shelters where the homeless sleep, to senior citizen centers, boxing clubs, and Indian children on the rez. I've carried them to public schools where kids have thrown enemy gang members through plate-glass windows, and into well-endowed private institutions where children write literature in at least three languages.

238

In a home for wayward boys on Chicago's Southside, I once met a thirteen-year-old whom the police had removed from his parents because he was found selling gum in restaurants and bars in Pilsen; he ran up and hugged me every week when I showed up for a poetry workshop. In a high-security juvenile facility in Omaha I worked with a sweet-faced silky-haired girl who one fair day went into a closet, grabbed the family shotgun, and calmly blew her sister away at the dining-room table. Her poems were quiet and romantic.

I remember walking dirt roads in upstate New York to reach the barracks where Puerto Rican migrant workers were taking their evening breaks. I walked into a recreation hall where several men sat around watching a baseball game on TV. These were hardened fans, shouting encouragements to their favorite team and making side bets for small change.

Somebody mentioned to the group that *el poeta* had come for the workshops. I got up and said it was okay, I would come back another day, that I could see they were in the middle of an important game. "No way," one of the men shouted. "You walked all this way for us." He turned off the TV and gathered the men into a circle, men who I knew would much rather watch baseball then listen to me and my poetry. But they sat and listened, and when their turns came, they recited their poems; I did not hear one complaint.

I have witnessed women who had been declared mentally ill and supposedly lost to substance abuse who never appeared as sane and as sober as when they read their poems.

"[Poets] have a task... to keep their attention on things that are happening, the living of lives, and the thinking that makes things happen," wrote Leslie Scalapino.[2]

In Chicago in the early 1990s I became the target of a backlash against poetry as popular art, particularly against the workshops I had been facilitating in homeless shelters for several years. The controversy began in 1992 when an article I wrote for *Poets & Writers* magazine about the workshops prompted an angry reply from a reader.[3] I also wrote about poetry and the homeless in *Letter eX*, the Chicago poetry magazine, and received negative responses from some local poets. And there was a review in Chicago's *New City* alternative weekly that criticized the publication of *With the Wind at My Back and Ink in My Blood*, an anthology of poems written by homeless people, which I had edited.[4]

One reader called my work with the homeless a "charitable act." She wrote that the homeless needed homes, jobs, and tangible means of survival, not poems. The *New City* reviewer concluded I had lowered "poetry's standards" by having people such as the homeless write poetry. He called the anthology "nothing more than a quaint souvenir."

Of course I never said the homeless and the poor should be given poems instead of homes. Food, homes, clothing—these should be made available to all who need them. And it will require much more than poems to obtain them. Since the homeless are denied homes, why not poems?

But poetry is about community. It is about spirit. It is about connecting. It is about how the words flower from the seeds of experience and the imagination. Everyone needs this—not just the well fed, the well educated, and the well placated.

There should be standards for poetry. The process of honing one's craft is an important and enriching one. But this should not be limited only to those with academic credentials. Poetry should never be the sole property of a few scholars and professionals. The root meaning of the word *standard* was to "extend" or "unfurl," as in a flag. When thinking of degrees of excellence, I can see the poignancy of this image. Each so-called standard should be a threshold to cross, not a door to be slammed in one's face. A poem may embody some literary acrobatics; but a poem is never more a poem than when it is also a cry from the heart.

Naysayers come and go. Today there is a growing movement to make poetry accessible and engaging for as many people as possible. The American Poetry and Literacy Project drops off free poetry books in Laundromats, airports, hotels, supermarkets, jury waiting rooms, and other supposedly unpoetic locations. The Poetry Society of America places poems on placards for buses and subway trains. And the most recent U.S. poet laureates—the late Joseph Brodsky, Rita Dove, Robert Haas, Robert Pinsky, Stanley Kunitz, and Billy Collins—have contributed tremendously to getting "poetry into the public sphere."[5]

Poetry should be on billboards, on the back of cereal boxes, on radio and TV—in place of so many commercials—in between screenings of popular films, and on public walls. Poetry should be read at sports events and at homecomings. *Poetry should be an everyday, everywhere, and every-occasion thing.*

The assaults against "public" poetry are nothing more than the perennial cry of the old guard to keep poetry pure and insulated, away from "the unwashed hordes." These critics echo those who condemned Walt Whitman and dismissed his belief that great poets need great audiences (to which Ezra

Pound later responded, Who cares about audience—it's something that has helped distort our sense of the ties between the personal nature of poems and their social context).

The backlash has never stopped me from taking poetry as far and wide as possible. I started doing this in 1980 with the Los Angeles Latino Writers Association and their Barrio Writers Workshops in Highland Park, East L.A., and Echo Park. Among the organizers were Victor Valle, who became a Pulitzer Prize–winning journalist and published poet; Helena Maria Viramontes, presently an award-winning short story writer and novelist; Marisela Norte, who is now among the city's best performance poets; Jesus Mena, a jet mechanic who turned into a journalist; Naomi Quiñonez, now an award-winning editor and published poet; and Roberto Rodríguez, who is the author of a number of books and, along with his wife, Patrisia Gonzales, publishes a nationally syndicated newspaper column.

In addition we collaborated with great artists like Barbara Carrasco, Patsi Valdez, Diane Gamboa, Guillermo Bejarano, Leo Limon, Harry Gamboa, Gronk, Willie Herron, among others.

In a couple of years I became one of their directors and editor-publisher of the literary arts magazine, *ChismeArte;* I had an office in the Self-Help Graphics & Arts Studio in East L.A., then run by the late Sister Karen Boccalero, a true champion of the arts in our community.

Another key participant was Manazar Gamboa, one of the country's leading voices against injustice and poverty—and a tireless worker for prisoners and the power of poetry and art. Unfortunately Manazar succumbed to liver and heart failure in December 2000 at the age of sixty-six.

A convict turned poet, Manazar spent the previous two decades conducting workshops in prisons, juvenile facilities, schools, and community centers. I worked with Manazar from 1979 to 1985. Besides the work we did at the L.A. Latino Writers Association and *ChismeArte,* I was on the board of Concilio de Arte Popular when Manazar was its director, and a founder and poetry curator of Galeria Ocaso, an art gallery and performance space that Manazar established in Echo Park.[6] For a time I lived next to him in a little room off his apartment in Echo Park; I was there when his daughter, Olmeca Sol, was born and for the first years of her life.

Manazar was an important Chicano poet. He was also one of my mentors. I related to him as a *veterano,* a shaman of Chicano barrio life and art. It was Manazar who took me to Chino prison to participate in the writing workshops that eventually led to my own work of the last twenty years among prisoners and juvenile offenders. *Manazar era un vato de toda madre.* In the street vernacular of the barrio world, he was both real and transcendent. He was a man who braved the barrio life of heroin and prison, yet he was also able to find the art, the soul, the immensity and complexity of this life. He had already walked the paths I was trying to enter. He was an important guide to what I was trying to do with my own literature.

According to the *Los Angeles Times*, Manazar directed more than 2,500 writing workshops for youths in the Los Angeles County juvenile justice system.[7] For thirteen years he also conducted workshops for prisoners at state correctional facilities such as Chino and Frontera in conjunction with the L.A. Theater Works, a nonprofit based in Venice, California.

After I left for Chicago in 1985, Manazar continued his work among the most hardened constituencies with art and poetry classes. In 1989 he became the artistic director at the Homeland Neighborhood Cultural Center in Long Beach, where he directed theater and literary reading projects and led writing workshops for adults and children.

Manazar was very close to his indigenous Chicano heritage and had strong Apache ties. It was through his connections that I first learned of the revival of the Sundance among native peoples in this country and of the Mexika indigenous traditions out of Mexico.

As a child, Manazar and his eleven siblings worked the crops throughout the San Fernando and Central valleys of California. The family eventually settled in the Chavez Ravine barrio in Elysian Park, where Dodger Stadium is presently situated. Like many other Chicanos, he was belittled in the schools he attended for only speaking Spanish. He eventually turned to stealing and selling weed. Manazar was especially affected by the destruction of Chavez Ravine in 1950, one of the most strongly contested and unjust removals of poor people in the country.

While some left the Chavez Ravine neighborhood after being told by the government to leave, others fought to the end, resorting even to gunfire. Eventually bulldozers and armed men razed the shanties and dirt-road streets. Chicanos did not forget the Battle of Chavez Ravine; for decades they refused to visit Dodger Stadium in any significant numbers. Only in the 1980s when the Dodgers recruited Mexican pitching sensation Fernando Valenzuela did this begin to change. Today the stadium is full of Chicanos and Mexicanos.

But the trauma of this uprooting always informed Manazar's anger and work. In 1954 (the year I was born), Manazar faced his first prison term. He was twenty years old. For the next twenty-three years he would spend seventeen of those behind bars. As did many barrio youth of the time, he became a heroin addict. One of the women he loved died in his arms of a heroin overdose in the early 1970s. Soon after, he went on a robbery spree and ended up back in prison.

But this time while incarcerated, Manazar began to read—the love that had been denied him in his few years of formal schooling. Reportedly he read everything he could get ahold of, including Keats, Shelley, Coleridge, and Blake. Eventually he started reading Shakespeare. Not deterred by the foreign-looking Elizabethan English, he studied the plays with an Oxford Universal Dictionary and began to unlock the magic of the words.

While still in prison, Manazar sent out many of his first poems. After close to forty tries, he was eventually published. The editor, a Brazilian professor at the University of Colorado, was the one who gave him the name "Manazar," a combination of words to indicate "Burning Man."

In 1977, Manazar was released from prison and became active in the L.A. poetry scene. From 1977 to 1981 he worked for Beyond Baroque, where he started the first cross-cultural reading series and edited the magazine *Obras*. Manazar published some of my first literary pieces in that publication.

Manazar died at a Long Beach hospice. I heard about his situation barely a week before from poet-journalist Ruben Martinez. I called Manazar right away. He was not lucid at the time and it was hard to communicate with him. I said I would see him by the end of the week. Manazar managed to suggest I come Monday or Tuesday of the following week. I called the hospice on Monday around lunchtime to see when it would be a good time to visit; they said he was walking around and generally well. I thought I would see him within the next two days. On Wednesday, the day I had planned to drive to Long Beach, Ruben called me to say he had passed away.

I felt terribly saddened that I couldn't see my friend. A genuine warrior. A man of words. A man close to the barrio and the heart of this great community. Someday his work and legacy will have its place; it's too bad that this will happen, as it has for many of our best artists, only now that he's gone. But for those of us who knew Manazar, who worked with him

and were taught by him, he remains one of the most important writers, organizers, activists, and visionaries this country has ever produced.

Descanse en paz, carnal.

In the early 1980s Susan Franklin Tanner, a longtime professional actress
and producer, and the United Steelworkers of America Local 1845 set up
the TheaterWorkers Project, which received widespread acclaim. Here steel
workers who had lost their jobs when Bethlehem Steel closed down in 1981—
it was the largest steel manufacturing plant in Los Angeles—wrote poems
and theater pieces, guided by Ms. Tanner. Some of them later performed in
a national tour of a play called *Lady Beth.*

From the mid-1970s to the mid-1980s there were many plant closures
in the Los Angeles area. The GM plants in South Gate and Van Nuys closed,
as did a Ford plant in Pico Rivera. Goodyear, Firestone, and Bridgeport, and
various other tire manufacturers left. So did metal factories, such as American Can, National Can, and American Bridge, and aerospace plants, such
as Lockheed. Whole communities were devastated.

Local 1845, then headed by George Cole, set up one of the largest food
banks in the country where some six thousand mostly Mexican families, were
fed weekly through the union hall. In addition local health officials said there
was a 25 percent rise in alcoholism—the plant already had a disproportionate
number of alcoholic employees—and eight suicides the first year. One steelworker friend reported how he came home one day to find his live-in girlfriend dead by a self-inflicted gunshot soon after the plant closed.

Since I worked at Bethlehem Steel for four years as an oiler-greaser and
millwright apprentice, I took part in some of the workshops. At one point
in 1984 Bruce Springsteen donated funds for the project, and even participated in a workshop with the rest of us. He invited several of us steelworkers
to raise more funds during his sold-out concerts at the sports arena from his
"Born in the USA" tour. We were given free tickets and a place of respect.
In between one of the songs Springsteen announced to the mostly white,
middle-class audience that Local 1845 members were in the house. He asked
people to donate to our food bank and writing workshops. We roamed among
the audience carrying large buckets. People graciously gave what they could.

An older steelworker named Cruz, who put in forty years at the plant
before it closed, turned to me and said, "I have never felt as honored being
a steelworker as I do now."

One evening at a workshop, I presented Springsteen with my poem:

Bethlehem No More

Bethlehem Steel's shift turn whistles
do not blast out in Maywood anymore.
Mill workers no longer congregate
at Slauson Avenue bars on pay day.

Bethlehem's soaking pits are frigid now.
Mill families, once proud and comfortable,
now gather for unemployment checks or food.

Bethlehem, I never thought you would be missed.
When we toiled beneath the girders,
we cursed your name.

But you were bread on the table, another tomorrow.
My babies were born under the Bethlehem health plan.
My rent was paid because of those long and humid
days and nights.

I recalled being lowered into oily and greasy pits
or standing unsteady on two-inch beams
thirty feet in the air and wondering if I would survive
to savor another weekend.

I recall my fellow workers who did not survive—
burned alive from caved-in furnace roofs
or severed in two by burning red steel rods
while making your production quotas.

But Bethlehem you are no more.
We have made you rich—rich enough to take our toil
and invest it elsewhere. Rich enough
to make us poor again.[8]

After I read the text to the whole group, Springsteen remarked, "The poem is very powerful for me; you are the only one who could have written something like this."[9]

In 1985 I left for Chicago to further my work as a writer, poet, and revolutionary. I spent three years editing and writing for the national political newspaper, *People's Tribune/Tribuno del Pueblo,* freelanced for local and national publications, and did reportage and wrote copy for the anchors at WMAQ-AM, All News Radio. I learned computer typesetting and worked throughout the city, including a few years for the Archdiocese of Chicago in their Liturgy Training Publications (LTP) offices.

And I continued writing poems and stories.

Doing what most young writers tend to do, I tried my hand at a novel and sent it unsolicited to major New York City publishers. I am the first to admit the novel wasn't any good. I ended up getting twenty-two rejection letters and would have gotten more, but I gave up after that. One letter from one of the country's largest publishers, however, proved to be quite telling. It said they had published an "Hispanic" novel ten years before and they thought they had done enough as far as "Hispanic" literature was concerned. I believe they didn't bother with the merits or lack thereof of my work. My name was enough for them to reject it.

It was these circumstances that compelled me in 1989 to start Tía Chucha Press, a poetry press named for my favorite relative, my aunt Jesusita. My first book of poems, *Poems Across the Pavement,* designed by my friend at LTP, Jane Brunette, with cover art by Puerto Rican artist Gamaliel Ramirez, came out and went through several printings. It also garnered a Poetry Center Award from San Francisco State University.

Other Chicago poets approached Tía Chucha Press with their own manuscripts. It has been an honor to have helped launch the first poetry collections of writers such as Patricia Smith, David Hernandez, Michael Warr, Rohan B. Preston, Nick Carbo, Andres Rodríguez, Kyoko Mori, Lisa Buscani, Terrance Hayes, and to publish established poets such as Elizabeth Alexander, Sterling D. Plumpp, Tony Fitzpatrick, and Afaa M. Weaver. In 1994 we produced a CD of various Chicago poets called *A Snake in the Heart: Poems and Music by Chicago Spoken-Word Performers.*

Jane Brunette, of German-Menominee descent, continued to be our designer for many years. Eventually Tía Chucha Press merged with the Guild Complex, and Northwestern University Press was contracted as our national distributor.

Beginning in late 1989 I traveled all over the United States, as well as to Canadian cities such as Toronto and Montreal, promoting my first book and our new press. One of the most interesting readings I did was with New York City performance poet Bob Holman (formerly of the Nuyorican Café's Poetry Slams) and Michael Warr at a hangar-shaped club called Chicken's in rural eastern Ohio. People said you didn't need an address; everyone knew where Chicken's was—you had simply to ask. More than two hundred mostly white, mostly unemployed, angry young people came to hear music, anticensorship speeches, and slam poetry. The night proved to be an eye-opening experience for me: these young people were open to new voices—even if urban and of a darker hue—as long as they were genuine and meaningful.

In 1991 I went to Europe for the first time to do readings in Paris and London bookstores, cafés, and university settings. I've read with Jamaican dub poets Linton Kwesi Johnson, Mutabaruka, and Jean Breeze as well as Amiri and Amina Baraka. I believe I was the only nonblack writer to read during one of the International Black Poetry events in London.

I read to audiences in former East Berlin—most people's second language at the time was Russian—where some didn't understand a word I was saying. But poetry finds its way, carrying its sentiments in cadences that sweep across like ocean waves that touch every shore.

One of the best experiences I've had was a two-week jaunt with several stops in cities throughout Germany and Austria as well as Amsterdam. San Francisco poet and impresario Alan Kaufman invited me to be part of this 1993 journey, which also included literary luminaries Paul Beatty, Neeli Cherkovsky, Dominique Lowell, and Patricia Smith.

The tour was a success. Not only did we bring home money, which is rare for poets, who have been known to accumulate more miles than moolah, we also attracted large and grateful audiences. In one bar people were lined up on the street outside and standing on top of parked cars.

But we had our misadventures as well. One of our poets, who shall remain nameless, was not allowed to enter Austria after said poet told off two border officers, who were checking passports in the train from Berlin to Salzburg. Poets are feisty, especially when there's too much alcohol in the system.

But the most memorable time was our trip to Amsterdam. We rented a van and made the long drive ourselves. I drove much of the way, around 120 kilometers per hour on the autobahn, with most cars still streaming past me and no police lights in the rearview mirror. Fueled on greasy schnitzels, and after getting caught up in holiday traffic, as everyone from Germany seemed to be on their way to the beaches of Holland, we finally entered the continent's party town. I maneuvered our van over the cable car rails, past crowds of drunken soccer fans from England, past street artists and acrobats, searching for a club called the Milky Way, where two of our company were expected to read. As was bound to happen, we got lost.

At one point we pulled up to a nice-looking Asian couple crossing the street, and in our abrupt U.S. manner, one of us jumped out the van and rushed up to the couple. "Where's the Milky Way?" he yelled out. They looked stunned. Then the man, his face a study in confusion, raised his hand and pointed to the sky. Man, we laughed about that for days! It was a great way to ease our anxiety. We eventually found the Milky Way (the club, that is) and the reading went on as planned.

Poetry is in the bones. Listen to children, the way they speak, using poetry without a command of language; the way they tap into feelings, concepts, things; their use of metaphor.

"Gee, Mama, you got scribbles on your head," my then four-year-old son Ruben said when his mother walked in with newly permed hair.

"My stomach is making angry faces," said Luis Jacinto, my other son, at age five, describing a bellyache.

"It feels like dancing," exclaimed a three-year-old upon drinking sparkling water for the first time.

Metaphor is one of the basic building blocks of human communication. Children embody this, as do many older cultures. Among Guatemala's Quiché Indians, for example, there is no word for spouse. One's love/sexual companion is known as "the keeper of my eyes."[10]

All people, by virtue of their creative and communicative capabilities, are born poets (not that they all will be). But today the classroom has become one of the biggest impediments to the nurturing of the poet in each of us; poetry, that complex word shaping that conveys the intimate life—the pains, glories, defeats, betrayals, triumphs—of a human being. The poet/artist refracts the myriad light rays of the natural world into a singular dimension: the poem. What pushes out a poem is what has been called "voice," which is something more than simply what comes out of the vocal cords.

Anne Schultz said this about voice discovery in a child: "We have a momentary glimpse of the writer... certainly tiny, easy not to notice because it is so small. But there is the beginning of voice here, and of a sense of audience that is real, however small; and if we listen and let this piece of writing stand, we are helping the writer to embark on a journey of discovery of his voice and his stories that will also be a discovery of the world around him and his place in it."11

What children say in their simple and direct manner may not be considered poetry; they are trying to convey fractured concepts, based on their real and imaginative circumstances. Let it stand, let it stand; it will eventually sink roots in the earth, unfold into a tree of constantly blooming, constantly ebbing, creative expression.

Yet in my countless visits to classrooms around the country, I've found poetry and other forms of writing reduced to a pedantic adherence to rules, syntax, and grammar—to the inert tools of language construction. Too many classrooms have become the domain of the static and the abstract over the living, vibrant, and breathing poet within each child.

As a result most children are denied their natural impulses for poetry. They are so often defeated on such things as spelling that they turn away from writing as a vital mode of expression. They grow up to be adults who would rather have their teeth pulled than write. Or, if they have learned their lessons well, some students become skilled writers, all *t*'s crossed and *i*'s dotted; yet they conceal with "proper" language what should otherwise be honestly revealed. "Good" writing may not always be expressive writing.

We've been talking a lot about the "gifts" within each child. But few seem to understand how these need to be carefully "led out"—the Latin root meaning to *educate*. Children are not blank slates for a teacher to write on. Nor are they empty vessels into which we pour knowledge. They are already called to a destiny that is about something great and beautiful. With the guiding light of knowledge and mentorship we can help them meet the challenge of this call, to "invite the genius out of a person," as Malidoma Somé wrote.12

In 1992 I conducted a six-week poetry residency at Gale Elementary School in the Chicago neighborhood of Rogers Park. The neighborhood is one of the most culturally diverse in the city. I worked with ten- and eleven-year-olds in a bilingual program; the students were mostly Spanish-speaking from Mexico. The first day, I asked the class, "Who does poetry?" No one would raise a hand. They were too "cool" for this; some were already members of local street gangs and designated as "troublemakers."

Later a Puerto Rican teacher asked me to come to his class of nine-year-olds, recently arrived from Mexico and Guatemala. I asked them the same question: "Who does poetry?" They all raised their hands. I then asked, "Who wants to recite some poetry?" They all clamored to be the first.

The image of one Mexican girl with strong Indian features stays with me. With her eyes closed, she recited in a performance style known as *declamación,* rocking and swaying with the rhythms of the Spanish words. I was deeply heartened by this. Then the teacher told me that in a year or two, these children would be just like the older, bilingual ones I had been working with.[13]

This brought to mind a visit in the early 1980s to an East L.A. classroom of Chicano thirteen-year-olds who were barely beginning to appreciate poetry due to the efforts of a vibrant teacher. Until then these children had little knowledge of any language art. A few months before, I had visited Nicaragua—the "land of poets"—where thirteen-year-olds, mostly poor, some in bare feet, recited from memory verse after verse of great poems.

What is it about our schools that takes the poetry out of our children? Poetry. Sometimes it's a hard sell.

There are schools where poetry is neglected or taught in such deadening terms that most students don't want anything to do with it. One Chicago high school where I had conducted weeks of successful poetry workshops brought in a new principal and zero-tolerance policies. The first thing this principal did was to stop the poetry workshops and remove copies of my memoir from the library. The link between eliminating poetry and expression and maintaining zero tolerance was clear.

More schools in this country dismiss or diminish the power of poetry than ones that don't. That's a sad fact. Despite this I've known high school students who carry their own personal journals with many poems, images, and ideas without having had a class assigment to do so. Poetry, like most art, happens even when education doesn't.

Michael Meade once said, "Education is never about buildings, standardized tests, and curriculums. It's about the human spirit willing to learn and the human spirit willing to teach. When the spirit of teaching is gone, zero tolerance is the result."

There are teachers who do bring life to the word, who use poetry to reach in and out of each student and his or her life, but also as a way of knowledge. One teacher in North Carolina brought Mimi, a thirteen-year-old Mexican girl, to a presentation I made at a local church. After the talk Mimi presented me with a poem she had written:

A Look in the Mirror

Are you the reflection of my strong proud ancestors?
Are your deep brown, caring eyes mine?
Is that peaceful expression I see
    the same as people see in me?
Are your friendly dimple and smiling mouth
the ones I use to say "hello" to the world?
And your hair—I know that's my hair—my wonderful
    thick, long dark hair.
Are you a hint of the strong, proud woman
I'm about to become?

She had carefully scripted the poem on pink paper, sealed it in plastic, rolled it up, and tied it with a ribbon. The delicate care she had taken had an inner wisdom that we often lose as adults. She just knew how to present her poem, what came from inside her.

In one Southern school I stood in front of a class of second graders considered "too rowdy" for poetry. Yet we got them to write down their lives in vivid terms. In one metaphor assignment I heard these lines:

My life is a wrecking ball.
When I'm with my friends, I feel like a pencil.
Being at home is like being in a washing machine.
Being at home is like being wrapped in a chocolate bar.

During a workshop I did at the Barium Springs Home for Youth in Statesville, North Carolina, a thirteen-year-old ward named Audie wrote this poem:

Grip of a Gang

The eyes of the cat glow in the dark
Your eyes see the sheet of lies but ignore its place
The sheet gets larger little by little like a flame comes from
    a spark

Who you were, you're them no more, your mind, your body,
   your race
...Upon the wings of an eagle you can sure escape
I tread the shining waters of an untouched hidden lake
Like the constant change of clouds that always change their
   shape
Like a war of endless nightmares you may finally awake

In the United States, poetry production, like most art production, has been relegated to the fringes—something to be done in galleries and cafés, artists' colonies or loft communities, under the banner of "bohemian," or in exclusive academic circles. Or, as is often the case, the arts are tied to commercial enterprises, to make products palatable, pleasing, and therefore sellable. And as everyone knows, arts programs are among the first to be cut when schools are having financial difficulties. One result of this is the exclusive concentration of artistic talent in particular individuals, and its suppression in the general population.

Discrimination based on skin color, nationality, or immigrant status has set up more barricades against human expression. In effect some schools have made a "liability out of difference."[14] The result is to break the creative spirit, to destroy the poet within, and make every neck ready for one leash. It's about the "control" of students, and about significantly restricting the growth of emancipatory human life activity.

Despite the many barriers, "flowers crack through the cement." The mural movement in East L.A., and other cities during the 1960s and 1970s— early on, Chicago established major wall works, including the famous "Wall of Respect" on the city's Southside—is one such bloom. East L.A. has more murals per square mile than any other community in the world. Tourist buses have made regular stops to places like the Estrada Courts and Ramona Gardens housing projects, where murals grace formerly drab federal housing walls, or the Self-Help Graphics & Art Studio and the Plaza de La Raza Arts Center and Museum.

At age seventeen, I was one of those budding street muralists, trained by Chicana artist Alicia Venegas and then briefly in the famous Goez Arts Studios under the tutelage of Cecil Felix, a leading Chicano muralist of the time. I ended up painting ten murals, most of them with thirteen gang youth in the Rosemead–South San Gabriel area, including the Bienvenidos Community Center, the Del Mar Public Library, and Garvey Park. All have been whitewashed; slides of these, however, are part of the Smithsonian Institution's Chicano Mural Documentation Project, housed at the Social Public Art Resource Center in Venice, California.

The rise of hip-hop culture from the late 1970s to the present is another of these arts explosions. Its core expression, rap, is a well-developed language art that took root in the rubble of places like the South Bronx, outside of existing learning institutions and English departments. "Whenever youth confront obstacles, they create music," a music promoter once said in a *Rolling Stone* magazine article.

Over the years dancing and primal beats were mixed to promote breaking, locking, New Jack Swing, house, techno, electronica, drum & bass. In a time when social programs were cut across the board in every urban community, when industrial jobs were destroyed by the millions, poetry and other arts continued to flourish.

Notwithstanding the commercialization of hip-hop, it is an important phenomenon that proves my point: We are all born poets and artists.

Similarly, in New York City, aerosol art—so-called graffiti—reached levels never before attained. This style has now spread throughout the world. In the Tor Bella Monaca suburb of Rome, Italy, site of some of the poorest housing projects in the area, several spray-painted murals were created in June 1995 during the Dionysia Project's youth arts festival called "quartieri, the hood, el barrio, ekasi."

On one of the walls some East L.A. aerosol artists, including Fabian Debora, spray-painted one of my poems and my words "Art is the Heart's Explosion on the World." On various sections of public space there, the heart indeed had detonated: Italian, South African, and U.S. youths put up numerous pieces in collaboration with some of the best known practitioners of spray-can art from the "old school," including Phase Two, Futura 2000, Lee Quiñones, Chico, and Stash.

At the invitation of Pat Murphy and the Beacon Street Gallery youth of Chicago, I attended the festival along with two members of YSS, Rocío Restrepo and my daughter Andrea. Other participants included aerosol artists from Tucson and L.A., as well as dancers, rappers, poets, theater artists, and visual artists such as Rhodessa Jones and Idris Ackamoor, Common, South Africa's Prophets of Da City, Next Diffusion, La Pina, Ice-One, Havoc and Prodigy, "Emakhishinia" from South Africa's domestic workers, Zanendaba

Storytellers, Cultural Harmony, Richard Lapchick and Dexter Jenkins of Sports in Society, and many others.

The young people were some of the most talented anywhere, with words, music, dance, artistry, and intelligence enough to move continents. I conducted poetry workshops with Italian youth offenders, who were allowed to attend despite having done some serious crimes—one had committed murder; another had sent a letter bomb through the mail. I asked the priest who had been escorting them why these young convicts didn't escape. He said it was because they had shown a measure of transformation and were trusted. In fact these young men were nothing but respectful, and wrote some of the most moving verses. In the United States, not even an incorrigible youth or purse snatcher, let alone a violent offender, would be given such trust.

We even had a run-in with some angry local youth, who accused us of using their walls without their permission; they almost jumped on a few of the festival participants, including Andrea, before we intervened. After we clarified our intentions, these young people eventually allowed us to spray-paint pieces across their community center in one of the housing projects.

With a cascade of colors, an ocean of voices, a nightfall of aerosol rain, we dreamed ourselves onto the walls. The art carried with it a vision, a sense of what can be, what must be, not merely to turn over the soil but to plant the ideal. In addition the music, dance, theater, and poetry transcended borders, barriers of language and skin color, and culture.

Three years later in Milan, rapper and artist Luca Massironi, known as FlyCat, invited me to speak at the Leon Cavallo Social Center for a panel on Chicano art and hip-hop, as well as to appear on TV and radio shows about the role of the arts in society. The Leon Cavallo Social Center had been an abandoned factory that members of the community, in particular young people, took over and transformed into a thriving and aesthetically rich hangout. There were several stages for live acts, a bookstore, a skating ramp, and rooms for workshops and panels. The old stone walls surrounding the structure were covered from top to bottom with some of the most elaborate and socially engaging aerosol art I'd ever seen.

Apparently police tried at one point to evict the youth from the factory, but some twenty thousand community people were mobilized to protect the occupants. After a public outcry the police reportedly backed off.

Later on that trip I recorded several of my poems for Skilz To Deal Records. One of them, "Civilization," was a selection on FlyCat's 1998 CD and vinyl, *Una domanda alla risposta—Come Through the Auratory Canal,* with a powerful hip-hop street beat created by FlyCat and DJ Kaos.

The "word" has also found other outlets with the rise of poetry slams and open-mike poetry readings. The original poetry slam was born in the mid-1980s in Chicago, the brainchild of poetry impresario Marc Smith (earlier versions included the Heavyweight Poetry Bouts, now held in Taos, New Mexico). Poetry slams and their various offshoots have now spread throughout the country, Canada, and Europe. Here oral poetic performances are judged, jeered, or applauded in bars, cafés, libraries, festivals, and even rock concerts. Some "Lollapalooza" events featured side tents with performance poets. An international magazine, Slam, has been published and international slam contests have been organized. Some high schools, such as Rio Grande High School in New Mexico, have set up "poetry cafés" where the students can read their work and slam.[15]

At the last poetry slam event I attended in Chicago—for the 1999 National Poetry Slam championships—several thousand people from around the country and parts of the world participated in slam events throughout the city, culminating in a highly charged finals slam at the famous Chicago Theater downtown.

In the early 1990s the Nuyorican Poets' Café in New York City opened its doors to poetry slams, getting attention on MTV, PBS-TV, and in places like *Time* magazine and *The New York Times;* I read there with poet Kimiko Hahn and folk guitarist/singer Richie Havens. The 1996 movie *love jones* was based on the open-mic scene of Chicago's mostly African-American word-jams in places like Spices and Anotha' Level/Literary Explosion; *Slam,* the 1998 film about an African-American convict poet, covered similar ground as did the documentary film *SlamNation* that appeared the same year.[16]

The Guild Complex and Tía Chucha Press converged with this movement and have been integral to it ever since. The Green Mill Lounge in Chicago's Uptown neighborhood continued to host poetry slams through the new millennium every Sunday night with "Slam Pappy" Marc Smith. For a few years we collaborated on Neutral Turf: The Chicago Poetry Festival, which sometimes attracted two thousand to three thousand people, and sent winners of slams, with the city of Chicago's backing, to cities like Okasa, Japan, and Prague.

And the success of PBS-TV's *The United States of Poetry* (with book and CD) and Bill Moyers's ongoing interviews with this country's leading poets during the Geraldine Dodge Poetry Festival in Waterloo, New Jersey, are further testaments to the power of poetry and performance in our lives.

Words transform lives and the things of life. The key for teachers or workshop facilitators who work with marginalized or oppressed communities is to begin with respect, which can't help but be a respect for individual cultures, languages, creativity, and capabilities.

I once heard a well-meaning teacher say she didn't recognize any differences among her students. But equality in these contexts doesn't mean everybody should be considered the same. See people for who they are, in all their glorious attributes, talents, and cultures. They should be appreciated and respected regardless of their differences. What a teacher needs to be aware of is the assigning of privilege and power *because* of difference. A teacher must also hear, and often heed, all the voices in this perpetual conversation called community.

"Children, whatever the color of their skin or the condition of their birth, bless us by their mere existence on our earth," wrote author and educator Jonathan Kozol. "The great, unanswered question of our age is whether our societies plan to bless them in return."[17]

It's fine when kids get mired in pedestrian things or questions; such inquiries can result in deeply moving responses. Children and adolescents should always get more than what they've asked for; it's really what they want.

Poetry must find its central place in the culture. Not just as a fun thing to do but, as poet Marie Howe once said, "as a life-and-death issue."

Chapter 22

Be Your Word

If you have not lived through something, it is not true.
—Kabir

In 1996 George Sanabria walked me around the Ramona Gardens Housing Projects in East L.A. Built in 1941, these are the oldest housing projects in the city. Off Interstate 10, near the California State University off ramp, for years a wide wall greeted visitors to East L.A. with elaborate gang graffiti, including the name of the one barrio gang that controlled the projects and much of the surrounding area: Big Hazard. This all disappeared recently when the city's "grafitti busters" program entered the picture.

Big Hazard was the setting for much of Edward James Olmos's 1992 film, *American Me,* about East L.A. gang life. Several youth from the neighborhood took part in the film. Unfortunately three people used as consultants, including forty-nine-year-old Ana Lizarraga, who also played a small role, were supposedly killed by prison gang members. Apparently they were unhappy with the movie's portrayals. Olmos was reportedly a target of a contract hit until federal indictments of alleged prison gang leaders in the mid-1990s put them away.

In the late 1970s, when I lived in the nearby Gerahty Lomas barrio, these projects were known as drug central. People from all over L.A. County would line up for blocks while local drug dealers sold their wares as if this was a drive-in food market. This rep was heightened through the 1980s and 1990s, even when other locations did the same thing.

There are many murals in Ramona Gardens, most going back to the late 1960s and early 1970s. One recent mural was for Smoky Jimenez, a twenty-one-year-old Ramona Gardens resident who was killed by sheriff deputies in

August 1991. This murder led to a three-hour melee in the projects that precipitated the much larger L.A. Rebellion of April 1992.

George, then a nineteen-year-old gang member, had turned his life around. He became active in Impacto, one of Proyecto Pastoral's programs that worked with many youth from East L.A.'s six housing projects, including the Aliso Village–Pico Gardens housing complex, and later with Inner City Struggle, run by Maria Teixeira.

By the year 2000, however, Aliso Village and Pico Gardens were being torn down for new subsidized housing, but also condos to entice the well-to-do to this poor urban core area. These housing projects skirted the eastside of the L.A. River and were only a short ride across the concrete bridges to the warehouse district, Little Tokyo, and downtown.

At a 2001 peace rally in Hollenbeck Park, a mother said that with the destruction of the housing projects, the community, instead of getting stronger, became scattered; families were forced to move all over the L.A. area; organized groups became disorganized; and she felt the community was being punished instead of helped.

I, too, have been ambivalent about the demise of Aliso Village and Pico Gardens. Much organized struggle orignated there. It was the site of a lot of important history, including intense battles during the Chicano movement, some of which I witnessed in the early 1970s when I organized youth in these projects.

Besides the more recent work of Proyecto Pastoral, there were a number of other active groups here that should not be forgotten, including Casa Carnalismo, Congreso Obrero, Los Tres del Barrio, Comite de Mujeres, to name a few.

Of course, these were some of the most violent and most neglected housing developments in the city, and something had to change. In the mid-1970s there was a battle between Mexican and African-American residents of the projects—an ongoing issue, even as the African-American population dwindled over the years—in which people were shooting at each other from the rooftops. A community peace gathering at the Mission Dolores that I was attending broke down into shouting matches and fistfights. Eventually peace came, but something would always get the tensions going again.

The barrio warfare and the drug trade have taken a mighty toll. Even during the demolition, surrounded by rubble and boarded-up buildings, the shootings and drivebys between rival gangs persisted.

Perhaps the most salient aspect of the renovations to the Aliso Village–Pico Gardens housing projects was that it was done from "outside" the community, to "free up" an area close to downtown, edged by several major freeways—the real estate has become more lucrative, and therefore more desirable.

As of this writing, the Ramona Gardens Housing Projects are still intact, although some sidewalks have been recently fixed. The issue for many is not "if" these projects will come down but when.

George participated in the *American Me* filming and was part of Olmos's documentary on Big Hazard called *Lives in Hazard.* An engaging and intelligent young man, George was filming a short video on guns and how they became accessible in the barrio. He himself had been severely stabbed, and he had a .22 bullet fragment in his arm from when he was shot.

On a warm summer day George introduced me to various people in Ramona Gardens who happened to be outside—there was a lot of street life in the projects. He pointed out a section of housing, known as Tecato Hotel, where heroin addicts had taken over abandoned apartments. He introduced me to an old wino—well known and respected in the neighborhood—as he sat against the wall of a local liquor store. I met some of the homeboys from Big Hazard, heavily tattooed, buffed, mostly jobless and mostly waiting for something to happen. One of the Hazard *vatos* I met had been blinded by a rival gang's bullet. George told me this young man still took part in shooting missions. He would have other homies point him in the direction of their enemies, then he'd fire away.

I met Bob Murrillo, who worked at the time for the housing authority. He was associated with the Southern Door Lodge, which held regular sweat ceremonies for ex-drug addicts, alcoholics, and gang youth. Bob had read my book and was pleased to meet me. Before I left, he handed me a large "dream catcher" as a parting gift.

At one point George and I went to the Resurrection Cemetery in Montebello on the edge of my old barrio, Las Lomas—it is known as the Homeboy Cemetery. It was opened in 1951, and fallen warriors have been put to rest there ever since. Barrio youth from all over East L.A. and the San Gabriel Valley are buried in this Catholic *panteon,* as the Mexicans say. There is a section where infants, toddlers, and younger children are buried. Although most probably died of disease or accidents, many of them were killed in the barrio warfare. George pointed to the more recent headstones of homeboys he knew, some with their pictures engraved on the marble slab.

In the fifty to seventy years that some of this warfare has existed, thousands of lives have been lost. The Resurrection Cemetery, along with other local burial grounds, serves the most intense gang communities in the country. As gang violence has grown throughout the country, particularly in the 1980s and 1990s, the violence in East L.A. and the San Gabriel Valley has grown along with it, both in numbers and intensity. One of the most devastating results of this was the 1995 slaughter of a man's whole family in El Monte, attributed to barrio/prison gang politics. Five people were killed, including a five-year-old girl and a six-month-old baby.

I spoke with George then, but he had already moved out of Ramona Gardens. Like many people whose personal interests are connected with their community, George didn't abandon the barrio and returned frequently in his capacity as a youth worker. He didn't turn his back on his neighbors; he simply grew up, which is true of many young people trying to lead a stable and healthy existence, after the intense dramas and traumas of an active gang life.

In YSS, as in all youth organizations, we repeatedly dealt with an ongoing issue: that people mature. As gang members enter other levels and phases of their lives, so, too, do those youth who work in empowerment and leadership development groups. I've met twelve-year-old kids who go on to graduate middle school, high school, and enter college or work while in the group. Soon their activities slow down. They aren't as available as they used to be. They have discovered new partnerships, jobs, study, and interests. These changes are natural. When youth or adults leave YSS, we try to send them off with prayers, blessings, love, and a sense of accomplishment. *Entering* and *leaving* are important aspects of any relationship and have to be given strict attention. Entering properly means being embraced, adequately oriented, and helped. Leaving properly means moving on without any outstanding issues, rancor, or feelings of unfinished business. We hope those who have left the group will never forget YSS and what we have learned together about life, sovereignty, and who they are.

It's important to remember also that for there to be proper change in people, there has to be an adherence to a continuous and consistent process. Knowing what is changing—the infantile ego into a mature adult ego—and what is constant are vital to any organization working with youth. This is why YSS maintains traditional indigenous knowledge and practices while incorporating new ideas and activities from the youth themselves.

As young people grow, so does the group. We are always being replenished with new people who will often take struggles to new levels, not just revisit old problems. You cannot be complacent about this work because new forces and issues are always coming in. Uppermost in our minds is the age-old concept that youth forges its own future. They have to make their own history.

Growing out of our education and experience, YSS takes a strong stand against drug use and alcohol abuse, disrespect—of women, races, sexual preferences, other gangs—breaking confidentiality, and committing violence with each other, in the home, or in the community. We established women's circles, parent-youth dialogues, and Peace Retreats, where twenty-five to thirty young people—oftentimes from different gangs—go to the mountains or forests and respectfully interact with caring adults, nature, and one another.

In December 1996, during one of our periodic leadership retreats, YSS members found an interesting way to discuss the issues uppermost on their minds. About forty people broke up into three groups. Each group discussed the question, "What does YSS mean to you?" They wrote down all their concerns.

Group One considered spirituality; learning one's culture; having family, someone close to talk to and a place to go; unity regardless of gang affiliation, race, sexual orientation; pride, no judgment, self-esteem, self-acceptance, being human, making mistakes and learning from them; friendship, companionship, not being lonely, having people understand you; fun, recreation; learning; respect; empowerment; and support.

Group Two pondered how to establish a unique revolutionary youth organization that does not discriminate against race, gender, age; how to set up conditions to get out of the streets; how to establish a place to express one's opinions, thoughts, and ideas that often cannot be expressed in society; how to have an organization that is run by and made up of youth, and where young people's intelligence is never underestimated, youthful vigor is appreciated, and their activities are rewarded.

Group Three considered stopping the violence; helping the community, including the homeless; setting up safe havens from the streets; establishing equal opportunities for all; stopping police harassment; and dealing with the causes of violence, including driveby shootings, robberies, abusive parents, rapists, and racists.

Each group was then asked to present to the whole gathering a quick, extemporaneous skit demonstrating their answers to these concerns. These were the skits they came up with: There was "YSS Man," in which someone would pop up out of nowhere with answers on a placard as two young people discussed problems they had with themselves and the community. "A Christmas Carol in the Hood" portrayed a gangbanger/drug dealer who meets three ghosts: one that takes him to the past, where he is a sweet and caring little boy; one to the present, where someone is dying because of the drugs he sold him; and one to the future, where he ends up dead from a gunshot wound—all these experiences help transform his life. And then there was "Who Are Our Real Enemies?" where homeboys were shown shooting at each other while they are surrounded by the powerful real estate interests, courts, police, and capitalists who actually decide the fate of their neighborhood.

These kinds of events kept the young people engaged and determined to carry out into their lives their work in the group. Although we couldn't follow all the youths around to "check" on them at home or in the streets, the key became for them to check themselves. If they valued the relationships, they usually did.

However, we had to be clear: We are not against gangs, drug users, prisoners, dropouts, or sexually active youth. We understand the economic, social, and psychological factors determining such activity. We are there to help transform people's lives, which also means working with those who need the most transformation. We are about change. To be effective, to be smart, and to win, we had to lay out a clear line of action that wouldn't later be closed off, when these young people had to do this for themselves.

"As I started developing myself, started getting knowledge of self, started understanding the words: *focus, determination, responsibility, respect, understanding,* and *communication.* I mean really started understanding the actual meaning of these words. Then I was able to make that change," said "Playmate" (Don Gordon), a former Grape Street Watts Crip and a participant in a Mosaic retreat and the healing procession we did in the Jordan Downs Housing Projects. "I'll never stop stressing that change is healthy. I don't care if you're eight, eighteen or eighty. It's never too late to change. Change is healthy, and it's something that we constantly have to do in everyday life."[1]

In 1998 the work in Mosaic and in YSS also inspired award-winning performance artist and storyteller, Antonio Sacre, to write and perform a monologue for the stage entitled, *Black, Brown, and White All Over.* This production had a successful run in Chicago before going around the country, including to New York's off Broadway. He incorporated the voices of the young men and teachers from a number of retreats and movingly showed how effective ritual, storytelling, poetry, and art can be to help turn violent youth away from harm and suicide, and toward their own unique destinies.

YSS works with anybody who agrees with the basic mission of our organization and who participates and enriches whatever program or plan of activity we are involved with, regardless of religious beliefs, gender, race, or class background.

The aim is to direct youth toward their art, which is also the territory of their wounds. Youth want to belong, to fit in—not just any place, but where their genius "fits."

Beyond this essential goal, our young people are also seeking the following:

- A new way of living more equitably, justly, and abundantly. They don't just want to fold into the old ways of doing things
- Meaningful activity and learning experiences; purpose and vision integral to what they do.
- Proper links between the group and the individual. The youth want to be "themselves," to express in their own way their own essence and to do so without being put down. Yet they also want to be accepted and embraced.
- Knowledge of what is known and also what is not known, how mystery is part of all life and how life is abound in mystery. Striving to understand these things is vital for many young people; just coming up with "answers" to fill the gaps would end up engendering more mistrust with adults.
- Adequate and passable bridges between the past and the future, elders and children, parents and their own kids, from not knowing to knowing.

Unfortunately today's adults, who have experienced only partial and incomplete initiations in their own lives, are forced through fear and misunderstanding to walk away from young people. And they are enshrining this distance in laws, policies, and conventional thinking. Once in Albuquerque, New Mexico, I spoke to an audience of youth and adults about these issues. At a certain point in the question-and-answer period, a well-dressed man in a suit and tie got up and commented, "These gang youth have no originality. I see them on the corners, in schools, and in the malls. They all wear the same baggy clothes, chains, and caps. Where's their individuality? Why do they imitate each other?"

I then asked the man what he did for a living.

"I'm an insurance agent," he replied.

"Well, I have to tell you," I said, "you look like every insurance agent I ever met."

The point was that wanting to be like one's peers is natural and normal. Adults do this as well as children. Teens are not the only ones wearing the newest "hip" styles. But when teens do this, we give them the impression that something is wrong with *them.*

"Once a community has taken a vow to acknowledge, support, and keep track of all its children, including the 'bad ones,'" writes Arturo Hernandez, "then it must acknowledge, support, and keep a keen eye on the places where these 'bad kids' will be served and transformed.... The 'good kids' will do well in this world. They receive our praise, our trophies, our financial aid packages, our trust, and our jobs; everything we have is theirs. But the 'bad kids' come home to us with nothing, and we have to let them know that they count. We have to let them know that we are glad they are home."[2]

In addition, Hernandez emphasizes that "Children must have a sense of a coherent world. This can only come from an adult world that has a clear and insistent direction for them... a mission, that what they [have] to do [is] important and shouldn't be shortchanged. Their work [has] real value in a real world, and its completion would be noticed, important, and celebrated."[3]

Individual coherency includes a more or less even development of character, style, discipline, and compassion. It's about *integritas,* a proper relationship between the parts to the whole, contributing to an *entire* person.

There should be no lost causes when it comes to our youth. Most of them need help. They need real and tangible options to the life in the streets, otherwise the "underground" initiations come to get them: addictions, incarcerations, rapes, gang warfare, abuse. Working toward these options is a major part of our mission at YSS. It is a major part of my personal commitment today—to get society to care for children and youth in the same way that any decent and moral society should value, care, and preserve its offspring.

It is the best environment for them to care for themselves.

There was a way that barrio youth and *pintos* (prisoners) used to represent "respect" when I was growing up in Los Angeles: *palabra* or "word." One who had *palabra* was the most respected—not necessarily the best fighter, the best shooter, or the loudest talker. Today young people talk about "being real." To me this is what they mean. Be your word. Have *palabra.* I'm not impressed by how many people anybody has hurt, how much time they've done in prison, or even how many university degrees they have. It's about their word.

Luis Ruan, a founder-director of Beyond Limits, Inc., of Santa Ana, California, and later a community organizer for Impacto in East L.A., says something similar in his *Youth At-Risk Workbook:* "The best way of destroying your credibility is by not following your word," Ruan writes. "The news spreads like fire when you go back on your word. These youths have had a lot of inconsistencies from adults in their environment. Do not make any promises you cannot keep. In this society, there are many examples of not being able to keep your word. Our leaders do it all the time.... Working with youth is a good place to apply this philosophy."4

Of course there are times when one has to change one's mind based on new information or outcomes. The key is to be honest about these things to the people you are involved with.

Ruan has taken Chicano gang youth to the Navajo reservation so that they can get close to nature, and learn traditional rites and teachings that may help steer them down a road of enlightenment, stimulation, and hope. He understands that Chicano/Mexicano/Central Americans are also indigenous, although many of them have been brutally "Hispanicized" and often "Anglicized." But they have Indian faces, inflections, and sometimes outlooks, which is not always recognized. Ruan has also lectured in various reservations and communities in the United States, including Hawaii, and Canada. In the summer of 2000, Ruan organized the first Youth Unity Gathering with the help of then Impacto director Frank Chavez, a former resident of the Primera Flats barrio, ex-heroin addict and ex-offender, who later obtained his master's degree and became one of the leading peacemakers in the country. When I first met Frank in Chicago, he was director of Latino Youth in the Little Village barrio and other violence-prevention and community organizations.

The Youth Unity Gathering brought together more than two hundred people from all over Los Angeles; representives from the Gila River Indian Reservation in Arizona; Lakota youth from South Dakota; Navajos from the Tsaile-Chinle communities of the Diné Reservation; and some forty people from the indigenous communities of British Columbia, Canada, who came by bus.

Diné teacher and elder Anthony Lee did some beautiful invocations and teachings. A number of people performed traditional songs and dances.

But it was the personal testimonies of former gang members like Chavez and another Primera Flats *veterano*, Mike Garcia, who brought many people to tears. They had seen so many of their family members and friends killed. They themselves had been shot and had also inflicted much damage to rival barrio gangs before they changed their lives.

The brave words of the guests from Canada, Arizona, and South Dakota, who have also experienced much death by violence, suicides, and drug and alcohol addictions, were also very moving. Particularly powerful was the testimony of a young Lakota man who accidentally shot his friend to death during a night of heavy drinking. And the tearful testimony of a Canadian indigenous mother whose son was facing several decades in prison touched everyone in attendance.

Perhaps the strongest presentation came from Rudy Buchanan, a Chicano/African-American father and grandfather as well as a longtime community leader in Phoenix, Arizona, who lost two of his sons to the madness. One was killed in a gang shootout; the other was slaughtered by Phoenix police only a few weeks after his first son was gunned down. Buchanan was working among the reservations near Phoenix and had brought some youth and mentors with him.

These stories proved to be strong medicine.

During this event I mentioned how we were gathering in the largest community of native peoples in the United States and Canada—East Los Angeles—where more than a million people of Mexican descent made their home. Although Mexicans are often mislabeled Latinos or Hispanics and are largely removed from their native traditions, they still have strong indigenous blood and spiritual ties, often more so than many recognized tribal peoples in the U.S. and Canada.

I also mentioned that East L.A.—about the size of Washington, D.C.—was the most gang-ridden area of the country. According to the Violence Prevention Coalition, within a two-mile radius of Boyle Heights, one of East L.A.'s many neighborhoods, there were fifty-six homicides in 1999; more than half of the victims were between the ages of ten and nineteen.

By the end of the gathering, people there felt like family, like the long-lost relatives we've all become, finally returning home to one another.

People like Ruan, Chavez, and Buchanan—who work daily against great odds in the poorest ghettos, barrios, reservations, and rural communities of the country—have taught me a great deal. They have pioneered innovative ways of working with violence, abuse, and neglect in our communities. They are usually able to incorporate a vital spirituality with a practical program that is in tune to young people's actual needs and concerns. "Being your word" is one of the most important aspects of this work. It cannot adequately be addressed in books or funding proposals; it is something that can only be seen in the actual day-by-day relationships in the community.

In *Kids Are Worth It: Giving Your Child the Gift of Inner Discipline,* Barbara Coloroso outlines some things that are important, not just in families and in schools but most definitely among juvenile offenders, gang members, and violent youth.

The major tenets of what Coloroso calls her "parenting philosophy" are:

• Kids are worth it.
• I will not treat a child in a way I myself would not want to be treated—the Golden Rule, which seems to be suspended when it comes to dealing with troubled inner-city youth
• If it works and leaves a child's and my own dignity intact, do it.[5]

About the last point, Coloroso writes, "Just because a technique works or appears to work doesn't make it a good one. A serious problem with the many parenting tools that control kids and make them mind is that both parents' and children's dignity and sense of self-worth are sacrificed in the name of behavior modification or behavior management. Behavior management is based on power and control. It is a way of manipulating children through bribes, rewards, threats, and punishment. It 'makes' children mind, but it emphatically does not leave their dignity intact. The 'good behavior' is purchased at a terrible cost."[6]

This manipulation is multiplied in all the homes, schools, churches, juvenile facilities, and the workplace. It is how we do things. And in return it has produced some awfully unstable relationships, organizational structures, and associations that have now reaped some devastating results, including the recent assaults by children against their classmates, teachers, and parents.

Parenting has two key aspects: one of ceaseless caring; the other, which flows from the first, of rearing a child to be a fully empowered, decent, and self-reliant person. This is nurturance. One aspect lets go, just loves. The other slows down and pays attention while imparting structure, knowledge, and awareness of the necessary limitations. Though linked, these aspects, like others within any entity or process, also pull and strain at each other; otherwise, parenting wouldn't be such a struggle—the most important one of our lives.

The main thing is to relate to our children by doing, not just talking. Again, this means accepting that there will always be enough for everyone and that this plenitude, like the creative capacities we all possess, is boundless.

Whatever you can do,
or dream you can, begin it.
Boldness has genius,
power and magic in it.

—Goethe[7]

PART FOUR

WHERE DO WE GO FROM HERE?

> yes is a world
> & in this world of
> yes live
> (skilfully curled)
> all worlds
> —e. e. cummings

Chapter 23
Children Whispering

Brother, stand the pain.
Escape the poison of your impulses.
The sky will bow to your beauty, if you do.
Learn to light the candle. Rise with the sun.
Turn away from the cave of your sleeping.
That way a thorn expands to a rose.
A particular glows with the universal.

—Rumi

More than a century old, the stoneblock Menard Correctional Facility is situated on the Illinois side of the Mississippi River, some thirty miles southeast of St. Louis. Heavy shrubbery lines the banks, and industrial barges stream silently across the wide and tranquil waters. Small rural homes, churches, and corner markets speckle the surrounding green landscape.

I have come here often, once on a bus from Chicago's Southside, where the mostly African-American passengers paid fifty dollars for each adult and thirty dollars for each kid on an all-night seven-hour ride to visit family members behind Menard's thick walls.

Another time, in 1999, Trini and I were escorted by guards to a special section of the prison. We entered an electronically locked room with a sign that read Condemned Unit. Although there was no longer a death row, this section housed an isolation tank for prisoners who had violated prison regulations. We came to visit my son Ramiro, then twenty-four years old. Unlike the one in the main facility, the visiting area here was enclosed with dense glass walls between the prisoners and their guests. Phones served as communication devices. While the other visiting area had tables and chairs where prisoners could sit and interact with their families, here prisoners could not be touched, could not be hugged.

Trini and I waited for a long time before guards brought out Ramiro.

Despite the barriers, Ramiro had chains and locks on his feet and wrists. The guards kept them on while Ramiro talked to us through an intercom that he had to get close to or else he couldn't be heard. I felt helpless as I listened to my boy, his face scowled, his voice a mechanical falsetto on a phone line. As Ramiro railed against his circumstances, all I could see was the face he had had at age ten, no longer innocent, but still a child. By age ten, Ramiro had already been physically abused by a stepfather and by one of his mother's live-in boyfriends. Living in South Central L.A., he tried to run away once to Chicago to find me, hopping a train; police found him before the train left the city.

Here was a boy forced into a man's shoes, whose feet were still encrusted with dirt from child's play. They said he was dangerous. A gangster. They said he couldn't be trusted. I only saw the searching eyes on his first day of school, the scraped knee, the first pimple, the first shave, the name on a chest tag for a grocery bag boy at a local supermarket.

I had contributed to Ramiro's predicament. I hadn't been entirely there for him since his mother and I broke up, when he was two years old and his sister Andrea was ten months. Although I would see my children on weekends, I also lived in other cities, slaving away in foundries and construction sites, then working for various newspapers, radio stations, in public relations, and as a poet and editor. I had other wives, lived with a half dozen other women. I drank too much and hid myself away in political study, writing, and community organizing. Eventually, at age thirteen, Ramiro came to stay with me, but things only worsened.

When we visited Ramiro that time, he had already spent several Christmases in one jail facility or another, including two and half years in the maximum-security division of the Cook County Jail. Since his seventeenth birthday Ramiro has also been in the state prisons of Joliet and Jacksonville, and the Green County Boot Camp. *Always Running* was largely written for him. A major impetus for creating YSS was to help Ramiro and his "nation" homies. In time Ramiro's difficulties helped pull together the family, including those in California from whom I had been removed from for many years.

I knew the source of his rage. I was part of it and I had to do everything I could to remedy this. In June 1993, after seven years of taking drugs and by then twenty years of drinking, I stopped. I had tried to do this before, but it never held. I've been sober ever since. Prior to this, I never considered deeply any spiritual concerns, although I grew up as a Catholic and had a brief foray into evangelical Christianity in my late teens. Yet not until my sobriety, some twenty years later, did I become spiritually aware and active, particularly in the more vibrant and open traditions. I found great solace and family in the native communal and earth-based ceremonies and cosmologies from Mexico and the United States.

While I don't belong to a Church, I've worked with many Christian churches as well as other groups for peace in our communities. I've given sermons, led workshops, participated in various rituals. In fact over the years I've taken part in Mexika naming ceremonies, Buddhist meditation retreats, Muslim Jum'a prayer, peyote prayer meetings, sweat lodge ceremonies, Santería rites, Passover, and gatherings of atheists. I now feel connected to the fellowship of humanity, in all its complexity and entanglements, that the Creator has sought fit for me to try and to understand.

Unfortunately most of this came somewhat late for Ramiro. Although Bob Boone—a teacher, friend of the Guild Complex, and founder of Young Chicago Authors—helped my son obtain his GED, and Ramiro got himself into Chicago State University and held several jobs, he was having a hard time keeping his life together. He raged all the time. He got into criminal acts, including robberies, shootings, and drug sales. By age twenty, Ramiro had three kids by three different women.

There was another side to Ramiro: Besides being a leader in YSS—he involved many of his friends—and doing poetry readings, Ramiro also took part in Mosaic events. Whenever he appeared on TV, radio, and various publications with me, he was intelligent and poignant. He was published in a couple of anthologies.[1] And once Ramiro acted in a film about Chicago's Latino gangs for an independent filmmaker (as far as we know, it was never finished).

But as Ramiro said, "I had a premonition everything was going to collide. It was like my life was a string…on fire. I just kept trying to hold on."[2]

It was a moment of madness that finally sent my son to Menard. YSS had organized a sleep-in retreat at the Jane Addams Community Center on Chicago's Northside, graciously assisted by then director Steven Guerra. Michael Meade and Orland Bishop were our guest facilitators. Ramiro was supposed to be there. We waited and waited. He never showed. We went ahead with the event. Late that night we received a phone call: Ramiro had been picked up. He had called my friend Michael Warr to say he was getting beat up by police—apparently this went on for eleven hours until our lawyer arrived at the police station. When we heard the charges, we were devastated: three counts of attempted murder, including shooting at two police officers.

Just before all this Ramiro seemed to be doing well. He had a new job. He was attending college classes. And he was trying to be a father to his children the best he could, considering he was estranged from the mothers. But the stress of keeping up with all this proved too much. Ramiro found it hard to handle certain kinds of pressures. He would snap, just lose it. To be honest, I had the same problem. I raged for many years until I learned to keep this to a minimum. It took a lot of strategizing and struggle—and being sober. So whenever I saw Ramiro, I saw myself.

At his arraignment Ramiro stood in front of the judge with black eyes, lacerated mouth, bruised arms, and caked blood around his face. Even the judge drew back when he saw my son. He allowed a medical checkup to make sure nothing serious was wrong with him. But he also imposed a $2.5 million bail. I seethed inside. Ramiro's lot in life had been getting beat up by police, yelled at by teachers, once being jumped by staff at a psychiatric treatment facility, and all that on top of whatever traumas and turmoils he had endured at home and on the streets.

It took a while for us to piece together what happened that day. I'm sure parts of it only Ramiro knows. But here is what we understand: Ramiro got into a verbal altercation with a truck driver at an intersection while on his way to the retreat. He apparently got out of the car, gun in hand, and walked up to the truck's cab and shot the driver. I had told him never to have a gun, especially when he was raging all the time. He told me later that since he had left his "nation," he needed it for protection.

Ramiro returned to his car and sped off, but sirens of an unmarked police car pierced the air behind him. Ramiro thought he had killed the truck driver, but fortunately, although he was shot through the arm and chest and had to be hospitalized, the man survived. Everything Ramiro had worked for collapsed in that instant, in that flash of rage. So he told himself it was time to die.

He turned the car around against traffic on a one-way street. Moving toward the officers, Ramiro shot at their vehicle. He said he didn't want to hit the officers, so he shot above them. He did this partly to get away, but another part of him wanted the police to gun him down. In the ensuing pandemonium the officers shot through their own windshield. Bullets were flying, but nobody was getting hit. Ramiro turned several corners, then pulled over. He stepped out of the car and did one last thing: He put the gun to his head.

How easily a world, a life, something precious, can fall apart. For those who have found their own ways of holding it together, this may be hard to understand. Many have done so by sacrificing their soul's purpose and internal nobility. Ramiro had an intensely noble nature. But in that moment of derangement he knew only one way out. When they speak of suicide, most people impute cowardice and unclear thinking. But if anyone believes suicide has no nobility, they know nothing about it.

Ramiro did pull the trigger, but in that instant, the gun jammed. It was not his time, as they say. Ramiro could have stayed there and waited for the police. But something wanting to live began to rise in him. He threw the gun under the car and ran into a liquor store. When the police arrived, they surrounded the store. They found Ramiro hiding in the cooler. Officers beat him inside the store, stripped him, and dragged him out naked into the winter air. To police the worst thing you can do is shoot at one of their own.

Fortunately none of the officers were hit. But now Ramiro was looking at forty years to life. He faced a third strike under state law for previously having three violent felony convictions—in Illinois, judges have discretion in these cases. He was twenty-one years old.

We spent the next two and a half years battling so that Ramiro wouldn't get a life term. Thousands of dollars went to lawyers, reports, and other fees. There were many jail visits, heart-to-heart talks, and psychiatric tests. We knew we couldn't get him off. In addition Ramiro's ploys of self-sabotage, such as challenging the police at his trial, seemed determined to garner him the longest possible time. The prosecuting attorneys were adamant about getting Ramiro the forty years plus.

At one point, while we were visiting him at the electronically enhanced maximum-security section of the Cook County Jail, Ramiro let down his mask of hardness and allowed himself to feel the pain of what he was facing. He asked me to save him. I had not always been there—and now I was unable to comfort my son and make it all go away. But he was entering manhood, and even if he wasn't there yet, he was going to have to grow up mighty fast, whether he was ready or not.

What I said amounted to this: *"M'ijo,* I can't save you. This is something you will have to go through. You will have to face the trial and all its ramifications. But I will say this: Regardless of what happens, I'll be there for you. I won't abandon you. And when it's over, when you finally get through this, you will know you have a family and a community to return to."

At several of the court dates we had close to thirty family and friends in the benches. Most of the time a close family member or friend was present. Although at one point the police officers in attendance called us a "circus," and would sometimes laugh at us whenever we showed up, we never failed to be there. There were many people who cared about Ramiro. We solicited the services of the Midwest Center on Correctional Justice (MCCJ) to do a report on the family's background, mitigating factors, and his state of mind, including analyses by professional therapists. It was hard to read some of the abuse and neglect attributed to me and his mother. But we accepted our end of this and took steps to redress these while finding our own balance and healing. And many people from the Mosaic retreats, YSS, community organizations, as well as teachers and poets who knew him, wrote letters on his behalf.

Finally, in September 1998, Ramiro faced the judge to finalize a plea. After the judge read the MCCJ report and saw how active we were in Ramiro's life, he was willing to entertain a sentence of twenty-eight years, but only if Ramiro pleaded guilty.

Our lawyer advised him to accept this offer. Ramiro at first agreed. But later he balked; he told the lawyer he wanted to plead not guilty and go to trial. This would have been crushing. The lawyer got the judge's permission to allow me a special visit to the bull pen to convince Ramiro to take the deal.

It was hard for me, a fighter for whatever is just in this world, to sit there and try to convince my son to take twenty-eight years in prison. There was an aspect of betrayal there, I understood that, but it was a compromise that had to be accepted for his own good. My son was intending to take on the system—and pay with his life. So for some fifteen minutes I calmly tried to persuade Ramiro, who was full of fire and righteous indignation, to let go of his "last stand"—a continuation of his suicidal impulses—and accept the lesser sentence.

Finally Ramiro said he would take the plea for the family, for all the people who stood by him, for me. But he wasn't doing it for himself. This, of course, was not the response I was looking for. Ultimately it was his life, not ours, that he was making a decision about. But at that moment it would have to do.

When it came time for Ramiro to go before the bench, his mother,

Camila, and I stood behind a counter near him. Deputies brought Ramiro in; he wore county jail–issued khaki clothing with *D.O.C.* (Department of Corrections) stamped on the pants and on the back of his shirt. As the judge read the charges, Camila began to sob and I held her. I pushed back my own tears as best I could. Ramiro pleaded guilty. After a few more words the sentencing phase began.

The judge noted the well-written document prepared for Ramiro. He said he wished more cases would do this in his courtroom. He also appreciated the family and community support. Then the judge gave Ramiro twenty-eight years in the state pen. The judge asked my son if he had anything to say. Ramiro indicated he did, and proceeded to apologize to the court, his family, the people he had hurt, and the rest of the community for what he had done. His voice was strong and unequivocal.

Then they took him away.

Outside the courtroom the truck driver who had been shot, and who was sitting on the "victims" side, walked up to a friend of mine in our group and said he was sorry that Ramiro got so much time. My friend told him to "talk to his father." In a rare and brave moment the man came up to me and said he was sorry about what had happened. I told him I was sorry he was shot. We shook hands.

Then family and friends gathered in a circle and prayed for Ramiro's protection and to give thanks—giving thanks for a sentence of twenty-eight years in prison—this is where our country's laws and policies, which are "deranged" in their own way, have brought us. A few wept.

Although many people have told me I wasn't responsible for what Ramiro did, I don't feel I can entirely escape reproach. Regardless of words to the contrary, I can never forget how I helped turn the prison key on my son's life.

Ramiro eventually got released from the isolation unit, but not before serving thirty days there. He had been accused of smuggling contraband while working in the commissary. He didn't do it. But partly because Ramiro was no longer active in gangs, he was an easy target. Someone dropped his name. Anyone accused of a violation would have to be placed in isolation for a minimum of thirty days while the incident was being investigated. After the probe, and after Ramiro passed a polygraph test, prison officials acknowledged his innocence.

Somebody in the facility, who knows who, must have figured out that Ramiro was trying to get his life back together. If he stayed in Menard, his own survival needs would push him to become more entrenched in this particularly harsh prison world. In a year's time Ramiro was transferred to a medium-security facility two hours closer to Chicago.

In this new institution Ramiro was able to take college courses, play organized sports (he even got to coach the volleyball team), and have longer visits. He was in a better place; he even took horticulture classes, which helped him to heal himself through taking care of plants; and he worked to beautify the facility's landscape. In a year's time he had gained a number of certificates for hours of study. He also assisted other prisoners by connecting them to YSS, and he wrote many letters to YSS members, often admonishing them not to end up like him.

Now, at the end of 2000, Ramiro has finished four years of his time. He has many more years to go. We're standing by him, as promised. I pray he will find his way, through his poetry, his studies, his indigenous spirituality, and the love of his family and his many friends around the country who, despite the walls and distance, continue to reach out to him.

I know Ramiro gets depressed. I know he has bouts of anger. He is only human after all. But presently he is much more in control of himself than he ever was before. He finally did tell me I was right in convincing him to take twenty-eight years instead of fighting the case, which would have gotten him forty years to life. I also know he has big hopes of reuniting with his children and other family and of giving back properly to the world.

Ramiro, like Andrea, is a good writer. He's written numerous poems. At one point he carried a small notepad in his back pocket to jot down lines whenever they came to him. He wrote this as a young teen:

> So many false hopes, so many false answers.
> Who am I? What am I? Did I come into this
> world unknown? Did I come into this
> world with a gun in my hand and a needle up my arm?
> Was I born to die, crying for salvation?
> Crying for hope? Is my pain ever going
> to be healed? Is my hurt ever going to be
> noticed? Walking along a lonely path
> into a lonely world, with a lonely hurt
> meant only for me.

As we enter a new era, a new millennium, the United States of America is one of the most important and dynamic places to be. This country holds a key to the vital revolutionary transformations the whole world is moving toward, inch by painful inch.

Holding a key to the future does not mean that the United States should take over everything and force everyone to adopt "our image," a process we're seeing today (there are McDonald's restaurants and Coke ads in Beijing as well as in San Salvador). There is a universal potential for abundance through technological advancements, and our imaginations can be instrumental in reconnecting us with nature as well as with our souls and specific geniuses. The problems we face in our society require solutions that draw on the creative wealth possessed by all of humanity.

As a Chicano I have a particular contribution to make. My roots are in the indigenous value systems and spirituality of this land, which should be central to helping us enter a path of peace, economic and civil justice, and a full human flowering. And because I'm Chicano, I don't care for national borders, which are mostly arbitrary, and for the advantage of a small ruling class that has divided peoples, tribes, and families throughout the centuries for the purpose of exploiting them. This social class ultimately derives its power and riches by enforcing borders to establish home markets they can control, and use as springboards to control other markets.

We don't all need to be molded into the same dull homogeneity, at the expense of the richness of our manifold languages, traditions, and cultural expressions. Many voices, skin colors, cultures, concepts, and stories inhabit this land. This is not about closing ranks but about opening up to the earth wisdom we all carry in our bones, the genetic memory of being that the industrial world has forced us to forget—one of the great crimes of our time. Honoring our differences, respecting one another, is the path to acknowledging and honoring what makes us all one people.

Regardless of our differences, we all have to live together. The issue before us, then, is how we can do so with dignity for all, with opulence of spirit, in health, creatively, with economy; and where the chaotic elements of decay and change are reconciled into a future we can all strive for.

As Joseph Campbell wrote, "A single song is being inflected through all the colorations of the human choir."[3]

I once read that the trick to our unity is to maintain our freedom in regard to nonessential things—I like to eat *chilaquiles,* someone else likes *mofongo,* and still another prefers hamburgers—and our agreement about the essential things, such as the well-being of our children. *Too often people consider nonessential things to be essential, and essential things to be nonessential.* It is something to think about, especially now that we are being dragged into a global economic system that is transforming the very nature of our existence and interactions.

With the vision of a blue-white planet as seen from the moon, perhaps we can view this world of ours with more objective eyes. It's true it is a world with borders, political regimes, nations, and local powers, as political maps in every school show us. But the "truth" of this exists only in the minds of human beings, not on the surface of the planet itself.

A greater truth—one that scientists, shamans, animals, and any life-form from space can see—is that we are on a planet with an ecosystem, unified yet diverse due to its relationship to the sun and moon and the rotation of its axis. The political maps were created by history and human struggles. The real planet was created by natural processes over a period of billions of years that continue regardless of who is ruling whom. It's time to acknowledge ourselves as inhabitants of *this* earth as opposed to the seemingly insurmountable political world that we have been made to believe is a "God-given" one. "The community is the planet, not the bounded nation," admonished Campbell.

This transmutation is lengthy and difficult. It's already playing itself out on military and political battlefields as well as on personal ones. Not surprisingly, more people are looking to indigenous thought as a beacon through the present chaos. Even the new sciences—chaos theory, quantum physics, complexity, and nonlinear systems—are penetrating to a kind of knowledge that indigenous people, with much lower levels of technology, have long grasped.

As certain writers have noted,

The old science portrayed a physical universe of separate parts bound to each other by rigid laws of cause and effect, a universe of things related by force and influence. The new science gives us the vision of an entangled universe where everything is subtly connected to everything else. Influences are felt in the absence of force or signal; correlations develop spontaneously; patterns emerge from some order within. Where the Newtonian scientist reduced everything to its component parts and a few simple forces acting on them, the quantum or chaos scientist focuses on the new properties or patterns that emerge when parts combine to form wholes. A universe where nothing new or surprising ever happens is replaced by a self-organizing universe of constant invention. The scientist learns that this fact or that part cannot be isolated from its overall environment or context, the way holism replaces reductionism and wholes are seen as greater than the sum of their parts. In the new science, organized simplicity gives way to self-organized complexity.[4]

Reflecting on the indigenous cosmology behind Navajo sandpainting, a Native American author wrote,

Basic to an understanding of how the sandpainting heals is the concept of time as cyclic and circular, a principle fundamental to Navajo thought; this embracing, surrounding quality of time leads to an emphasis on dynamic process over static product. Furthermore, everyday and spiritual realities are fused: the spiritual world informs not only ceremonial experience but also everyday experience. Emory Sekaquaptewa, the Hopi scholar, uses a beautiful phrase to express the sense of inclusive multidimensional truth with which many Native Americans view the world—"mythic reality"...this more inclusive perspective embraces the coexistence of a mythic, spiritual world along-side the physical, quantifiable world. This viewpoint also expresses a circular concept of time as opposed to Western linear temporal notions, a perspective founded on the coexistence of past and present, which is the basis of the integral, reciprocal relationship Native Americans have with the spiritual world, and the environment, and their immediate and extended families and clans. To understand the sacred, living nature of the sandpainting and its power to heal, it is essential to suspend the Western notion that equates the 'real' with the measurable. Only by accepting the possibility that time and space can have richer dimensions than the Newtonian ones can we begin to grasp the depth of the Navajo sacred sandpainting.[5]

These cosmologies have provided me with the methodologies, tone, and temperament of this book. There is a sense that we cannot go forward unless we take a significant look back. Anything else will only keep us from getting to where we have to go. As Trini says, "We as a culture have clawed and crawled to the place that indigenous people have been at already."

Humanity is a world—not nations, states, provinces, sets, or turfs. And still we face this truth: Humanity manifests itself in the local and the provincial and the neighborly. Yet while we try to set up "nice neighborhoods" and "good communities" in this country, in the world we act as a global bully. We want it both ways, but one end of the contradiction erodes the other.

The main task we face as a world community is a radical realignment of our primary relationships so that they reflect mutual association, concern, and compassion. The multitude of experiences known to the many cultures that people the United States contain an extremely vital lesson for the profound changes we all must undergo: The world is meeting at the "crossroads" called the United States.

A crucial part of this task is the radical alteration of our relationship with youth. In the U.S., we have both good and bad examples of how to do this. The fact that we incarcerate more youth than any other industrialized nation should be brought to the table. But there is also a growing movement for peace with the leaders of major street organizations, the hip-hop community, among churches, and in some schools, who are committed to community building from the ground up. Many are incorporating spirit-centered rituals and teachings, breaking through the glass wall of our nation state— not just from the Americas, but from Africa, Asia, and indigenous Europe as well.

Human will must now be joined with the heart and spirit to reimagine and recreate a society and culture worthy of all our children and their gifts and dreams. The great spiral of life has taken us to this point, where such a statement resonates with renewed truth and vigor. We are being propelled toward a new world, whether we like it or not. What we do now is as simple—and as difficult—as organizing to go where we are supposed to go in the first place.

We have been through this struggle before. Drawing on the ancestral fire that burns bright within our youth, realizing that a demand for young people to lead is a demand for elders to teach, we can work to achieve the vision of equity, peace, and justice that hope has kept alive in us since time immemorial.

The great hands of the best of humanity are on our collective shoulders.

The great minds and the great hearts are demanding that we rise to the song they have sung so long ago. We have always been ready; we have only to say yes, and a way opens up. A profound truth is that we are equal to anything the world puts in front of us. Moreover, it is precisely where we have stumbled, in our personal despair, where we will find our answers. Heaven is laid out across the earth, and as Jesus says in the Gospel of Thomas, we do not see it.[6] It will not come by expectation. It's already here, now.

We are living in times when our heroes—men and women, poor and rich, from the four directions, people of all colors—rise to the task that is before us at all times: to meet the particular and seemingly insurmountable challenges of our time. "One has only to know and trust, and the ageless guardians will appear," wrote Joseph Campbell. "Having responded to his own call, and continuing to follow courageously as the consequences unfold, the hero finds all the forces of the unconscious at his side. Mother Nature herself supports the mighty task. And in so far as the hero's act coincides with that for which his society itself is ready, he seems to ride on the great rhythm of the historical process."[7]

I was intrigued with the outpouring of books, articles, and movies in the mid-1990s on "horse whispering," inspired mostly by the publication of *The Horse Whisperer*, a novel by Nicholas Evans, and *The Man Who Listens to Horses*, by Monty Roberts. Horse whispering is the art of stabilizing a reluctant, shy, or traumatized horse so that it will respond positively to a human handler—"the craft of taming the untamable and transforming the ornery into the obedient."[8] This is a hell of a job, sometimes taking hours of patient, slow, and meticulous work to convince a horse, mostly through soft tones and easy handling, to do what a whisperer wants it to do. These books are as much about relationships between humans as they are about relationships between people and animals.

Frank Bell, forty-eight, a horse whisperer from Larkspur, Colorado, said, "I help horses back to being OK, instead of [them] going to auction... or for dog food." Bell calls himself "an equine psychologist who helps horses through problems people have gotten them into in the first place.... I put a huge emphasis on bonding. If you get a relationship and trust going, the chance of getting the job done is dramatically increased." When he came across a particularly tough horse, he said, "I'm fighting a lot of history here."[9]

In many respects we can do no less for our fellow human beings. We know many raging youth who are responding to various forms and degrees of abuse, neglect, or humiliation. Some of it is personal, but much of it is institutional and cultural. Like almost any other animal that has been similarly mistreated, these people become "hard to handle." Instead of "putting them out to pasture" or sending them away to be destroyed—long prison sentences amount to the same thing—they can be taken through a careful process of trust building and management through self-control. *We need some children whispering going on.*

Because human beings are presumably more complicated than horses, bringing them around to a state of trust and participation is also more complicated. But let's stretch the process out over months—even years, if need be—and we will see similar changes in people who have been challenged by poverty, trauma, and powerlessness.[10]

A society that makes time for this will resolve many of its issues about violence. Such an approach to the crises that teens face will result in better and more responsive people. In effect the hodgepodge of relationships and interests we are presently enmeshed in should improve from the bottom up.

During the thirty-year period from 1970 to 2000, for many urban areas—and a growing number of suburbs—violence has become the main shaping feature of life. In 1995 renowned psychiatrist Dr. Carl Bell did a study of a poor Chicago neighborhood. He found that 45 percent of the high school students surveyed had witnessed a murder; 71 percent indicated that a friend or family member had been raped, robbed, shot, stabbed, or killed; and 27 percent said they had been victims of violence.[11]

According to the fall 1995 issue of *Great Cities* newsletter, the researchers at the Institute for Juvenile Research of the University of Illinois at Chicago (UIC) found that this kind of "violence is, in a sense, a rational response to the inner-city environment."

"Anyone living in these places would want to fight and protect themselves," said Nancy Guerra, one of four principal investigators for UIC's Metropolitan Area Child Study. "The aggression can be self-protection gone awry and it spirals into other behaviors."

According to Guerra, averting violence in a violent environment is like "want[ing] to lose weight, and you liv[ing] in a candy store—it's probably going to be very hard." The article points out that violent children live in a "'store' whose shelves are stocked with arbitrary aggression, violence, poverty, gangs, poor education, broken families, and lack of nurturance…. What's been surprising to us from an academic theoretical perspective is how often we neglect to consider that children in some neighborhoods must adjust to stark fear. I don't think researchers who operate in nice comfortable settings know what it's like to be constantly afraid. We develop these elaborate theories about dealing with aggression and violence, but we don't understand what it's like to live in these environments."

While large numbers of teachers, social workers, psychiatrists, and artists have worked tirelessly to help traumatized children and their families cope and thrive in such environments, we need the kind of clarity that Guerra talks about if we are to understand why many more people have fallen through the cracks. Clarity is a major first step for people to do something positive and focused about their conditions.

Unfortunately a new wave of thinking swept the land at the same time that the social environment became more "violence friendly." Let's turn our backs on the poor, the dispossesed and the troubled. This thinking justified the vast transfer of funds previously earmarked for social programs in the blighted areas to support the interests of an increasingly smaller group of people and corporations, many of whom left the inner city in previous decades to develop "safe" refuge in the suburbs. A result was the loss of tax revenue in the cities. For years afterward most cities were unable to establish new sources of revenue while state and federal governments failed to provide funds for these programs. The answer of urban redevelopment, mostly by gentrification or designating economic zones for tax relief, only shifted the problem.

Social compassion became an antiquated concept. People and politicians clamored for harsher prison sentences for the most traumatized youth. Testimony about contributing factors in cases involving violence were frequently disallowed in court. Drug treatment programs and prison rehabilitation efforts were gutted during a time when the worst drug addictions were occurring due to "crack," "crank," and other lethal drugs.

This period also featured two major campaigns: a "war on poverty" and a "war on drugs." But their results were more poverty and more drugs, despite the massive allocations of tax dollars and resources. With this experience what expectations can we have for a "war on crime"? People can complain about "politically correct" language and positions all they want, but the most PC of all has been the ferocious chorus to put "criminals" away—no exceptions, no excuses.

Horses were being whispered to while our children were being shouted down.

Is there another way? How about being prepared at all levels of our being to undergo the ordeals and rigorous work to get strength, wisdom, and confidence so that we can become adept in improving our own lives and the lives of our families, friends, and communities? Aligning and strengthening mind and spirit to overcome the body, instead of the other way around. Not numbness. Not no. And not letting go. But an affirmation: Show me the way, give me the tools, help me with the signs and images, stand by my existence with all its pains and glories so that I can know what it is to be truly alive, to have clarity and purpose, and to thoroughly and genuinely belong.

Chapter 24

New Economy, New Outlooks

Most industrialized people, eyes ever on the clock, fragmented by the pressing problems of a split-second, microchip society, have little time or inclination, it seems, to speculate on the communal nature of the universe.

—Richard Erdoes and Alfonso Ortiz[1]

North Carolina is a land of many terrains and diverse climates, from snow-capped mountains to sun-drenched beachheads. Winds strike the trees and mountainsides at all angles, and separate shades of sunlight trace its skies. Varied soils, plants, animals, and birds grace the landscape, while its people speak with differing accents and tongues.

The state also has a large agricultural and industrial base, with textiles, food processing, turkey and chicken farms, furniture manufacturing, tobacco, soybeans, and corn. And Charlotte is one of the largest financial centers in the world.

For more than two months I drove from the Blue Ridge Mountains, to the Piedmont, to the outer banks, and felt much of its rich history and natural allure. The state was also undergoing substantial cultural convulsions from a large migration of people from Mexico, Central America, Puerto Rico, the Dominican Republic, Colombia, and other Latin American countries. In ten years these people had managed to become the main workforce in the lower-end jobs in almost all of the industries.

Racial, class, and cultural tensions abounded. But I also saw many people, churches, and institutions come together to help welcome and integrate the new transients. A few North Carolinians were learning Spanish, and I met a few Mexican migrants conversing with North Carolina accents.

Among the many industrial sites I visited was a large turkey farm, where

287

hundreds of workers in plastic head caps and uniforms milled around a large lunchroom. At a bedding plant I spoke to several ESL students taking classes there. In the main facility there were rows and rows of industrial sewing machines with multicolored hoses and lines of threads dangling from the ceiling, while mostly Mexicans and Central Americans leaned across massive tables to power huge, bobbing needles into thousands of feet of cloth.

In the schools, efforts to incorporate many of the Spanish-speaking children were often blocked. The ridiculous "English only" state law forces some teachers to teach their charges in Spanish clandestinely, even having to erase Spanish words from the chalkboards when guests happen to visit their classrooms.

Some kids are also pressured to leave school—sometimes in the younger grades, but mostly in high school—so that they can work the fields and factories, and help with the family income. Away from any real place called home, unschooled, and largely out of sight, these people were fast becoming some of the "lost ones."

Parts of North Carolina reminded me of California when my family first settled there—cornfields at the end of the street, being nine years old and working, and everybody in the household contributing to the family income. Still, North Carolina's people made my visit most memorable: When I entered the lives of strangers, I found family; when I gazed into eyes of frustration and helplessness, I found hope; where I laughed along with the bountiful chuckles of children and, through the tears, listened to two nine-year-old girls considering suicide (nine years old?); where many tongues—Spanish, English, Hmong, Russian, Chinese, Vietnamese, and Cherokee—flowed like the most ancient of rivers.

The interesting thing about North Carolina was the fact that all this was going on in the midst of a New Economy, where "the move from an economy based on the production of physical goods to an economy based on the production and application of knowledge"[2] was going to leave many of these people straggling.

A young person entering the job market today can expect to move from job to job. He or she will change jobs more frequently than in the previous generations—temporary work is the fastest rising category of work in the country. The chances of getting a life-long job, staying at it long enough to know its intricacies, and perhaps move up the ranks, are increasingly nil. As a result people will have many job experiences, go through many work relationships, and endure an overwhelming lack of longevity or permanence. This will affect their outlook about themselves and the world. With this situation built into the work world they are entering, a young person shouldn't be judged as lacking a "work ethic" or being lazy.

But it does mean there should be new ways of approaching work issues that take into account what young people are presently experiencing. We have to adjust our thinking to consider what work really is now, and to discover how jobs can still be made meaningful and long term. Today jobs have the potential to be aligned with one's particular path, practice, and art, instead of being the kind of soul-draining, purposeless grind—from the hamburger stand to the office—that we have come to expect from employment.

When I first entered the workforce as a teenager, I had to learn everything the hard way. That is to say, I learned a lot without proper support. I made many mistakes that could have been avoided, even hurting myself and others in the process. When I worked as a millwright and carpenter's apprentice, there wasn't the kind of journeyman-apprentice relationship in which people took care of one another and where they patiently and respectfully worked together toward the same goals. Instead I learned by shouts, indignities, game playing, tricks, racial and personal attacks, betrayals, and mistrust.

At one of my first industrial jobs I almost lost my eyesight when a welder neglected to tell me not to look at an arc weld he was making. I was sent off to do tasks that were often degrading and unnecessary. Once, in a steel mill, I unsteadily climbed thirty feet of an electric furnace to grease the bearings on top while the furnace was still hot, although this didn't need to be done until the furnaces had cooled for twenty-four hours or so. I have been electrocuted, knocked out cold by toxic fumes, and narrowly escaped having air bubbles drilled into my veins when a supercompressed air hose broke and pounds of pressurized air struck my arm. On top of that I was called names and belittled for every little misunderstanding or mishap.

Eventually I learned my jobs, learned to lick my wounds, and keep going. But I also held a lot of resentment against my fellow workers and bosses, who often pitted one employee against another, devising elaborate schemes to keep their positions of power over the entire workforce. I had bosses whose every word to me was an insult. I encountered fellow workers who set me up to be fired when they didn't like me. Of course, as always, the majority of my fellow hard hats were decent and supportive. And I had a boss or two who knew how to treat people with dignity. But there seemed to be something about the kind of work we did that required a hard and demeaning style of communication.

Young people are eager to learn, and at their age they are most open to doing so. Most are willing to abide by the rules and requirements of a workplace. Many adults, however, end up pushing them into no-win situations and then degrading them, so that they respond in very bad ways, mostly by quitting or getting fired. In my many years of working in factories, steel mills, foundries, and construction sites as a young man, I gave up many a job and was fired from a few others. My generation expected this. It was the way it was. Today it is unnecessary for any young person to have to go through that. Nobody can truly and adequately learn in an environment of coercion and humiliation.

The new technological changes in the workplace should afford an opening up of creativity and soul satisfaction that we have not seen in "work" before. This is part of an economic revolution that can serve as a foundation for energizing the whole of our society and our intimate and social relationships as well. If not, then technology will become a chain around our necks.

"Imagine a world where pursuing our passions pays the bills," declared Andrew Kimbrill. "An important starting point for any effort to re-envision work is to remember that there is nothing natural or preordained about our modern system of jobs.... In searching for ways to put meaning back to work, we might want to revive the term *vocation* (from the Latin for 'voice' or 'calling'). Today, 'having a vocation' or 'answering a calling' usually means embarking upon a religious life—an unfortunate narrowing of the concept. We all deserve to be involved in work to which we have been called by our passions and beliefs."[3]

But this must be planned for and organized so that it can be realized. Instead of pressuring individuals to simply fold into the needs of a larger, abstract process or system, we should look at the inherent potential—what in Spanish are called *poderes*, "powers"—that each person brings to a situation, and integrate it with the aims and interests of the whole community. It should not be limited to the confines of an association, office, firm, corporation, or government or nongovernmental agency.

Yet at a certain point, meeting one's particular calling, we enter a terrain of our own making. "This is the path of no path, the gateless gate," Joseph Campbell said, "the unmapped life of an individual quest and an individual realization—we must all learn to incubate our destinies."[4]

In late June 2000, my family and I moved from Chicago to the Northeast San Fernando Valley to be closer to my wife's vibrant family there. The area includes a large Mexican-Latino community—80 percent of the 400,000 people who live here. There is one incorporated town, San Fernando, with a population of 25,000, and several Los Angeles communities such as Pacoima, Arleta, Sylmar, and Sun Valley. Pacoima is one of the poorest communities in L.A.

Soon after we arrived, a number of community leaders, artists, and developers—Otto "Tito" Sturcke, Enrique Sanchez, Maria Florez, my wife Trini, and I—came together to create Tía Chucha's Café Cultural. Our aim was to establish an institution that would enhance the intellectual, cultural, aesthetic, and technological life of the community.

Like many deprived areas, this section of the northeast valley did not have movie houses, bookstores, cultural centers, or enlightened community centers of ideas, the arts, and literature. There were instead the usual video stores, food stands, vacant lots, dollar stores, storefront churches, used-car lots, and bars. As a former mayor of San Fernando said at a fundraising event, "You would have to drive twenty-five minutes on two freeways to see a first-run movie."

Previous attempts to bring in major bookstores had apparently failed. One bookstore-chain representative told a local developer that the people of the Northeast San Fernando Valley "don't read." It appears they required a critical percentage of college graduates and higher income brackets in the population for them to set up shop.

While students in the local public schools had some of the lowest scores in the vast Los Angeles Unified School District, the refusal to bring in such cultural institutions greatly lowered the expectations for these students' success, despite the fact that most of them wanted to learn, craved being able to conjoin with their roots and cultures, and were more than willing to partake in whatever the future holds. This is precisely why we wanted to set up Tía Chucha's Café Cultural in the northeast San Fernando Valley. Such an institution can thrive in these communities because the people are hungry for intellectual and artistic stimulation, after being excluded from such places for so long. For the children, for the community's future currency in the world, we had to try.

In the beginning of our endeavor there were, of course, the usual retorts: Nobody reads here. Who's going to buy your coffee? Artists are unreliable.

And how are you going to make profits? Of course we knew that people here *do* read, that artists do come through, and that many people would love to have access to a variety of interesting and tasty coffees. And if the issue was solely about profits, we wouldn't be in this kind of work. Although we knew we had to be self-sufficient, able to sustain our institutional goals for a long time, Tía Chucha's Café Cultural has another more important reason for being: the overall political, cultural and economic advancement of this community.

We also wanted to open up a dialogue about new kinds of work and new kinds of teaching, about how to direct our children outside of the existing jobs and educational programs that tended to push students into dead ends and static career boxes.

Our one-page promotional statement reads:

> Tía Chucha's Café Cultural is a dream of community empower-ment.... Our aim is to provide great books; workshops on the arts and literature; spoken word; musical and theatrical performances; an art gallery and workspace; and a technological center to help bridge the digital divide in our communities. And it's going to be a place where one can find great-tasting coffees and drinks. We want a place where the community can dialogue, share ideas, organize, and get skillful in the various communicative and visual arts. A place where families can be stimulated to read books, participate in intellectual endeavors, and be surrounded by the healing power of art and the word. A place where creativity can be brought fully to bear and where we can positively transform the quality of our individual lives as well as the lives of our diverse communities. Everyone we've talked to—from high school students, to teachers, businesspeople, family men and women, profes-sionals, artists, university students and academics—have said the same thing: "We need a place like Tía Chucha's Café Cultural." Tía Chucha's will proudly feature the best of Chicano/Latino art, literature, and theater presented by well-established and emerging artisans. We will also have a cutting-edge multimedia center that will draw from our rich past and help guide us into the future. Our doors are open for every-one as we welcome all nationalities, cultures, and communities to partake in what this growing community has to offer in arts and liter-ature.... Books. Art. Music. Dance. Theater. Computers. Poetry. And good coffee, too.

The idea had such resonance that when word spread about what we wanted to do in the San Fernando Valley, people in East L.A.—my old stomping grounds—and other communities wanted us to open other Tía Chucha's Café Culturals. Perhaps in time we will. And friends came through to help us, like labor activist and writer Suzan Erem, writer and technology activist Jeff Park, longtime San Fernando Valley resident and activist Debra Fisher, curator and community organizer Christina Ochoa, world-renowned Chicano artist Chaz Bojorquez, teacher and organizer Angel Cervantez, singer and activist Angelica Loa, community educator Maria Elena Tostado, Reuben Martinez of Martinez Books in Santa Ana, the Midnight Special Bookstore in Santa Monica, the Guild Complex, Mosaic Foundation, and Eliott Bay Books in Seattle.

At the Border Book Festival in Las Cruces, New Mexico, organized in March 2001, Chicana novelist Denise Chavez, who was also festival director, helped arrange a major auction of rare and first-edition Chicano/Latino books, magazines and other similar items from the John Randall Collection that benefited the Border Book Festival and Tía Chucha's Café Cultural. John Randall, a friend to Chicanos and activists everywhere, graciously offered this to us. And the Liberty Hill Foundation provided us funds for construction and other needs. People like these sense that possibilities are everywhere, and they're seeking ways to be prepared as these possibilities converge on their lives.

We are living in a time of momentous challenges, a time in which the values of our society must clash. What can guide us? Study, study, and more study. It's time for the dispossessed to lead. You, the abandoned mother. You, the hungry and tired. You who are without a job or place called home. Study and be free. If you can imagine it, you are already on your way. Hold fast to your dreams. Deepen your knowledge. Imagine. Organize. And win.

Chapter 25

Safe and Sacred Space

It's easy to see how to do away with what we call crime.... It can be done by giving the people a chance to live.

—Clarence Darrow

For a few years now I have been active with groups like the Community Renewal Society's Churches-in-Community Unit, with the reverends Art Waidmann, Nidza Chavez, and Marilyn Pagan, trying to organize sanctuaries for youth in trouble with their families, the law, and their communities. We explored the various aspects and components of what such sanctuaries should be about, look like, and accomplish. In many respects Youth Struggling for Survival has been a sanctuary in its embryonic state.

Sanctuary has been described as a "holy place," a place of protection, rest, and contemplation. There are sanctuaries for endangered birds and animals. There are holy places in churches and temples. *Sanctuary* has also been defined as a "sacred place where a fugitive from the law or a debtor was secured by medieval church law against arrest or violence."[1]

Sanctuary is an old idea that needs to be revived for the present violent situations in our communities. There has to be a workable alternative to prisons, detention homes, boot camps, and mental institutions; a place that takes into account the development of the whole person, with resources and assistance to quicken the psychological, environmental, economic, political, cultural, and spiritual dimensions of everybody involved.

A sanctuary should be seen as a temporary sustainable community within a larger community, which is fraught with frayed relationships and shattered expectations. It should be a place that mitigates repressive policies, one that offers positive alternatives. The Mosaic Foundation describes sanctuary as "the occasional temple, the vestibule or house of genius where the soul is

present." The goal should be to get a person back into the world, emboldened to struggle and achieve a greater wholeness for the world.

In sanctuary the laws of the land are temporarily suspended and the laws
of spirit are consciously and actively engaged. This is not to say we should
harbor a known fugitive without spelling out what is involved in such an act;
it may mean preparing such people for the initiation of a trial they must go
through, as well as providing proper representation in court. It is a place to
help people master their emotions and impulses, so that they can contribute
to the healthy development of their abilities and of their communities.

The moral imperative for such a sanctuary has to be greater than the
laws that may be suspended. Criminal codes, immigration laws, unilateral
agreements, and unjust treaties must *not* be the binding factors in our decisions to safeguard someone who may be a victim of those very codes, agreements, and treaties.

There are practical considerations of course. In the 1980s, when sanctuaries were set up in the Southwest for refugees from war-torn Central
American countries, the government tried to force sanctuary workers to turn
over refugees, threatening them with indictments, injunctions, and possible deportation.

In 1988 Demetria Martinez, a social activist and fellow poet, was indicted
on charges related to the smuggling of two Salvadoran refugees into the
United States. Demetria had apparently accompanied a Lutheran minister,
active in the sanctuary movement, to the border to bring the refugees into
the country. At the time Demetria was working as a journalist in Albuquerque, New Mexico. In court the U.S. government tried to use her poem
"Nativity, for Two Salvadoran Women" against her. Of course, deporting the
Salvadoran women back to their country was not an option—this would
surely have meant torture and possible death. Demetria was later acquitted;
she never backed down in her resolve to safeguard these women's identities
and the sanctity of her words.

For the most part the sanctuary movement ensured that those working
in the movement were adequately represented in court and in the media. At
the same time a greater moral imperative—most of this movement consisted
of clergy and laypersons—allowed them to maintain their mission and
integrity in the face of fire.

During the pre–Civil War period in the United States, when slavery was
the overriding political and moral issue, similar sanctuaries were set up to

safeguard fugitive slaves as well as abolitionists threatened with jail or death. The proprietors of these sanctuaries, or safe houses, were aware that their actions, despite the existing laws—particularly after the 1857 Dred Scott Decision made it a crime for anyone in the U.S. territories to harbor an escaped slave—put their own lives at stake.

We have to do the same thing for our youth suffering from a rash of three-strikes-and-you're-out legislation, truth-in-sentencing, accountability laws, and being tried as adults.

There has to be a great moral imperative behind our present urban sanctuary work.

In addition sanctuaries should have access to health care, both for the mind and for the body. Decent diet, exercise, and healthy habits have to be instilled; anger management skills taught; trauma reduction practiced; and, when needed, carefully prescribed psychiatric drugs made available. My experiences with existing psychiatric treatment facilities in poor communities is that brutal techniques—shackling of clients, scattered beatings, and the overuse of drugs—are too frequently used.

According to a statement in a workbook by the Anti-Violence Initiative of CRS, "Violence is organized in childhood and *acted out* in adolescence." The traumas of childhood, then, have to be transcended—not by dismissing them and saying "get over it," as I once heard a TV preacher say—but by working through them.

Rituals geared to this process can help take the punch out of any hate and violence that can arise from such traumas. By beauty-making and a *re-placement* of the issues, things change. Sanctuary should be a place where these rituals can be conceived and acted on, and where true transformations are possible.

Most of this can be done in collaboration with institutions, churches, schools, and organizations. Anything less will not go deep enough, will not meet the level of the crisis we are currently embroiled in.

In early 1996, with representatives of Christian protestant churches and Catholic dioceses, we endeavored to do our first-ever sweat lodge ceremony with active Chicago gang youth. Some seventy young people participated, including rival gang members, along with ten adults. Our facilitator was Julio Revolorio, a Guatemalan Mayan who was also a Sundancer, taught by Lakota elders in South Dakota. We gathered in a secluded camp area run by the Community Renewal Society in Woodstock, Illinois.

At first there was tension in the group. A few of the kids began to mad-dog each other—"eye boxing" as one prisoner friend described it. Words were exchanged. In attendance were factions of the Latin Kings and the Two-Six Nation as well as youth from "nations" in Pilsen and Humboldt Park. "Folk" *and* "People." We even got word that one participant had supposedly shot another participant in a previous street battle. A couple of the adults wanted to end the whole thing and send everyone back home. But we decided to proceed.

Julio had everyone make a circle and began to teach us about the significance of the sweat lodge—the purification aspects that are so vital for anyone. He got us all to say a few words about why we came and what our expectations were. It took hours to get everyone's voice in, but in "ritual time" the clock is largely ignored.

Then Julio taught the group how to build a sweat lodge from the ground up, and how to fire up the rocks in the traditional manner. The newness of the experience—even though most of the youth were of Mexican-indigenous descent—and the sacredness in the way this was handled helped calm the attitudes.

At one point Julio related how his first wife and family were killed by Guatemalan national guardsmen during the civil war that claimed some 100,000 lives over a two-decade period. He openedly wept, breaking down many of the tough veneers in the group. Since we all had to work together, it was a sight to see enemies from the street talk to one another and cooperate in creating the lodges.

Julio had the males do one lodge, the females do another. While the male lodge looked somewhat crooked compared to the female lodge—we attributed this to higher levels of trust and cooperation among women than men—everyone managed to pull it off. We also created numerous prayer ties for all the participants, which were to be hung from each of the lodges.

Finally the men were allowed to change into shorts and the women into long cotton dresses to take part in the ceremony. Each carried their own towel. In the male lodge I saw "enemies" standing behind one another as they entered, a few with tattoos on their backs, visible without their shirts. By the end of the ceremonies no one held grudges or had hatred in their hearts. Their spiritual searching was being honored.

Then just before our communal meal a few of the youth who had previously challenged another group walked up to them and apologized—something they did on their own. After this success we decided to hold similar ceremonies with other youth from violent communities in and around Chicago.

Sanctuaries are predicated on the idea that, freed from fear and punishment, most people will heal. Sanctuary is a healing place. A child in a poor urban environment is constantly bombarded by beatings, bullets, threats, and abuses. You can't begin to heal under such a bombardment.

Luis Ruan, who works with gang youth in Orange County and East L.A., has taken some hard-core violent youth to the Navajo reservation in Arizona for a long-range "time-out," away from the pressures of the barrio.

One young man, Felipe, was a twenty-year-old shot-caller for his barrio gang. He was a drug dealer, shooter, and substance abuser. When I met Felipe in 1997, he had just finished a year on the rez, working and living with a local family in a trailer located in a particularly sparse area. He appeared healthy, calm, and confident. Unfortunately he needed to go back to the neighborhood to see his family—he had not seen his mother in six years, five of which had been spent in a youth prison. This turned out to be major setback for Felipe, but Luis and I both felt that the time-out on the rez would always be there for him; he could learn to gather himself when he needed to.

The Navajos are very traditional people. They taught Felipe some of their ways, inviting him to prayer meetings and sweat ceremonies. Luis also introduced him to Anthony Lee, our respected Diné elder. Felipe, in turn, tried to help some Navajo youth who were becoming active in their own gangs, such as Indian Power, the Cobras, and the Dragons. Many of them were also linking to Brown Pride and Sureños or other Chicano/Latino gang structures in Los Angeles, Phoenix, and Chicago.

On the day Felipe left, the family and friends who had taken care of him on the rez gave him a tearful sendoff, something he had never experienced. This experience is now part of any arsenal he may need to help him maintain a decent and wholesome life.

I saw the value of taking such violent youth—for however long it is necessary—away from gang and family pressures, removing them from their traumatized environment and bringing them back into nature, into ritual, and closer to spirit. On the Navajo reservation these youth learned new skills, underwent rites of passage, found an art and a practice, and learned healthy and sane methodologies for growth.

A number of us have talked about setting up such venues, particularly in open spaces, so that youth can commune with the earth again and be surrounded by caring adults, elders, and other youth. It's invaluable.

"True sanctuary either does or doesn't exist within an individual human spirit. If we're really at peace, the world can't destroy that peace. If the fear is ringing in our ears, no amount of outside safety will make it stop. But the skills of creating sanctuary can be learned from other people, and from time spent in a place of safety and rest."[2]

In Mosaic, we also started a "Walking With" component that involves young prisoners who have been to our retreats. Here we established lines of communication and ways to get books and tapes into the institutions. We help with letters of support, jobs when released, and assistance in court. Our aim is to bring more and more communities to "walk with" their sons and daughters in various correctional institutions. We believe when such prisoners do get out, they will wish to be part of a community—to give and not take—and to be involved from the strength of their own capabilities. Malidome Somé called this, "a crusade for self-retrieval."

At the same time, certain things should be in place so that when such youths return, they have gone far enough into their initiation and practice that they can never go back to the old habits, patterns, and rages that debilitated them in the first place. It's a "walking with" till they can walk on their own. As Michael Meade has stated, "a procession, rather than a prosecution."

One of the most striking examples of a "walking with" approach involved Delbert Leo Hosteen, a young Navajo man who had attained a level of notoriety when he was convicted in the slaying of a police officer on the Navajo reservation. Although he had no connection to Mosaic's work, his return to a meaningful life involved the ongoing support of one of his teachers, my friend Priscilla Aydelott.

In fact Leo's case was the reason Priscilla and I first connected. For more than a decade she taught at Monument Valley High School in Kayenta, Arizona. Leo was sitting in her class when she read my book to the students. Later when Leo was awaiting trial, she sent him a copy, which he liked. I also wrote to Leo while he was in the federal prison facility in Dickinson, North Dakota.

I first met him after his 1999 release; he worked at a fast food stand in Flagstaff. In April 2000, during one of my appearances at the Flagstaff Literary Festival, I had dinner with Leo and his fiancée. At the time, Leo was managing a company that built and replaced underground gasoline tanks for gasoline stations. During dinner Leo looked calm and confident, a far cry from the image of him as a crazed teenager being taken away for a particularly vicious crime. Leo said he had barely had the job a month when his employers decided to put him in charge. He later started his own business cleaning and installing window blinds.

Leo is a born leader, a quick thinker, and a hard worker. He learns fast and takes full responsibility for his work. At twenty-two, Leo is on a good path and in a good way. While this is hard for most ex-cons, Leo has already overcome extraordinary pain and suffering to get to this point. He has already taken some courageous steps to become a decent and contributing member of his community. Despite a few setbacks, such as a couple of minor parole violations, Leo is clean and strong.

During his incarceration Priscilla and I stayed in touch. He even wrote Ramiro as my son underwent his own prison ordeals. Unfortunately Leo's victories had to be built on top of some stark and brutal experiences. Like many prisoners and gang youth, Leo's world was one of violence, fear, and uncertainty. Growing up poor on the rez, he saw his mother beaten by an abusive stepfather. This man once broke Leo's nose when the boy tried to intervene on his mother's behalf. But the most devastating thing in the boy's early years was the untimely death of his younger brother, a death that Leo accidentally caused when he was around seven years old.

Leo had no proper counseling or other help with this. He had only his mother's love, which never abated even when her younger son died and Leo was taken away from her. He had to deal with the pain and guilt on his own. He turned to alcohol and drugs. He ditched school, got involved in gangs, and participated in numerous fights, shootings, and other violent acts. The first time he met Priscilla, she pulled him aside to address his quick temper. Eventually this teacher's caring and consistency broke through Leo's defenses. He didn't like school, but he did like being in Priscilla's class.

This all changed on January 6, 1996. On that day, after several days of drinking, drugging, and robbing, Leo and a partner were pulled over at gunpoint by a tribal police officer. The officer allegedly threw Leo to the ground, cuffed one of his hands, and shoved Leo's face into the sand so that he couldn't breathe. Leo managed to reach around with his free hand and pull the officer to the ground. In the ensuing scuffle, Leo beat the officer with his flashlight. He dropped the flashlight and was going to let the officer go, but the cop again tried to subdue his suspect. Leo was able to get the officer's gun and put it to his neck. After an exchange of words and tearful pleadings, Leo dropped this weapon as well, whereupon the officer pulled out a Mace bottle and sprayed Leo in the face.

Although blinded, Leo reportedly swung wildly at the officer, at one point connecting and dropping the man. Then Leo choked him—for what he thought was around five minutes—until the officer died. Leo and his friend took the gun, some ammunition, and rode off in the police car, which they wrecked by the side of the road.

They ran into the jagged rocks and massive stone formations of the nearby canyons. A couple of hours before dawn Leo woke up to the sound of two helicopters shining spotlights on the other side of the canyon. He also saw "like a mile" of police vehicles just below where he was holed up. There were men with flashlights and dogs, including what he thought was a SWAT team, searching the terrain. By the time the sun came up, Leo and his friend had been spotted and arrested.

Leo was placed in a federal maximum-security juvenile facility in Florence. Three times prosecutors tried to get him tried in adult court, once going to San Francisco to find a judge who would agree. In adult court Leo would have faced a life sentence without parole or else the death penalty. But in the end this didn't happen. Leo says the death penalty was ruled out after intervention by the tribal government. The tribe had told federal prosecutors that many Navajos had died in various wars defending America's interests; in World War II they were the leading members of the Indian code talkers that confused the Japanese and strengthened U.S. defenses. The tribe had done enough dying, they said. No death penalty.

On October 21, 1996, Leo received convictions for first degree premeditated murder, first degree felony murder, conspiracy to commit burglary, burglary, theft of a law enforcement vehicle, credit card fraud, and murder of a federal officer. The judge also ordered him to pay $26,098 in restitution to the Kayenta Police Department for damage to the police car.

Leo's sentence was slated to end on his twenty-first birthday in the year 2000. But while doing his time, he obtained a GED and enrolled in college courses. He also wrote letters and poems. And he worked to take care of his restitution. With good time, Leo was able to get an early release. Despite the terrible nature of his crime, with the assistance that came his way, particularly from Priscilla, the tribe, and his family, Leo was able to walk out of the federal prison system a changed person.

During his imprisonment Leo spent a long time thinking, suffering, risking, to overcome the terrible beast within that had done a terrible act, that still carried the dead eyes of his brother in his head, that still carried his mother's tears from the beatings but also from the loss of her son, tears from the day he was convicted and forced to leave after embracing her, tears that always affected Leo to his core.

Based on what Leo's done, it may be hard to see him as a redeemable human being. But we must. He's young and he will have much to learn and much to go through. But he has already visited many hells and many prisons, real and psychic, and he'll not want to revisit them anytime soon. For now he has to think about a new wife, a new job, and a new city—important and vital steps for anybody.

Perhaps the following passage from Leo's writings may shed light on his violent past, and also on why he's changed. It's a glimpse of what he has had to think about, day in and day out, and perhaps will as long as he lives. It's about what happened between him and his younger brother:

My younger brother was three or four years old. I was about seven or eight. We were sitting outside the house when I ran inside and found a gun, put a bullet in and walked back outside. I really didn't know about the safety or anything about a gun. My brother sat in front of me, happy and all. The next thing you know, the gun goes off. I saw a shocked look on my brother's face. I started to cry. He cried, his lips turned purple. He yelled my name. He was walking around and saying my name. I tried to pick him up and help him walk around. I lifted his shirt and saw blood on his back—and blood trickle down from his chest. I put him in a truck and ran off. I ran to my Auntie Ella. I told her what happened and we ran back to the house. By then my brother was almost dead. I held his head and hand as he whispered my name for the last time. He slowly closed his eyes forever, and I sat there trying to call him, moving him around, his blood on my hand and his head on my lap.

Chapter 26

Between Two Worlds[1]

*When a refugee told his or her story, it was not psychoanalysis, it was
testimonio:* story as warning, facts assembled to change not the self
but the times.

—Demetria Martinez

The faces of the young men and women were hard and discomforting.
They were dark-skinned with strong Indian features. Some had their heads
shaved. One of the girls, in her early twenties, was called Baby Crazy. She
had tattoos on her lips and cheek as well as harsh mascara and dark lip paint.
Her arms had tattoos in old English letters and in the barrio gang style, including the initials of her gang and the names of her boyfriend and two children.

One of the young men had tattoos across his arms, back, and chest. On
his face he had tattooed tear below one eye and the three dots signifying "Mi
Vida Loca" below the other eye; the initials of his gang were on his chin.
The others were similarly marked, some with scars of bullet wounds and knif-
ings. They wore the loose and oversized clothing known as the cholo style.
They had names like Diablo, Pelon, Villain, Clever, and Whisper.[2]

They were Salvadoran gang members attired in the same L.A.-gang style
that has brought chills to many an outsider in the United States and in parts
of Latin America. Only these particular youth weren't in Los Angeles. They
were participants in a 1996 summit on youth and violence in San Salvador,
El Salvador's capital.

Donna DeCesare and I had located these young people so that they could
take part in an important gathering that involved government officials, members of the newly formed National Civilian Police, nongovernmental agencies, churches, social workers, and representatives of various political parties.
It was called La Juventud Salvadoreña Enfrentando La Violencia (Salvado-

ran Youth Confronting Violence). Some of these youth also attended a reading and talk that Donna and I gave at the Intercambios Culturales in San Salvador, where Donna's award-winning photos of Mara Salvatrucha and Mara 18th Street gang members were on display. Donna and I had been collaborating on bringing to light the phenomenon of L.A.-based barrio gangs in El Salvador. She also went on to photograph the growing globalization of U.S. gang culture in Belize, Haiti, and other countries.

It was Franklin Torres, a twenty-year-old Salvadoran dying of AIDS in El Salvador who prompted this collaboration. Donna met him while producing a photographic study of AIDS in that country. He was not like the others she had photographed during four years of the civil war. Franklin was covered with tattoos, including one that proclaimed "18th Street." U.S. immigration authorities had deported Franklin, who was undocumented, at age seventeen because of his police record and gang affiliation in the United States. At the time he had full-blown AIDS, which he contracted from using infected tattoo needles.

It was a death sentence for Franklin to get deported to a country that had no adequate means of dealing with AIDS. It has happened before. Andres Bustamante, a Los Angeles immigration lawyer I interviewed in early 1994, said, "[Since the mid-1980s] changes in the law, including the addition of aggravated felonies, have allowed the federal and state governments to work hand in hand in deporting as many of these people as they could. There is definitely more aggressiveness by the INS to seek out and deport these youth."

Bustamante went on to claim that in 1992–93 some four hundred alleged gang members were deported from L.A. While most of them went to Mexico, about forty were sent to El Salvador.

Franklin was dying when he gave Donna the names of his homeboys and family in L.A. for her to visit. She then conceived the idea of doing a photo/text project on the plight of Salvadoran gang members in L.A. and its impact on El Salvador. In early 1993, Donna approached me to work with her.

On this bright May day, members of MS and 18th Street suspended their rivalry to sit on a panel together. They came to tell their story. One of the 18th Street gang members picked up his arm to reveal a mangled hand. He said he had tried to lob a hand grenade at MS rivals when the explosive blew before he could let go.

While El Salvador had known almost fifteen years of civil war, the country had not seen this kind of warfare: drivebys, hand grenades thrown into crowds, AK-47s in the hands of children, and dead and tortured tattooed bodies. In 1993 one hand grenade blast reportedly killed nine people.

During the panel discussion other young people spoke eloquently about their struggle to survive in a poor country they hardly knew; most had come to the United States as infants. They were without resources or jobs, and faced the wrath of police, who beat and tortured them, including burning off tattoos with irons and cutting off their "homeboy" braids. They also talked about the death squads who hunted them down.

The audience was rapt. Here, for the first time, directly from the mouths of those involved, they heard why these gangs existed, why they did what they did, and how many of them were seeking ways to live peaceful and meaningful lives. It was this spirit that helped create Homies Unidos a short time after.

Since 1993 the major news media in the U.S. and El Salvador had been putting out articles, reportage, documentary pieces, and other information on MS and 18th Street. Similar "exposés" were coming out in Guatemala, Honduras, and Mexico, where MS and 18th Street members had also been deported. Most of these were inflammatory and distorted, making these youth look like the most devastating criminal element in the world.

Like all gang youth I've met and worked with, the Salvadoran youth were capable of great havoc. But I also felt safe and respected by them. For our documentary we entered their closed-off enclaves in abandoned buildings, empty lots, and drug dens. In the two prisons we visited—one was Mariona, the country's largest and most dangerous, located in the capital city—the youth were eager to talk, to tell their side of things, to discuss the brutal world they had been forced to live in. But also how they held answers in their hands— practical strategies as well as visions of peace and visions of healing.

Once in the late 1990s I did a presentation in Chicago for a Latin American issues conference. When I mentioned the Mara Salvatrucha, one of the Central American journalists in attendance jumped up and exclaimed: "How dare you bring up this band of killers and thieves! They are totally unredeemable."

This journalist, however, had never bothered to listen to these young people, had never stayed in their makeshift homes, or walked the dirt roads leading to their hangouts, or witnessed their parties in vacant trash-strewn lots; he had never been to the prisons and hospitals where they were thrown away and forgotten. This is why Donna and I made sure these kids could be part of the panel at the San Salvador summit—so that others could see they are our children, our hope, our legacy. We made them; now we have to find ways to embrace them.

San Salvador's dust fell like ash on cars, homes, stalls, people. Anyone driving in the *trafison*—the terribly erratic and backed-up traffic into the capital—had to use their windshield wipers to remove the dust in order to see. In late 1993 two million people—including some of the poorest on the continent—called San Salvador home.

After driving from the airport past miles of mountainous green scenery, we arrived at the city where blocks and blocks of corrugated tin-roofed shacks lined the main roads. People warned us to be wary of bandits, who were known to stop vehicles leaving the airport and rob their occupants, sometimes killing them. We also heard about airport personnel giving signals to their accomplices about who had brought valuable items from abroad. Uniformed men with AK-47s guarded the few gasoline stations and markets along the way.

In the Central American summer of December, the heat drooped over everyone like a wet blanket—weather for *la fiebre,* the dengue fever, and other tropical ailments. With Christmas and New Year's approaching, an unbelievably large number of stalls sold the typically destructive *mortares*—large, red-papered, explosives used as holiday fireworks. As the mosquitoes partied on our skins, the children played, and wafts of *pupusas* smells struck you at all angles, the city's center came to life.

Multicolored shawled women and equally colorful but ancient buses crammed into the narrow streets. *Microbuses,* small vans used to transport a smaller number of people, pulled in and out of traffic and pedestrians; hanging off the micros' running boards, the usual young man or teenager would pull in passengers, get their *colones* (Salvadoran currency), and chase away any possible pickpockets.

Donna and I were on the prowl for L.A. gangbangers. We met many of them in the barren and oxen-populated communities of La Libertad, Santa Ana, Sonsonate, Soyapango, and Usulutan. Most were hidden in their dirt-floor shacks or in special hideouts where the very visibly tattooed MS and 18th Street guys could talk, party, recruit, and just relax without being spotted or hounded.

The capital brought in people from all over the country as well as Guatemala, Honduras, and Nicaragua to sell their wares, food items, and fireworks. In late 1993 the country was so poor that most people made a living, not by working or growing crops but by selling. When money was short, they often bartered items they didn't need for items they did. Some stalls had pointless Mickey Mouse toys, Bic pens, and gaudy U.S.-made ceramics that relatives brought from Los Angeles. All sorts of T-shirts—with pop art from Metallica to Nike—were hawked. Nobody had money, but everybody had something to sell.

Like most Latin American cities at the time, there were plazas and side-streets filled with sleeping orphaned children. I didn't see too many over the age of fourteen—they say by that age most were dead. Some were as young as three or four; a large number were seven or eight. They were orphans of war, but more likely of poverty, abandoned by their stricken parents on church steps, left alone in a plaza, or left behind while the child was visiting friends.

The civil war took its toll on many parents and left many children who had witnessed atrocities such as seeing their father's head being hacked off, or their mother raped and then shot, or their siblings dismembered. Those memories, not that old, seemed faraway that December. The overriding concern seemed to be survival—at the barest levels imaginable.

And as in the border towns of Mexico and the U.S., and mega-cities such as Mexico City, Guadalajara, Guatemala City, Bogotá, and São Paolo, these homeless children continuously dulled their pain by sniffing glue, mostly from the kind used to make shoes, a product manufactured in the United States and readily available throughout the Americas. The glue, we found out, is given to the kids by unscrupulous vendors so that the children won't feel like eating, like fighting, like doing anything but dying.

One day I noticed two *huelepegas* (glue sniffers), who appeared to be six or seven, trying to cross a bustling intersection. As the traffic cleared for a moment, the younger kid held up the older one as they traversed the street. In that instant, a deep sorrow overwhelmed me—I knew that fellowship. I had been a sniffer of glue, gasoline, and other toxins in my East L.A.–area barrio when I was a preteen. These kids looked like my kids—my son Ruben wasn't even six yet. For the first time in my life I grieved for that life I had led when I was in the streets, for these children, and for all kids.

In our quest Donna and I met with many MS and 18th Street members—Scoobie, Boxer, Topo, Chuco, Negro, and Cara Loco (Crazy Face). All their stories were similar: how when they were small, they had been brought to L.A., during the height of the civil war; how they grew up in some of the city's worst barrios; how they fought with the Chicano gangs and how eventually they got into their own gangs; how as teenagers they were arrested, set up at times, and then deported.

I heard the *calo*-tinged slang of L.A. barrio youth in remote areas of El Salvador and met many L.A.-based guys in the prisons of San Vicente and Mariona; the facilities were battered and worn, the guards had rusty rifles (I wondered if they worked), and the prisoners often had to construct their own *chambas* (shacks) in open-air courts that they defended with makeshift arms, machetes, and, if they had money, more lethal weapons.

Two months before we arrived, a bloody riot had broken out at another prison, which led to the death of at least two dozen prisoners, most of them dismembered; officials said the trouble began over one gang trying to take over the institution from another one. Although it didn't appear to involve L.A. gang members that time, they are often the target of attacks by locally bred criminal organizations.

At San Vicente I met a leading member of the Hollywood Locos set of MS. He was serving a twenty-five-year prison sentence—there is no parole system; he had to serve the whole time—for a rape-murder he says he did not commit. "The police arrested me only because I was from L.A.," he said. "I was asleep and nowhere near where the crime occurred—and they knew it. But they wanted to get as many L.A. guys as they could."

I also interviewed a man considered the most feared and respected inmate in Mariona. This guy received his rep mostly because of the savvy he picked up on L.A.'s streets. He was serving twenty-four years for stealing two cars—twelve years per car, he explained (I heard later that he was murdered in the joint).

We got close to the family of one guy named Scoobie. When Scoobie was six years old, he saw his father killed by National Guardsmen during the civil war. Afterward, as a refugee in L.A., his younger brother Ulises was killed by Chicano gang members. On one arm he had tattooed an R.I.P. for his father; on the other he had an R.I.P. for Ulises.

At the time, Scoobie's sister, Jessica, was serving a prison term in a CYA facility in Ventura, California, for armed robbery; she was thirteen and hooked on crack when she got arrested. Donna took many photos of Scoobie and his half sister and cousin in El Salvador, as well as of Jessica in Ventura, when her five-year-old son, Carlos, and her mother visited from Pico Union. Jessica wrote me a couple of letters about how she wanted to get out to be a good mother to her son.

But one day in 1996 I got news that Scoobie was shot and killed when he tried to jack a car in San Salvador. Soon after this occurred, I talked to Jessica, who had already been released. She was devastated, but said she wanted to hold everything together for her mother—who had lost the three men closest to her—and for her son, Carlos, so he wouldn't end up like this.

Another young eighteen-year-old I interviewed in El Salvador, Jorge, had been a member of a tagging crew from L.A.'s San Fernando Valley. With close-cropped hair, baggy shirt and pants, and surrounded by tin-roofed huts and seated near the blue and yellow flames of an outdoor fire, Jorge seemed to be from another world.

Inside a small makeshift funeral parlor his mother was laid to rest, her lifeless face visible through a glass window on the upper part of the coffin. Allegedly gang members believed to be affiliated with 18th Street gang had shot her.

Jorge had just arrived in the country when he was picked up and taken to the funeral parlor. He had only made sporadic visits to El Salvador since he was a child. His mother, who had stayed in the old country, was an organizer in a new housing development set up by the government. She was shot apparently after confronting the supposed gang youth who had overtaken a children's play area. We went to the housing development to talk to the woman's neighbors and heard from a few of them that a rival community organizer may have instigated her killing.

Jorge hardly knew his mother, or the younger half siblings who cried there at the funeral parlor. During the all-night vigil Jorge didn't cry. "It's all like a dream," he said while looking at his mother's face through the glass of the coffin.

One person Donna and I located in El Salvador was a twenty-five-year-old former MS member who had spent five years in a California Youth Authority prison. Victor Manual's story was told to us by officials at the Hemen Stark Youth Training Facility (YTS) in Chino. The youth was reportedly convicted of an attempted murder charge at age seventeen. Although Victor Manual insisted he didn't do the deed, police came into his high school classroom, pulled him out, handcuffed him in front of the whole school, and hauled him away. He had never been in trouble before and was supposedly an exemplary student.

In any case, he did exceedingly well at YTS. In the time he served, Victor Manual obtained a high school diploma (he was chosen class valedictorian), a welding certificate, several awards, and an associate of arts degree.

But as soon as Victor Manual's sentence was up, U.S. immigration agents showed up. Although teachers and others who knew the youth wrote glowing letters on his behalf, the INS demanded a large bond from his family, who couldn't afford it. The young man was soon deported to El Salvador.

"We spend time and money on these young men—$32,000 a year to house and educate them—then the INS comes and takes them away," a YTS teacher told me. "They've done that to several of my students. If we're not going to keep them in this country as citizens after all the trouble of educating them, why bother?"

When I met Victor Manual, he was unemployed, living in a *colonia* in Usulutan along a muddy road. He slept in a small square room in a crumbling compound belonging to his grandmother, who had several chickens, goats, and dogs. None of his U.S. credentials were recognized in El Salvador. He tried to show them to government officials and at a few job prospects, but the documents were only cheap paper to them. He had no money for legal assistance—in El Salvador this is nearly impossible to obtain. And he couldn't return to the United States because of his prison record. He seemed condemned to a country that, although born there, he hardly knew—with no recourse but to take his chances and leave.

Victor Manual sat on a dusty chair in the middle of his room, surrounded by his certificates, his degree, and his high school diploma. He didn't smile very much, even in the face of these accomplishments. Yet despite feeling justifiably cheated, Victor Manuel was nothing but considerate to us the whole time we were there.

Back in the U.S. there were homeboys amid the cornfields.

On a vast expanse of Oklahoma earth a number of Mara Salvatrucha members were working beneath a torrid sun under the caring eye of a fifty-seven-year-old Muscogee Creek man whose land these so-called gangsters were helping to seed and harvest. It was the summer of 1994.

Chuck Coleman was like a surrogate father to members of the Hollywood Locos set of Mara Salvatrucha. Coleman, who retired the following year, worked for the Los Angeles Unified School District's Office of Student Integration. He also taught for twelve years at LeConte Junior High School, which catered to many of the first Salvadoran families moving into Hollywood's seediest neighborhoods.

As an English as a Second Language (ESL) instructor in the evening, Coleman ended up teaching Salvadoran kids during the day and their parents at night. Over the years he saw the kids grow up, and get into the gangs, then get shot, hospitalized, jailed, and, finally, deported.

Unfortunately he was one of only a few adults in the area willing to take these young people in, to assist them in court, to provide their families with groceries if needed, and to get them jobs and schooling programs.

Coleman was one of the precious few whom the MS could trust.

One day I visited Coleman's apartment on a street behind the Mann's Chinese Theater complex on Hollywood Boulevard. Seven MS youth had been sleeping on the floor; a couple more were on makeshift beds in the living room. Among them were dudes named Raskal, Boomer, Flaco, and Triste, which in Spanish means "sad" and whom Coleman lovingly called Crispy.

When their schools, their employers, law enforcement, and even their families abandoned them, Coleman was still there. Once I saw him stop to talk to MS members at a popular Mexican fast food stand near the intersection of Western and Santa Monica. He was often counseling kids at the parking lot, in their homes, at their hangouts, including an abandoned apartment complex in the shadow of the famous "Hollywood" sign. This time he was explaining to one baby-faced boy how to get back into school and stay there.

In the ten years before his retirement Coleman would pile half a dozen kids into his van and drive them several days to his Oklahoma family farm, a farmhouse built in 1907. He estimated he'd brought around 250 mostly Salvadoran youth to the area. They stayed anywhere from three days to several months. Coleman had inherited the land from the sixty acres the government gave Muscogee Creeks after they and members of four other tribes were forced to leave the Southeast region of the country in the 1800s; this mandatory evacuation is infamous as the Trail of Tears.

Even if some MS youth may have been hiding out from the law, they all worked the fields, helped maintain his two houses on his share of the land, and attended local powwows and other Creek Nation activities.

"I have pictures of them with the tribal chief," Coleman said. "The tribe has sort of adopted them. These kids see us eating our Indian food, and they say, 'Hey, that's like what we eat.' They're Indians, but they don't know it."

Coleman's impulses to help and not demonize the MS youth stemmed from this connection, as well as the fact that he saw many injustices meted out to Salvadoran immigrants when they first came to the country.

"Police have told these kids, 'I have a warrant out on you, don't mess with us,'" Coleman related. "Then they let them go. But when I check with our own computers, I find there is no warrant. What the kids don't realize is that the police are duty bound to take you in if they have a warrant. They can't just stop you, threaten you, and then let you go."

Coleman said he attended community meetings where law enforcement officers told the audience that the Mara Salvatrucha were former soldiers from El Salvador who brought guns into the country and were trained killers.

"It's all lies," responded Coleman. "Many of these kids grew up in L.A. Sure, there are former soldiers and former guerillas among them. But I tell you the vast majority are like any other U.S. kid. They only use the lies to justify the deportations."

Coleman has also gone to court with these teens, even when a parent can't or won't take them. "It makes a difference if somebody, some adult, is there for them," Coleman said. "Sometimes this will influence the sentencing, to know there are people who care."

"In one case an MS member got ninty-two days in Tracy Prison for a shooting," Coleman explained. "Witnesses told police that MS did the shooting. Police then picked up the kid, although six people knew where he was at the time of the shooting. He was eventually let go by the judge, but not before he risked his life in Tracy for more than three months."

In another case Coleman appeared in court to help a Mexican member of the MS named Nacho. This young man had gone nine times to court on a car theft. They put a $45,000 bail on him that his family couldn't obtain, even with the one percent a bail bondsman would take. While in jail Nacho was charged for a murder, although witnesses had different descriptions and stories about what happened.

"In the preliminary hearing, a police officer identified another guy in court who was there by mistake," Coleman said. "After they found out the guy wasn't supposed to be there, they brought in Nacho, and the cop pointed to him as the culprit—and the court let this stand."

In turn, some law enforcement personnel have chided Coleman for endearing himself to these immigrant youth in and out of the school system. "He takes a soft approach," one probation officer told me. "They need tough treatment—that's the only thing they understand."

Whatever Coleman was doing, many MS members, some of whom have done some major damage in their day, opened their hearts and homes to the tall Native American. This explained why many MS youth would venture out to Coleman's farm to meet his family, learn to ride horses, and get away from the familiar but uncertain realities of Los Angeles or El Salvador.

"I feel safe and wanted here," said Cartoon while eyeing rows of watermelons at Coleman's farm. "I never feel that way at home or in my country. This is the only place I can find any peace."

"We respect Coleman," Largo added. "He respects us."

This led to one Salvadoran family helping Coleman when he needed a place to stay for a while. For several months in 1993 Coleman lived with the family of twelve people, including grandparents. This was the home of a then eighteen-year-old MS member whom Coleman first met at Hollywood High School. For years this school was a predominantly white school. By the mid-1990s the student population was 40 percent Salvadorans, 20 percent Mexicans, and 20 percent Armenians.

"The rules at the house were based on respect," Coleman said. "Everyone did his or her share of work, including me."

Coleman was unique as far as other adults in the area went. Most people turned their backs on these youth. Most people wanted to deport and remove MS and other Central American gangs from their neighborhoods. In El Salvador two major death squads—the Angels of Death and the more notorious Black Shadow[3]—targeted L.A. gang youth for torture and death. I heard of bodies being found in shallow graves, by rivers, in garbage dumps. At the Rosales Hospital in San Salvador, English-speaking tattooed youths who have been tortured and shot confirmed the dangers they faced.

In L.A. the Salvadoran youth faced wars with rival gangs, including the many Chicano barrio organizations that they eventually learned to emulate. But one of the most insidious dangers came from the police, particularly the notorious Rampart Division in the Pico Union-MacArthur Park area, where many Central Americans made their home.

One day I was at a Mexican fast food hangout. Largo and Cartoon were just standing there; a young man in a wheelchair with no legs or lower body, also dressed in black cholo-style clothing, was next to them. This dude was known as Half Dead. A police car pulled up and two officers jumped out, swaggering toward the young men. The officers made them spread out on the asphalt, except for Half Dead, who had his wheelchair probed while he was being interrogated. Coleman walked out to talk to the police. I couldn't hear what was said, but after a while the police turned around and left. It was a routine stop that was intended mostly to humiliate and anger the youth.

Soon a nineteen-year-old guy known as Junior entered the take-out stand. He had been an MS member for eight years. Coleman greeted him with a smile and invited him to sit down with us.

Two months before, somebody had shot Junior. The bullet apparently hit his spine, but only struck a nerve. The bullet did other damage: He had a colostomy bag strapped to his body. Junior told me he had tried to stay out of the area since the shooting, but he came in that day to see his girlfriend at a nearby hospital. She had been shot in the stomach two weeks before.

"Junior was hooked on crack, real bad," Coleman said. "He smoked it in the pipe. Sometimes I'd drive through here and see him laid out in the street."

Coleman sent Junior to Oklahoma. He quit the pipe. Coleman's family got close to Junior. Coleman's brother and sister wanted him to stay on the farm. His mother, in a nursing home nearby, treated him like one of her own children.

"He's a charmer," Coleman added. "They wanted him to join Four-H, give him cows to take care of. But unfortunately he came back here instead." It was soon after that last trip that Junior was shot.

Another Salvadoran that Coleman introduced me to was a pretty, slim mother in her late teens named Ana Maria. Coleman saw a lot of intelligence in this girl. She loved to read books. However, when he first met her at age eleven, she was lost, constantly in trouble, in the streets, and on drugs. She became one of the first MS *locas*—one willing to act out, to attack and hurt people. At the age of fifteen Ana Maria was arrested for gang-related charges and was sent to a juvenile facility. Coleman stuck by her until she got out. Then he helped her get a GED and improve her writing skills.

When I met Ana Maria, she was living in a clean but cramped apartment with her baby and a young husband, who apparently was helping her stay out of drugs and trouble. She didn't seem crazy or irresponsible. She wore nice clothes and had her hair in long soft black curls. She had a journal in which she was writing her thoughts and ideas. She appeared calm—looking toward something bright in her future, unlike in the past.

"If it wasn't for Mr. Coleman," Ana Maria said. "I'd be dead."

Chapter 27

Nurturing the Genius

For it is important that awake people be awake,
or a breaking line may discourage them back to sleep;
the signals we give—yes or no, or maybe—
should be clear: the darkness around us is deep.

—William Stafford

With the twentieth century over, the world greeted the new millennium with celebrations—from the pompous to simple prayer—as well as books, fashions, and songs. The start of a new century is marked by radical changes and social alterations, what Michael Meade called "a rush of endings and beginnings."[1]

At the closing of any era you can sense the start of the new. It is a time when things get condensed. In the past this was marked by great apprehension as well as great hope. The French called this *fin de siècle,* which suggests mostly turn-of-the-century dread and doom. But these transitions haven't always been worthy of pessimism. All beginnings are endings, and all endings are the places of new birth. All tombs are also wombs.

"Willingly or not, we are all attendants at the funeral of the last era and the birth of the next. We are all mid-wives placing the shroud on a body soon to disappear and anointing the next birth with our prayers, fears, denials, and hopes. The radical dismantling of institutions, boundaries, beliefs, and ecosystems that characterizes the end of the era is an extended funeral that we can consciously attend or try to deny," wrote Meade.[2]

So here we are, at the beginning of the end of the industrial age, at the last stages of an economic system that also gave us a world of concepts and symbols tied to material gain and material power that for well over five hundred years has dominated almost every relationship, war, conquest, political decision, presidency, religious conflict, and social resolution. What characterizes the significance of this age is not the date assigned to it but the transition from one kind of imagination, one set of possibilities, to another—from inequity to plenitude. It is times like this when spirit—the mysterious, invisible, but palpable energy igniting all of life, all processes, all movements—appears to move in.

The current spiritual interventions being witnessed around the world, particularly in the United States, are linked to being at the door of a new era—even if some still appear bound to monetary interests and a passing order. This is illustrated by the recent growth of spiritual literature, a developing interest in Eastern religions and indigenous cosmologies, a revival of Talmudic and Koranic teachings, and deeper investigations into the actual words and deeds of Jesus—in contrast to a widespread fundamentalism in almost all organized belief systems in the face of uncertainty and instability. Alongside this there is a healthy increase in skepticism, free inquiry, and ardent challenges to the religious and political images, stories, and ideas of the past. That is as it should be.

The "things" of spirit, including its challenges, become paramount when the physical pursuits and patterns cannot adequately sustain our souls, our inborn need to go beyond what we can see. These narrow and superficial pursuits and patterns have become barriers to attaining our complete humanity; they continually drain from us the capacity to become thoroughly creative and compassionate beings. Our present incompleteness as human beings, indeed, has contributed to making us quite fragile and destructive beings.[3]

We must welcome these interventions. But the same spirit of change, of opening up and encompassing, must also become part and parcel of whatever decisions, plans, and policies we devise concerning our relationships with our children.

We really only have two choices in this matter: Do things the old way—which cannot work under the present conditions—or proceed with a new orientation and develop a different social consensus based on a coherent worldview that incorporates the possibilities of the new rising period.

These changes are not about more prisons, zero tolerance, detached relationships, or abandoned lives. They are not about helicopters maintaining watch above our heads, driving our youth underground and with them the hope of lasting change. We are not talking about closed ideas, more shopping malls, stagnant readings of sacred texts, expedient solutions, megachurches, or a gross national product as the best gauge of our collective worth.

Whenever there is a new threshold to cross, there is fear. This is why we have so many hero stories in the culture, why we have all the mythologies and philosophies that show us how to act during crisis and change. These lessons are inherent in the ancient stories and texts, as they are in many modern philosophical writings. Courage and character need to grow like many-branched trees from within our hearts. If there was ever a time to be brave so that we can be free, it is now.

No one will grab the hand of an elder if that hand is unsteady, unwise, if it does not heed the pull of his or her own path. Moreover an elder's "wisdom" is not just "answers" to practical problems. It is a poetic knowledge, a level of language and experience that enters the mythological and metaphorical and therefore has an impact at a deeper level. We need more poetry from elders, strong enough and encompassing enough to meet the vigorous poetry of our youth, whose raps and verses are presently subject to frequent attacks and repression.

Unfortunately, because there are not many elders whose hands and hearts can carry us forth, today people don't just die at fifteen, they die from being fifteen. During the PBS-TV *Making Peace* segment on YSS, my son Ramiro said, during the burial of a sixteen-year-old YSS leader, "This is our way of living, our way of dying." And young people have accepted this way because it appears as the only viable one for them.

The intense loyalty to a gang or cult often comes from the psychological need to establish relationships that are significant when there are no other significant relationships to be had.

So it's time to get smart with heart. To allow compassion to rule again, guided by the wisest folly. Governments and banks worry about inflation, but ours must be an inflation of soul, not of money. We need pain that doesn't cancel out someone else's pain, but joins it. We need light and darkness—seeds grow in darkness toward the light. We need passion and purpose. It's time to redefine power and beauty—remembering that real ugliness comes from the abuses of beauty and power.

Malidoma Somé once said, "Where this Spirit is taking us is lethal, as if the body is dispensable." Spirituality is serious business—we can't afford to address this superficially or piecemeal. By denying, by forgetting, by not doing what is required to move us toward the often fragile bridges between present and future, between scarcity and abundance, between paralysis and movement, we are daily losing whatever remnants of our sovereignty may still exist. The body may be intact, but the internal impulse to aspire to one's destiny is soon diminished.

This is an initiatory path upon which we must all, as part of society, embark in order to emerge alive and newly awake on the other side. The object is to begin a bigger life for us all by nurturing the seeds of destiny within each of us.

There is an old saying that a culture is made around what we do with young people. This book is meant to help us envision and remake a culture around what our youth have been feeling, saying, struggling, and dying for. Young people carry the dreams of the whole society. If we don't establish and maintain a space for those dreams, the community as a whole loses its dreams and their attainment.

But this is also about establishing a vital place for elders, for teachers, for mentors. It is about the lived wisdom that comes from a conflicted life.

Part of any initiation is having one's self revealed to oneself. This applies to cultures as well as to individuals. The mask is removed. The cosmetic blushes are washed away. Now we are looking into the mirror of the culture—blemished and scarred—and we do not like what we see. We turn away from government, that "sleeping kingdom" in Washington, D.C., where debts and lies abound. We turn pale with anger and fear at thirteen-year-olds shooting classmates and teachers, ten-year-olds throwing kinder-gartners out of housing-project buildings, or babies dying in the arms of screaming mothers, victims of driveby shootings. We do not like what we have become.

Although we must suffer the circumstances that are intended for our life to grow, it's crucial to understand that these horrors and betrayals are not *the* problem. They are symptoms of a world out of balance, a society out of touch, a "darkmotherscream" from the entrails of the earth, saying it's time to change or pay the piper.

It's important to remember that it is the *sacred* linked to *sacrifice* that will consecrate and "make holy"—whole—the ground of our lives. When we do not pay attention, the sacrifices are often our own children, our souls, our own sense of self. There's a lot of sacrifice in our culture, but not enough rebirth.

"If you really want to help this world, what you will have to teach is how to live in it. And that no one can do who has not himself learned how to live in it in the joyful sorrow and sorrowful joy of the knowledge of life as it is," wrote Joseph Campbell.[4]

There is no real "gap" between generations. Even when adults turn away from youth, youth learns something. As adults we continue to impart values and beliefs about the essence of our relationships and what is truly important in this world. Each generation gives something of a life-giving relevance to the others; every new generation is the ground where we plant the seeds of change or stagnation.

"It was a human fact, understood by most cultures, that when youth go through their transition, everyone is affected and involved," writes Michael Meade. "All celebrations must wait; usually, all other conflicts must wait. In the meantime, everyone prays or offers assistance, support, or guidance. The youth must cross from innocence to self-knowledge; from simple dependence to the challenges of independence on one hand and community involvement on the other.... If elders and mentors cannot hold the doors of community acceptance open, how can youth trust any authority or deeply value their lives and the lives of others? Why should young people suffer the ordeals of self-knowledge if there's no one waiting to welcome them home."[5]

One of the biggest obstacles we have to implementing these concepts is what I call the *tyranny of indifference.* In many respects indifference allows a small group of people who can't see hope in our children, who only want to punish and put them away, who actually profit politically and monetarily from the misery of the poor and deprived among us, to make the decisions by which we all must live.

Indifference is a greater force to overcome than evil intent. I recall a few mean teachers when I was growing up—their words and deeds have stayed with me for a lifetime. But it was the indifference of most of the other teachers and adults (sometimes parents) who let this situation continue without so much as a protest, without standing up for children who couldn't sufficiently do so for themselves.

Every child wants to be seen for who she or he is. "See me!" is the deeper cry of most suicides, violent outbursts, or silent screams. Young people may need to seek out peer relationships and peer approval, but they find something exceedingly important and powerful in an adult who truly sees them.

To see the gang. To see the Eric Harrises and Kip Kinkels. To see the Franciscos and Jeremiahs, the Ricks and Leos, the Doloreses and Ana Marias. To see the "good" youth as well as the most troubled.

"If genius is the expression of the sacred in an individual, then the individual's link to the Other World is the spiritual umbilical cord that cannot be cut until its owner is fully awakened into his gift," wrote Malidoma Somé. "Just as our umbilical cord cannot be cut until we are fully in this side of reality, we must nurture and maintain the genius until its complete birth in this world."[6]

Just before our departure from Chicago, the family went to visit Ramiro. The hardest thing was to leave my son behind in the Illinois correctional system. But Ramiro encouraged us. He knew it was better for his younger brothers to be around Trini's large family in the San Fernando Valley. He also knew they needed to relate to their grandmother, my mom, who had been diagnosed with lymphoma the year before. Ramiro was saddened, but he didn't want us to feel bad.

I was also leaving knowing that Ramiro was in a much stronger state of mind. Despite his imprisonment I was proud of him. He had mostly stayed out of trouble, reading and writing, and getting an education in the new facility.

I reminded Ramiro to align himself with the cosmos—its rhythms, pulses, contradictions, and changes; this is the essence of Mexika indigenous spirituality. The plants that Ramiro tends have lessons for how to live. They breathe in the poison in the air (carbon dioxide) and turn it into oxygen—what we need to exist. I told him to see his life as having taken in a lot of hurt, abuse, neglect, fear, and hate, but also how he can bring the beauty out of this ugliness. The grace out of the rage. The songs out of the silences. Already his children were proof that, regardless of what has transpired, he has helped create some wonderful people.

Even in his own private (and not so private) hell, Ramiro can—if he wholeheartedly takes in this knowledge and his experiences—find his peace, his place, and his purpose.

Before the move, we also attended the college graduation of my daughter Andrea. It was the culmination of hard years of struggling for her B.A. degree as a single mother and an energetic organizer among youth and community, despite having suffered some of the same kind of abuse and neglect her brother had gone through, as well as dealing with immature and unappreciative men. As she strolled onto the stage to receive her diploma—happy, young, and full of life—I became emotional with the weight if it all.

For years Andrea and I hadn't communicated well. She, too, harbored resentments, but she tended to deal with them by shutting down. I tried to find out why. She finally told me: "Where were you when I needed you? Where were you when I needed a father to hold me, to be there for me?"

My heart just broke. I didn't know how to respond. But I knew I had to try. I told her I couldn't make up for that time and I will suffer an eternity for that. But I wanted to be her father now. I wanted us to learn how to talk to each other, to love and be there for each other, even though she was already a young adult. We finally did. She eventually opened up to me and I listened. We've become closer since then—a real father and daughter—and I thank the Creator for this.

Yes, we can make some horrendous mistakes—and I've made my share. But the nature of life—in the fullness of the Great Spirit energizing and animating all things, in the nobility built into all processes and experiences— is that people and relationships and this world can heal.

I never graduated from college. I didn't even graduate properly from high school—my diploma was handed to me at the principal's office. In fact I never wore a cap and gown until my early forties, when I was asked to do the commencement speech at Chicago's Robert Morris College. Andrea is the first member of the next generation of the Rodríguez family in the U.S. and Mexico—my father had close to thirty grandchildren spread out in both countries—who finally finished college.

In the audience that day was Andrea's four-year-old daughter, Catalina, who sat on the lap of her grandmother, Camila; Andrea's best friend, Jessica, who stood up to videotape; one of Ramiro's kids, Anastasia, who was also present with her mom, Laura; and, next to them, my wife, Trini, and our young boys, Ruben, almost twelve, and Luis, six.

Andrea and Ramiro are living proof of the caliber of our youth. I say this as a deservedly biased father, but also as an embattled warrior for community who knows how hard it is to recognize such qualities in our young. They're there. They're there. They have always been there.

So despite much print, weekly sermons, countless lectures, and many "experts" to the contrary, I believe we *can* stop the violence, suicides, and addictions among our children, our young people, and even among adults.

It means continuing to focus the youth and their elders in the direction where their pains and strivings are already taking them. It means looking toward the unfolding discoveries awaiting us as we participate in the great human adventure.

The social erosion stops at our door. To build from there, we're going to need a different ethos in this country. Not "kill or be killed," which some youth take literally, but one that values and nurtures every child. One that teaches us to work for the decent survival of all, for therein lies our best chance for survival. An ethos that says we must place all our resources, all our institutions, at the disposal of one child, any child, crying out.

Notes

Introduction

1. Rick Moody, "In Guns We Trust," *Details* magazine, Oct. 1998, p. 166.

2. Ibid., p. 193.

3. Kalle Lasn and Bruce Grierson, "America the Blue," *Utne Reader,* Sept.–Oct. 2000, pp. 74–81.

4. "16-Year-Olds Lead in Teen Car Fatalities," *Chicago Tribune,* April 15, 1998.

5. From "We Must Ask What the Craziness Is," in *To Be a Man: In Search of the Deep Masculine,* edited by Keith Thompson (Los Angeles: Jeremy P. Tarcher Publishers, 1991), p. 42.

6. Luis J. Rodríguez, *Always Running: La Vida Loca, Gang Days in L.A.* (Willimantic, Conn.: Curbstone Press 1993; paperback, New York: Touchstone Books/Simon & Schuster, 1994).

7. Mike A. Males, *Framing Youth: Ten Myths About the Next Generation* (Monroe, Me.: Common Courage Press, 1999), pp. 4–6.

8. "For all the talk of the fragmentation of America, there is only one division that is dangerously getting worse, and that is the gap between rich and poor," from "UnAmerican Thoughts," *The Economist,* Oct. 26, 1991, as quoted in Jeffrey Reiman, *The Rich Get Richer and the Poor Get Prison* (Needham Heights, Mass.: Allyn and Bacon, 1998), p. 29. Reiman adds, "In 1970, the poorest fifth of the nation's families received 5.4 percent of the aggregate income, and the richest fifth received 40.9 percent. In 1980, the share of the poorest fifth was 5.1 percent of aggregate income, that of the richest fifth was 41.6 percent. By 1994, the share of the poorest fifth had declined to 4.2 percent, while that of the richest fifth had risen to 46.9 percent. During this period, the share of the top 5 percent rose from 15.6 to 20.1 percent. By 1995, the number of poor Americans was 35.6 million, up from 30.1 million in 1990, and 25.2 million in 1980." (p. 29.)

9. As quoted in Michael Cole's Foreword to Urie Bronfenbrenner's *The Ecology of Human Development: Experiments by Nature and Design* (Cambridge, Mass.: Harvard University Press, 1979), p. vii.

10. From Osip Mandelshtam, "Tristia," *Selected Poems* (New York: Penguin Books, 1991).

Chapter 1

1. This piece originally appeared in a different form in *The Nation,* Nov. 21, 1994.

2. The Young Lords Party and Michael Abramson, photographs by Michael Abramson, *Palante: Young Lords Party* (New York: McGraw-Hill, 1971).

3. Since its founding, Youth Struggling for Survival has received a 1998 Neighborhood Award from the Chicago Council on Urban Affairs and a 1999 Self Education Foundation Award (cofounded by William "Upski" Wimsatt). In 1997 the group was designated as one of the eleven most promising youth leadership programs in the country by the Center for Youth Development and Policy Research in Washington, D.C. In addition YSS has been supported by sources like the Mott Foundation, Chicago's Community Trust, Crossroads Fund, Donnelley Foundation, the Milarepa Foundation, the Red Moon Theater, and, most importantly, members of the community, primarily in the form of hours and hours of volunteer time.

Chapter 2

1. Some of this history came from the following publications: Joel Rose, with fifty-seven top comic artists, *The Big Book of Thugs* (New York: Factoid Books/Paradox Press, 1995); T. J. English, *The Westies: Inside the Hell's Kitchen Irish Mob* (New York: G. P. Putnam, 1990); Steven L. Sachs, *Street Gang Awareness* (Minneapolis: Fairview Press, 1997); Sidney Zion, *Loyalty and Betrayal: The Story of the American Mob* (San Francisco: CollinsPublishers, 1994); Edwin G. Burrows and Mike Wallace, *Gotham: A History of New York City to 1898* (New York: Oxford University Press, 1999); and various articles in the Illinois-based *Journal of Gang Research* of the National Gang Crime Research Center.

2. See David Wyatt, *Five Fires: Race, Catastrophe, and the Shaping of California* (New York: Addison-Wesley, 1997), pp. 78–106.

3. There are a number of good books documenting the Mexican response to Anglo indiscretions following the 1848 U.S. war against Mexico. They include Alfredo Mirandé, *Gringo Justice* (Notre Dame, Ind.: University of Notre Dame Press, 1987); Rodolfo Acuña, *Occupied America: A History of Chicanos* (New York: HarperCollins, 1987); and a self-published study by UCLA professor and author James Diego Vigil, *Early Chicano Guerrilla Fighters,* which he graciously shared with me.

4. William Ayers, *A Kind and Just Parent: The Children of Juvenile Court* (Boston: Beacon Press, 1997), p. 24.

5. It is estimated that upward of one million people were killed and another million emigrated to the United States during the Mexican Revolution (1910–21), at a time when Mexico had about fifteen million people. See Lawrence A. Cardoso, *Mexican Emigration to the United States, 1897–1931* (Tucson: University of Arizona Press, 1980), pp. 38–39. For a good account of the birth of the largest barrio of Mexicans in the United States, and of its first so-called gangs, see Ricardo Romo, *East Los Angeles: History of a Barrio* (Austin: University of Texas Press, 1983). And for an important addition to the often terrible and wanton history of uprootedness and removal among L.A.'s Mexican

communities, see Don Normark, *Chavez Ravine, 1949: A Los Angeles Story* (San Francisco: Chronicle Books, 1999).

6. See also James Diego Vigil, *Barrio Gangs: Street Life and Identity in Southern California* (Austin: University of Texas Press, 1988); and Joan W. Moore, *Homeboys: Gangs, Drugs, and Prison in the Barrios of Los Angeles* (Philadelphia: Temple University Press, 1978).

East L.A.'s old barrios—some going back to the 1920s and 1930s—have been associated with a number of street organizations, including Primera Flats, Cuatro Flats, La Tercera, White Fence, Evergreen, Little Valley, Clover, Cypress Park, The Avenues, Happy Valley, El Hoyo Mara, Marianna Mara, La Rock Mara, Lopez Mara, Kern Mara, Ford Mara, Lote Mara, Lomita Mara, Arizona Mara, El Hoyo Soto, Gerahty Loma, Big Hazard, Lomita Primera, Eastside Los, and Varrio Nuevo Estrada.

7. A good book on the causes and effects of the attacks on zootsuited youth by sailors and police is Beatrice Griffith, *American Me* (New York: Houghton Mifflin, 1948). Utilizing short stories, true-life accounts, and research, the book is unparalleled in bringing to light the plight of the Pachucos and their impact on the post–World War II youth culture. (The book, now out of print, is not connected with the 1990 movie *American Me,* starring Edward James Olmos.)

8. COINTELPRO was a federal undercover operation that is believed responsible for most of the destabilization and ruin of "antiwar" and "antiestablishment" organizations during the late 1960s and early 1970s, including the Black Panthers, Students for a Democratic Society, Brown Berets, American Indian Movement, the Young Lords, Nation of Islam, and many civil rights organizations.

9. Joseph T. Hallinan, *Going Up The River: Travels in a Prison Nation* (New York: Random House, 2001), p. 24.

10. Some of this information came from personal correspondence with Texas prisoners, from the mid-1990s to the present. Most of this was corroborated in a book of prisoner testimonies entitled *From Crime to Christ: Chronicles of Christ's Work in the Hearts of Inmates,* compiled by Chaplain Al Gibbons (Waco, Texas: Davis Brothers Publishing, 1999).

11. A book that describes the roots and horrors of that riot is Roger Morris, *The Devil's Butcher Shop: The New Mexico Prison Uprising* (Albuquerque: University of New Mexico Press, 1983).

12. A 1998–99 research project by the National Gang Crime Research Center called Project GANGMILL showed that in the twenty-two juvenile facilities and adult jails surveyed (from the states of California, Georgia, Kansas, Michigan, New Jersey, Ohio, and Wisconsin), most gang members claimed to be allied with Crips, Bloods, People (Brothers), Folks, Sureño, or Norteño (the makeup of the respondents was roughly 41 percent African American, 37 percent white, almost 10 percent Latino, more than 3 percent Native American, almost 1.5 percent Asian, and the rest of mixed parentage). See "Preliminary Results of Project GANGMILL: A Special Report of the

National Gang Crime Research Center," *Journal of Gang Research* [Peotone, Ill.] 7, no. 4 (Summer 2000).

13. From "Fire Sale: America's Unchecked Gun Market," *Chicago Tribune,* Dec. 11, 1997. It is a matter of deep concern how poor urban youth were able to rapidly obtain such powerful weapons. Besides heists of gun shops, homes, and armories, many street organizations have found direct access to gun manufacturers and dealers. One gang member claimed that suburban licensed gun dealers often visited the "hood" to sell guns out of the trunks of their cars. Most of these weapons were apparently "overruns" from shops and gun shows.

In addition, there have been many claims that police officers have routinely participated in the vast urban gun market. In Chicago, police who picked up youths for crimes would often extort guns from them in lieu of arrest. Some of those guns ended up back on the street.

When I raised this issue once, in a talk I was giving at a small North Carolina church, a member of the audience became incensed, insisting that licensed gun dealers would never do such a thing. While I believe the vast majority of gun dealers (or police) do not sell guns out of the back of their cars, I also pointed out how prevalent this practice had become. Fortunately a local police chief in attendance supported my claims with his own experiences, saying the community should not be in denial about how most of these guns are getting into the hands of our youth.

14. In June 1998 sociologist John Hagedorn caused a stir with the publication of "The Business of Drug Dealing in Milwaukee," *Wisconsin Policy Research Institute Report* 2, no. 5. His study concluded that illicit drug activity in the inner-city for the most part is not that of "drug kingpins" with mansions and fleets of fancy cars. These "criminal" acts have mostly to do with supporting a basic living arrangement when most legitimate jobs have disappeared in the poorest urban neighborhoods. Although politicians and the media constantly refer to low-level drug crews and street gangs as if they were Al Capone or major organized crime outfits (see "Gore Vows Federal Help in Tracking Down Drug Kingpins," *Chicago Tribune,* Aug. 11, 1998), Hagedorn's study shows that "the work of drug dealing in the central city is in many ways an innovative, entrepreneurial, small-business venture." In addition, "most drug entrepreneurs are hard working, but not super rich.... [T]he majority of their employees are daily drug users, are not paid in money, and have difficult working and living conditions." Even though this report was published by a prestigious conservative think tank, a number of prominent people, including the mayor of Milwaukee, decried it.

15. See Michael Krikorian, "Violent Gang Is Stain on a Proud Ethnic Community," *Los Angeles Times,* Aug. 17, 1997, and "Gang Gains Reluctant Respect from Some," *Los Angeles Times,* Aug. 18, 1997.

In the early to mid-1990s, Armenian gang youth, although smaller in number, were warring heavily with Salvadoran and Mexican gang youth. At the same time the most estranged Armenian youth had gravitated toward the cholo culture of the Mexican and Salvadoran youth. (This has also been true for disaffected

African-American youth, Cambodians, and even whites; it appears that for many new arrivals, the cholo culture has been the most expressive of their own traumas and identity needs.) By the year 2000, however, the highly publicized stabbing and killing of a seventeen-year-old Latino youth outside of a Glendale high school by alleged Armenian gang youth opened up a major dialogue to find threads of unity and comprehension, and to help end the violence, between the two groups.

16. Luis J. Rodríguez, "Los Angeles' Gang Culture Arrives in El Salvador, Courtesy of the INS," *Los Angeles Times,* May 8, 1994.

17. Ruben Martinez, "Mexico's Little Americas," *Los Angeles Times,* Aug. 17, 1997. "The Chicano style has been noticeable for some time in the provincial cities and towns of Southwestern and Northern Mexico, in states like Jalisco, Michoacan, Zacatecas and Guanajuato," wrote Martinez. "But with the economic crisis touched off by the devaluation of the peso in December 1994, people in and around Mexico City have been forced to travel the migrant routes northward."

See also Rogelio Marcial, *La banda rifa: Vida contidana de grupos juveniles de esquina en Zamora, Michoacan* (Michoacan, Mexico: El Colegio de Michoacan, 1997), on the influence of L.A.-style gangs upon the growing *banda* street gang activities in central Mexico.

18. Robert L. Jackson, "Nationwide Spread of L.A. Gangs Is Alarming," *Los Angeles Times,* Apr. 24, 1997.

19. Other White Supremacist groups include the Aryan Nations, Christian Identity, the Church of Jesus Christ Christian, and the PEN1 (Public Enemy Number One) Death Squad. Many are cloaked as "religious" institutions or inspired by Nordic and Nazi symbology.

20. Some prison officials designate these groups as "Security Threat Groups" along with other prison and street gang organizations, despite their overt religious or political foundations. On the other hand, street groups heavily involved in criminal activities often use religious beliefs and political positioning in their written literature and ceremonies.

21. Andrew Martin, "Gangs May Be Too Diverse for Single Remedy," *Chicago Tribune,* Apr. 13, 1997.

22. Examples of this are described in articles such as Michael Krikorian, "Bloods' Infighting Pulls in Some Crips—To Stop the Killings," *Los Angeles Times,* Apr. 5, 1998; Michael Krikorian and Greg Krikorian, "Watts Truce Holds Fast Even As Hope Fades," *Los Angeles Times,* May 18, 1997; and Luis J. Rodríguez, with Cle Sloan and Kershaun Scott, "Gangs: The New Political Force in Los Angeles," *Los Angeles Times,* Sept. 13, 1992.

Also the efforts of African-American, Chicano/Mexicano, and Salvadoran gang members in bringing peace resulted in the formation of the 1997 Peace Process Network in California, which has worked with state legislators such as former State Senator Tom Hayden, and various community organizations of gang and nongang youth. By 1997 Hayden, with members of the Crips and the Bloods, Chicano and Salvadoran barrios, and representatives of groups such as Barrios Unidos, went to El Salvador to meet with gang youth organizers there who are working on similar peace efforts such as Homies Unidos.

Unfortunately Homies Unidos, which has worked with mostly Salvadoran gang youth in L.A. and El Salvador, was targeted from its inception by the Los Angeles Police Department (included in the recent Rampart Division scandal) as well as officials and death squads in Central America. The very real dangers they faced were dramatically illustrated by the 1999 murder in El Salvador of the Homies Unidos director, Sigfredo "Ringo" Rivera. A week prior to his untimely death, a professor friend of mine who was visiting there had given Ringo a copy of my 1993 memoir in Spanish, *La Vida Loca.*

23. See John J. Dilulio Jr., "Moral Poverty: The Coming of the Super-Predators Should Scare Us Into Wanting to Get to the Root Causes of Crime a Lot Faster," *Chicago Tribune,* Dec. 15, 1995. Dilulio claimed that by 2010, some 270,000 more juvenile "superpredators" will be roaming the streets of America. He called for 150,000 new placements in secured confinement between the next five to seven years. Among others, Frank E. Zimring, a University of California law professor, countered such "faulty arithmetic and conceptual sloppiness." (See editorial "Crying Wolf Over Teen Demons," *Los Angeles Times,* Aug. 19, 1996). "If politicians and analysts can believe in 'superpredator' toddlers," writes Zimring, "they can believe in anything."

In my view, some envision children yet to be born and want to lock them up. Others, on the other hand, see the promise of an enriched, open, and more just society in every newborn.

24. Eric Lichtblau, "Youth Crime Rate Plunges, Justice Dept. Study Says," *Los Angeles Times,* Dec. 15, 2000. See also Robert L. Jackson, "Violent Crimes by Juveniles Down First Time in 17 Years," *Los Angeles Times,* Aug. 9, 1996. And Marlene Cimons, "Youth Violence Is Down, Report Says," *Los Angeles Times,* Jan. 18, 2000.

An article addressing the misguided panic to gangs in New York City is Kit A. Roane, "Despite Fears, Little Evidence Is Seen of a Rise in Gang Violence," *The New York Times,* Oct. 12, 1997. Even the idea that killers are becoming younger is in question. According to the FBI Uniform Crime Reports, as published in the *Chicago Tribune,* Aug. 11, 1998, there were 241 children ages five to fourteen arrested for murder across the country in 1991; by 1996 the same age group produced sixteen murder suspects.

A few good books on how the current hype around crime, particularly youth crime, does not reflect the actual numbers are Michael Males's *The Scapegoat Generation: America's War on Adolescents* (Monroe, Me.: Common Courage Press, 1996) and *Framing Youth: Ten Myths about the Next Generation* (1999), as well as *The Real War on Crime: The Report of the National Criminal Justice Commission,* edited by Steven R. Donziger (New York: HarperPerennial, 1996); and Peter

Elikann, *Superpredators: The Demonization of Our Children by the Law* (New York: Insight Books/Plenum Press, 1999).

25. Eric Zorn, "'Legal Fiction' Lets Prosecutors Shun the Truth," *Chicago Tribune*, Nov. 14, 2000.

26. Mary Ellen Egan, "Gang Bang," *City Pages* [Minneapolis], Dec. 10, 1997.

27. On how unemployment impacts gang violence, see Greg Krikorian, "Study Ranks Joblessness Top Factor in Gang Toll," *Los Angeles Times*, Oct. 28, 1997. "Of all the factors contributing to gangs and their epidemic of violence in Los Angeles, none is more significant than the staggering rates of unemployment in their communities," wrote Krikorian. The study, funded by the California Wellness Foundation and the University of California, examined eight social, economic, and demographic factors against the gang homicide statistics compiled within each of the Los Angeles Police Department's eighteen geographic divisions during the five-year period ending in 1992 when there were 1,702 "gang-related" killings.

28. By 1997 the National Youth Gang Center claimed there were 25,000 street gangs and 665,000 gang members in the United States. Los Angeles County was believed to contain 25 percent of these members with 1,250 identifiable street gangs (in other statistics, more than 6,000 homicides from 1990 to 1998 were attributed to L.A. gangs). About 80 percent of this growth in gangs occurred during the thirty years of massive job losses from the early 1970s to the present.

29. Much of the statistical information on Chicago-area gangs comes from the National Gang Crime Research Center, based in Peotone, Illinois, which also publishes the *Journal of Gang Research*. NGCRC is perhaps the leading gang crime resource center in the country. It is behind the 708-page *An Introduction to Gangs*, by George W. Knox, Ph.D. (its fifth edition was published in 2000 by New Chicago School Press).

30. Statistics from "Supreme Court Should Squash Anti-Gang Ordinance," *Chicago Defender*, Apr. 23, 1998. The U.S. Supreme Court on Apr. 20, 1998 agreed to hear the city of Chicago's appeal of the Illinois Supreme Court's decision that struck down the law. Police officers, prosecutors, mayors, and various community organizations went to Washington, D.C., to ask the justices to reinstate the law. Many other people and organizations arrived there to oppose it. The city of Chicago called the law an indispensable tool for law enforcement in stemming gang violence; opponents said the law was "vague and overbroad," and violated the constitutional rights of free assembly and due process. The U.S. Supreme Court sustained the state court's ruling. However, taking a lead from Justice Sandra O'Connor on how to make the law pass constitutional muster, the city council enacted a new "antiloitering" law in February 2000 (further revised in March 2000).

31. David Rosenzweig and Matea Gold, "Sweeping Order to Limit Activity of 18th Street Gang," *Los Angeles Times*, Jul. 12, 1997. This injunction against 18th Street has become the largest of its kind in the country. Ben Ehrenreich in

"Chained Gang: Can the City Attorney's Injunction Stop Pico-Union's 18th Street Gang," *L.A. Weekly,* Jan. 15–21, 1999, wrote, "Now, whenever [18th Street gang members] find themselves in the square mile bounded by Ninth Street and Washington Avenue to the north and south, and by the Harbor Freeway and Hoover Street to the east and west, [they] are prohibited from publicly associating with each other or with any other known gang member, from being out after 10 P.M. (or after 8 if they're minors), from carrying pagers or cell phones or screwdrivers or felt-tip pens, from being on private property without prior written permission from the owner, from being within 10 feet of an open beer can, from climbing a tree, from using 'abusive language,' and, of course, from 'whistling, yelling, or otherwise signaling... to warn another person of an approaching law-enforcement officer.'" However, as Ehrenreich pointed out, "[the injunction came about] when gang-related crime was already on the wane. [When] residents were actively taking back their streets and becoming involved in the life of the community." In fact a year before the injunction, gang-related crimes had dropped 28 percent compared to the previous five years. And it wasn't the community, or even the police, that called for the injunction, but then Los Angeles Mayor Richard Riordan. "It's politics—the D.A. wants to be D.A. again, Riordan wants to stay mayor," said an alleged 18th Street gang member.

"The rapidly multiplying injunctions continue to pose a wide host of civil rights concerns, particularly given that thus far they have been used only in black and Latino communities," wrote Ehrenreich. "'The orders are so broad,' says Alex Ricciardulli of the L.A. Public Defender's Office, 'that every time they detain these people there's going to be something they're doing wrong'; it's nearly impossible not to be in violation."

See also Hector Becerra, "Gang Members Barred from Meeting Publicly," *Los Angeles Times,* Aug. 5, 1998.

32. Carl Ingram, "Wilson Proposes Overhaul of Juvenile Justice System," *Los Angeles Times,* Apr. 10, 1997. See also Vincent J. Schodolski, "Two California Officials Suggest 13-Year-Olds Face Death Penalty," *Chicago Tribune,* Apr. 15, 1997. According to Scholdolksi, besides the United States, only Bangladesh, Barbados, Iran, and Iraq presently allow the execution of minors.

33. Quoted in Mike Dorning, "U.S. Rewrites the Rules on Youth Justice," *Chicago Tribune,* May 7, 1997. For more on the rise of juveniles sentenced as adults or on blended sentences (a combination of juvenile and adult incarceration), see also Christi Parsons, "Youth Could Face New System of Justice: Reform Plan Targets Juvenile Offenders," *Chicago Tribune,* Jan. 14, 1998. In addition, with the rise of school shootings, many communities are posting law enforcement officials in schools, using informants, and sharing information of potential "troublemakers." See Jack Leonard, "Deputies to Join Schools' Anti-Crime Efforts," *Los Angeles Times,* Jan. 7, 2001.

34. By the year 2000 the U.S. Justice Department reported that more than two million people were behind bars in this country. The United States had a

greater incarceration rate than any other country in the world, including Russia (the U.S. incarceration rate was 690 people per 100,000 residents, whereas Russia's was 678 people per 100,000). This present rate is quadruple the U.S. incarceration rate from 1980. See "The Prison Paradox," *Time* magazine, Nov. 13, 2000; and Dan Baum, "Invisible Nation," *Rolling Stone,* Dec. 7, 2000.

The Associated Press on Aug. 8, 1997, also reported that corrections officials from throughout the country built 213 state and federal prisons between 1990 and 1995. "There were more people coming in the door and fewer people going out," stated U.S. Justice Department statistician James Stephan.

The main contributor to this vast growth in prisons was tougher sentencing laws, which resulted in prisoners getting longer sentences, and getting released at a slower rate, despite a drop in crime in the 1990s, according to a 1999 study of the new laws released by the U.S. Justice Department. The enactment in a number of states of "truth in sentencing" laws effectively ended the indeterminate sentence for certain crimes. In Illinois, for example, a violent felon must serve 85 to 100 percent of his sentence, whereas in the past he may have been eligible for release in half the time. In addition some states have eliminated parole boards.

"The fundamental thing the report shows," said Franklin Zimring, director of the Warren Legal Institute at the University of California at Berkeley, "is that the changes in the American prison population are the result of a shift in policy, rather than any basic change in the nature of criminals or the crime rate." See "Longer Terms Boost U.S. Prison Population: Tougher Sentencing Laws Cited," *Chicago Tribune,* Jan. 11, 1999.

It should also be noted that the present prison population explosion is largely due to the so-called War on Drugs, which began under President Reagan in the early 1980s. This has resulted in thousands upon thousands of low-level, nonviolent drug offenders sentenced to long prison terms. Presently the primary offense of 58 percent of federal prisoners and 21 percent of state prisoners is drug-related. Dan Baum, "The Invisible Nation," *Rolling Stone,* Dec. 7, 2000, p. 44.

"The sea change came in 1984, when Congress enacted the most sweeping reform of federal sentencing laws in American history. Sentencing Reform Act of 1984 eliminated parole for all federal crimes committed on or after Nov. 1, 1987. Anyone convicted after that would have to serve at least 85 percent of his or her sentence. The new law also radically curtailed the freedom of judges to set sentences. Taken together, these two changes would spark an unprecedented boom in the nation's federal prison population.... In 1987, when the first of these reforms began to take effect, there were 44,000 federal prisoners. By 2000, there were nearly 140,000," wrote Joseph T. Hallinan in *Going Up the River: Travels in a Prison Nation* (New York: Random House, 2001), pp. 38–40.

And, again, we have to state, poor people, particularly those from the African-American and Latino communities, are disproportionately represented in our country's jails. While whites made up 70 percent or so of the general population, they made up around 30 percent of the prison population (and these were overwhelmingly from the poorest communities). African Americans were 13 percent of the general population, but half of those were in prison. Latinos (mostly Mexicans and Puerto Ricans, with growing numbers of Dominicans, Cubans, Colombians, and Central Americans) comprised 11 percent of the U.S. population while close to 20 percent were behind bars. And Native Americans, with 1 percent of the general population, were double this (2 percent) among our prison population. (Asians, like whites, were imprisoned at a lower percentage—1 percent—than their numbers in the U.S. population—4 percent.)

"Minorities are sent to prison at up to thirteen times the rate of whites. This is partly due to police targeting of low-income neighborhoods and sentencing disparities.... According to Human Rights Watch, 'In seven states... blacks constitute between 80 and 90 percent of all drug offenders sent to prison,' despite the fact that whites use drugs at a higher rate than blacks" (Ibid., p. 45).

Chapter 3

1. Based on the essay "Treating L.A.'s Gang Problem: We Need 'Root' Doctors," *Los Angeles Times,* Feb. 9, 1997.

2. Rich Connell and Robert J. Lopez, "The 18th Street Gang," *Los Angeles Times,* Nov. 17–19, 1996.

3. Sarah Downey, "Cicero Turns Its Failed Anti-gang Ordinance into a Curfew Law," *Chicago Tribune,* Aug. 25, 1999.

4. Michael Meade, *Thresholds of Change: Finding Purpose and Inner Authority in Troubled Times* (Pacific Grove, Calif.: Oral Traditions Archives, 1995), audiotape, read by author.

5. Joseph Campbell, *The Hero with a Thousand Faces* (Princeton, N.J.: Princeton University Press, 1949). In this section of his most well-known book Campbell illustrates the vital role of persons (women, mentors, elders), angels, deities, or spirits in assisting the protagonists of hero adventures, what James Joyce termed the monomyth, which is the archetypal narrative line of most of the world's folktales and myths. In the story of the "Labyrinth and the Minotaur," the hero Theseus was aided through the maze with the help of a thread of linen that the labyrinth's creator, the artist-scientist Daedalus, gave him to tie at the entrance, and that he unwound as he maneuvered through the labyrinth's treacherous twists and turns. Campbell then writes, "The flax for the linen of his thread was gathered from the fields of the human imagination. Centuries of husbandry, decades of diligent culling, the work of numerous hearts and hands, have gone into the hackling, sorting, and spinning of this tightly twisted yarn. Furthermore, we have not even to risk the adventure alone; for the heroes of all time have gone before us; the labyrinth is thoroughly known; we have only to follow the thread of the hero-path" (pp.24–25).

6. The biggest issue cited about the fractured family structures of today, particularly in poor urban communities, has been the lack of fathers. However, I

contend that poor men, particularly fathers, have been highly marginalized in society—first by the economy, then by social services, and finally by people who accept the perilous notion that "we don't need men."

Public services tended to push this concept for years by penalizing welfare recipients for having men in the house, forcing men to seek work outside the community, not having more men assist with children in schools or social agencies (as if they can't be trusted with children), and increasingly detaining and removing men who are idle, active in gangs, or in illegal trades.

Unfortunately this means that women carry the physical, financial, and emotional burdens of raising the children and keeping the community intact (and for the most part they've done a massively heroic job). It's true that many men buy into this and act accordingly: We don't need any more abusive, irresponsible, and cowardly men (a situation that, ironically, in many subtle and not-so-subtle ways is given a green light in this culture). But we can't walk away from men either. We need compassionate, astute, and courageous men. We need strong men and strong women.

7. James Hillman, *The Soul's Code: In Search of Character and Calling* (New York: Random House, 1996).

Chapter 4

1. Part of this section first appeared in "Adult Prisons Are Not the Place for Juveniles," *Chicago Tribune,* Aug. 5, 1999; and "Don't Send Kids to Adult Prisons," *Judicature* magazine, Jul.–Aug. 1999.

2. Otto L. Bettmann, *The Good Old Days—They Were Terrible!* (New York: Random House, 1974), pp. 90–91.

3. As quoted by Shannon Brownlee, "Inside the Teen Brain: Behavior Can Be Baffling When Young Minds Are Taking Shape," *U.S. News & World Report,* Aug. 9, 1999, pp. 44–54.

4. Quoted in William Plummer and Leila Cobo-Hanlon, "Miracle of the Loaves: In East L.A., A Priest Turns Gang-Bangers into Bakers and Businessmen," *People,* Dec. 15, 1997, pp. 139–140. Father Greg Boyle is a Jesuit priest who instituted perhaps one of the most famous gang peace efforts in the country, Jobs for a Future, which oversees several businesses run by gang youth, including Homeboy Industries, which includes a bakery and a tortilla factory. Jobs for a Future's motto is "Nothing Stops a Bullet Like a Job." See also Celeste Fremon, *Father Greg & the Homeboys* (New York: Hyperion, 1995).

5. One such survey, conducted by Junior Achievement of Central New Jersey, involved 267 sixth, seventh, and eight graders in the New Jersey counties of Monmouth, Mercer, and Hunterdon. According to an article by Dina Maasarani, "Poll Finds Youngsters See Economic Unfairness," *Asbury Park Press,* Jul. 31, 1998, "Forty-five percent of those surveyed said they do not feel the country's economic system is fair, while 52 percent believe the system benefits the rich. Thirty-three percent said the system benefits the middle class, while 8 percent

said it favors the poor." The article also pointed out that half the students felt the government should have a big role in the nation's economy.

6. A number of books now exist outlining this process. One of the better recent ones is Jim Davis, Thomas Hirschl, and Michael Stack, eds., *Cutting Edge: Technology, Information, Capitalism and Social Revolution* (New York: Verso Press, 1997).

7. Low-paying jobs aren't the only result of the new economy. See Karen Brandon, "Housing Crunch Keeps Many Out in the Cold: In Orange County and Elsewhere in the U.S., Many Low-Wage Workers Find the Booming Economy Actually Works Against Them," *Chicago Tribune*, Apr. 25, 1999. The article details how the economy that has forced housing costs to skyrocket has adversely affected working families in many suburban communities. Those affected included the Scotts, a family of five children and two adults who had to live in a motel for around $1,400 a month—leaving very little for other necessities. "The strong economy has exacerbated the plight of the poor by pushing up housing prices and rents, to record levels in some regions," wrote Brandon. "Nationally, rents rose at double the rate of inflation from 1997 to 1998, according to the U.S. Department of Housing and Urban Development. [Meanwhile] the wages of the lowest-paid workers in particular have stagnated. As a result, the federal government estimates that some 12.5 million people, a record number, face what it terms 'worse case needs.' That is, they live in households earning less than 50 percent of the area median income and either paying more than half of their income for rent or living in substandard housing, or both."

8. "Penal philosophy in the latter half of the nineteenth century did not advance with technology," wrote Otto L. Bettmann in *The Good Old Days—They Were Terrible!* (New York: Random House, 1974). "Prisons were strictly for punishment, which was carried out with medieval excesses. Public opinion as a whole supported this view, and criminals customarily were treated as a subhuman species.... Starvation, floggings, chainings and torture were blandly routine. Although prison reform did have some devotees, and isolated experiments in rehabilitation had been carried out—notably in the Philadelphia and Auburn systems—unyielding repression was the rule" (p. 104).

9. There are many labor-history books out there. One I have consulted over the years is William Cahn, *A Pictorial History of American Labor: The Contributions of the Working Man and Woman to America's Growth, from Colonial Times to the Present* (New York: Crown Publishers, 1972).

10. Excerpted from an interview with Michael Meade by Annie Brown on Colorado Public Radio, KAJX-FM, Nov. 20, 2000.

11. Again, see Dr. John M. Hagedorn, "The Business of Drug Dealing in Milwaukee," *Wisconsin Policy Research Institute Report* [Thiensville, Wis.] 11, no. 5 (Jun. 1998). In this important study Dr. Hagedorn maintained what people in the streets have long known: "Poor people in Milwaukee have responded to the loss of 'good jobs' by starting thousands of new, mainly off-the-books busi-

nesses," according to the report's executive summary. "The most profitable business in this informal sector of our economy, unfortunately, is the business of drug
selling."

More specifically, the study showed that "(1) Much of what we call 'crime' is
actually work; (2) The work of drug dealing in the central city is in many ways
an innovative, entrepreneurial, small business venture; (3) Most drug entrepreneurs are hard working, but not super rich; (4) Most drug entrepreneurs aren't
particularly violent; (5) Drug entrepreneurs have reduced their risk of arrest; (6)
Women do not seem to be entering the ranks of drug sellers in large numbers;
(7) Drug dealing by whites in the suburbs and youth culture is more about party-
ing than economics" (pp. 1–2).

Although controversial, the study is helpful in objectifying what's behind
"inner city" drug trafficking in contrast to the theoretical notions often portrayed
in the media. The drug trade—although it has grown to its highest levels in U.S.
history—is not as lucrative, as violent, or as prevalent as people may believe.
Another conclusion of the report helps put this in perspective: "One lesson of
economic restructuring is that without better education and training, workers in
poor communities will not be directly helped by the 'good jobs' being created by
today's information-driven economy" (p. 3).

12. Soon after the 1992 L.A. Rebellion, I met with African-American members of Crips and Bloods as well as Mexican and Salvadoran youth on how to
rebuild Los Angeles. The Crips and the Bloods, as an outcome of their truce, had
proposed a plan. While attacked by law enforcement, politicians, and some sociologists, the plan did not call for reestablishing the taco stands, the liquor stores,
or the overpriced markets that had previously dotted South Central. The plan
included razing the burned-out buildings and putting up new structures, including career counseling-centers and recreation areas; resurfacing all pavement and
sidewalks in disrepair; increasing lighting in city streets and alleyways ("We want
a well-lit neighborhood"); putting in new trees and landscaping; using pest control and cleanup crews on a regular basis; building new hospitals and health care
centers; replacing welfare with state work and product manufacturing plants; giving a complete face-lift to all parks, stages, pools, and ball courts, as well as
twenty-four-hour security; and reconstructing and refurbishing city schools,
including providing up-to-date books and supplies. Besides helping implement
the plan, the Crips and Bloods would see that drug trafficking and street violence
were stopped.

This proposal, with minor adjustments, could have been a strong step toward
truly rebuilding South Central L.A. Unfortunately millions of dollars were
thrown into the Rebuild L.A. project after the uprising (which did not involve
any of the youth, and which personally benefited non–South Central residents,
such as Rebuild L.A. cochairman Peter Ueberoth). The plan was ignored and
derided. It was an opportunity for healing that was squandered for narrow political concerns. The net result was that the crucial issues leading to the fires and

deaths in 1992 have not been fully addressed. You can't have peace in these streets without also addressing concerns such as jobs, skills, educational opportunities, drug and psychological treatment, and decent health care—what we know is required to have a quality of life in these modern times. Instead the over-priced and highly exploitative businesses were rebuilt, and vastly more money went into law enforcement, antigang units, and prison construction.

See "Bloods/Crips Proposal for L.A.'s Face-Lift," in *Why L.A. Happened: Implications of the '92 Los Angeles Rebellion,* edited by Haki R. Madhubuti (Chicago: Third World Press, 1993), pp. 274–282.

Chapter 5

1. See Robert Becker and Rob D. Kaiser, "Cicero Taking Its Gang Fight to Court: Suits Seek Millions and Judicial Orders to Restrict Activities," *Chicago Tribune,* May 12, 1999.

2. Gary Marx and Peter Kendall, "Cicero Top Cop: Corruption Rife," *Chicago Tribune,* Apr. 26, 1998. See also Eric Slater, "Chicago Suburb Living Up to Its Legacy," *Los Angeles Times,* Jun. 16, 2001.

3. General Colin L. Powell, "Let's Show Our Goodness," by General Colin L. Powell, *Parade* magazine, Apr. 27, 1997, pp. 4–6.

4. Bill Alexander, "On and Off the Wagon: America's Promise at Two," *Youth Today* 1 (Jul./Aug. 1999), pp. 34–36.

5. Mimi Hall, "Plight of Needy Kids Is Powell's Battlefield," *USA Today,* Feb. 24, 1998.

6. Amy Beth Graves, "Schools Scrutinizing Gothlike Kids: ACLU Swamped with Calls Over Possible Violations of Students' Rights," *San Francisco Chronicle,* May 9, 1999.

7. "Girl Scouts Fit Mall's Definition of a 'Gang,'" Los Angeles Daily News, 1995.

8. See also "Many Inmates Have Suffered Abuse, Neglect," *Chicago Tribune,* Apr. 27, 1998.

9. By early 2001 a number of important organizations have come out against "zero tolerance." One, the American Bar Association, overwhelmingly voted for a resolution calling on Congress "to enact legislation encouraging local school boards to do away with the controversial policies." As Michael Johnson, chairman of the bar association's criminal justice section, was quoted as saying, "the demands of society to be safe can be satisfied by making our system more responsive, not less human." From Jessica Garrison, "Group Opposes Zero-Tolerance School Policies," *Los Angeles Times,* Feb. 20, 2001.

10. The sponsors of the residency, the Multicultural Resource Center of the Philadelphia Area Independent Schools, and its director Kit Reath, were most gracious during my visit. They made sure the students were prepped and that I had a receptive audience in all my presentations. I commend their efforts to deepen the dialogue about race, culture, and class in our society.

Chapter 6

1. Expelling and suspending students was a growing phenomenon, particularly among younger pupils and for fairly minor infractions, way before the high school shootings such as those in Littleton, Colorado. See Mitch Martin, "School Suspends Pupil Over Toy Weapon," *Chicago Tribune,* Apr. 5, 1998. According to this article, the number of expulsions for elementary school students in Illinois almost tripled in five years—from 273 during the 1991–92 school year, to 731 in 1996–97. In one particular case, a thirteen-year-old was suspended for a year and a half for bringing to school a fake hand grenade (similar to what is sold at any toy store). And if this isn't incredible enough, how about the two teenagers in Evans, Georgia, who were suspended in early 1998 for wearing "Pepsi" shirts on "Coke" Day? (Editorial, "A Bad Call in Coke Country," *Chicago Tribune,* Mar. 31, 1998).

2. Jon Nordheimer, "Arrest of Girl, 5, Was Way to Get Her Aid, School Says," *The New York Times,* Feb. 22, 1998.

See also "Forget Sticks, Stones—Names May Get You Jail Time: 10-Year-Old Girls Warned by Judge," *Chicago Tribune,* Dec. 2, 1997. In this article, Circuit Judge Michael Schwartz in Mt. Clemens, Michigan, told two fifth-grade classmates after they were involved in a hair-pulling, name-calling dispute, "If one of you looks cross-eyed to the other, you're going to come back here." Schwartz then reportedly said, "No more harassment, no more threats, no more obscenities or vulgar names, no more pulling hair, no more threats to the family, no more threatening calls to each other or relatives. If one of you causes problems to the other, I'm going to put you in the juvenile hold." However, one prosecutor claims this was an abuse of the court system. Educators were concerned this could subvert their efforts to teach children how to get along. "Where did we get this idea that every dispute between children has to wind up before a circuit court judge?," a prosecutor asked.

In another case an eighth grader in Granite City, Illinois, in her living room dressed in pajamas and wrapped in a sheet, was confronted by a police officer. "Get your clothes on, you're going to jail," the officer said. The girl was arrested for allegedly missing fourteen of the first forty-one days of school. From "Granite City's Schools Arrest Truancy Problems—With Arrests," *Chicago Tribune,* Nov. 28, 1997.

And in yet another bizarre incident of overkill, a McHenry County, Illinois, teenager was expelled from school, booked at the county jail, and held for seven hours in a lockup for shooting a paper clip at a cafeteria cashier. (Jeremy Manier, "Student Is Expelled for Paper Clip Incident," *Chicago Tribune,* May 13, 1998.)

3. "Man Who Blamed Fear for Killing Has Sentence Commuted," *Chicago Tribune,* Dec. 25, 1997. Maryland governor Parris Glendening commuted the five-year prison sentence of Nathanial Hurt, sixty-five, who had shot to death a thirteen-year-old boy that Hurt said had "terrorized him." Hurt claimed he suffered from "urban fear syndrome." After his conviction in 1995, Hurt report-

edly received hundreds of calls and letters from people who thought the sentence was too harsh. When Glendening freed Hurt, he had served only fourteen months of his sentence.

One of the most startling cases involved a thirty-five-year-old man, William Masters, who in 1995 shot two youths in L.A. who had been "tagging" beneath a Hollywood freeway overpass. Eighteen-year-old Cesar Arce was killed; the other, David Hilo, twenty, survived, although he had been shot in the back. Masters claimed self-defense, although it was he who had pulled out the gun on the unarmed youth; he also had a previous conviction for carrying a concealed weapon. Masters never went to trial—prosecutors refused to press charges. "Where are you going to find twelve citizens to convict me?" Masters asked rhetorically after being released.

4. From Richard A. Underwood, "Living by Myth: Joseph Campbell, C. G. Jung, and the Religious Life-Journey," in *Paths to the Power of Myth: Joseph Campbell and the Study of Religion,* edited by Daniel C. Noel (New York: The Crossroad Publishing Company, 1990), pp. 18–19.

Chapter 7

1. James Hillman, *The Myth of Analysis* (Evanston, Ill.: Northwestern University Press 1972), p. 206.

2. James Hillman and Michael Ventura, *We've Had a Hundred Years of Psycho Therapy—and the World's Getting Worse* (New York: HarperSanFrancisco, 1992).

3. Ibid., p. 8.

4. See Joanne Archibald, "The High Costs of Jailing Mothers," *Chicago Tribune,* Apr. 20, 1998.

5. I have a friend in Phoenix, Arizona, Rudy Buchanan, Sr., of Chicano and African-American descent, whose twenty-two-year-old son, Rudy Jr., was shot at eighty-nine times and hit thirty-three times by police in early 1995 following a domestic dispute. The young man was allegedly despondent at the time (ninety days before, his younger brother Chris had been killed by a rival gang). Rudy Jr. walked out of his home with a loaded shotgun and walked several blocks, firing three times into vacant lots. The police, however, cornered Rudy Jr. and, although he had dropped his weapon, continued to shoot. See Bill Hart, "Buchanan Shooting Leaves Many Questions," *Phoenix Gazette,* Mar. 14, 1995; and Ruben Hernandez, "A Case of Overkill? The Buchanan Trial Set to Unfold," *New El Sol,* Jul. 28, 1998. Yet a police review panel in May 1995 exonerated nine of the police officers involved and only censured four others. In addition the U.S. Department of Justice's Civil Rights Division in January 1998 ruled that the case lacked "prosecutive merit" for possible violation of federal civil rights laws. However, in March 1999 an unlawful death lawsuit against the Phoenix Police Department by the Buchanan family was settled out of court for more than half a million dollars—following nationwide outrage at this and other deaths by Phoenix police officers.

According to Ray Stern, "Cops Shoot, Kill More in Phoenix," *The Tribune,* Aug. 30, 1998, the Phoenix Police Department shot and killed more people per capita than other large police force over the prior three years. Even though New York, Los Angeles, and Chicago police killed more people (these cities are seven times, three times, and two times larger, respectively, than Phoenix) the rate of suspects shot dead by police was 2.16 per 100,000 in Phoenix, 1.89 per 100,000 in Los Angeles, 1.10 per 100,000 in Chicago, and 1.03 per 100,000 in New York. In addition, the percentage of suspects killed by Phoenix police from 1995 to 1998 was 58 percent—the highest of any other major city in the country.

6. From 1974 to mid-1998 Chicago police killed 414 people (a total of 1,642 had been shot). See William Recktenwald, "Shootings by City Cops Edging Up," *Chicago Tribune,* Apr. 30, 1998. However, according to the article, the number of police killings in Chicago have been in a near-steady decline during this period. On a national level, while there were 332 "justifiable homicides" by police in the U.S. in 1996, this number was reportedly the fourth lowest reported in thirty years. Recktenwald wrote that "improved police forces are reasons for the overall decrease in shootings, experts said. 'They have better training, and better educated people,' [Criminal Justice Professor John] Doherty said."

There are also other ways to do damage. Besides police shootings and killings, Amnesty International (AI) recently declared the United States "a world leader in high-tech repression." (Terry Atlas, "Abuses in America Put Under Scrutiny," *Chicago Tribune,* Oct. 5, 1998). In its first worldwide campaign aimed at the U.S., AI claimed official abuses included "widespread and persistent" police brutality, physical and sexual violence against prisoners, and unequal racist application of the death penalty as well as the use of electroshock devices and chemical sprays to control suspects or force confessions. The U.S. Department of Justice vehemently challenged AI's findings.

In the Dec. 2000 issue of *CounterPunch* 7, no. 21, Karen Saari maintained that the 350 or so people killed by police every year is grossly undercounted. Many law enforcement agencies aren't included in these numbers, including "the Border Patrol, DEA agents, park police, FBI agents, BATF agents and the myriad other kinds of police." The numbers also don't include killings by security guards, who are often off-duty officers. Ms. Saari's own search of on-line newspaper databases and collected news stories on deaths by law enforcement found that in one twelve-month period—October 1, 1997, to October 1, 1998—close to 700 people were killed, including about 80 due to excessive application of restraint techniques.

7. Robert Bly, *Iron John: A Book About Men* (New York: Addison-Wesley, 1990), pp. 96–98.

8. James Hillman, *Myths of the Family* (New York: Sounds Horizon, 1997), audiotape.

9. Far too many people have been killed by police for being "mentally ill." Although police often cite a high level of fear for their safety when confronting

such people, a recent study found so-called mentally ill people are no more violent than other people. See "Study Belies Stigma of Mentally Ill as Violent,"
Chicago Tribune, May 15, 1998.

10. Paul Chevigny, *Edge of the Knife: Police Violence in the Americas* (New
York: The New Press, 1995), p. 250.

Chapter 8

1. *Increase the Peace: A Primer on Fear, Violence, and Transformation* (Springfield, Ill.: Illinois Prevention Resource Center, 1994). See the chapter entitled
"The Chemistry of Fear," pp. 21–29.

2. Ibid., 21.

3. Ibid., 24.

4. From "Adolescent Assault Victim Needs: A Review of Issues and a Model
Protocol," *Pediatrics* 98, no. 5 (Nov. 1996): 991. The article also states, "The
belief that the treatment of adolescent victims of violence is hopeless in, in some
ways, a self-fulfilling prophecy" (p. 991). And further, "The consequences of
poverty encourage violence. Overcrowded and poor-quality housing, dangerous
living structures, limited access to transportation and lack of access to parks and
recreational facilities increase fear and isolation. Alcohol and other drugs, used as
an escape from despair, are involved in the majority of homicides and nonfatal
assaultive injuries. In high-risk communities, the experience of multiple losses of
loved ones to violent or nonviolent death, prison, and substance abuse is common. This experience in turn becomes a risk factor for violent injury and other
injuries and also for maladaptive psychological reactions to violent injury" (p.
996).

5. *Increase the Peace,* p. 25.

6. Despite the effects of increased trauma in urban areas, American jurispru-
dence has for the most part turned its back on such environmental and physiological factors in criminal prosecution—even though these factors play a major
part in cases involving people with wealth, resources, and, too often, a "privileged" color of skin. Paul Harris, a California lawyer, helped pioneer an urban
rage defense (sometimes called the black rage defense, although, as Harris himself concedes, this term does not accurately describe the scope of economic,
social, racial, and social-class pressures in the lives of people who commit
crimes). He says such factors must now be given a legitimate berth in our court-
rooms if we are truly to become a just and equitable society. If we understand
these factors—and the courts' discounting of them—we may better understand
why our jails are made up of mostly poor people, both whites and people of
color, rather than accepting the inane explanation that "blacks and poor people
are prone to do wrong."

As Paul Harris writes, "In a country divided by color and class, racial oppression and poverty have always been causal agents of theft and violence. However,
lawyers, have had difficulty translating these consequences of racism into the lan-

guage of the criminal courtroom. The law does not allow the simple fact of racial discrimination as a defense to murder. Long-term unemployment is not accepted as a defense to bank robbery. French novelist Anatole France's famous ironic quote about the law is an accurate explanation of the inequality of the American legal system: 'The law, in its majestic equality, forbids the rich as well as the poor to sleep under bridges, to beg in the streets, and to steal bread.' Although legal doctrine has maintained a claim of class neutrality and a facade of colorblindness, in some cases lawyers have been able to break through the criminal law's resistance to allowing social reality into the courtroom." From Paul Harris, *Black Rage Confronts the Law* (New York: New York University Press, 1997), p. 2.

7. From the four-part TV series "Crime and Punishment," which aired on *Nightline,* ABC-TV, Mar. 25–30, 1998. The particular segment I quoted from, hosted by Ted Koppel, was subtitled: "Is This Where We Want to Go?"

8. This process is part of a "war" mentality, whether in the streets or in overseas conflicts. From 1988 to 1992, including during the short-lived Persian Gulf War, I was a news writer for an all-news radio station in Chicago, then operated by CNN. I got disgusted with the aerial views of bombs being dropped onto various targets in Iraq. They were done mostly by computers, similar to video games operated by kids. I called these attacks "the Great Drivebys." The attackers did not have to see the bodies, the faces, the crying, or the deaths of those they hit when the bombs fell. Later it was disclosed that at least 100,000 Iraqians, including many women and children, were killed in these operations. But these people were considered "dogs," "animals," and "less than human" (terms I actually heard in the newsroom). The justification was in. "They deserved what they got," became the general sentiment.

9. George Lakoff and Mark Johnson, *Metaphors We Live By* (Chicago: University of Chicago, 1980), p. 4.

10. Ibid., p. 4. Another take on this: Words can most definitely illicit certain emotions, resulting in certain kinds of action. Images and metaphors are carried from language into our lives and relationships. See Robert Lee Hotz, "Watching the Brain Bring Emotions to Life," *Los Angeles Times,* Nov. 30, 2000. Hotz writes, "Mapping the brain's emotional landscape, researchers are learning how [emotions like love] alters the brain's neural activity. They have detected the inner turmoil that strong words can stir. They can see how the biochemistry of feelings clouds the brain's ability to think clearly or create accurate memories. They are discovering how the brain must change its emotional ways to master the dark disturbances of depression."

My concern is also how this works for so-called normal people. If words can stir emotions and, as Hotz says, "each emotion generates a unique pattern in the brain," we are hitting on a powerful means by which those who control the media can also control what we feel, what we think, and eventually how we act or don't act.

The word *industry*—the mass media, including books and the Internet—

make fantastic profits in drawing on the most prurient or violent aspects of our nature, including the scurrilous, vile, gross, lurid, ribald, titillating, and crude. These aspects exist and they can't be denied, but they are cleverly manipulated whenever you set yourself in front of a TV or watch movies. The immediate responses to these feelings then serve as strong foundations for commercials and other profit-directed activity to bring out certain calculated responses, such as buying a product. We're confronting one well-oiled and maintained manipulation machine, grinding and winding through our feelings, sentiments, desires, and needs.

Yes, I understand that not all people involved in the media are guilty of this. But they are definitely overwhelmed by the predominant forces behind the media today (and "family" fare is not immune either). Powerful images and metaphors that convey strong emotions and desires in a more positive manner are much lacking in our culture. "Why," as I once heard Father Greg Boyle ask, "can't we conjure up an image that a young person can hold into the future?"

11. From Sam Keen, *Faces of the Enemy: Reflections of the Hostile Imagination* (New York: Harper & Row, 1986), p. 11.

Chapter 9

1. See Steven A. Drizin, "Should We Demand Juveniles to Cry Us a River?" *Chicago Tribune,* Apr. 27, 1998. A supervising attorney with the Children and Family Justice Center at Northwestern University Legal Clinic, Drizin addressed why demanding remorse from young people may be unrealistic—not only may they be developmentally incapable of true remorse but they may perceive it as something that may hurt them later on.

"While… guilt, empathy and sympathy appear in rudimentary forms in very young children, it is not until late childhood or early adolescence that children first become aware that others have personal identities and life experiences beyond their own," wrote Drizin. Other factors also abound: "Apologies and tears may be particularly difficult for adolescent males, who make up the bulk of the delinquent population. Such emotions may subject them to ridicule by those whose opinions matter the most to them—their peers. In some high-crime communities, such emotions may be seen as signs of 'weakness,' which may make these youths targets of violence. Furthermore, extreme depression is common to adolescents after incarceration and often is a major factor in a child's lack of affect during court proceedings."

In one recent case of an eleven-year-old accused of murdering a thirteen-year-old neighbor in Antioch, California, some people were upset because the child kept coloring pictures with crayons while two attorneys argued out his case. But what else can we expect of an eleven-year-old? (I know of adults who don't pay attention to their own serious cases in court.) See Tim Tyler, "Envy Cited as Antioch Killing Motive," *Contra Costa Times,* Jul. 24, 1998.

2. This practice is extremely lucrative. According to the Chicago-based

Prison Phone Project, Illinois' Cook County, which administers the largest jail in the world, signed a contract in 1999 with the Ameritech phone company for exclusive phone service to the jail for five years. The county will collect an approximate 45 percent commission from every collect call made by a prisoner and a $200,000 bonus each year of the contract. Ameritech, by overcharging calls made from jail, will garner more than $30 million in profits over the life of the contract. The state, in turn, will get about $24 million. Similar gains from collect phone calls are obtained from almost every jail, penitentiary, and juvenile facility in the country. Most of this is coming from poor people, as a kind of supertax, just to be able to communicate with their loved ones, although this doesn't necessarily translate into better or extended services. I know, since I have to pay exorbitant fees just to talk to my son, Ramiro, on a regular basis.

3. From Mike Rose, *Lives on the Boundary* (New York: Free Press/Macmillan, 1989), as quoted by Michael Ventura, "The Age of Endarkenment," in *Crossroads: The Quest for Contemporary Rites of Passages,* edited by Louise Carus Mahdi, Nancy Geyer Christopher, and Michael Meade (Peru, Ill.: Open Court/Carus, 1996), p. 52.

4. Michael Meade, "Latima: The Inner Heat," in *Crossroads,* p. 57.

5. Randall Sullivan, "A Boy's Life: Part 2," *Rolling Stone,* Oct. 1, 1998, p. 48.

6. There have been various gatherings around the country of youth, practitioners, and professionals on moving youth, families, and communities "from risk to resiliency," including the "Building Hope: Exploring Resiliency in Youth and Communities" conferences, sponsored by Kaiser Permanente at the University of Maryland. According to one of their promotional brochures, "An increasing body of research from psychology, psychiatry, social work, and education is showing that children, youth, and adults can bounce back and experience life success—even if they are now involved in violence and criminal behavior; alcohol or other drug abuse, or experiencing school failure, teen pregnancy, or other risk factors. To facilitate resiliency, families, schools, communities and all youth organizations need to provide specific protective assets that aid the internal traits that foster resiliency and that buffer environmental stress." Again, with a proper interaction of resources, tools, collective support and a person's own transformative powers, people can overcome some of the most debilitating traumas, habits, and addictions.

7. Emily Dickinson, "Much Madness Is Divinest Sense," in *The Rag and Bone Shop of the Heart: Poems for Men,* edited by Robert Bly, James Hillman, and Michael Meade (New York: HarperCollins Perennial, 1992), p. 10.

Chapter 10

1. Some of the material in this chapter first appeared as "Writing Off Our Youth," *Prison Life,* Oct. 1994, pp. 8–9.

2. Mircea Eliade, *Rites and Symbols of Initiation* (New York: Harper Torchbooks, 1958).

3. Many of these laws and policies were predicated on the supposed rise in juvenile "superpredators." But this has proven to be more hype than reality— with devastating results nonetheless. "[M]any criminologists and other juvenile justice experts now say that the get-tough policies are driven as much by politics as reality and are occurring at a time when the rate of juvenile crime is dropping after years of dramatic increases," writes Gary Marx in "Young Killers Remain Well-Publicized Rarity: 'Superpredators' Fail to Grow into Forecast Proportions," *Chicago Tribune,* Feb. 11, 1998. "Moreover, they say the small number of pre-teen killers suggests that the threat posed by superpredators appears to have been overstated."

Recent FBI figures showed homicide rates for juveniles dropped 16 percent in 1997, while juvenile arrests for all violent crimes declined for the third year in a row ("Youth Violence in U.S. Drops in a Third Year," *Chicago Tribune,* Nov. 20, 1998).

But according to Gary Marx, several studies in the early 1990s suggested that the country would experience a phenomenal rise in juvenile criminals, which in turn fueled more juvenile justice legislation, including that which encouraged trying youths as adults. "One study completed in 1994 by the highly respected National Center for Juvenile Justice in Pittsburgh used arrest rates and the nation's growing juvenile population to predict that the rate of murder and other violent juvenile crime would double again between 1992 and 2010," wrote Marx. "'We issued the report and people went bonkers,' said Melissa Sickmund, a senior research associate who worked on the 1994 study. 'The media grabbed on to it bigtime.'" Yet Sickmund admitted that part of the study was misinterpreted. "While most criminologists say legislators' concerns about violent juvenile crime are justified," according to Marx, "they question whether too much emphasis is being placed on increased penalties for juvenile offenders rather than crime-prevention programs."

See also Beth Shuster, "Living in Fear," *Los Angeles Times,* Aug. 23, 1998, which explores why many Americans still feel threatened by crime although violent crime is declining and highly concentrated. Shuster writes, "Police stoke fear in part because they take crime seriously, but also to prime their budgets; politicians feel deeply about the issue, but also manipulate it to win votes. News organizations amplify fear by ratcheting up their crime coverage, even as crime declines, because it helps ratings. Security companies, theft detection manufacturers and others tap into deeply held fears and end up turning a profit. In some respects, the merger of profit and political advantage has turned the crime business into the domestic equivalent of what President Dwight Eisenhower once described as 'the military-industrial complex.'" See also Mike Males "Why Demonize a Healthy Teen Culture," *Los Angeles Times,* May 9, 1999; and "Early Figures Show 7th Straight Drop in Crime Rates, FBI Reports," *Chicago Tribune,* May 17, 1999. See, in addition, Peter Elikann, *Superpredators: The Demonization of Our Children by the Law* (New York: Insight Book, 1999).

4. J. Taylor Buckley, "Growing Up... and Growing Old in Prison," *USA Today*, Apr. 9, 1997.

5. Ibid.

6. Maura Dolan, "Justices Curb Law on Prosecution of Youths as Adults," *Los Angeles Times*, Feb. 8, 2001.

7. Eric Lotke and Vincent Schiraldi, "An Analysis of Juvenile Homicides: Where They Occur and the Effectiveness of Adult Court Intervention," *NCIA Report*, Jul. 16, 1998, p. 1.

8. Ibid.

9. Ibid.

10. William Ayers, *A Kind and Just Parent: The Children of Juvenile Court* (Boston: Beacon Press, 1997), p. 24.

11. From January 16 to April 9, 2000 (with a two-week break in between), I spent ten weeks driving from one end of North Carolina to the other, giving from fifteen to twenty-one readings, talks, and workshops a week. It was the longest writers' residency in the state's history. I talked at public schools, libraries, universities, colleges, work sites, churches, ESL classes, prisons, juvenile facilities, recovery programs, youth centers, and several locations on the Cherokee Reservation. The project was called "Word Wide" and was sponsored by the North Carolina Literary Consortium, the N.C. Arts Council, the National Endowment for the Arts, the N.C. Humanities Council, and the Josephus Daniels Charitable Trust of the Triangle Community Foundation.

12. From Joseph Campbell, *Mythology of the Individual* (High Bridge: Joseph Campbell Foundation, 1996), audiotape. I believe that a strong reason why this myth of the individual has taken hold in our culture is that it allows us to override collective interests with personal ones, so that the individual becomes the first block to united revolutionary action. Although long a part of Western—that is, European—intellectual history, the emphasis on "individualism" in the twentieth century was a direct response by the American ruling class to the triumph of Soviet power in 1917. Ayn Rand's *The Fountainhead* was a well-known literary work that argued for this ego-driven individualism, unbound by "mass" sentiments for justice and equity, where "selfishness is a virtue, altruism a vice" (from Merriam Webster's *Encyclopedia of Literature*, 1995, p. 929).

But as indigenous people and many social scientists have long known, there is no real antagonism between an individual and the community. An imbalance exists because there is an imbalance between the economic impulses of the community and its cultural and social makeup (in other words, between the tools, technology, and level of skills in the community, on the one hand, and the way people relate to one another in the process of basic production on the other). To emphasize one aspect over the other is to undermine further the balance of tensions between individuals—who bring their own unique insights and imprints to the world—and the community, which should ensure the full and well-rounded development of each person so that it is enriched, not diminished, by the individual. The confluence of collective interests and individual callings is a powerful dynamic for human interaction and growth. If you take care of community, you take care of individuals; if you take care of individuals, you insure community.

13. See Joseph Campbell, *Transformations of Myth Through Time,* (High Bridge: Joseph Campbell Foundation, 1990), audiotape, for more on these issues concerning the "spontaniety of the noble heart" that is inherent in everyone, versus forcing people into a common set of rules and lifestyles, into a cultural homogeneity that often sucks the life out of personal heroism and growth.

14. T. S. Eliot, *The Wasteland and Other Poems* (New York: Harcourt Brace & Company/Harvest Books, 1934), p. 42.

15. This process, not insignificantly, begins in school. In the nineteenth century, schools were fashioned around the needs of the harvest. In those days most Americans lived on farms. But for most of the twentieth century, schools prepared children for the factories, warehouses, and assembly lines that existed in the major urban centers of the country, where the majority of people moved to. Similarly, despite any unique talents and attributes a child may have, most everyone was pulled into the same metaphorical/mythological terrain. The privileged and powerful had their own institutions built around their own mythic images and symbols, along the lines of their so-called destiny to rule. However, with neither harvests nor factories to pull communities along as before, prisons today have become a major directing force of such education, particularly in the urban core neighborhoods. I've even heard young people tell me they were "destined" to be in prison. This doesn't just occur from nothing. They have these beliefs based on the social pressure toward these kinds of institutions. While schools once looked like factories—with desks set up in rows like assembly lines—today many schools feel and look like prisons, with metal detectors, police substations, and locked gates.

A striking example comes from Mt. Prospect, Illinois. "The announcement over the Prospect High School intercom just after lunch... sounded like a prison warden's call—'we are now in a lockdown'—and students knew immediately what to do," wrote Dimitra DeFotis in "Not Your Ordinary Drill at High School," *Chicago Tribune,* May 12, 1999. "Those in classrooms got away from windows and watched as teachers locked the doors. Those caught in the hallways walked calmly to the cafeteria or nearest room and waited for the all-clear, which came five minutes later."

16. The Associated Press, "4 Million in Nation on Probation, Parole," *Chicago Tribune,* Aug. 23, 1999.

17. Jennifer Connerman, "Welcome to Huntsville, Texas: Death City, U.S.A.," *Vibe,* Aug. 1998.

18. According to many reports, privately owned correctional facilities, to save costs, can be extremely poorly kept and hazardous. For example, see Fox Butterfield, "Profits at a Juvenile Prison Comes with a Chilling Cost," *The New York Times,* Jul. 15, 1998. Butterfield wrote, "Here in the middle of the impoverished

Mississippi Delta is a juvenile prison so rife with brutality, cronyism, and neglect that many legal experts say it is the worst in the nation." Louisiana's Tallulah Correctional Center for Youth, which housed 620 boys and young men ages eleven to twenty at the time the article was published, is privately owned and run. To cut costs, Butterfield claims, Tallulah had allocated only one percent of its $15 million budget in 1998 to education and counseling and 4 percent to health, while 17 percent went to administration and a whopping 78 percent to "other" (mostly construction). Because of this, meals were meager, poorly paid staff routinely beat the boys, and psychiatric visits were limited to only one day a week, although a fourth of the juveniles at Tallulah were mentally ill or disabled. But as Butterfield noted, "Tallulah appears unexceptional, one new cookie-cutter prison among scores built in the United States this decade." Earl Dunlap, president of the National Juvenile Detention Association, agreed, saying, "The issues of violence against offenders, lack of adequate education and mental health, of crowding and of poorly paid and poorly trained staff are the norm rather than the exception."

Of course, these kinds of problems don't just affect privately owned institutions. In early 2001, the U.S. Justice Department's civil rights division launched an investigation into Los Angeles County's juvenile detention facilities after a series of articles by the *Los Angeles Daily Journal*, a legal newspaper, and a report by the L.A. County Grand Jury claimed substandard housing and improper treatment of children at various county juvenile facilities. More than one hundred juvenile corrections systems have been investigated across the country over the last twenty years. See David Rosenzweig, "U.S. Probes County Youth Detention Conditions," *Los Angeles Times*, Feb. 6, 2001.

19. Joseph T. Hallinan, *Going Up the River: Travels in a Prison Nation* (New York: Random House, 2001), p. 145.

20. Jeff Ferrell, "Youth, Crime, and Cultural Space," *Social Justice: A Journal of Crime, Conflict & World Order* 24, no. 4 (1997): 31.

21. Clarence Darrow, *Address to the Prisoners in the Cook County Jail* (Chicago: Charles H. Kerr, 1975), pp. 37–38.

22. Urie Bronfenbrenner, *The Ecology of Human Development: Experiments by Nature and Design* (Boston: Harvard University Press, 1979), p. 16.

Chapter 11

1. See also Steven A. Drizin, "Race Does Matter in Juvenile Justice System," *Chicago Tribune*, May 13, 1999. "[The] fight against racism in the juvenile justice system is far from over," wrote Drizin. "As the intense media focus on the Littleton, Colo., shooting brought home, the fight needs to be stepped up—rather than abandoned. The middle-class white children responsible in the Columbine High School shootings and other school shootings have been called 'lonely,' 'alienated,' 'disturbed,' or 'disaffected,' while the black and brown children involved in the 'gang' violence of the early 1990s were 'morally impoverished' and 'remorseless superpredators.'"

2. Jeffrey Reiman, *The Rich Get Richer and The Poor Get Prison: Ideology, Class, and Criminal Justice* (Needham Heights, Mass.: Allyn and Bacon, 1998), p. 1.

3. Ibid., p. viii.

4. Unfortunately, with the rise of accountability laws, more than one person are taken in for the actions of an individual involved in a criminal activity. For example in Illinois people who happen to be in the same car with someone who does a driveby or an armed robbery can be judged not just on their particular actions or involvement (which deserves some serious consideration); they could wind up facing the same charges and sentencing as the person who actually pulled the trigger. Four, five, and even six guys could theoretically get the same time for one person's stupid acts.

Recently, in California, a highly publicized murder case involving three white middle-class youth dramatized the injustice of these kinds of laws (although they have been used against blacks and Latinos for years). In 1995 Jimmy Farris, sixteen, was stabbed to death during a brawl in Orange County's Agoura Hills over an attempted theft of marijuana. One youth, Jason Holland, then eighteen, confessed to stabbing Farris with a pocketknife to assist his smaller younger brother, Micah Holland, fifteen, who was being beaten. The other defendants—Brandon Hein, then eighteen, and Tony Miliotti, seventeen—didn't know that Jason had a knife or that a stabbing had occurred during the fight. Yet they were all found guilty under the state's felony murder rule, which specifies that all involved in the commission of a felony can be charged with first-degree murder if a death occurs as a result of the crime. The mandatory sentence is twenty-five years to life.

In May 1996, Jason Holland, Brandon Hein, and Tony Miliotti were convicted and sentenced to life in prison without possibility of parole. Micah Holland received twenty-five years to life. Although an appellate court reduced Micah's sentence to fifteen years to life, it upheld the convictions and sentences for the other three youths.

According to Rocky Jaramillo Rushing, a legislative consultant on juvenile justice, "[The felony murder rule is] a barbaric law whose origins date to Elizabethan England. Such was the state of law then that a defendant was not permitted defense witnesses. Those convicted of most felonies, such as burglary and larceny, were hanged. In 1957, England abolished the felony murder rule.... [Under the felony murder rule] it makes no difference if the killing was unplanned or accidental. Those playing a lesser role in the underlying felony share the same responsibility for the death as the killer. One person is held responsible for the unagreed upon and unforeseen acts of another. The purpose of creating varying degrees of murder charges is to punish intentional killing more severely than accidental killing. So how is it right that an unplanned death be treated the same as a premeditated, cold-blooded murder?" See Rocky Jaramillo Rushing, "Tragic Slaying, Tragic Sentencing," *Los Angeles Times,* Feb. 11, 2001.

Besides these "accountability" laws, there are new laws demanding punishment for the parents of the accused, their counselors, their coaches, and their best friends. You end up imprisoning even more people who had no direct link to the criminal activity in question. See Peter Applebome, "Holding Parents Responsible as Children's Misdeeds Rise," *The New York Times,* Apr. 15, 1996. "Frustrated by rising juvenile violence and crime, states and cities around the country are rushing to enact laws making parents responsible for the misbehavior of their children," writes Applebome. "But some criminal justice experts and groups are saying the laws are little more than political grandstanding. 'Most of these laws are a complete waste of time,' said Barry Krisberg, president of the National Council on Crime and Delinquency. 'It's country-club criminology. It sounds good in the suburbs but in reality it's an empty threat because if you carry it out you just further endanger and pull apart families.'"

The term *the long arm of the law* now has new meaning. Even whole communities get criminalized for the acts of a few. I've seen instances in which the actual perpetrators of a deadly crime are let go or given far less time for cooperating with the police than their so-called accomplices. Someone who was in the backseat of a car in which another person fired a gun, for example, could end up doing that other person's time after the actual perpetrator had struck a deal. These laws sound good to politicians, the media, and even in hypothetical arguments. But in real life they are farcical and unjust.

5. "Place" has a real impact not just on the quality of life but also on the length of it as well. As reported in "Short Life Spans in Some U.S. Areas Puzzle Experts," *Chicago Tribune,* Dec. 4, 1997, Harvard scientist Christopher Murray told a gathering organized by the Centers for Disease Control and Prevention that men in parts of South Dakota and the eastern cities of Baltimore and Washington, D.C., live about as long as men in such developing countries as India and Bolivia. "That's an absolutely staggering range," Murray is quoted as saying.

The areas with the shortest life spans were the inner cities, the South, and Indian reservations, Murray declared. According to the article, "Male Indians living in the worst South Dakota counties had a life expectancy of just 56.5 years and black men living in the nation's capital 57.9 years, as low as in parts of Africa." Murray then asks "Why does the United States have a bigger spread than any other high-income country? Even if you took all of Europe, you would not find this variation."

6. Bruce Rubenstein, "Lost in Translation," *Chicago,* May 1990, p. 119.

7. Ibid.

8. Parker J. Palmer, *The Active Life: Wisdom for Work, Creativity, and Caring* (San Francisco: HarperCollins, 1990).

9. Ibid., p. 124.

10. See V. Dion Haynes, "No-Jail Drug Policy Works, Arizona Says," *Chicago Tribune,* Apr. 21, 1999. According to Haynes, "In a report that likely will increase debate on the merits of imprisoning substance abusers, the Arizona Supreme Court... issued a study concluding that the state's new mandatory treat-

ment law has broken drug users' habits in the short term and saved the state millions of dollars.... Proposition 200 grew out of a study sponsored by some prominent Arizonians, including University of Arizona President John Sperling, to find alternatives to incarcerating drug offenders." California voters did the same thing by passing Proposition 36 in November 2000; this law allows most minor drug offenders to get treatment instead of jail.

This concern also corresponds to the recent calls of a number of trauma surgeons and activists to push assaults with guns as a health issue, not just a law enforcement issue. See John Barrett, Richard Fantus, and M. Geno Tellez, "Trauma Surgeons Call Gun Violence a Public Health Emergency," *Chicago Tribune,* Apr. 29, 1999.

Chapter 12

1. *Rudy Arthur Rosales vs. John Cherry, M.D., et al.;* case number 400CV3164, in the United States District Court for the District of Nebraska; Oct. 2000.

2. See also the editorial, "Violent Crime Down, No Thanks to Three Strikes," *USA Today,* Feb. 24, 1997; and "Repeat Offenders Strike Out in California," *Parade* magazine, Jan. 19, 1997. By 1998, however, California courts began changing the most draconian sections of the state's "three strikes" law. See "Let the Punishment Fit the Crime" editorial in the *Orange Country Register,* Aug. 3, 1999.

3. Jeffrey Reiman, *The Rich Get Richer and the Poor Get Prison* (Needham Heights, Mass.: Allyn and Bacon, 1998), p. 3.

4. From Fraser Boa, *The Way of Myth: Talking with Joseph Campbell* (Boston: Shambhala Publications, 1994), p. 9. "I have a friend," Campbell said, "who recently gave me a list of things which let you know you're getting old. One, you sink your teeth into a juicy steak and they stay there; another, the little old lady you're leading across the street is your wife; a third, your back goes out more often than you do. But the real killer is this one. You've got to the top of the ladder and found it's against the wrong wall."

5. Michael Ventura, "The Age of Endarkenment," in *Crossroads: The Quest for Contemporary Rites of Passage,* edited by Louise Carus Mahdi, Nancy Geyer Christopher, and Michael Meade (Peru, Ill.: Carus Publishing Company, 1996), p. 53.

6. Jon Marshal, "Poetry and Prayer as Antidote to Gangs: How One Chicago Resident Uses Years of Writing Experience to Turn Kids Away from Violence," *Christian Science Monitor,* Jun. 15, 1998.

Chapter 13

1. Kate Richards O'Hare, "Crime and Criminals," in *Prison Writing in 20th Century America,* edited by H. Bruce Franklin (New York: Penguin Books, 1998), pp. 85–86.

2. See Judy Daubenmeir, "Study Says Michigan Arts Can Help Cut Crime, Boost Test Scores," *Kalamazoo Gazette,* Jan. 6, 1997. "A report done for the Michigan Council for the Arts and Culture Affairs says many of the state's large cultural organizations offer programs for at-risk-youth as part of their contribution to improving community life," wrote Daubenmeir. The report, prepared by the Center for Art and Public Policy at Wayne University, said "involving at-risk youth in the arts helps cut crime by teaching empathy and respect for others, self-discipline and self-expression." Furthermore, the center's director, Bernard Brocke, was quoted as saying, "It seems to me the study suggests that arts are an integral part of a person's way of living, add quality to a person's life and should be part of daily activity."

See also Bob Pool, "Teens Find Poetry Is a Path to the Soul," *Los Angeles Times,* Feb. 5, 2001. In that article poet-teacher Sita Stulberg, forty-six, is quoted as telling a group of seventh graders, "Your work is powerful, you have a voice. You have worked with things that are really tough, and you've had the courage to share. Now you won't walk around all your life thinking you're alone."

3. Julia Cameron, *The Artist's Way: A Spiritual Path to Higher Creativity* (New York: Jeremy P. Tarcher/Putnam, 1992), p. xiii.

4. Julia Cameron, *The Right to Write: An Invitation and Initiation into the Writing Life* (Los Angeles, Audio Renaissance, 1999), audiotape.

5. From Maralyn Lois Polak, "Michael Meade: A Different Drummer," *Philadelphia Inquirer* magazine, Mar. 13, 1994.

6. William Stafford, "You and Art," *The Way It Is: New and Selected Poems* (St. Paul, Minn.: Graywolf, 1998), p. 7.

Chapter 14

1. Sections of this chapter originally appeared as an opinion piece by Luis J. Rodríguez, with Cle Sloan and Kershaun Scott, entitled "Gangs: The New Political Force in Los Angeles," *Los Angeles Times,* Sept. 13, 1992, and as an article for the *People's Tribune* 25, no.11 (Nov. 1998).

2. As in many of these street conflicts, few if any of the combatants knew what actually started the wars they were embroiled in. Mostly what kept these young men and women in the conflicts were the family and friends who had been killed while they were active in the gang. Still, I had to find out why Lomas and Sangra had become such enemies to the point that childhood friends and even family members shot at each other.

Through a friend of mine who once worked with various barrio gangs in this part of the San Gabriel Valley (including older associations such as Sangra, Lomas, Monte Flores, Bassett, Jimtown, Bolen, Canta Ranas, El Jardin, Pico Viejo, and Pico Nuevo, to name a few), I located an older man who claimed to know the origin of the Sangra and Lomas gang war. What he told me was astounding. Yet it correlated with other origins stories I had heard—that despite the great suffering and death that came from these conflicts, they had often started over insignificant things. In this case the man claimed that in the early 1950s, when young residents of the Lomas barrio had supposedly started a bike club, someone from Sangra had stolen a bicycle from someone in Lomas. Fights ensued, mostly with fists. But over the years these had escalated to stabbings and eventually shootings.

So that was it? A stolen bike. That was the reason so many people over half a century have lost their lives, ended up in prison, and have became largely immobilized by fear and hatred for several generations, and, very likely, for generations to come.

3. See also Michael Krikorian, "Ex-Gang Members Work to Bring Peace to Streets: They Get Little Recognition, but Former Gangbangers and Grass-Roots Groups Contribute to Drop in Homicide Rate," *Los Angeles Times,* Jan. 26, 1998. "In tattered storefront offices from Pico Boulevard to Central Avenue, in apartments in the city's toughest housing projects in Watts, in attractive homes in Southwest Los Angeles and on the city's deadliest corners, the work of promoting peace goes on night and day," Krikorian writes. In his article, he quoted Janine Watkins from the Watts Labor Community Action Committee, who said, "The solutions are coming from those that are suffering, not from those that are creating legislation that perpetuates the problem. These guys that started the treaty, that work in the trenches all over the city, they are the solution. They have lived up to their word. You can bring in the National Guard, but if the neighborhoods aren't organizing the peace, it is not going to happen."

4. In 1997, the House of Representatives passed the controversial Juvenile Crime Bill; the Senate version came out of the Judiciary Committee in July 1997. However, the bill died on October 15, 1998, when Democrats and Republicans failed to agree on key provisions. See Gary Fields, "Partisan Disagreement Kills Juvenile Crime Bill," *USA Today,* Oct. 16, 1998. Since then, however, similar bills continued to be introduced in Congress.

5. The Kensington Welfare Rights Union (KWRU), the Poor People's Economic Human Rights Campaign, and the International Campaign for Economic Justice (based in The Hague, Netherlands) spearheaded the Poor People's World Summit to End Poverty in New York City during November 2000. Hundreds of people from around the country and parts of the world converged on Riverside Church on the Upper West Side. They also helped organize a National Poverty Summit in Philadelphia in October 1998, as well as countless marches, housing takeovers, tent cities, and other organizational efforts of the poor. A documentary, *Outriders,* produced by Sky Light Pictures in the early 1990s, highlighted some of KWRU's work. Several thousands of people, including singers, artists, rappers, and poets, and a diverse group of community organizations representing the most economically deprived people in the land, have participated in these events over the last two decades. They've gathered to outline a program for united action, including the implementation of the Human Rights Initiative, presented to the United Nations, which called for a basic level of subsistence and

dignity for all people. When the richest country in the world is expected to have some 3.5 million people experience homelessness in the year 2001, according to the National Coalition for the Homeless, it's time that the poor begin to claim back their lives, their homes, and their dignity.

6. "The brothers in Watts, way back in December of '91, was talking about a truce between the three primary housing projects: Nickerson Gardens, Jordan Downs, and Imperial Courts.... The FBI had knowledge of it, and that's when they started sending those FBI agents down here to the city. That was in February of '92 when they first infiltrated Watts. Then they implemented the Weed and Seed program. The Weed and Seed program that they implemented here was to seed in certain individuals, and to weed out other individuals, that's what it is. Plant something to get rid of something else. Just like an antidote for a disease. So what they were doing was hiring individuals, bringing down the FBI to work at getting rid of certain gang bangers who had resources." This quote was attributed to "Angelo," a Blood from Compton, in *Uprising: Crips and Blood Tell the Story of America's Youth in the Crossfire*, edited by Yusuf Jah and Sister Shah'Keyah (New York: Scribner, 1995), p. 74.

7. In an article by Ron Russell, "La Eme: Murder, Mayhem, and the Mexican Mafia: Can the Feds Really Cripple America's Deadliest Prison Gang?" *New Times Los Angeles*, Dec. 12–18, 1996, Russell notes, "Although officials disagree about the extent of the group's success, few quarrel with the notion that la Eme changed the face of gang warfare in greater L.A., where Latino gangs now make up 84,000 of the county's estimated 150,000 known gang members. Cops began to notice the change in 1993, after a series of celebrated outdoor meetings in which [Eme] leaders issued an edict to thousands of Latino gang members to halt drive-by shootings or face the organization's wrath." The article goes on to say how authorities believed the edict was "an elaborate system of taxation and extortion designed to expand la Eme's control."

8. Ward Churchill, James Vander Wall, et al., *Agents of Repression: The F.B.I.'s Secret Wars Against the Black Panther Party and the American Indian Movement* (Boston: South End Press, 1988).

9. I got involved with the Salvadoran youth peace process with members of the Mara Salvatrucha and Eighteen Street gangs in El Salvador through a collaborative project with New York City photographer Donna DeCesare, for which we garnered a Dorothea Lang/Paul Tayler Prize from the Center for Documentary Studies at Duke University. Beginning in 1993, Donna and I paid several visits to the barrios of El Salvador and the Central American communities in Los Angeles. In the course of this work we met many of the young people who would later become active in Homies Unidos, including one of its most visible leaders, Alex Sanchez. Still, Homies Unidos became the target of a concerted police effort to destroy the group and its leaders. Sanchez was eventually set up by members of the Rampart police division for arrest and deportation. Community support, including many letters, eventually allowed

Sanchez, a reformed gang leader, to be released. I've participated in retreats and panels with Sanchez, who is a clear, heartfelt, and intelligent voice for peace in the barrios.

In 1995 DeCesare and I also made presentations in Paris, France, and at the Center for Documentary Studies in Durham, North Carolina, around the "globalization" of the L.A. gang culture through deportations (I made a separate presentation in Taxco, Guerrero, Mexico). Donna, who has won major photojournalism awards, including an Alicia Patterson Journalism Fellowship, a Mother Jones Photo Fund Grant, and an Open Society Fellowship, continues to give presentations and slideshows throughout the country and internationally. In addition in 1996 we addressed government, religious, community, and nongovernmental agencies in San Salvador during an historic conference on gangs in that country that helped shape a more humane policy toward street youth.

See also, Luis J. Rodríguez, "Los Angeles' Gang Culture Arrives in El Salvador, Courtesy of the INS," *Los Angeles Times,* May 8, 1994; Luis J. Rodríguez, photos by Donna DeCesare, "The Endless Dream Game of Death," *Grand Street* 13 (Spring 1995); Ken Guggenheim, "Salvador Gang Members Unite," *Associated Press,* Jun. 30, 1998; and Donna DeCesare, "The Children of War: Street Gangs in El Salvador," *NACLA Report on the Americas,* Jul.–Aug. 1998.

There are also a number of books in El Salvador on this subject, including by Homies Unidos, Instituto Universitario de Opinión Pública, Radda Barnen de Suecia, and Save the Children de Estados Unidos, *Solidaridad y violencia en las pandillas del gran San Salvador: más allá de la vida loca* (San Salvador: UCA Editores, 1998) and Marcela Smutt, Jenny Lissette, and E. Miranda, *El fenómeno de las pandillas en El Salvador* (San Salvador: UNICEF/FLACSO, 1998).

10. See Leslie Berger, "San Fernando Valley Gangs Maintain Precarious Peace," *Los Angeles Times,* Sept. 27, 1994.

11. See the *Associated Press,* "Murder Rate Declines to 30-Year Low," *Chicago Tribune,* Nov. 23, 1998.

12. As quoted in Hugo Martin, "Reaction Deeply Split on Killer's Nobel Nomination," *Los Angeles Times,* Dec. 7, 2000.

13. From "Youth Struggling for Survival—Chicago Youth Peace Plan," also published in *Representin* 2, no. 4 (Fall 1996), a publication of the Youth Empowerment Network, Chicago.

14. The United Nations recently reported that up to 300,000 children are currently serving as combatants around the world, many with automatic weapons. They also claimed that two million children have been killed in armed conflicts since 1987, with three times that number seriously injured or permanently disabled. See "300,000 Children Are Fighting in Wars Worldwide, Study Says," *Chicago Tribune,* Oct. 21, 1998.

15. From a brochure announcing a presentation by James Hillman and Michael Meade at the Chicago Historical Society, Rubloff Auditorium, Sept.

7–8, 1996, sponsored by the Institute for the Study of Imagination and Green Street.

Chapter 15:

1. Parker J. Palmer, *The Active Life: Wisdom for Work, Creativity, and Caring* (San Francisco: HarperCollins, 1990), pp. 124–125.

2. Ibid., p. 125.

3. Tlakaelel, with Isabel Luengas, Gertrudis Zenzes, and Patricia Heuzé, *Nahui Mitl: The Journey of the Four Arrows* (Chaplin, Conn.: Mexicayotl Productions, 1998), p. 75.

4. *The Active Life*, p. 124.

5. From the German poet Hilde Domin, as quoted in Mihaly Csikszentmihalyi, *Creativity: Flow and the Psychology of Discovery and Invention* (New York: HarperCollins, 1996), p. 245. Here is part of her quote on how words and symbols can save a writer, or anyone for that matter, from cold, raw, and often unbearable realities and experiences: "[The emotion] gets fulfilled.... You know what was in you, and you can look at it now. And it is kind of a catalyst.... You are freed for a time from the emotion. And the next reader will take the place of the author.... If he identifies with the writing he will become, in his turn, the author. And he then also gets freed. Like the author gets freed. The emotion may not be exactly the same, but it is somehow, how would you say, in harmonic resonance."

Chapter 16

1. Quoted in Mihaly Csikszentmihalyi, *Creativity* (New York: HarperCollins, 1996), p. 260.

2. Robert Bly, *The Sibling Society* (New York: Addison-Wesley, 1996), p. 164.

3. "Throw Yourself Like Seed," by Miguel De Unamuno, translated by Robert Bly, in *The Rag and Bone Shop of the Heart: Poems for Men,* edited by Robert Bly, James Hillman, and Michael Meade (New York: HarperCollins Perennial, 1992), p. 234.

Chapter 17

1. Some of this material comes from the *Youth Struggling for Survival Program Guide,* published for the *Making Peace* TV series, which first aired nationally on the Public Broadcasting System during March 1997.

Chapter 18

1. I learned many writing exercises as part of Anne Schultz's team of poets, storytellers, and artists, who assisted teachers in the Chicago public schools (grades K through 12) in her capacity as director of the Writing from the Source Program of the Chicago Teachers' Center/Northeastern Illinois University.

In early 2001 Schultz wrote a paper called "Chicago Public Schools,

2001—A Consultant's View of the State of Things" on the forced testing of public school children that had unfortunately gained much steam throughout the country. Here is part of what she wrote: "The history of the current purpose of the tests is rather interesting. [At first] they were supposed to provide a tool for assessment and diagnosis of where a child had difficulties and needed extra help; or, if there were many children with the same kinds of difficulties, the teacher would know what she or he needed to teach this particular thing differently. The tests were not supposed to have any evaluative purpose at all. There was not supposed to be judgment attached to the tests, and their intention was to be helpful to both teachers and students. But in this capitalist culture which is quick to judgment, and divides people as quickly and efficiently as possible between the winners and the losers, this idea didn't stick.... And this whole dreadful dehumanizing business is not necessarily about what the children are really learning in school. It's *all* about test scores, and *only* about test scores.... There is much noise about the importance of independent thinking—but do we want it? Do we really want students to leave the schools able to think for themselves? Or is it more in line with capitalist interests to have a nation of test-takers, who are willing always to be defined by someone else—a compliant population who will neither doubt nor probe, nor challenge the way of things?... I know how much work is being done to try and keep students in school, and if they've dropped out already, to try and get them back. But I don't believe that this work, splendid though much of it is, is able to address the systemic cause of why students drop out in the first place. Unless we do address that underlying cause, and turn in an entirely different direction; unless we take upon ourselves a different vision of the aim of education, in which we educate for excellence in whatever each individual person can get to be excellent at, rather than compliance; unless we regard the hopes and dreams of our children as being of the utmost importance to the way we plan the curriculum; unless we arrive at forms of evaluation in which there are no 'norms', and consequently no divisions into winners and losers; unless our aim is towards the ultimate goal of helping our children become literate, sensate, joyful, and compassionate human beings; and unless there is nothing more sacred to us than a human being's capacity to fully realize his or her own life, and to be a responsible member of the larger community—we will never have an education system worthy of the name."

2. A. Alvarez, *The Savage God: A Study of Suicide* (New York: Random House, 1972), pp. 121–122.

3. Simon Wiesenthal, *The Sunflower* (New York: Shocken Books, 1976), pp. 40–41. I first came across this and the Alvarez quote in the essay "The Thousand and First Face," by Walter B. Gulick in *Paths to the Power of Myth: Joseph Campbell and the Study of Religion,* edited by Daniel C. Noel (New York: Crossroad Publishing, 1990), pp. 39–40.

Chapter 19

1. In Chicago, many street organizations allow a member to leave by having a five-minute beat-down. During this beating, the "violated" member cannot strike back at his assailants. If he should be seriously hurt before the five minutes are over, the clock is stopped. He is taken to the hospital. After a reasonable recuperation period, he will have to submit to more beatings until the alloted five minutes are done. While this has led to some serious injuries—I've known of young men having brain damage after being beaten for trying to leave the gang—most people who don't make an issue of leaving simply "remove" themselves for another life of companionship, kids, work, and home.

Chapter 20

1. Julie Parson-Nesbitt, Luis J. Rodríguez, and Michael Warr, eds., *Power Lines: A Decade of Poetry from Chicago's Guild Complex* (Chicago: Tía Chucha Press, 1999).

2. Ibid.; excerpted from the introduction and back cover copy.

3. Jon Anderson, "Workshop Offers Writers Refuge from Frequent Despair of City Life," *Chicago Tribune,* Sept. 4, 1998.

4. Anna West, ed., *Rescuing the Word: An Anthology of Writing from the Prism Writers Workshops 1997–2000,* foreword by Luis J. Rodríguez (Chicago: Young Chicago Authors, 2001), p. 9.

5. From a brochure of a Mosaic Foundation event called "Walking the Grounds of Practice," held in Mendocino, California, from Aug. 21–26, 2001, and featuring Michael Meade, Malidoma Somé, Jack Kornfield, and Luis Rodríguez.

6. Luis J. Rodríguez, "Self-Discipline," *U.S. News & World Report,* Aug. 1, 1994, pp. 36–37.

7. See Luis J. Rodríguez, "Liberation Radio in America: Arresting the Airwaves," *The ROC—Voice of Rock Out Censorship* [Jewett, Ohio] no. 9 (Summer 1992); and "Rebel Radio: Rapping in the Hood," *The Nation,* pp. 12–19, Aug. 1991.

8. "Congress Kills Low-Power Radio: Sen. John McCain Calls the Decision 'A Gross Injustice,'" *Rolling Stone,* Feb. 15, 2001, p. 28.

9. There is a growing concern that the United States now prescribes drugs like Ritalin and Prozac at dangerous levels. Not withstanding the benefit of these drugs for some people, we should seriously consider changing the circumstances that require people to need such drugs in the first place.

"In the United States, attention deficit disorder (ADD) accounts for almost half of all child psychiatric referrals.... Studies indicate that 1 of 20 children aged 6 to 10 and about 3 percent of all children under 19 are on ADD medications like Ritalin or Cylert. Prescriptions are currently at 1.5 million and climbing dramatically.... Some schools have as many as 10 percent on Ritalin," from Eric Jensen, *Teaching with the Brain in Mind* (Alexandria, Va.: Association for Supervision and Curriculum Development, 1998), p. 49.

Yet many doctors and scientists believe ADD may mask poor hearing, bad eyesight, inadequate nutrition, and a longer DNA sequence in the receptor gene for Dopamine. Some ADD may be genetic, according to Jensen. It is most certainly affected by large classroom size, too much "focused attention" expected of children (children and teens need from five to fifteen minutes of direct instruction and a reasonable time after this for the brain to process the instruction and to rest, Jensen contends), and social pressures to curtail certain behaviors.

I once met an eighteen-year-old college student from a well-off family in Connecticut who told me she had been on Ritalin since the age of ten. Apparently her parents felt she needed the drug when, during a particularly long and boring first communion rehearsal at their church, they saw her do a somersault. But when she entered college, the school retested her by giving her a placebo. She indicated that she felt quite calm and able to concentrate with what turned out to be a water pill. The general appraisal was that she may not have needed Ritalin in the first place.

The controversy over ADD, Ritalin, and the use of drugs like Prozac, and its sister drugs Zoloft or Paxil, is far from over. Today there is a large and growing body of literature on the subject. One thing is certain: We are living in a high-stress, high-expectation society. TV, video games, and the fast-food culture have conditioned us to insist upon faster and more intense stimuli. Fewer and fewer of us know how to slow down and fully appreciate the beauty and other extended joys around us.

"Today, we expect more *for* our children, and we expect more *of* them," wrote physician Lawrence H. Diller, "Running on Ritalin," *DoubleTake* 4, no. 4 (Fall 1998), pp. 46–55. "At the same time, the old network of social supports for children and their families has been undercut. A ten-year-old patient of mine, upon hearing about the idea of a 'chemical imbalance' underlying ADD, produced this insight about his own situation: 'It's not a chemical imbalance, Mr. Diller, it's a *living* imbalance.'... I'm not 'against' Ritalin.... However, I am against employing Ritalin as the first and only treatment for a host of behavioral and performance problems in children. I'm concerned that we might be too successful in medicating away the negative consequences of our obsession with performance. If this is true, we might further delay addressing some of the larger issues that affect all of us, such as public school funding and support for parents who stay home. What most worries me is the sense that we are postponing some later reckoning with the 'living imbalance' our children are experiencing today."

10. Diné Roadman Anthony Lee explained this concept further in a letter dated Feb. 7, 2001, that he wrote to my wife, Trini—his adopted spiritual daughter—and me: "The Navajo Language can express metaphysical and spiritual meanings, and express notions of intrinsic relationships in ways that the English language cannot. One has to move beyond the symbol, beyond metaphorical levels of understanding, in order to look at the complexity of human consciousness and cognition. For instance, *hozho,* does not simply mean the 'good.' It is a

dynamic interplay of order and chaos, and it can be best understood through experience. The Diné traditional mind is organized in accordance with the natural order. Traditional knowledge tells us that we are part of the eternal cosmic process of dawn, midday, dusk, and night. Our physical being is part of the dawn process, as well as part of the air process. One has to breathe in order to think, and when one goes deeper into that organization of knowledge, one's mind becomes one with light. This is when one can look at a bucket of water and find clarity. Ultimately, the knowledge doesn't have to be written, or even spoken. The relationship is just a natural occurrence."

Chapter 21

1. Eavan Boland, "Warning, Witness, Presence," *Poets & Writers,* Nov.–Dec. 2000, pp. 52–55.

2. Leslie Scalapino, "The Cannon," *American Poetry Review* 27, no. 3 (May–Jun. 1998), pp. 9–12.

3. Luis J. Rodríguez, "Poetry Workshops with the Homeless," *Poets & Writers,* Mar.–Apr. 1992.

4. Luis J. Rodríguez, ed., with Michael Warr and Marvin Tate, *With the Wind at My Back and Ink in My Blood: A Collection of Poems by Chicago's Homeless* (Chicago: Coalition for the Homeless, 1991).

5. See Glen Elsasser, "Poetry Project Has Simple Mission: Spread the Words," *Chicago Tribune,* Jun. 12, 1997, on the work of Andrew Carroll and the American Poetry and Literacy Project, which gave out thousands of volumes of poetry free of charge as part of a national "poetryseed" tour during National Poetry Month in April 1998. See also Barbara Mahany, "This Woman Wants to Put Poetry in Your Face," *Chicago Tribune,* Jan. 23, 1998, on the work of Elise Paschen and the Poetry Society of America. And see Robert Pinsky, "Poetry in the Public Sphere," *The New York Times,* Apr. 10, 1997, which was later reprinted in *Journal of the Poetry Society of America,* Aug. 1997.

6. Manazar, myself, and others created Galeria Ocaso in a renovated warehouse on Sunset Boulevard. We organized some of the most exciting and well-attended performances, exhibits, readings, and art gatherings of the time. It closed its doors in 1985 for lack of funds—the big art collectors around West L.A.'s gallery row would not venture into the barrio funkiness of Echo Park, except on a few rare occasions.

7. Elaine Woo, "Manazar Gamboa: Poet Wrote About Chicano Experience," *Los Angeles Times,* Jan. 7, 2001.

8. Luis J. Rodríguez, *The Concrete River* (Willimantic, Conn.: Curbstone Press, 1991), pp. 101–102.

9. See Anne Japenga, "Springsteen Pays a Visit to Union Hall," *Los Angeles Times,* Nov. 8, 1984; and Dave Marsh, *Glory Days: Bruce Springsteen in the 1980s* (New York: Pantheon, 1987), p. 280.

10. The concept is written as *nu guachaxil,* and was related to me by Roberto

Mendoza, a professional interpreter based in Chicago. Mendoza, originally from Guatemala, studied the Quiché language after realizing that all his life, despite his Indian heritage, he knew nothing about the culture or the people. In doing so, he discovered that the modern tribal dialects—there are twenty-eight Mayan dialects in his country—consist almost entirely of metaphors, and are among the most poetic tongues on earth.

11. Anne Schultz, *Writing From the Source: A Content Approach to Teaching Writing* (Chicago Teachers Center, 1992), p. 2. Concepts such as "whole language" and "writing from the source" have recently come under attack. In late 1998 the California Board of Education abandoned its whole-language approach in favor of phonics. Although this should not be an either/or issue—many teachers would agree that phonics *with* whole language can work—changes in political winds continually throw these issues into disarray. Children pay a heavy price in the long run for these swings in educational policy, which are mostly based on political agendas, not educational ones. See "California Decides Phonics Wholly Better for Kids," *Chicago Tribune,* Dec. 11, 1998.

12. Malidoma Somé, *The Healing Wisdom of Africa: Finding Life Purpose Through Nature, Ritual, and Community* (New York: Jeremy P. Tarcher/Putnam, 1998), p. 127.

13. Part of this incident is recounted in my children's book, *América Is Her Name,* which also included experiences with Spanish-speaking children and their parents in workshops I conducted at Yungman Elementary School in Chicago's Pilsen community. This also involved classes with mostly illiterate mothers and their six- to eight-year-old children. These women couldn't write or read in either Spanish or English; one mother did her "poems" with images cut out of magazines. And it included a few home visits. In particular I relied on my experiences with the Huizar family, who lived in a boarded-up building next to dilapidated warehouses. During our sessions a young mother and three children (ages eight, five, and two) gathered around the kitchen table to "do" poems. Even the two-year-old scribbled on paper; she later read her markings as if they contained actual words.

14. Carlos J. Ovando, "Politics and Pedagogy: History, Politics, Theory, and Practice," *Harvard Educational Review,* 1990, p. 341.

15. See also Erika Hayasaki, "Voices from Everywhere: Crowds Attest to the Passion of Poetry as Performance," *Los Angeles Times,* Mar. 2, 2001. Hayasaki describes the phenomenally large crowds—upward of three hundred—that have been attending a recently opened poetry venue called Da' Poetry Lounge, located at Fairfax High School's Greenway Court Theatre in L.A.'s Westside. According to the article, "Da' Poetry Lounge draws actors, singers, modern dancers, tap dancers, screenwriters, comedians, rappers and anyone else who wants to say something through poetry. Admission is free; donations help cover stage costs and are given to a Fairfax High School film program." One eighteen-year-old poet, Codi Chavez, was quoted as saying, "I fell in love with expression and the fact that people can leave their souls on stage and just be embraced."

16. Two of my poems were put on a CD and audiotape box set called *In Their Own Voices: A Century of Recorded Poetry*, compiled by Rebekeh Presson and David McLess for Rhino Records/Word Beat. Produced in 1996, the box set includes recorded readings of the poems of Walt Whitman, William Carlos William, Langston Hughes, Elizabeth Bishop, and Allen Ginsberg, among others.

17. Jonathan Kozol, "A Call to Action," *Reaching Today's Youth* 1, no. 1, p. 5.

Chapter 22

1. From *Uprising: Crips and Bloods Tell the Story of America's Youth in the Crossfire*, edited by Yusuf Jah and Sister Shah'Keyah (New York, Scribner, 1995), p. 93.

2. Arturo Hernandez, *Peace in the Streets: Breaking the Cycle of Gang Violence* (Washington, D.C.: Child Welfare League of America, 1998), p. 147.

3. Ibid., p. 190.

4. Luis R. Ruan, *Youth At-Risk Workbook: Training the Trainers Guide* (Santa Ana, Calif.: Beyond Limits, Inc., 1998), p. 12.

5. Barbara Coloroso, *Kids Are Worth It: Giving Your Child the Gift of Inner Discipline* (New York: Avon Books, 1994), p. 11.

6. Ibid., p. 17.

7. "Until One Is Committed," by Johann Wolfgang von Goethe in *The Rag and Bone Shop of the Heart*, edited by Robert Bly, James Hillman, and Micheal Meade (New York: HarperCollins Perennial, 1992), p. 235.

Chapter 23

1. Ramiro's words have appeared in Anne Schultz, ed. *Open Fist: An Anthology of Young Illinois Poets* (Chicago: Tía Chucha Press, 1994); and Sydney Lewis, *A Totally Alien Life Form: Teenagers* (New York: The New Press, 1996).

2. Quote from Marc Spiegler, "Losing Ramiro," Chicago, January 1999.

3. Joseph Campbell, *The Hero with a Thousand Faces* (Princeton, N.J.: Princeton University Press, 1946), p. 390.

4. Ian Marshall, Danah Zohar, and F. David Peat, *Who's Afraid of Scrödinger's Cat?: An A-to-Z Guide to All the New Science Ideas You Need to Keep Up with the New Thinking* (New York: Quill/William Morrow, 1997), p. xxvii.

5. Trudy Griffin-Pierce, *Earth Is My Mother, Sky Is My Father: Space, Time, and Astronomy in Navajo Sandpainting* (Albuquerque: University of New Mexico Press, 1992), pp. 6–7.

6. The Gospel of Thomas was found among the papyrus texts discovered in 1945–46 at Nag Hammadi near the Nile River. It was published in 1959 and consisted of 114 sayings by Jesus, including words not preserved anywhere else. These works were believed buried in the fifth century by Christian monks to protect them during a hunt for unorthodox literature. Some of the sayings include, "The Father's Kingdom is spread out upon the earth, and people do not see it," "Love your brother as your self, guard him as the apple of your eye," "Woe to the flesh

which depends upon the soul; woe to the soul which depends upon the flesh," and, "If you bring forth what is within you, what you have will save you. If you do not have that within you, what you do not have within you will kill you."

Most of this information came from John Bowker, ed., *The Oxford Dictionary of World Religions* (New York: Oxford University Press, 1997). See also Marven Meyer, trans., *The Gospel of Thomas: The Hidden Sayings of Jesus* (San Francisco: HarperCollins, 1992); and Elaine Pagels, *The Gnostic Gospels* (New York: Vintage Books, 1979).

7. Joseph Campbell, *Hero with a Thousand Faces*, p. 72.

8. From an article by Mary Daniels, "Horse Whispering," *Chicago Tribune,* May 13, 1998.

9. Ibid.

10. Many successful prison programs involve taking care of and working with animals, particularly horses. At the Salt River Pima–Maricopa Reservation in Arizona, for example, Leif Hallberg runs the Esperanza Equine Learning Center. Hallberg has taken incarcerated and other troubled youths and adults to work with the breeding and training of horses on a thirty-five-acre farm, located south of the Salt River. She has seen the healing power of connecting humans with horses, including how these relationships can teach honesty, compassion, problem solving, discipline, self-worth, and respect.

Similarly, at the Blackburn Correctional Complex in Lexington, Kentucky, dope dealers, burglars, and assailants who want to make good work at the prison barn and take care of sixty-two horses. "The barn smells of manure and hay, and 15 inmates in grungy work clothes spend all day, every day, there," writes Stephanie Simon in "Program Mends the Spirits of Broken Men, Broken Horses," *Los Angeles Times,* Feb. 20, 2001. "The convicts groom and exercise the horses. Grow alfalfa to feed them. Muck out their stalls, tend their injuries, and, unabashed, nuzzle them nose to nose.... In the prison barn, there is hope." Simon reports that the horses are former thoroughbreds that have been slated for slaughter for being too old or broken to race. "About 7,000 thoroughbreds, some of them champion racers, end up in the slaughterhouse each year, hung by one leg and slit open," writes Simon. "They are not in demand as studs. And feeding them is expensive. So their owners sell them for a few hundred dollars for human consumption abroad. Perhaps the classic example is the race horse Exceller, who won $1.7 million during his career in the 1970s, but ended up sold by the pound to the slaughterhouse."

The Thoroughbred Retirement Foundation spent some twenty years trying to save these horses. With a million-dollar annual budget put together entirely with donations, they buy washed-up Thoroughbreds at meat auctions, bring them back to health, and seek loving owners to take care of them. "The prison gets a job-training program. The foundation gets free land and free labor. The horses get devoted care. And the men get a chance to feel good about themselves," adds Simon.

11. From an unpublished manuscript by urban architect Paul Alt entitled "Death and Rebirth: The Du Sable High School Urban Ecology Sanctuary," copyright 1998 by Paul Alt. Used with permission.

Chapter 24

1. Richard Erdoes and Alfonso Ortiz, *American Indian Myths and Legends* (New York: Pantheon Books, 1984), p. xi.

2. Part of a quote by U.S. Treasury Secretary Lawrence H. Summers, from Jonathan Rauch, "The New Old Economy: Oil, Computers, and the Reinvention of the Earth," *Atlantic Monthly* 39, Jan. 2001. "Economists agree that to the extent the economy has changed, 'information technology'—the computer and its many offshoots—must have a good deal to do with it," wrote Rauch. "In the three decades since 1970 the power of microprocessors increased by a factor of 7,000. Computing chores that took a week in the early 1970s now take a minute. According to the Federal Reserve Bank of Dallas, the cost of storing one megabit of information, or enough for a 320-page book, fell from more than $5,000 in 1975 to seventeen cents in 1999."

3. Andrew Kimbrell, "Breaking the Job Lock," *Utne Reader,* Jan.–Feb. 1999, pp. 47–49.

4. Joseph Campbell, *The Lost Teachings of Joseph Campbell,* vol. 3, tape 2B, an audio recording (Redmond, Wash.: Zygon International, 1993).

Chapter 25

1. All definitions from *The Oxford Dictionary and Thesaurus* (New York: Oxford University Press, 1996).

2. *Increase the Peace: A Primer on Fear, Violence, and Transformation,* (Springfield, Ill.: Illinois Department of Alcoholism and Substance Abuse, 1994).

Chapter 26

1. Some of this material first appeared in "Los Angeles' Gang Culture Arrives in El Salvador, Courtesy of the INS," *Los Angeles Times,* May 8, 1994; "A Tale of Two Cities," *Rock and Rap Confidential,* Apr. 1994; "The Endless Dream-Game of Death," *Grand Street* 13, no. 4 (Spring 1995), with photos by Donna DeCesare; and Genevieve Fabre, ed., *Cultures de la rue: les barrios d'Amerique du Nord* (Paris: Cahiers Charles V, Universite Paris 7-Denis Diderot, 1996).

2. In 1995 I lectured in the class of Kristine Stiles, an assistant professor of art history at Duke University. Ms. Stiles later gave me a paper she had written entitled "Shaved Heads and Marked Bodies: Representations from the Cultures of Trauma." It was published in the scholarly journal *Stratégie* II, nos. 64–65 (Jul.–Dec. 1993), pp. 95–117. Ms. Stiles states that tattoos, shaved heads, and other "images and attendant behaviors constitute the aggregate visual evidence of the cultures of trauma," as if they were the inside wounds outside the body. Speaking about one youth who had the word *Romania* emblazoned on his body

during the conflict following the overthrow of the Ceauşescu regime, Stiles writes, "[The tattoo is] an indeterminate sign signifying the synchronicity of a visible wound and a mark of honor. A symbol of resistance and icon of marginality, it is a signature of capture, a mask that both designates and disguises identity." I find this to be similar to the visual expressions of many gang youth in the United States, particularly the cholos, who have been known to extensively tattoo themselves, shave their heads, and use outlandish, but stylish clothing and idioms in the face of abuse, racism, violence, neglect, and marginality. "Where such continuous peril exists, trauma is constant," Stiles says. "The task is to undermine its invisibility. For its concealed conditions, its silences, are the spaces in which the destructions of trauma multiply." And further, "the body and its languages may transform victimization into personal agency. 'Write yourself,' [French feminist theorist Hélène] Cixous declared. 'Your body must make itself heard.'"

3. In the first six months of 1995 the Black Shadow (La Sombra Negra) was believed to have killed some twenty-five alleged gang members. See Ray Sanchez, "Marked for Death: El Salvador's Tattooed Teens Face 'Shadow,'" *Newsday*, Jul. 4, 1995. During the civil war, death squads, mostly directed by government and military officials, were reportedly responsible for the deaths of thousands of suspected leftists. With the rise of L.A.-based gangs in El Salvador in the early 1990s, the death squads targeted those who they believed belonged to these gangs. Again, human rights officials and opposition politicians claimed these new death squads had the government's blessing. A legislative assembly member in 1995 said, "[Death squad murders are] still state-run terrorism. You cannot carry out these killings without intelligence information and institutional support." The assembly member also declared that the death squads weren't really battling organized crime or drug smuggling. "They are hired killers," he said. "But where do their orders come from? Who have they killed up until now? Barefoot delinquents!" Recently Salvador officials have claimed that the Black Shadow no longer exists—but some of the youth have told me that, even though the Black Shadow's activities have fallen over the last few years, they are still very much a threat in the country.

Chapter 27

1. From Michael Meade's foreword to Mircea Eliade, *Rites and Symbols of Initiation: The Mysteries of Birth and Rebirth* (Dallas: Spring Publications, 1994), p. xvii.

2. Ibid.

3. For those who don't believe how extensive our destructiveness has been, see "Costliest Year for Disasters; Researchers Cite Humans," *Chicago Tribune*, Nov. 28, 1998. The article states that research by the Worldwatch Institute, an environmental research group, and Munich Re, the world's largest reinsurer, blamed human meddling for much of the $89 billion damage from violent weather that killed an estimated 32,000 people and displaced 300 million in

1998—the worst year for weather-related disasters in recent history. Total losses from storms, floods, droughts, and fires for the first eleven months of the year exceeded the losses from such events in all of the 1980s.

According to the article, "The report says a combination of deforestation and climate changes has caused this year's most severe disasters, among them Hurricane Mitch, the flooding of China's Yangtze River, and Bangladesh's most extensive flood of the century.... When hillsides are left bare, rainfall will rush across the land or into rivers without being slowed by trees and allowed to be absorbed by the soil or evaporate back into the atmosphere."

"In a sense, we're turning up the faucets... and throwing away the sponges, like the forests and the wetlands," one of the researchers was quoted as saying. The report also cited conditions that forced people to settle on "vulnerable flood plains and hillsides."

Moreover, in an equally startling statistic, more than 30 percent of the natural world has been destroyed since 1970 by human beings, including depletion of the forests, and freshwater and marine systems on which life depends.

Although a small group of people are directly responsible for this terrible destruction—they happen to be very powerful people—the rest of us may also be complicit at one level or another. This is mostly because of ignorance of the facts and of the role played by such people and their power, due to a general lack of interest—"If it doesn't affect me directly, why should I care?"—or even an actual agreement and participation. In the end it takes a lot of people to lay waste to a forest: companies, bureaucrats, woodcutters, equipment operators, their families, and consumers.

4. Joseph Campbell, *Myths to Live By* (New York: Penguin Books, 1972), p. 104.

5. Michael Meade, "Introduction," in *Crossroads: The Quest for Contemporary Rites of Passage,* edited by Louise Carus Mahdi, Nancy Gever Christopher, and Michael Meade (Peru, Ill.: Open Court, 1996), pp. xxi–xxv.

6. Malidoma Somé, *The Healing Wisdom of Africa: Finding Life Purpose Through Nature, Ritual, and Community* (New York: Jeremy P. Tarcher/Putnam, 1998), p. 103.

About the author

Luis J. Rodríguez is the award-winning author of the memoir *Always Running: La Vida Loca, Gang Days in L.A,* as well as several poetry collections, two children's books, and a short story collection. In 2001, Luis was one of fifty people from around the world recognized as "An Unsung Hero of Compassion," a designation presented by His Holiness, the Dalai Lama.

To contact Luis and to find out more about the various social-change institutions, literary projects, and peace efforts he's presently involved in, write: Luis J. Rodríguez, c/o Tía Chucha's Café Cultural, P.O. Box 328, San Fernando CA 91341.

Other books by Luis J. Rodríguez

NON-FICTION

Always Running: La Vida Loca, Gang Days in L.A. (1993)

POETRY

Trochemoche (1998)
Concrete River (1991)
Poems Across the Pavement (1989)

JUVENILE FICTION

It Doesn't Have to Be This Way: A Barrio Story/No tiene que ser asi: Una historia del barrio (1999)
América is Her Name (1998)